An Introduction to Linguistic Theory
and Language Acquisition

Blackwell Textbooks in Linguistics

An Introduction to Linguistic Theory and Language Acquisition

Stephen Crain and Diane Lillo-Martin

 BLACKWELL
Publishers

First published 1999

2 4 6 8 10 9 7 5 3 1

Blackwell Publishers Inc.
350 Main Street
Malden, Massachusetts 02148
USA

Blackwell Publishers Ltd
108 Cowley Road
Oxford OX4 1JF
UK

Library of Congress Cataloging-in-Publication Data
Crain, Stephen, 1947–
    An introduction to linguistic theory and language
    acquisition / Stephen Crain and Diane Lillo-Martin.
        p.   cm. — (Blackwell textbooks in linguistics ;
    15)
    Includes bibliographical references and index.
    ISBN 0–631–19535–1 (cloth : alk. paper). — ISBN
    0–631–19536–X (pbk. : alk. paper)
    1. Language acquisition.   2. Grammar, Comparative
    and general.   3. Psycholinguistics.   I. Lillo-Martin,
    Diane C. (Diane Carolyn), 1959–   II. Title.
    III. Series.
    P118.C6747   1999
    401'.93—dc21   98–34401
                                                          CIP

British Library Cataloguing in Publication Data
A CIP catalogue record for this book is available from the British Library

Typeset in 10 on 13pt Sabon
by Graphicraft Limited, Hong Kong
Printed in Great Britain by TJ International, Padstow, Cornwall

This book is printed on acid-free paper

Contents

Preface

The goal of this text is to examine the nature of the human capacity for language. This goal is pursued using linguistic theory. Therefore, the contents of the text introduce linguistic theory and summarize many important results from the literature on language acquisition. The text is designed to be used in general introductory courses – the type that are sometimes referred to as Language and Mind courses. In these courses, it is assumed that much can be learned about the human mind by studying one of its most significant functions: language. This text is also designed to serve or supplement courses in language development and the psychology of language.

The scientific study of language is called linguistics, and the study of language and mind is often called *psycholinguistics*, short for the psychology of language. In this book we take a psycholinguistic approach to the study of the human mind. We consider language to be a part of human psychology. The linguistic behavior of children and adults is a small but significant part of their larger behavioral repertoire, which includes other cognitive skills such as mathematical reasoning, musical skills, spatial skills, social relations, and so on. Approaching the study of language from a psychological perspective enables us to gain important insights into the nature of the human mind.

In our view, understanding language has been enhanced by the availability of a detailed theory of the nature of language, called the theory of *Universal Grammar*. Since the mid-1960s, linguists working within the theory of Universal Grammar have developed and extended a rich and complex system of principles that pertain to natural languages (as opposed to artificial languages, such as programming languages). Most importantly, some of these principles are common to all natural languages. These linguistic universals form the core of the theory of Universal Grammar.

Linguists and psycholinguists have been at the forefront of the Cognitive Sciences. Much of this is due to recent developments in the theory of Universal Grammar. The results of empirical evaluations of these recent developments are quite impressive, in our view. Psycholinguists, including us, have applied the theory of Universal Grammar in attempts to understand and explain the complex linguistic capacities of our species. In so doing, many of the precepts of the theory of Universal Grammar have been empirically confirmed. In addition, aspects of the theory have proven useful in helping us to understand the process of language acquisition. This book will summarize many of these achievements.

We hope to give you the flavor of the book in the paragraphs that follow. The first part is called *Linguistic Knowledge*. This unit provides an overview of some of the facts to be explained by any viable theory of language and mind. We will present some of the kinds of mental processes that are accomplished by anyone who learns a language, which includes just about every person on earth. In fact, it is probably because nearly everyone is capable of learning to speak and understand language that it may seem to be simple. But, just the opposite is true – language is one of the most complex of all human abilities. There are a myriad of things we do with language, things which we all take for granted but which are, nevertheless, quite difficult to explain.

It is not obvious how to explain even the basic observation that every child acquires language, and any child can acquire any language. The universality of language is puzzling, because it stands in contrast to other cognitive abilities, such as the ability to paint, or to play music, or to perform complex mathematical calculations. These other abilities are hardly universal, and fail to be mastered even by many college-educated people. Language stands in contrast to these other abilities, then, because everyone masters a language. This is one of the mysteries about language that any theory should attempt to explain.

One reason we adopt the theory of Universal Grammar as our focal point for discussing language development in this text is that this theory takes seriously the project of explaining the universality of language acquisition. Another prominent feature of the theory is that it highlights those aspects of linguistic knowledge that cannot be learned from experience. If this knowledge is not learned from experience, we are led to conclude that it must be innately specified, as part of the genetic endowment of the species. In this respect, then, the theory of Universal Grammar invites us to consider the nature versus nurture controversy, as it pertains to the acquisition of linguistic knowledge. As we progress through the book, we will raise many other issues related to language acquisition.

Several basic facts about language acquisition, such as those raised here, are introduced in the first part. We state these facts first in general terms, but we return to consider them in greater detail in later parts. The list of facts serves as a data-base to test the adequacy of alternative theories of language and mind. As one alternative, we consider Behaviorism as a theory of language acquisition. It will become apparent that Behaviorism does not begin to account for most of the facts in our data-base. This sets the stage for a detailed examination of the theory of Universal Grammar. This theory, unlike Behaviorism, is remarkably successful in explaining the linguistic phenomena in the data-base.

Parts II and III are concerned with the details of the theory of Universal Grammar (UG). We describe in some depth both *Constituent Structure* and

Transformational Syntax, the core components of the UG theory. In these chapters, we acknowledge the fundamental contributions of one linguist, Noam Chomsky, to the development of the theory of Universal Grammar. In 1957, Chomsky published a small book called *Syntactic Structures*, which is often said to have begun an intellectual revolution because it so dramatically changed the field of linguistics and related studies of mind. Chomsky introduced several new concepts to the study of language and mind. One of his technical innovations was the notion of a transformational rule. Because of this type of rule, one area of linguistic research is often referred to as *Transformational Grammar* (or *Generative Grammar*). Transformational grammar differs in fundamental ways from the traditional, "descriptive" grammar that existed before the Chomskian revolution. Prior to Chomsky, linguists concentrated much of their efforts on describing the easily observable properties of language: the sound system, the vocabulary, and how some words are derived from others. Linguists in this tradition rarely looked at patterns of sentence structure, which can be very abstract, and they certainly never went as far as studying in detail the meaning relations in language. Because of this, traditional linguistics missed much of the richness of languages, including the complexity of sentence structure and sentence meaning. The formal mechanisms that Chomsky devised enabled linguists to explore these uncharted waters. As we will see, these mechanisms explain several important aspects of human language – its expressive power and flexibility – that make it quite unlike the communication system of any other animal. In short, one of Chomsky's main innovations was to give linguistics the formal tools to study the more complex aspects of language.

Chomsky's contributions to linguistic theory go well beyond technical innovations in the study of linguistics, however. Another of Chomsky's major contributions was to point out that language is a window to the mind. When we learn a language, we internalize a system of rules. When we use language in speaking or hearing and in reading or writing, we use the language system that we have internalized. Chomsky proposed that by providing a formal account of the properties of human language, we can make inferences about the kinds of minds that can learn and use language. There are many alternative systems which *could* be used for successful communication, but which are not part of human language, and therefore are not learned or used by people. For example, it is possible to imagine rules that exchange the first and last words of a sentence, in order to form questions. No known language has rules of this kind, however. Human languages incorporate only a *limited* number of the possible computational devices that are among the logically possible communicative systems. It seems, then, that language must be the product of *special* kinds of mental processes. Chomsky's point was that by studying the product we can understand these processes.

As noted earlier, one of the fundamental goals of the theory of Universal Grammar is to explain how languages are acquired. An important area to examine for linguistic universals is to see if learners acquire knowledge about the properties of language that they could not have acquired on the basis of their linguistic experience. Like certain aspects of human physical development, properties of language may emerge in all language learners whatever their environment is like, as the result of the biological endowment of the human species. We will examine several of these properties throughout the book. In particular, we will ask when these properties are known by young children. It is worth looking at young children, for the following reason: if all young children, with their various sets of limited experiences, come to know something about language, especially something that looks to be quite complicated from a pre-theoretical point of view, then this would add support to the claim that this aspect of language is biologically given.

For the most part, we will discuss children's acquisition of English. Obviously, English differs from all other languages in many respects. Thus, in order to reach generalizations about how "language" (any language) is acquired, our real focus should be on those aspects of English that also appear in all other languages. In other words, we are interested in children's acquisition of language universals. We can circumvent the problem of focusing too narrowly on English by comparing the course of acquisition by children learning English with the course taken by children learning languages quite unlike English. With this in mind, in Part IV we will discuss how universal linguistic principles apply in the visual-gestural language used by deaf people in the United States, American Sign Language (ASL). We will see that, despite the profound differences between signed and oral languages, they share a common core of principles, which are acquired in much the same way. Clearly, these principles are likely candidates for linguistic universals.

In addition to the study of the structure of language, and its acquisition, we will discuss the *meanings* of linguistic expressions. This is the topic of Part V. Broadly speaking, all the issues we consider fall under the scope of what is called *Semantics*. An important aspect of semantics is the meaning of proper names like "Arnold Schwarzenegger" and definite descriptions such as "the greatest living actor." These names and descriptions combine with predicates to form sentences; ultimately, our goal is to offer an account of the meanings of complete sentences. One important property of sentences is their truth or falsity. As the sentence "Arnold Schwarzenegger is the greatest living actor" makes apparent, the truth or falsity of sentences depends on the entities being referred to. It is less apparent how the meaning of a sentence is formed from the meanings of its constituent parts. This process, called *compositionality*, will be spelled out in detail in order to illustrate one aspect of the semantic component of UG. As before, technical discussion of semantics will be complemented by considering the findings of empirical investigations into how children acquire knowledge of the principles of this component of the grammar. Since semantic structure also involves purportedly universal properties, we will again ask whether young children show evidence of early mastery of these properties. In some ways, the acquisition of semantic knowledge seems more abstract than syntactic acquisition, and overt evidence on which children base their decisions might seem even more rare. However, it appears that children are biologically endowed with semantic knowledge, just as they are biologically endowed with syntactic knowledge. Thus, examining how children come to have adult knowledge in semantics is just as important as it is in syntax. In our view, semantics is just another component of Universal Grammar.

This surveys, in broad strokes, the topics covered in this text. It should be noted that we will not cover all of the concerns of linguists. For example, we will not discuss the sound patterns of language (phonology), or how languages change, or how to teach a second language. These are important areas of linguistics, but we have chosen to exclude them in order that we might spend more time discussing the other aspects of linguistic knowledge we have mentioned. We discuss only selected topics in this book for two reasons. One is that they offer examples where linguistic theory has been applied with considerable success. Probably the more important consideration, however, is that these are areas in which we conduct our own research. We hope that our interest in these topics will be apparent, and will make the text more enjoyable to read.

Acknowledgments

We are indebted to many people for helping in the formation of this book. First, we wish to acknowledge Janet Fodor, who originally developed the course out of which this text grew. Although the course and the text went through many transformations as we co-taught it after Janet left the University of Connecticut, we can truthfully say she started it. We would also like to extend thanks to our many colleagues and students who contributed in various ways to the book while we taught "Language and Mind" at the University of Connecticut, and later at the University of Maryland where Stephen now teaches. Specific thanks go to David Michaels, who provided written comments on a draft, and to Željko, Bošković, Norbert Hornstein, Howard Lasnik, David Lightfoot, and William Snyder, who provided comments when they taught the course or portions of it. Elizabeth Laurençot and Roger Martin provided valuable editorial and reference assistance at an early stage.

Since the text presents some of our own research, we also thank the colleagues who were involved in that research with us. They are cited at the appropriate places, but Rosalind Thornton deserves special mention, since much of the language acquisition work reported in Part III was conducted in collaboration with her. Portions of the research reported here were supported by the University of Connecticut Research Foundation, and National Institutes of Health grant #DC00183 to Lillo-Martin. Portions of the work by Stephen Crain were supported by a Program Project Grant to Haskins Laboratories from the National Institute of Child Health and Development (HD-01994).

At a personal level, we are grateful to our colleagues, students, and families, who sometimes had less than our full attention while this text was being prepared.

Part I Linguistic Knowledge

Introduction

In this part, we begin by laying out some basic facts about language acquisition which any theory of linguistic knowledge must be able to explain. We then consider a common-sense answer to the question of how children acquire language, and show that although it is intuitive, it does not begin to explain the facts we have set out. As an alternative, we present the theory of Universal Grammar, which posits innate knowledge of certain linguistic principles that guide the language learner. We will show that this theory fares far better in explaining the remarkable facts about language acquisition with which we start.

There are some important points of terminology which need to be clarified at the outset. In the field of linguistics as a whole, and particularly in this text, we make a distinction between linguistic **competence** and linguistic **performance**. Linguistic performance consists of the utterances which we actually make (or might make). This performance is fraught with limitations of attention, time, and resources – that is, we often make mistakes when we talk, such as forgetting the beginning of our sentence, or letting a new thought interrupt, or failing to complete a sentence due to a cough, sneeze, or headache. Although such performances are "real," they are not the basis for our theory of linguistic knowledge. Instead, we seek to understand our linguistic competence – the rules in our head which govern our speaking attempts – what it means to "know" a language. The full extent of our linguistic competence is never seen, since we are capable of producing an unlimited number of linguistic utterances. The rules which underlie these potential utterances are what we seek.

Don't be fooled by our use of the word "rules," however. Our aim is to produce a **descriptive** grammar: a list of the rules we have internalized during the course of language acquisition. Our grammar *describes* linguistic knowledge. We do not seek to produce a **prescriptive** grammar, listing the rules we *should* follow in order to speak "correctly." We do not judge. Whatever rules the language users employ are the rules of the language, as far as we're concerned.

We turn now to the beginning of our overview of linguistic knowledge.

1 Introduction to Language Acquisition

Introduction

One of the most remarkable characteristics of human beings is that virtually every single one acquires language at a very young age. This fact is even more remarkable considering the full complexity of the system which is acquired. If you doubt any part of these assertions – that everyone acquires language, that we acquire it at a young age, that the system is complex – be assured that we will soon back them up with evidence. For now, assume that they are true, and ask yourself, "How?" How does every single very young child acquire such a complex system? You might think that parents teach their children language, but this is not correct, except in so far as the parents may provide a language model by talking to and around their children. What we will argue in this book is that children acquire language so readily because it is in their genes. That is, we will argue that children are born with innate knowledge which guides them in the language acquisition task. This innate knowledge, known as the **Language Acquisition Device** (LAD), includes principles common to all human languages, called **Universal Grammar** (UG). What is innate does not have to be learned – hence language acquisition consists of learning what is peculiar to the language environment (e.g., the particular words of one language or another), and applying the universal principles.

The theory of innate linguistic knowledge which we will discuss in this book is largely due to the thoughts and influence of Noam Chomsky, a linguist at the Massachusetts Institute of Technology. Chomsky's 1957 book *Syntactic Structures* revolutionized the field of linguistics by introducing new technology and new goals for the study of the properties of language. His book *Aspects of the Theory of Syntax*, published in 1965, laid out the reasoning for a theory of innate knowledge, and since then much of his work and volumes of work inspired by him have added to our understanding of this theory and its implications.

In this chapter, we begin our presentation of this theory of language acquisition. We start by looking at what is known about the course of language development in general. These facts will lead to a more detailed presentation of the proposed innate language faculty. For now, our discussion will be fairly general, but the arguments for innateness should be clear. We will return to take a more thorough look at very specific aspects of language acquisition in later chapters, where we will discuss the syntax of these constructions in detail. Overall, our goal is to test the tenets of Universal Grammar.

The knowledge that a child brings to the task of language acquisition, the LAD, is the means by which the child/learner analyzes the linguistic input (from parents and others). The linguistic input to the learner is called the **Primary Linguistic Data** (PLD). On the basis of these data, the LAD hypothesizes a series of grammars. The last grammar that is formulated is the adult grammar, or Final State. The process can be represented schematically in the following way:

Input (PLD) → LAD → Final State

We should specify what we mean by "language." When we talk about a language, we are not talking about sentences in a textbook or on a blackboard – or even a list of all the sentences any speaker might produce. Language is not a concrete set of things out in the world that we can point to or measure. Rather, it is something inside our brains or minds. In linguistics, we attempt to describe what we know when we know a language by formulating a **grammar**. A grammar is a set of rules which characterizes all and only the sentences of the language that we as speakers are able to produce and understand. We take it as given that to learn a language is to master the rules of the mental grammar. Sometimes the mental grammar is called a "Generative Grammar," because it is a system of rules that generate (= produce) sentences of the language.

Against this background, the most basic questions about language acquisition are: Who learns language? How and when is it learned? What is the course of language acquisition like? Only when these questions have been answered will we begin to examine the properties of the Primary Linguistic Data, the LAD, and the Final State. Even the answers to the more tractable questions turn out to be quite remarkable if we approach them without any preconceived notions. At this point, it will be important to suppress any preconceptions you may have about how children learn language. Try to hold in abeyance any beliefs you may have, for instance, about the "baby-talk" of toddlers or young children, how they speak in only simple sentences, and use incorrect grammar, such as saying, "I runned home" instead of "I ran home." As we shall see, young children's grammatical successes are vastly more impressive than their mistakes. Also try to erase any preconceptions about the parents' role in teaching children to speak in grammatical sentences. The actual role of parental input to children is probably not what you believe it to be. Perhaps it will be useful to approach the topic of child language development as if we were scientists from another world who have been assigned to study the communication system used by people on

Earth. In preparing to report back the basic facts about how this communication system is acquired, we are simply summarizing what we have observed in our studies of Earth children. At this point we will concentrate on "Just the facts," as Joe Friday from *Dragnet* says. We will collect facts about language acquisition to prepare us to develop a theory, or model, of this process, which is our ultimate goal.

1   Characteristics of Language Acquisition

What would our report say about children's transition to the Final State? Perhaps the most remarkable fact is that, without special training or carefully sequenced language input, every normal child acquires a natural language. We refer to this property of language acquisition as the **universality** of language. The universality of language stands in glaring contrast to the limited attainment of arguably simpler cognitive skills such as the ability to perform basic calculations or to tie knots. A related observation is that every child in a linguistic community succeeds in converging on a grammatical system that is equivalent to everyone else's, despite a considerable latitude in linguistic experience. Finally, we will see that children acquire language quite rapidly and with few wrong turns, considering the number of potential pitfalls that exist.

Despite the diversity of natural languages, this picture of the course of acquisition has been observed so often across languages that we are certain of its truth. But this in no way renders it less astonishing for a parent watching the process unfold, or less difficult for a scientific theory to explain. What is special about natural language, and about children, that guarantees that almost without fail they will master a rich and intricate system of rules for language production and comprehension by the time they reach school age, i.e., at a time when they are receiving their earliest instruction in other complex cognitive skills? This is one of the puzzles which our theory of language must solve.

The next observation concerns the primary linguistic data – the environmental experience within which children learn language. Some children spend a lot of time in their first few years with adults, who give them extensive individual attention. If these were the only children we encountered, we might reach the conclusion that children are taught language by their parents or caretakers. But other children receive less individual attention, even if adults are around to care for them, and they nevertheless develop equal facility with language as the children who received much more individual attention. In other situations, children spend most of their time with other children, and not in situations in which an adult speaks directly to them very often. In yet other cases, children are spoken to in one language by some adults, and in another language by other adults. In all of these circumstances, children manage to acquire a native language – and rather quickly at that. Some of the differences between children's experiences are cultural, some social, and some accidental. After studying many children, our report would conclude that even children growing up in the same linguistic community, and ultimately learning the same language, may have a wide variety of experiences with language during their early years. Despite the variety in experiences, however, the report would note that every child in every linguistic community acquires the language of that community.

A related point is that every child in the same linguistic community learns the same language. This means that the grammars they have internalized are nearly equivalent. Otherwise, mutual understanding would not be possible. Children's uniform convergence on equivalent grammars is all the more striking in view of the fact that children all receive different input (= primary linguistic data). How is it that all children manage to learn to speak and understand a language, despite being raised in environments that vary considerably?

These observations lead us to ask whether *explicit* instruction is required at all for language acquisition. In this context, it is worth remarking on the linguistic achievements of the children of immigrant parents. Even in cases where adult immigrants exhibit great difficulty in mastering more than the rudiments of the language of a new community, it is normal for their young children to acquire the new language without any difficulties at all. Clearly, these children are not using their parents as models, yet they learn all the complexities of the language spoken around them just as successfully as children whose parents are native speakers.

Here, then, are the first two facts about language acquisition. First, it is universal (within the human species) and, second, there is a considerable latitude in the kind of environmental inputs that permit children to develop language. A theory of language and mind, to be viable, must be responsive to these observations.

Another observation that would be in our report is that some children learn many languages, although most children learn only one. In communities where more than one language is spoken, children acquire all of the languages of the community. So, in this way at least, language clearly IS a function of the input – if a child's primary linguistic data is limited to one language, she learns just that language. But if a child is exposed to two languages, she learns both; and if exposed to three, the child learns three, and so on. If a polylingual child moves to another speech community, she may no longer be in a position to use all the languages she has been exposed to, and she may quickly forget one or more of them. But children who are exposed to and use more than one language will acquire (and retain) all the languages. As far as we know, *any* child can become polylingual.

Another observation is that every language is learned with equal ease. No particular language is so difficult that it is only acquired by a subset of the children who are exposed to it. It is sometimes said that Russian, or Japanese, or English is hard to learn. And it may be true that English-speaking adults find it more difficult to learn certain languages than others. But it is important to note that every child exposed to Russian acquires Russian, and that it is mastered as rapidly and effortlessly by Russian children as English is acquired by English or American children. The same is true of every other language.

We should note also that children who learn more than one language learn each of them with equal ease. Thus, the language of a child's parents doesn't determine the language of the child except in the most obvious sense that children speak whatever language (or languages) is spoken to them. That is to say, every child exposed to English learns English, and every child exposed to Chinese learns Chinese. One final point reinforces this conclusion. This is the observation that if a child born of English-speaking parents is taken to China, and raised there, the child speaks Chinese, not English. And this will be true, as noted earlier, whatever the level of linguistic achievement of the child's parents turns out to be. The observation that the language of the community is sufficient for language development calls into question one of the most common misconceptions about language – that children need explicit instruction in order to learn a language. To sum up, the facts about the process of language acquisition (with respect to differences in language exposure) all show that language acquisition is *uniform* across languages. Let us call this set of properties, then, the uniformity of language acquisition.

The universality and uniformity facts about language acquisition are quite interesting, but they are only the tip of the iceberg. As hypothetical scientific observers, we will have uncovered some other facts that make these facts pale by comparison. First, language acquisition is quite *rapid*. Almost all of the complexities of language are mastered by children before they begin school, by age 3 or 4. Of course, there are many *words* that children don't know – but even college students (and their professors) are still developing vocabulary. Also, children usually only begin learning to read and write when they are 5 or 6, and they may not be particularly eloquent in their speech. But, this should not make us lose track of the fact that most 5-year-olds can produce and understand sentences of considerable length and complexity. By age 5, children have mastered nearly all the different types of structures used in their language. At the same time, children of this age are only beginning to count, many of them can't tie their own shoes or draw human figures, and so on. So the rapid mastery of language by the preschool child is another important fact with which to confront a theory of language and mind.

A fourth important fact about language development is the *sequence* of steps children go through in mastering the language of their community. Children learning the same language all follow an almost identical pattern. They progress through the same stages of acquisition, and in the same order. It is true that the rate at which individual children pass through these stages may differ, however. In other words, stage and not age is the better indicator of a child's level of language development. This fact, too, must be accounted for by any model of language acquisition.

2　How Does Language Acquisition Proceed?

We have collected a number of facts about language acquisition which we would like a model to be able to account for. Now, let's consider some possible mechanisms which might be proposed as the basis for this remarkable process. We will start with mechanisms which have some intuitive appeal, but we will show that none of them is able to explain the facts we have presented so far. In the following chapters, we will introduce a theory which is up to the task.

Trial and error

The fact that children progress through similar stages of language acquisition suggests that language acquisition is not a trial-and-error process. If language acquisition was done simply by trial and error, then we wouldn't expect all children to go through the same steps, that is, make the same trials and errors in the same order. We should have anticipated this conclusion already, even if we hadn't observed that children pass through an invariant sequence of stages. It is unlikely that language is acquired in a trial-and-error process, because, if it were, the children learning the same language wouldn't all converge on the same grammatical rules. Children who reached their conclusions by trial and error would surely sometimes fail to communicate with each other, because they would have reached different conclusions. But, as far as we know, this does not happen. As we noted earlier, children in the same linguistic community all learn the same grammar. (There may be small differences, but these too are systematic.) This uniform convergence on the same Final State would be mysterious if children were free to entertain different hypotheses about the processes underlying language.

　　It is worth noting that we have already ruled out two ways in which trial-and-error learning procedures could be used successfully by children to come up with the same set of hypotheses. First, this could happen if the input to children were fixed, that is, if every child received the same experience. But we have already seen that this is not the case. We emphasized that, to the contrary, language acquisition takes place with diverse environmental experiences – children receiving quite varied input all settle on the same hypotheses.

A second logical possibility is that the Final State is so simple that it can be reached universally even using a trial-and-error approach. This, too, is incorrect. We will see abundant evidence of this in the chapters to follow.

Another source of evidence against trial-and-error learning is the fact that children make so few grammatical errors in language acquisition, at least considering the number of logically possible wrong turns that they could conceivably take – that is, considering the number of hypotheses that are compatible with the data at some stage of acquisition, but which turn out to be incorrect in the light of further data. Somehow, children know to avoid most potential pitfalls. Later we will discuss several examples of linguistic hypotheses that children systematically pick out from among a host of logically equivalent alternatives.

One of the main goals of Universal Grammar is to explain why so few errors occur. Of course, the errors that do occur are more prominent than ones that do not occur, because we simply don't take note when children say exactly what we say. But it is important not to let the errors children make play too prominent a role in the theory. For one thing, we all make errors, even as adults. But these mistakes, too, are not random. Our errors follow from the nature of the mental apparatus we have for learning and using language. The theory must explain both what does and what does not occur. As we will see, in many cases it is more difficult to explain the latter. The kind of errors that we have in mind are subtle grammatical errors, ones that you probably would never expect children to make. They are not the kind of errors we often hear, like saying "pasketti" for "spaghetti."

For now, the point to remember is that, from the standpoint of grammar, language acquisition is relatively *error-free*. It does not conform to a scenario in which each child is free to consider a large and varied set of alternative hypotheses. By all indications, then, it seems that children's hypotheses are not determined by trial and error.

Corrective feedback (negative evidence)

Many people believe that children learn to speak correctly because their parents correct them when they say something wrong. This cannot be the basis of language acquisition for several reasons. First, we have just observed that acquisition is relatively error-free. If children do not make certain kinds of mistakes, we can hardly expect their parents to correct them!

What about the errors that children do make? Researchers have found that parents do not systematically correct children for their grammatical errors (despite your recollections otherwise). Since the early 1970s, dozens of children have been observed, tape-recorded, and videotaped, for hundreds of hours by many researchers within the field of psycholinguistics. All of these data have been combed through, at great effort, looking for facts to support or contradict particular hypotheses, such as the hypothesis that parents reward children for improving their language skills.

One study of the availability of corrective feedback (or negative evidence) to children, by the psychologists Roger Brown and Camille Hanlon, looked at parental responses to children's utterances. First, these researchers recorded all the cases where the parents' response revealed a misunderstanding of what the child was saying. They found that there was *no* correlation between the parents' understanding and how grammatically well formed the child's utterance was. Parents seem to be able to understand the language of their child perfectly well, however babyish and oversimplified it is.

Brown and Hanlon also recorded all the instances of approval or disapproval in the parents' responses. What they found was that the approval responses didn't distinguish between well-formed sentences and incorrect baby-talk. Parental feedback did distinguish between true sentences and false sentences, regardless of whether these sentences were grammatically well formed or not. For example, one child studied by Brown's group said, "Mama isn't boy, he a girl." Despite the ungrammatical utterance, her mother replied, "That's right." On the other hand, when another child said, "Walt Disney comes on Tuesday," his mother said, "No, he does not" (since, as we know, Walt Disney comes on Sunday). In short, parents do give negative feedback, when children do not tell the truth, but they *don't* distribute positive and negative reinforcement in a way that could be causally related to children's language learning.

There is further evidence against corrective feedback as a major contributing factor in language development. Evidence of this kind is quite convincing, even if it is anecdotal. It is often noted that children fail to respond on the occasions when their parents do try to correct them. For example, one child was heard to say, "Nobody don't like me." Since her parent was a linguist, the parent of this child attempted to respond to the grammaticality of the child's sentence rather than its truth-value. The parent tried to correct the child, saying, "No, say, 'Nobody likes me'." The child responded saying, "Nobody don't like me." This went on for eight repetitions, until finally the child thought she understood the correction. She said, "Oh! Nobody don't *likes* me."

This anecdote offers considerable insight into the problem children would confront if they were to use parental input as the basis for correcting their own grammatical mistakes. As the example shows, it is one thing for the child to know that she has made a grammatical mistake and quite another to know how to go about instilling changes in her grammar so as to eliminate the mistake. The example points out a distinction that needs to be drawn, between **input** and

intake. Even if corrective feedback, say, were present in the input to children, what they make of the input, their intake, is another matter.

Imitation

It is often suggested that children develop grammatical knowledge through imitation. That is, children learn language by imitating their parents' talk. While there might be a grain of truth to this proposal, it cannot be the whole story. One source of evidence against the claim that children learn by imitation comes from children's **overregularizations**. As one example, children produce incorrect past tense and plural forms such as "goed" and "foots." These forms are clearly not the product of imitation, since they do not appear in the input from adults. These non-adult forms are evidence that children form generalizations (i.e., rules) that enable them to produce linguistic utterances they have not encountered. In this case, children have clearly attained the adult rules for past or plural, but have incorrectly applied them to stems which irregularly do not take them in the adult grammar.

It is interesting to note that non-adult utterances such as "goed" and "foots" continue to appear in children's spontaneous speech for several months, sometimes even years. Apparently they are expunged from children's grammars only after children encounter a number of occurrences of the adult irregular alternative. Somehow, these alternative forms are in competition with the errant forms emanating from the child's grammar. It has been suggested that children's errant forms are jettisoned because their grammars contain a **blocking principle**, or a **uniqueness principle**. According to this type of principle, the presence of the irregular form blocks the rule-generated one. Both forms of expression are permitted simultaneously only if there is abundant evidence (in the input) for each of the alternative forms of expression. Clearly these principles apply in the adult grammar as well as the child's, accounting for the adult acceptance of both "dived" and "dove", but not "singed".

Later in this book, we will discuss in more detail the creative aspect of the child's emerging linguistic system, which is called **productivity**. As we will discuss, children not only produce novel forms that are not part of the adult language, but they develop a system of linguistic rules that is capable of producing an unlimited number of sentences that are acceptable in the adult language. This means that the non-adult utterances children produce pale in comparison to the adult utterances they produce, but which have not previously been encountered in the linguistic environment.

Another example of a construction used by children, but not by adults, concerns their questions. Children sometimes ask ill-formed questions such as, "Where he is going?" What makes it interesting is that children who ask questions like this also ask correct questions of other types, such as, "Is he going?" This means that they have internalized the rules that are needed in forming these questions. Yet, they often fail to apply the rules correctly in forming questions. These forms are a product of the child's internal grammar (and possibly their performance limitations) and do not reflect their attempts to imitate what they encounter in the input.

It has also been found that some English-speaking children around the age of 3 or 4 consistently insert an "extra" word in some of their questions, such as, "What do you think what pigs eat?" The appearance of the extra word in the language of children learning English cannot be explained as children's response to the input. Although these constructions are not grammatically well formed in English, structures like this are found in certain dialects of German and other languages. It is worth noting that, if the innateness hypothesis is correct, then there is no *a priori* reason to expect children's grammatical hypotheses to be closely tied to their linguistic experience. However, if children make non-adult hypotheses, these should be consistent with the possibilities allowed by UG. This is true whenever the difference between children's productions and the target language mirror differences that occur across languages.

Expansion

Another possible explanation of how children develop language is that the parents *expand* their child's talk, turning the child's simple forms into proper sentences. For example, if the child said "Daddy chair," the parent might respond, "Yes, that's right dear, you're sitting on Daddy's chair." Although parents sometimes do this, it cannot be a mechanism that is crucial for language development. This was shown in a study with preschool children. One group of adults was asked to speak to their children by regularly expanding what the children said. They did this five days a week for three months. Another group of parents served as a control group. For this group, expansions were not given. The main finding was this: the experimental group of children showed no improvement in their language relative to the control group that did not receive expansions of their utterances. Thus, even if some parents do sometimes expand on their children's utterances, this does not seem to be a primary factor in language development.

Motherese

A related suggestion is that parents **simplify** their speech to their children. The idea is that parents use simple forms at the early stages, and gradually increase the complexity of their own sentences to match the child's development. In this fashion, the child moves ahead a little at a time. Adults do talk differently to children than to other adults, using what is sometimes called "Motherese," or "baby-talk." Adults mumble less to children, they use fewer incorrectly formed sentences, they use shorter sentences, and they frequently use different intonation patterns with young children. However, in many studies it has been found that they do not *invariably* use grammatically simpler sentences. Also, in studies comparing children whose parents used Motherese to those whose parents didn't use Motherese, no difference was found in language development. So it doesn't seem that Motherese serves to pace the information presented to the child, in order to help her learn the language in easy steps.

There is a more fundamental problem with this proposal. By simplifying the linguistic input, a parent is actually making the child's task harder, not easier. Simple input is consistent with a greater variety of grammatical hypotheses than is complex input. We will see an example of this later, in our discussion of structure dependence in chapter 3. It will be shown there that the formation of simple yes/no questions, such as, "Is Bill going to the show?", from their de- clarative counterparts, "Bill is going to the show," is compatible with both the correct, structure-dependent principle and the simple, but ultimately incorrect, structure-independent operation: move the first "is," "will," "can" etc. to the front of the sentence. The structure-independent operation produces the wrong yes/no questions with more complex input. For example, the application of the structure-independent operation to declarative sentences with a restrictive rela- tive clause, such as, "The man who is running will win," yields the question, "Is the man who running will win?", not, "Will the man who is running win?" This example shows that more complex input can help the learner eliminate errone- ous hypotheses. It should be clear that Motherese would not be helpful, and could be detrimental to language development in certain cases.

Conclusion

What can we conclude, then, about *why* and *how* language is acquired? The main conclusion we would draw is that language development seems to be internally driven. It comes from within the child, rather than from anything parents provide from the outside. It seems that children are just built to learn – they don't respond in any obvious way to external pressure or rewards. Rather, they are internally motivated to pick up information from what they hear, and record it and use it in their own behavior. We will see more evidence for this conclusion when we present the results from experimental studies of child language development. We will argue that the success at language acquisition which children's spontaneous productions reveal is actually an underestimate of children's abilities. For example, experimental procedures enable us to ascertain that children attain knowledge of grammatical principles that are not attested in their linguistic environment.

We will discuss in some detail the solution to this puzzle advanced by the theory of Universal Grammar. According to this theory, children's hypotheses about language are taken to be constrained in advance, in the sense that hypotheses are limited by biological characteristics of the human species. According to this viewpoint, there are innate restrictions on the hypotheses that children may entertain in forming their grammatical system. In this way, the remarkable linguistic feats that children accomplish in their first few years can be accounted for. We will consider further evidence for this position throughout this text.

Bibliographical Comments

Chomsky (1957) and Chomsky (1965) are two of Chomsky's most influential works laying out the theory of language presented here and in the rest of the text. There are many books reporting data on the process of language acquisition; among them are P. Bloom (1993), Brown (1973), Goodluck (1991), Slobin (1985). The original study on negative evidence was presented by Brown and Hanlon (1970); a more recent review of negative evidence is presented by Morgan and Travis (1989). The anecdote about children's failure to be corrected is from McNeil (1970). The proposal that a blocking principle applies to children's overregularizations is made in Pinker (1995). Children's non-adult questions mentioned here will be discussed in detail in chapters 20 and 22. One study of the potential effects of expansion on children's language acquisition is reported by Brown, Cazden, and Bellugi (1969). The phenomenon of Motherese and the limitations of its effects on language acquisition mentioned here are discussed by Newport, Gleitman, and Gleitman (1977); other studies of this phenomenon are collected in Snow and Ferguson (1977).

2 Knowledge in the Absence of Experience

Introduction

In this chapter, we discuss aspects of linguistic knowledge which all language learners come to know, but for which there is apparently no corresponding evidence in the linguistic environment. Phenomena of this kind are introduced to bolster the theory of innate knowledge, introduced in the previous chapter.

First, we will discuss people's awareness that some sentences have multiple meanings; such sentences are said to be **ambiguous**. It is easy to demonstrate that any English-speaking person realizes, after a few moments' reflection, that some sentences are ambiguous. It is difficult to explain, however, how anyone could have gained this knowledge on the basis of their experience, because it is not usual for people to point out the alternative meanings of sentences. A second kind of linguistic knowledge concerns the ability of language users to tell which sentences are well formed and which are deviant. We will treat these two phenomena in turn.

1 Ambiguity

Example (1) contains two kinds of ambiguous sentences. Figure 2.1 illustrates the alternative interpretations (readings) of the ambiguity in (1a).

(1) a. They fed her dog biscuits.
     b. Washing machines can be dangerous.

One reading of example (1a) can be paraphrased: *They fed some biscuits to her dog*. The other reading is: *They fed dog biscuits to her*. The ambiguity in example (1b) can be seen in the following paraphrases of the alternative meanings: *Washing machines is dangerous*, OR *Washing machines are dangerous*. On the

Figure 2.1　Two meanings of an ambiguous sentence: "We fed her dog biscuits"

first meaning, we are talking about a kind of activity: to wash machines. On the second meaning, we are talking about a kind of object: machines that wash.

The observation that with little effort everyone is able to identify the alternative interpretations for these sentences is quite remarkable. Where did we learn to do this? Is it reasonable to suppose that each of us was exposed to sentences like these at some point in our childhood? Presumably not. But if not by experience, how does everyone learn to make these judgments? The proposal of Universal Grammar is that the rule system we have internalized can be called on to produce multiple meanings for certain sentences, though the rules themselves were learned on the basis of unambiguous sentences. This is an empirical claim, of course, and one that we will go into in more detail later. For now, we are simply making the point that it is highly improbable that everyone has learned to resolve each of the possible ambiguities in language through his or her experience. So ambiguity resolution is at least a likely candidate for innately given linguistic knowledge.

2　An Ambiguity Lost: Wanna Contraction

On the other side of the coin, sometimes a sentence has only a single interpretation, where we might expect more than one. Some sentences of this kind can be found in the linguistic phenomenon known as **wanna contraction**. The examples we will use involve WH-questions. As their name suggests, these are questions beginning with WH-words like *who*, *what*, *where*, and *why*. Read example (2). Can you find more than one interpretation?

(2)　Who did the coach want to shoot at the end of the game?

Example (2) can be asking two different questions. One of the interpretations of this question can be depicted as in figure 2.2. The alternative meaning of example (2) is depicted in figure 2.3.

The ambiguity in (2) is due to the interaction of a complex set of factors. It arises, in part, because (2) is a WH-question and in part because it contains the

Figure 2.2   Who did the coach want to shoot at the end of the game?

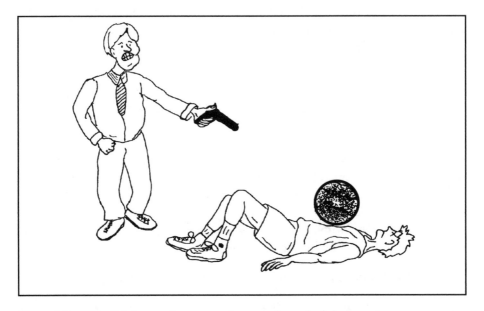

Figure 2.3   Who did the coach want to shoot at the end of the game?

verb *shoot*. The verb *shoot* is ambiguous. It can be used either as an **intransitive verb** or as a **transitive verb**. An intransitive verb is one that never appears with an **object**. An example is *sleep*. We say, "The Terminator never sleeps" but not, "The Terminator never sleeps the bed." In contrast, a transitive verb always appears with an object. An example is *hit*. We say, "The Terminator hit the wall" but not "The Terminator hit." The verb *shoot* can be used in either way.

The other factor involved in the ambiguity in (2) is the grammatical role of the WH-word *who*. Suppose *who* is taken to be the object of *shoot*; that is, suppose that *shoot* is taken to be a transitive verb. In this case, the question asks about the identity of a person such that the coach wants to shoot that person at the end of the game. There is another possibility, however. The verb *shoot* can be analyzed as an intransitive verb. If so, the WH-word *who* cannot be an object (there is none for intransitive verbs, as we saw). Therefore, the WH-word must be the **subject** of the shooting. On this analysis, the question asks about the identity of the person who the coach wants to do the shooting at the end of the game. When we read (2), we simply can't tell which analysis of the verb *shoot* is intended, so we cannot determine a unique grammatical role for the WH-word. There are two different ways to interpret the question being asked, as we have seen.

Now observe that (2) contains the verbal elements *want* and *to*. In many linguistic contexts, these words can be **contracted**, to form *wanna*. When *want* and *to* are contracted to form *wanna* in (2), this alters the range of possible interpretations that can be assigned to it. Consider how you would interpret (3). It may help to say the sentence aloud.

(3)　Which player did the coach *wanna* shoot at the end of the game?

If you are like most people, (3) has only one of the interpretations that could be given to (2), namely the interpretation according to which the coach wants to shoot some player. With the contracted form *wanna*, then, one of the meanings of question (2) seems to have vanished. We will discuss the constraint on *wanna* contraction in more detail in chapter 23, and we will show evidence that children obey this constraint in chapter 24.

Now let us consider another example like the last one, in which an ambiguity comes and goes depending on the construction involved. The present example is a phenomenon called **backward pronominalization** or **backward anaphora**. Pronominalization has to do with the **reference** of pronouns (i.e., what they pick out in the world). Sometimes, pronouns can have the same referent as (or are **coreferential** with) another phrase (such as a proper name) in a sentence. But in some sentences, the pronoun must have as its referent an entity that is not mentioned in the sentence. This contrast can be seen in the following pair of sentences:

(4) a.   After she ran, Jackie had a lot of money.
     b.   She ran after Jackie had a lot of money.

Notice that *she* can (but isn't required to) refer to *Jackie* in the first sentence, but it cannot in the second sentence. To explain this contrast, Howard Lasnik, a linguist at the University of Connecticut, proposed a **non-coreference rule** to account for these facts. The idea behind this rule is that in a certain configuration, a pronoun and a name must not refer to the same thing. Lasnik coined the term **disjoint reference** to refer to the phenomenon, which we will discuss in greater detail in chapter 14. For now, the point to take away is that sentence (4b) exhibits a case of potential ungrammaticality which hinges on the meaning of an utterance, not just the words it contains. The string itself is fine, but its interpretation is restricted in a way that sentence (4a) is not. In (4a), the pronoun and the name can corefer, but in (4b) they cannot.

We would ask again how we all come to know this linguistic fact. The answer is, apparently, that we did not LEARN it because the kind of evidence that would be needed to learn it is not available. The requisite data would presumably consist of feedback from parents or other caretakers informing the learner that sentences could NOT be given certain interpretations. It is far-fetched to think that every one of us who can make these judgments about what meanings canNOT be assigned to sentences such as (4b) has, at some point in our lives, had the relevant instruction – that a pronoun and a name cannot refer to the same thing in certain linguistic contexts. We will buttress this argument in Parts II and III, by demonstrating that even very young children exhibit the same judgments in these matters as adults. This renders it even more implausible to think that these judgments are learned.

3   Judgments of Grammaticality

This brings us to another aspect of linguistic knowledge that seems likely to be acquired without corresponding experience from the environment. This is the ability to detect sentences that are grammatically deviant. To illustrate this ability, we will return to WH-questions involving *wanna contraction*. Consider example (5).

(5) a.   Who did the coach want to shoot?
     b.   Who did the coach wanna shoot?
     c.   Who did the coach want to shoot the basketball?
     But?
     d.   *Who did the coach wanna shoot the basketball?

Example (5d) sounds quite awkward to our ears, as indicated by the asterisk(*).[1] When the ambiguous verb *shoot* is followed by an object (*the basketball*), contraction of *want* and *to* is awkward at best. This oddity is limited to WH-questions, however. Both of the following **declarative** sentences are natural.

(6)   a.   Donyell will want to shoot the basketball at the end of the game.
      b.   Donyell will wanna shoot the basketball at the end of the game.

Another way of making the same point is to replace the ambiguous verb *shoot* either by a verb that is unambiguously transitive, such as *beat*, or by one that is unambiguously intransitive, such as *win*. In WH-questions, the verbal elements *want* and *to* can be contracted when they precede a transitive verb, as in (7b), but not when they precede an intransitive verb, as in (7d).

(7)   a.   Which team did the coach want to beat?
      b.   Which team did the coach wanna beat?
      c.   Which team did the coach want to win?
      But?
      d.   *Which team did the coach wanna win?

Soon we will see that the oddity of contraction in WH-questions is a reflection of a grammatical principle. The result of the principle is that contraction of *want* and *to* is prohibited in certain constructions, such as the one we just examined. That is, contraction of *want* and *to* is prohibited before an intransitive verb, but contraction is optional (permissible, though not required) when the verb that follows is transitive, as long as the object is not overtly mentioned in the question.

Another example involving *wanna contraction* might help, because the intuitions underlying this phenomenon are quite subtle, and may elude you at first. Read the following sentences aloud. Be sure to pronounce the *wanna* in the first example, and omit the "answers" on the first reading.

(8)   a.   Who do you think the Red Sox will wanna play first?
            (Answer: anyone but the Oakland A's)

      b.   Who do you think the Red Sox will want to play first?
            (Answer: anyone but Bill Buckner)

If we are correct, you should have interpreted the word *first* in the first example as an *ordinal*. This question asks about the *first team* the Red Sox will want to face. The second question with *first* also permits this interpretation, but the word *first* may also be interpreted as a noun in the second question, shorthand for *first base*.

4　The Innateness Hypothesis

We should not lose sight of the basic question we began with: How did it come about that everyone who speaks (American) English has knowledge of the kind of linguistic phenomena illustrated in this chapter? That is, how is it that any speaker can judge that certain questions sound okay but others sound odd? And, why is it that all speakers assign some questions only one interpretation, while other questions are taken to be ambiguous? It seems unlikely that either type of linguistic knowledge could have been derived from our experience. If it had been, this would mean that all of us would have needed to experience the requisite input from the environment, since all of us know the relevant facts. However, as we pointed out in chapter 1, researchers have found that parents *don't* provide the kind of negative information which would be necessary to children. They may sometimes tell children to speak properly, but the kinds of corrections parents make have nothing to do with many of the kinds of linguistic knowledge that we have been discussing. Therefore, we are invited to infer that these grammatical distinctions are mastered without recourse to experience.

If the kind of linguistic knowledge we have discussed in this chapter is not learned by experience, then how IS it acquired? According to current linguistic theory, the answer is that this knowledge is *innate* – it is part of Universal Grammar, the human genetic blueprint for language acquisition. Following the line of argument we outlined in the last chapter, linguists argue for innateness by pointing to the disparity between what language users come to know and the input they receive. Focusing on the limitations of experience, the argument that some linguistic knowledge is innate is called the argument from **the poverty of the stimulus**. In those instances in which children and adults know things about language for which they have no evidence, it is said that their experience **underdetermines** their knowledge.

5　The Poverty of the Stimulus Argument

To put these ideas concerning innateness in clearer perspective, let us return to some terminology we introduced earlier. As we stated, the mechanisms that are used in language development are contained in the Language Acquisition Device (LAD). The LAD is the means by which the child/learner analyzes the linguistic input (from parents and others). The linguistic input which the child receives from the surrounding people is called the Primary Linguistic Data (PLD). The LAD uses these data to hypothesize a series of grammars. The last grammar that is formulated is the adult grammar, or Final State. Recall that the process can be represented schematically in the following way:

(9)   Input (PLD) → LAD → Final State

Now we have a way to represent linguistic facts that we come to know without decisive evidence. Those will be properties of the Final State that are not also properties of the input. Knowledge of these facts somehow follows from the mechanisms within the LAD. One of the main goals of linguistic theory is to explain the nature of the device – the Language Acquisition Device (LAD) – that uses whatever data it has at hand to converge on the adult grammar. We have seen already that there are many facts about the LAD to be explained. It must be capable of promoting a fast transition to the Final State, taking an invariant route for every child in the same linguistic community, and it must accomplish this feat with only limited wrong turns along the way. Although we will not be able to specify every piece of knowledge in the LAD, in later chapters we will describe certain of its components in some detail.

Conclusion

The examples of knowledge in the absence of experience which we have discussed in this chapter strongly motivate the theory of innate knowledge which we have briefly outlined. Further evidence comes from more extensive study of the course of language acquisition – what paths children take, which errors they don't make, and so on. In the next chapter, we will give an overview of the stages children go through in language acquisition. This will serve as important background for the theories we will consider. We will come back to look at details of the child's acquisition of complex syntax throughout the text.

Note

1   As is standard practice in linguistics, we use an asterisk (*) preceding an example sentence to indicate ungrammaticality, i.e., a sentence which doesn't sound right to a native speaker.

Bibliographical Comments

The syntax of "wanna contraction" has received considerable attention; one review of much of the work on this topic is presented in Postal and Pullum (1982). This issue, and children's knowledge of the constraints on contraction, will be discussed in chapters 23 and 24, and additional references will be given there. The non-coreference facts mentioned here were observed by Lasnik (1976). We will discuss the issues and children's knowledge of the facts illustrated here in chapters 14 and 15. The poverty of the stimulus argument for the innateness hypothesis will be developed more fully in chapter 6.

3   Stages of Language Acquisition

Introduction

In this chapter, we will outline the basic milestones which children have been observed to pass by in their development of language. The data for this chapter come mainly from studies of children's natural, spontaneous productions. As we will see later, experimental investigations have some advantages for more complex issues. We nevertheless believe that it is profitable to outline the stages that children have been found to go through in producing words and sentences in naturalistic settings. We should point out that the timing of these events can vary by several months from child to child. However, the sequence that children go through is remarkably constant from one child to the next. As we proceed through the stages of development, we will compare language acquisition with children's development in non-linguistic areas at each stage. This is to see the extent to which language develops independently of other cognitive systems.

1   The Milestones of Language Acquisition

First few months

During the first few months, children cry and coo, and they begin to babble certain sounds. **Babbling** is the utterance of linguistic sounds without any meaning attached.

On the comprehension side, experimental studies of children learning diverse languages have shown that they have particular linguistic ways of perceiving speech sounds. There is evidence that even before they have heard much of their native language, much less done any analysis of it, they are prepared to attend to linguistic distinctions that will be crucial in analyzing the speech stream into appropriate segments. Some of the strongest evidence comes from the work of

Peter Eimas. Eimas showed that 2-week-old babies could discriminate between a so-called **voiced** consonant such as "ba," where the vocal cords begin to vibrate early on, as compared to an **unvoiced** consonant such as "pa," where the vocal cords begin to vibrate only at the vowel, /a/ (ahh). The phonemic contrast, voiced versus unvoiced, is used in natural languages to distinguish between words; for instance, the English words "pat" and "bat" differ only in **voicing**. Voicing is just one of many ways of marking categorical boundaries that distinguish between words, so this ability by infants to distinguish phonemic boundaries is called **categorical perception**.

What about children's non-linguistic development at this stage? Infants will smile, and grasp at things. Also, infants can recognize human faces, an ability that is also regarded as innate by many researchers.

Approximately 6 to 10 months

At about 6 months of age, children have more varied babbling. They babble different syllables which they will repeat over and over, sometimes changing the syllable by one phoneme (e.g., ba, ba, ba, bi, bi, bi, bu, bu, bu). Children in all language environments seem to do the same kind of babbling. In fact, even *deaf* children babble vocally at this stage, even though they're not getting any linguistic input from speech. This fact indicates that babbling is an internally driven behavior, not a response to external stimulation.

At about 10 months, babbling changes. Children in different linguistic communities begin to babble differently. Each child only babbles sounds that are used in her own linguistic community. Children also babble using the stress and intonation contours of their language community. At this age, deaf children *cease* vocal babbling.

In non-linguistic development, during this stage the child is able to laugh, and progresses from wiggling on the floor to real crawling and sitting.

Approximately 1 year

At about the age of 1 year, the child begins to produce her first words. These will generally be words for things in the immediate environment, such as "Mommy," "Daddy," "cookie," "doggie," and so on. The child also uses gestures to communicate at this stage; for example, reaching upwards to indicate that she wants to be lifted up, or reaching outwards for "gimme." She may also combine some words with gestures. For example, the word ("more") is often combined with an open hand or with an open mouth. This combination of word and gesture happens most often with pointing gestures, which are combined with the name for the object being pointed to. For example, the child might point to the dog and say, "doggie." During this time, the child also continues to babble according to the sounds of her language. At this stage the child also has a fast-growing comprehension of language, so she can obey simple commands at this time (such as "point to your eyes").

At this age, children can "cruise" (walk holding onto things), stand, and wave bye-bye.

Approximately 1½ years

At about 1½ years, the child will start to put together two successive single words, e.g., "Mommy . . . cookie." The intonation pattern used for each of these words is a single word pattern, with falling intonation at the end of each word and a pause between the words. The child seems to be picking out the components of a complex situation, and seems to apprehend the meanings of words. However, these word combinations are apparently not yet sentences; rather, they are the *precursors* of sentences. At this stage, vocabulary is increasing quickly.

Before long the child puts two-word combinations together to form primitive two-word "sentences." A difference can be observed in intonation: the pattern has now changed so that both words are included in one intonation group, with falling intonation only at the end of the two-word sequence, and without a pause between the words. Using these primitive sentences, the child is able to ask for things with language. For example, the child might say, "more milk," or "Mommy up."

There is reason to believe that throughout development, there is a **computational bottleneck** which prohibits the child from expressing all that she knows. We use the term "computational bottleneck" because it seems that the child knows many things about the language, but can't get them all out at once, just as the liquid in a bottle can't flow out all at once because of the bottleneck. In acquisition, at about a year and a half, the child might be ready to put together two-word sentences, but this computational bottleneck limits her to single words. As this stage progresses, the bottleneck widens, and the child begins to produce two-word utterances.

As we will see, the child has to face similar bottlenecks in other areas. For example, there may be a bottleneck in the number of words she can put together into sentences, and later there may be another bottleneck in the use of rules to form new sentences. These bottlenecks can be attributed to some limitation in a non-linguistic cognitive capacity, such as attention span or memory span. The idea of a computational bottleneck also influences adult behavior in some circumstances. It is difficult to do two demanding tasks simultaneously – such as driving a car down a twisty road and discussing a philosophical issue. Apparently, children have such bottlenecks at a much lower level.

Non-linguistically, at this age the child can walk, feed herself, and in drawing, she can make scribble lines with crayons.

Approximately 2 years

The late Roger Brown of Harvard University conducted a ground-breaking study of children's language development in the period of early sentence-formation. He showed that starting at about 2 years, it is more appropriate to talk about language development in terms of **stages** rather than in terms of *ages*. This is because children differ enormously in the age at which they achieve various levels of language mastery. For a long time, looking at children of the same age obscured the fact that the developmental sequence is almost *invariant*, even though some children pass through certain stages faster than others do.

Brown's study discovered that the stages correlate very highly with the *length of a child's utterances*. What is correlated is not the maximum length of any utterance the child might make, because a child will produce an occasional sentence that's much longer than her normal performance. But if we take the average or *mean* length of the child's spontaneous utterances, we can differentiate such stages. This measure is called **Mean Length of Utterance**, and is abbreviated MLU. MLU is determined by recording a large number of speech samples from a child, writing down her utterances, and finding the average number of words that appear in the utterances.

Presumably, MLU is a measure of a child's computational capacity – how far her memory and attention spans have developed. It seems that children develop at different rates because of differences in their processing capacity. But at a given processing capacity, the kinds of utterances they produce are just about constant. It should be kept in mind, however, that MLU is probably not an accurate measure of a child's grammatical competence. Occasionally, a child will produce sentences that exceed her MLU considerably. In our view, such sentences may provide a more accurate assessment of grammatical competence. But, MLU can be used as a guide; it provides us with approximate information about a child's stage of language development, relative to other children.

At about 2 years of age we say the child is at Stage I in development. At this stage, the child has a vocabulary of about 400 words, and an MLU of 1.75. The child is producing many single-word utterances, such as naming objects, as well as two- and three-word "sentences" which express the semantic concepts that are usually contained in a single clause. For example, the child might say, "Ball all gone," or "Daddy sit chair." Children's *word order* consistently follows adult word order, but grammatical words such as "is" and "the" are not used.

In non-linguistic development, the child at this age usually can run, pull off their socks, and scribble in circles.

Approximately 2½ to 3 years

At the age of about 2½ years, children usually reach Stage II. At this stage, their MLU is about 2.25, and their vocabulary is about 900 words. During this stage, the child acquires some grammatical devices, such as determiners, pronouns, the progressive ending "-ing," and the past tense. The child can say sentences like, "Cat sitting there," or "He goed in the house." Notice that the verb form "goed" is incorrect – it is an overgeneralization of the regular past tense form "-ed" on a verb which takes an irregular past. It is also worth pointing out that the pronoun "he" may be used to refer to a female. Children can talk about absent objects and past events, and can ask questions about things around them.

The development of grammatical words (= morphemes) at Stage II follows a remarkably stable course. Most children learning English first learn the progressive marker "-ing." Next, they begin to use the simple locative prepositions "in" and "on." Next, the plural marker "-s" appears, and so on through the entire set of grammatical morphemes. Children continue to learn grammatical morphemes over several stages, but the order of acquisition is remarkably consistent for different children.

Another aspect of the development of grammatical morphemes deserves further comment. This is the observation that children form generalizations based upon the input they receive. For example, when children learn the past tense marker "-ed," they apply what they have learned to make other past tense forms that they haven't yet encountered. For word pairs like "walk" and "jump" the generalization (apply "-ed" to the verb stem) gives the correct past tense forms, "walked" and "jumped." However, children also use the generalization to create past tense forms for other verbs, like "go." Here, the result is not benign; it leads to the erroneous form "goed." Similarly, the plural marker "-s" is applied too broadly: children produce "foots," for example. These non-adult forms are referred to as **overregularizations**, because children have extended the generalization *too far*. The existence of children's overregularizations are important, however, because they invite us to infer that they have deduced a rule based on the input they have received.

During Stage II, children still produce sentences of just one clause. Notice that there is no *a priori* reason for development to go this way. Why shouldn't children begin to produce multi-clausal sentences, or even sentences with complex operations, *before* they start to produce grammatical morphemes? They do develop in these areas eventually, but not until later in development, as we will see.

During Stage II, children can jump, pull off their clothes, and they can draw closed figures. Children usually cannot count, although they are sometimes taught to hold up two or three fingers, to indicate their age.

Approximately 3 to 3½ years

At approximately 3 years of age, children go through Stage III of language development. During this time their MLU = 2.75 and their vocabulary consists of approximately 1,200 words. Children continue to go through acquisition of auxiliary verbs, prepositions, and other grammatical morphemes. They also begin to use **syntactic transformations**. We will discuss transformations and their acquisition in some detail in Part III. For now, we will give a simplified example. Think of transformations as rules which create new sentence types out of basic declarative sentences. For example, children use a transformation (called Subject–Auxiliary Inversion) to form yes/no questions, such as, "Is Daddy mad?" from corresponding declarative sentences, i.e., "Daddy is mad." They use another transformational rule (called WH-Movement) to form WH-questions such as, "Where is he going?"

Let us assume that a variant of a declarative sentence underlies the WH-question, "Where is he going?" The underlying declarative form is, "He is going where." On this assumption, the child can ask correct WH-questions such as, "Where is he going?" only if they know both the rule for forming WH-questions (WH-Movement) and the rule for forming yes/no questions (Subject–Auxiliary Inversion). The first transformation moves the WH-word "where" to a position at the beginning of the sentence, yielding "Where he is going?" This is not a well-formed question, however. A second transformation is needed to invert the subject "he" and the auxiliary verb "is." The end result is the well-formed WH-question, "Where is he going?":

Underlying Form:	He is going where
WH-Movement Transformation:	Where he is going
Subject–Auxiliary Inversion Transformation:	Where is he going

Interestingly, Stage III children sometimes produce the intermediate WH-question, "Where he is going?" in addition to correct WH-questions, such as "Where is he going?" This error is frequently found with "why" questions, such as "Why they can't run?" We will discuss this error type in chapter 20, where we examine the acquisition of WH-questions in more depth.

At this stage in the non-linguistic area, children can learn to ride a tricycle, wash their own faces, and hop on one foot.

Approximately 3½ to 4 years

At around 3½ years, children move into Stage IV (MLU = 3.50, vocabulary = approximately 1,500 words). At this stage, children begin to use multi-clause sentences, such as relative clauses, complement clauses, and conjoined clauses. They still overregularize many irregular forms of verbs, however.

Non-linguistically, children at this age can catch a ball in their hands, use scissors, or do jigsaw puzzles. They also begin to tell stories.

Approximately 4 to 5 years

At approximately 4–5 years, children go through Stage V (MLU = 4.0, vocabulary = 1,900 words). During this stage children produce more conjunctions, including subordinate clauses with temporal terms such as "before" and "after." They engage in more social conversations with peers at this time. They also begin to learn some **metalinguistic** abilities such as defining words, and correcting their own grammatical errors. These abilities are called "metalinguistic" because they involve conscious awareness of the properties of language.

The development of metalinguistic skills underscores an important point about language acquisition: that it is not a conscious process. For the most part, before Stage V, young children can't say what is wrong with an ungrammatical sentence (even though we know they unconsciously know and use the relevant rules, since they produce the correct forms). Even older children can rarely articulate the rules they have discovered – but then, neither can a typical adult.

Non-linguistically, children at 4–5 years begin to learn basic mathematical notions, but still fail Piagetian cognitive tests of conservation of quantity.

After 5

After Stage V it is difficult to explain language acquisition in terms of stages which are connected with the development of MLU. The problem is that children's sentences continue to show more complexity, without becoming longer. Furthermore, so much of the basics of grammar are acquired by the age of 5, that it is difficult to point out areas which still show development. During the age period from 5 to 10 years, vocabulary continues to increase, though at a slower rate. Also during this time, children learn most of the exceptions to rules which they have overregularized. Although rule learning is more or less complete by about 5 years, the learning of exceptional forms is not complete until after 10 years (e.g., many teenagers still say "We won the other team," instead of "We beat the other team"). After puberty, there is very little change in syntax or pronunciation. Vocabulary continues to grow, as does the ability to use language stylistically. Of course, vocabulary learning continues throughout the teenage years and (at a much slower rate) through adult life. This presumably is because the concepts associated with many words are not accessible to children. But it is also probably because vocabulary learning is fundamentally memorization. It is the general rules that underlie the productivity of human languages that children are especially well equipped to cope with.

During this time period conceptual development continues; for example, children at this stage begin to give logical explanations.

Conclusion

This overview of the stages of language development as they are displayed in the spontaneous speech of children reveals certain properties of language development. It is apparent that language development is remarkably fast and consistent across children. Various studies examining the acquisition of numerous languages have found strikingly similar steps of development at similar age ranges. Furthermore, the strategies which children seem to employ in acquisition are similar cross-linguistically. The child somehow sifts through the language she hears, selectively picking out those aspects of it that are relevant to the properties of the grammar she is working on at the time. Finally, note especially the kinds of errors which children do and do not make. Overregularization errors are common. Such errors tell us two things. First, overregularizations show that children are rule-makers; they are able to detect regularities in the input, and to go beyond them to produce novel, rule-governed forms. Second, they show that certain language-particular idiosyncrasies are the source for potential errors of commission. In contrast, children are not observed to make errors in other areas, such as word order, complex clauses, and transformations. They may omit certain options which are available, such as failing to apply a transformation, but they rarely err in the form of the transformation, once it is used. This is an important contrast, which we will illustrate in more detail and reinforce in the following chapters, and in the chapters of Part III.

Bibliographical Comments

An overview of much of the research on the acquisition of English summarized here is given in deVilliers and deVilliers (1985). The study of infant speech perception is presented in Eimas (1985), as well as other works by Eimas and his colleagues. A summary of studies of children's babbling is given in Vihman, Macken, Miller, Simmons, and Miller (1985). The original Harvard study of children's early syntax is reported by Brown (1973) and other works cited there. Most of the work reported in this chapter was carried out in that project.

4 Why Language Does Not Have to be Taught

Introduction

Shortly we will begin presenting in some detail Chomsky's theory of language and mind, Universal Grammar. Understanding the theory of Universal Grammar will require you to learn quite a lot of technical machinery. We think it is worth the effort and we would like to take the opportunity to convince you that it is. To achieve that goal, we will first consider a very different theoretical approach to language from Chomsky's theory. The alternative is much simpler and less technical, so it is worth demonstrating that it is not up to the task of explaining the set of facts we have gathered together as our data-base against which to evaluate Chomsky's, or any, theory. We will indicate several specific places where the simple alternative approach is unable to explain the facts we have before us. Lacking a simpler alternative, we are motivated to consider a more complex theory.

In addition to its simplicity, however, the theory we discuss first appeals to common sense. Many people intuitively believe that something like what this theory maintains actually is involved in language acquisition. So, for this reason, too, it is important to examine it closely. Theories that sit well with our ordinary observations should be taken seriously, and abandoned only if there are good reasons for doing so. The simple theory is the **Behaviorist** theory of learning. According to this hypothesis, children *learn* language in much the same way as they learn mathematics or music – that is, someone, usually their parents, *teaches* them. If this is so, then learning language should follow a similar course as the learning of mathematics or music. Children would use general principles of learning which apply across domains. They would make many errors, which could differ widely from one child to the next, depending on each child's particular environment. In addition, the level of ability achieved by different individuals would not be the same. Just as people differ widely in mathematical knowledge, and musical ability, they would differ widely in linguistic abilities.

We have already suggested that language acquisition does not appear to proceed in this manner. Everyone achieves a similar standard of skill, and they proceed through similar stages in attaining it, regardless of the latitude in environmental input. These observations suggest that language is not learned – rather, it is acquired through the interaction of innately specified linguistic principles and exposure to language in the child's environment. Thus, this view requires hypothesizing a special-purpose language acquisition mechanism. In order to support this claim more fully, it will be useful to see just how the learning hypothesis fails.

In order to make our case tangible, we will consider a particular variant of Behaviorism, as espoused by the late American psychologist B. F. Skinner of Harvard University. Before Chomsky, many psycholinguists and linguists believed that the principles of Behaviorism would ultimately explain a great many important facts about language. Behaviorism is worth exploring as a theory of language and mind even if it, in fact, has proven not to work. There are several reasons to take Behaviorism seriously. It postulates few mechanisms. It meets with common sense. And, it has broad applicability, having proven successful in the hands of Skinner and others in modifying many different animal and human behaviors, even ones that appear to be quite complicated. Because our concern is with Behaviorism as an account of verbal behavior, we will review only those principles and research techniques that have been used in explaining some linguistic phenomena.

The most fundamental tenet of Behaviorism is that the mind is not a proper object of study. Behaviorism studies only overt observable actions, and relates these actions to other overt observable actions. Behaviorism considers research on mental states as "unscientific," since it is based on putative mental processes which are unobservable. Behaviorism claims that the postulation of mental processes is not necessary for the description and explanation of behavior. It claims that there are physically mediated correlations between environmental **stimuli** and behavioral **responses**, and that these correlations can provide a scientific explanation, in principle, for all behavior. If this is true, then Behaviorism would be a strong, parsimonious theory, because it requires us to postulate few mechanisms to achieve the correct results. However, although Behaviorist psychology has demonstrated some correlations between certain stimuli and particular responses, it has been unsuccessful in accounting for much complex human behavior, including language, as we will now discuss.

1   Classical Conditioning

One of the central methodologies of Behaviorism is **classical conditioning**, discovered by the Russian researcher Ivan Pavlov. Here's the familiar prototypical

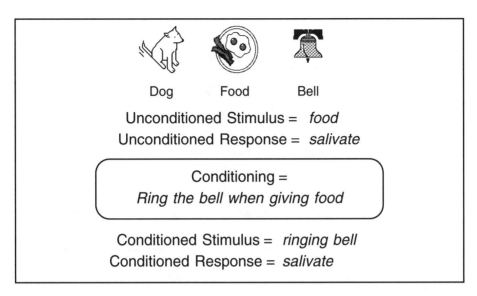

Dog Food Bell

Unconditioned Stimulus = *food*
Unconditioned Response = *salivate*

Conditioning =
Ring the bell when giving food

Conditioned Stimulus = *ringing bell*
Conditioned Response = *salivate*

Figure 4.1 Classical conditioning

experiment he performed. Pavlov knew that dogs will naturally salivate when food is placed before them. Because it occurs without any outside interference from the experimenter, any naturally occurring behavior such as salivating is called an **unconditioned response**. The stimulus for an unconditioned response is called an **unconditioned stimulus**. In the present example, this is the food that is placed before the dog. The term "unconditioned" is used because the experimenter has not yet done anything to change the animal's behavior. Pavlov took advantage of this natural behavior to experimentally condition (or train) dogs to respond in the same way, that is, to salivate, even when no food was present. To do this, he sounded a bell every time the dog was presented with food. After a certain number of trials, the dog associated the sound of the bell with the presence of food. So, the dog would salivate when he heard the bell, regardless of whether any food was given. At this point in the experiment, the bell is called the **conditioned stimulus**, and the salivation is now a **conditioned response**. (See figure 4.1.)

Pavlov's work showed that you can condition an animal's (or a human's) natural response by changing the environment in specific ways. Let us consider how classical conditioning could be used to explain a linguistic phenomenon: learning the meaning of a word. As an example, let us suppose that a parent is using the technique of classical conditioning to teach her child the word "water."

How would the parent go about this task? The goal seems straightforward: to get the learner to respond to the word "water" in the same way as she would

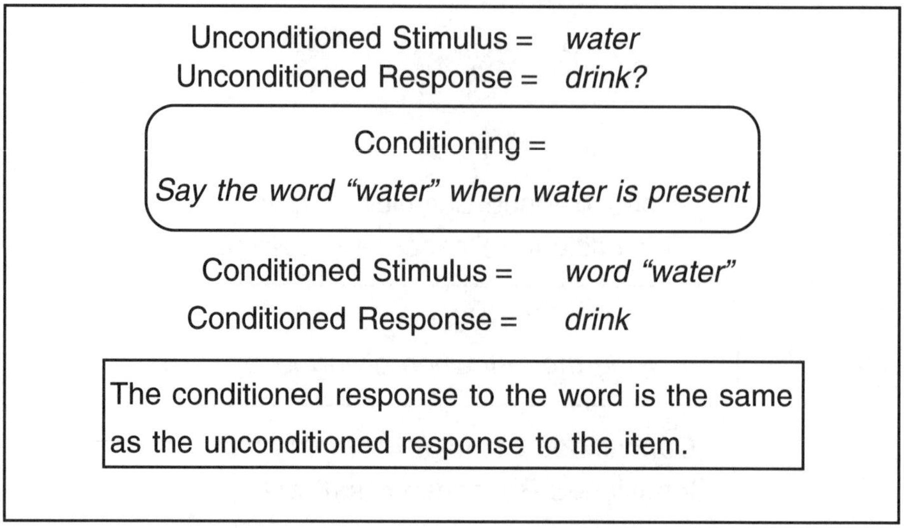

Unconditioned Stimulus =   *water*
Unconditioned Response =   *drink?*

Conditioning =
Say the word "water" when water is present

Conditioned Stimulus =   *word "water"*
Conditioned Response =   *drink*

The conditioned response to the word is the same as the unconditioned response to the item.

Figure 4.2   Classical conditioning in language learning

respond to the object water, the parent simply has to utter the word "water" whenever the child is in the presence of water. Thus, we can diagram the various components of the classical conditioning process as in figure 4.2.

As this example indicates, Behaviorism supposes that to understand a verbal stimulus is to produce a behavioral response appropriate to the associated object. Is this true? One problem with this idea is that it is difficult to identify the unconditioned response a child is supposed to produce in the presence of water. In fact, of course, children produce a variety of behaviors in response to water. They might drink it, or splash it around, or spit it out, and so on. Are any of these behaviors likely to become associated with the word "water"?

It also seems counter-intuitive to say that someone who knows the meaning of a word performs similarly in response to the word as they perform in response to what it refers to. Note what this would mean if we understood someone's words, but chose not to produce any behavioral response at all. It seems that, according to a Behaviorist, a child who did not respond to "water" in the same way on each occasion does not understand the meaning of the word. This is clearly incorrect. Even if we just sit quietly watching the news on TV, we usually understand it.

Another undesirable consequence of the Behaviorist account is that it cannot explain another common experience, when we understand what someone says but do not believe it. Notice that Behaviorism *can't* explain how we can fail to believe what we hear, because the essential idea is that we are conditioned to act in the same way to every occurrence of the same word(s). We should therefore be unable to produce a response other than the one that is appropriate to the physical stimulus. But, not believing what we hear is, in Behaviorist terms, behaving in completely the opposite way we would behave in response to the physical stimulus.

Given these observations, it makes more intuitive sense to suppose that understanding words and sentences is something going on in our minds (brains). We depend on what else is going on in our minds – what we believe or disbelieve, what we care about, and so on – in order to decide to produce a specific behavioral response or, perhaps, to produce none at all.

2   Operant Conditioning

A second technique used to build up habits for associating environmental stimuli with behavior is called **operant conditioning**. This form of conditioning is associated with B. F. Skinner. In operant conditioning, the techniques of conditioning are extended to behaviors which are normally not associated with any particular stimulus.

Let's go through an example of an operant conditioning experiment, which is often conducted with pigeons. A pigeon is placed in a cage, which can be called a Skinner box. Test animals are usually deprived of food throughout an experiment: this is so food can be used as **positive reinforcement** for some behavior to be learned. As the hungry pigeon stands in the cage, it begins to move around. Its movements are relatively random. But after a period of time, by chance the pigeon pecks at a disk in the wall of the cage. When it does this, food drops into a tray in the cage, and it can eat. The food is called positive reinforcement because it is a (positive) result of the pigeon's action. The pigeon continues its random behaviors, and after a period of time it happens to peck the disk again. Every time it pecks the disk, it gets food. After a series of such pairings, the pigeon associates pecking the disk with the receipt of food. It now pecks consistently at the disk when it is hungry, receiving a food reinforcement each time. In this study, the initial pecking of the disk is called a **free operant**, because it is a behavior the pigeon does entirely on its own. It wasn't a natural response to the presence of the disk, just a random behavior. After many trials, however, this behavior has become a **conditioned operant**.

Behaviorists have conducted many impressive experiments using operant conditioning, and have demonstrated that it can be extended to all kinds of complex behaviors, called **habits**. To evoke more complex behaviors, Behaviorists have added another element to this conditioning paradigm, called **shaping** (progressive approximation). This technique is used to teach animal behaviors that are not free operants; that is, behaviors that might not occur if the experimenter

Figure 4.3   Operant conditioning

simply waited for the response that she wanted to reinforce and condition.
Suppose the pigeon never happens to peck after turning a figure eight, and this
is the behavior the experimenter chooses to reinforce. What Behaviorists do in
this case is to employ a **shifting criterion** for the reinforcement, starting with a
likely free operant, and moving closer and closer to the desired conditioned
response. To train the pigeon to execute a figure eight, say, she starts by rein-
forcing any step in the right direction. As the bird becomes conditioned to step
to the right, the experimenter withholds reinforcement until the bird executes
more of a circle. Once the clockwise circle is conditioned, the experimenter must
condition the pigeon to execute a counter-clockwise circle. Ultimately, only after
both behaviors are executed in sequence does the pigeon receive food. Using this
procedure, pigeons can be trained to do any number of things. For example,
pigeons have been trained to play ping-pong – but, since their actions are simply
responses to their training to perform, the pigeons play without cheating. (See
figure 4.3.)

According to Skinner even the most complex behaviors such as language may
be conditioned in somewhat the same way. For example, he argued that verbal
behavior is acquired through operant conditioning with shaping (progressive
approximation) of utterances. In language learning, shaping uses a shifting criterion for reinforcement to produce closer and closer approximations to the
correct, adult way of speaking. That is, suppose that a child is initially reinforced
by her parents for producing an utterance which is somewhat in the direction
of the desired production – for example, "wawa" for "water." As the child
becomes more proficient at "wawa," the parents change the criterion: soon they
will only reinforce the child for saying "wada" and, later, only for "water." As
the child grows yet more, they will shift the criterion still further, and only
reinforce her when she also says "Please." (See figure 4.4.)

Figure 4.4 Operant conditioning in language learning

Does this technique of progressive approximations toward the target utterance explain how children actually learn to speak? In most cases, the answer is clearly, no.

First of all, it should be noted that children develop vocabulary too rapidly to explain what happens in these simple Behaviorist terms. Children learn as many as nine words a day during certain periods of early childhood. This far exceeds what they should be capable of if they were relying on reinforcement. It has also been demonstrated experimentally that children can sometimes learn a new word after only one exposure to it. This should not be too surprising since people create entirely new words on demand, to describe new objects and situations. New words are coined with surprising frequency; consider "Xerox," "fax," and "yuppie," for example.

There are other observations about word learning that pose a challenge to the Behaviorist account. It is well known that children use words appropriately in different forms, even if they have never heard them used this way before. For example, it was shown in the late 1950s by the researcher Jean Berko that 3-year-old children produce the appropriate plural form of words that they have never encountered before. In one experiment on this topic, children were shown a cartoon-like picture of an unknown creature that the experimenter described as a "wug." Then, children were shown a picture of two of them, and asked to complete the experimenter's phrase, "There are two . . ." By age 3, children say that two of the creatures are called "wugs," never having heard the (plural) form "wugs" before.[1]

It is also pertinent to point out that children speak and understand entirely novel *sentences*. According to the Behaviorist account, children's understanding would be limited to sentences they have heard before – i.e., those which they have been conditioned to understand. Suppose it rained at the day-care center, causing the child to report to the teacher, "The roof is falling down." Assuming that the child hadn't encountered this particular situation before, she obviously hasn't built up the habit of saying it. But, she can easily produce it if need be.

This raises an interesting problem, in principle, for the Behaviorists. The fact is that people are constantly forming new sentences of considerable length and complexity. One process that allows this to happen is **recursion**. Notice that I can repeatedly add, "I think that . . ." or, "I know that I am supposed to think that . . ." to any simple declarative sentence, making it longer and more complex. This is an aspect of our linguistic competence that falls far beyond the reach of a Behaviorist explanation.

3   Response Chaining

The fundamental principles of Behaviorism cannot readily account for many of our linguistic abilities, including the ability to produce and understand sentences that we have never encountered before. Skinner tried to cope with this "creative" aspect of language by extending the principles of Behaviorism. Part of his proposed solution was to say that we have learned habits for sequencing words. Through years of experience, we have gradually built up associations, not simply between words, but also between groups of words. We have learned which group of words can be used to begin a sentence, and which group can appear second, and so on. Having produced the third word in a sentence, for instance, the entire set of possible fourth words is triggered, and any of them can be accessed, depending on the context. Recall our example, "The roof is falling down." Even if the speaker had never uttered this particular sentence, she will have uttered related ones, beginning with "a roof . . ." or "the boy is . . ." Given this set of experiences, the speaker has gradually built up a set of habits. She has learned that the word "the" can begin a sentence, and that the word "roof" can come in second position. This means that she can produce the sequence "the roof" even if she has never heard it before. The word "roof," in turn, triggers another set of words, which includes the word "is," even if "roof is" was never encountered. By this long process of associations, the learner is able to produce the novel utterance, "The roof is falling down." In this process, each word acts as a stimulus for the next response, so it is called **response chaining**.

Notice that response chaining conceives of sentences as strings of words – like beads on a string. If the first word is the stimulus for the second word, and the second word is the stimulus for the third, then there is no particular relationship between the first and third words. But such a procedure often results not in grammatical sentences, but in ill-formed strings of words like (1).

(1)   This baby rocks are playing cards have friends.

This is called a first-order approximation to English, because one word triggers the next, and so on. Perhaps, however, each word is a response to the two words before it (= a second-order approximation), or even the five words before it (= fifth-order). A fifth-order approximation to English would be simulated by the following childhood party game. First, cards are handed out to fifteen people. The first guest simply writes down a word that can begin a sentence, and hands her card to the next guest. The second guest hands both cards, in order, to the third guest, who writes down a word, and hands all three cards to the fourth guest. Likewise, until the seventh guest. This person is given the cards of guests 2 through 6, so she cannot see the word written by the first guest. The eighth guest sees the words of guests 3 through 7, but not the first two words, and so on. In short, each person bases her decision on the five words that came before (or on all the words that came before, for guests 1 through 6). But even in this case the result is not always a correct rule-governed sentence. Instead, one result might be as follows:

(2)   Rabbits were running away from a policeman that I took the ticket to Mary and her brother are good dancers.

Clearly, this is not how people talk. But it would be how people would talk if their linguistic skills were a matter of response chaining.

There is additional evidence that response chaining cannot account for our linguistic knowledge. We are constrained in the linguistic hypotheses we generate, in that our hypotheses must refer to the hierarchical structure of sentences rather than simple left-to-right word order. We refer to this constraint by saying that our linguistic hypotheses must be **structure-dependent**. Here is an example of a linguistic phenomenon that could, on first appearances, be interpreted according to either a structure-dependent or a structure-independent process. The example involves the formation of yes/no questions.

(3)   a.   Bill is going to the show. → Is Bill going to the show?
      b.   Bette can sing very well. → Can Bette sing very well?

In order to produce the yes/no questions on the right-hand side from the declaratives on the left-hand side of example (3), we need to postulate a process which moves auxiliary verbs (such as "is," "have," "can," "must," etc.) to the beginning of the sentence. The examples in (3) are consistent with either a structure-dependent or a structure-independent formulation of the rule. It's possible to say, for example, "move the first (auxiliary) verb to the front of the sentence to form a yes/no question from a declarative." It is not necessary to refer to structure at all in this formulation – only left-to-right order is mentioned. However, anyone who adopted a structure-independent hypothesis for yes/no question formation would produce INCORRECT question forms when they began to ask more complex questions. For example, they would produce the wrong question forms in converting the following declarative sentence into a yes/no question:

(4)   The man who is running will win.

Applying the structure-independent rule to this example results in an ungrammatical sentence:

(5)   a.   *Is the man who ____ running will win?

The correct yes/no question form of the declarative in (4) is given in (5b):

(5)   b.   Will the man who is running win?

This form can be generated by a structure-*dependent* rule which says to invert the main clause auxiliary and the subject. Since the subject is the phrase, "the man who is running," and the main clause auxiliary is "will," this rule produces the correct result. No structure-independent hypothesis will do the trick in all cases of yes/no question formation. In short, people do not treat sentences as unstructured sequences of words, as response chaining would have it.

We will see in chapter 17 that correct yes/no question forms can be generated in all cases only if we refer in our rule to abstract structural notions such as Subject and Main Clause. A yes/no question is derived by the application of a structure-dependent rule which treats entire phrases, such as "the man who is running," as a single constituent. Furthermore, we will see in that chapter that children respect the principle of structure dependence – they do not make the error that the structure-independent hypothesis would predict. Hence, the principle of structure dependence is a prime candidate for UG.

Because response chaining is structure-independent, associations can only develop between words that are close to one another. An entire sentence can be conceived of as a continuous sequence of strictly local associations. In natural language, on the other hand, there are many linguistic phenomena that involve relationships at a distance. The class of such relationships is sometimes referred to as **long-distance dependencies**. One dependency that occurs at considerable distances is number agreement. In simple sentences, number agreement between nouns and verbs is often *local*, sometimes between adjacent words:

   (6) a.   The student IS clever.
         b.   The students ARE clever.

In other cases, however, agreement holds between nouns and verbs that are widely separated. Notice that in the following questions, there is number agreement between linguistic constituents despite the fact that the intervening material includes other nouns (the teachers, the coach):

   (7) a.   Which student did the teachers hear the coach say IS clever?
         b.   Which students did the teachers hear the coach say ARE clever?

In the first example, the singular noun "student" agrees in number with the verb "is." In the second example, the noun "students" is plural, so the form of the distant verb that it agrees with must also be plural ("are") for the question to be well formed. The nouns that intervene are simply ignored for purposes of agreement. For the present, we will just add this interesting linguistic phenomenon to our stockpile of linguistic facts to be explained, but we will give an explanation for it in Part III. The point is that long-distance dependencies like this are a clear threat to the Behaviorists' goal of accounting for complex human linguistic behavior by extending the basic principles of association to include processes like response chaining.

Conclusion

We considered a simple, common-sense account of language development – one which many people might come up with if asked how they thought children learn language. It's not just a layman's theory, however, since it was also the proposal of a well-known behavioral psychologist: B. F. Skinner. Skinner thought that it would be possible to account for verbal behavior using the tenets of Behaviorism. However, we have given evidence that the Behaviorist theory is too simple to account for the complexities of linguistic knowledge. There are additional reasons to abandon Behaviorism as a theory of linguistic behavior. We will see in the next chapter that several other aspects of verbal behavior fail to conform to fundamental laws of conditioning discovered for some other animal and human behaviors. This evidence also shows that a more powerful theory of language is needed.

Note

1   Children also have the ability to form new *compound words* on command. For
    example, a child who is told that the object in front of her "makes apples," and is
    asked what a device that does this is called, will respond "apple maker." It is highly
    unlikely that this ability is based on their having heard expressions like this before.

Bibliographical Comments

Pavlov's famous experiment with dogs is reported in Pavlov (1927). Skinner is another of
the most well-known psychologists of our age. His conditioning work is reported in
Skinner (1938), and his proposal that language is learned by conditioning is given in
Skinner (1957). Chomsky (1959) provides an extensive rebuttal to Skinner's proposal.
The study reported here showing that children have a mental rule allowing them to go
beyond the data presented to them was published in Berko (1958).

5 Dispelling a Common-Sense Account

Introduction

The previous chapter outlined several arguments against adopting Behaviorism as a theory of language behavior. In this chapter we will illustrate how people's verbal behavior appears to systematically violate two laws of conditioning which are generally considered basic to Behaviorism: **reinforcement** and **stimulus generalization**. Although both of these principles have been discovered to hold for other animal behaviors, they cannot be extended to human linguistic behavior.

1 Reinforcement

We have seen that, in animal experiments, behavior is shaped by reinforcement. Reinforcement comes in two forms. First, a behavior can be reinforced by presenting a reward (= positive reinforcement) if the animal's behavior approaches the response that the experimenter is after, and no reward if it doesn't. An additional kind of reinforcement is called negative reinforcement (= punishment). Negative reinforcement can be administered if the experimenter wants to diminish or eliminate some unwanted behavior that the animal is performing. If a habit is not reinforced or receives negative reinforcement, it becomes **extinguished** (by the process of **extinction**).

In discussing language behavior, Skinner suggested that both positive and negative reinforcement are at work, but in more subtle ways. That is, the original model of conditioning was extended by Skinner to make it relevant to language behavior. It was obvious to Skinner, for example, that parents don't in fact use a specific reinforcement, such as food, for a specific behavior such as saying "water" correctly. So, one extension of the model was to expand the range of experiences that count as reinforcement. In the case of language, according to Skinner, reinforcement is given in less obvious forms. He suggests that parents reinforce certain language behaviors by approval or disapproval. Whenever they observe language behaviors that conform to their expectations, they reward their child with a smile or a nod or by saying, "unhuh," and so on. As a consequence, these behaviors are learned, and ones that are not reinforced, or are "frowned upon," become extinguished. The idea is that language acquisition can be explained if we just acknowledge a broader range of reinforcement and punishment contingencies in linguistic development than are needed to explain the results of the conditioning experiments with animals. Skinner also remarked that several types of reinforcement may be given to the same behavior. For example, if a child says "please," he may be reinforced with a cookie, or a hug, or a smile. It is not necessary for there to be a one-to-one correspondence between actions and reinforcements in the development of verbal behavior. This is necessary for Skinner, because these are the conditions under which verbal behavior is found.

As we mentioned in chapter 1, researchers have examined whether or not children receive various forms of positive reinforcement for their grammatically correct utterances, and negative reinforcement for ungrammatical ones. Two psychologists, Roger Brown and Camille Hanlon, were among the first who investigated this. Brown and Hanlon specifically looked for parental approval or disapproval for ungrammatical utterances. They analyzed hours of tapes of children interacting with their parents, and found that the children were rewarded – with attention and approval from their parents – when what they said was *true*. This was the case even if the children's utterances were ungrammatical. So if a 2-year-old child said, "Doggie sit chair," and the dog in question was indeed sitting on the chair, the mother or father might say, "Yes, that's right," instead of saying, "No, don't say it that way, that's an ungrammatical sentence." But if the child said, "Johnny got a cookie," which is perfectly grammatical, but in fact Johnny didn't get a cookie, the mother would reject the utterance and say, "No, he didn't." It appears, then, that adults do indeed reward children selectively for what they say, but the pattern of rewards fails to explain how children attain knowledge of the grammar.

Recall, also, that there are many facts about the language for which there are no environmental stimuli. For example, children must somehow learn that we don't say "wanna" in certain linguistic contexts. And they must somehow learn what meanings cannot be given to certain sentences; for example, that, "He admires what John Wayne did" cannot mean the same as, "John Wayne admires what he did." But, it is evident from the findings of the Brown and Hanlon study that parents don't provide the kind of feedback that would be useful in learning linguistic facts of either sort. Moreover, the absence of negative reinforcement in the course of language development raises a serious problem for the learner. What happens if a child forms an incorrect hypothesis about the grammar of her language? Putting the question another way: how would a child who makes a mistake in the course of language development ever realize that an error had been made, and expunge the incorrect hypothesis?

Consider the formation of WH-questions. It has been observed that young children sometimes produce questions such as (1a) in place of the grammatical (1b):

(1)   a.   *Why he can go?
      b.   Why can he go?

Notice what has gone wrong in the child's question – the auxiliary verb "can" should (ordinarily) be inverted with the subject "he" in questions of this sort. This error of failing to invert the subject and auxiliary verb has been reported in the literature to occur in the speech of many young children learning English and to continue to be present in their productions for several months, perhaps even years. Thus, it seems clear that it is not just a slip of the tongue, or an utterance that appears just when children lose track of what they are saying. Rather, this appears to be a *bona fide* grammatical mistake that children make at some early stage of development. Perhaps children form the wrong hypothesis for "why"-questions because "why" is similar in meaning to "how come," and with the latter, there is no inversion:

(2)   a.   Why is everyone staring at me?
      b.   How come everyone is staring at me?
      c.   *How come is everyone staring at me?

Whatever the reason, let us assume for the purposes of argument that children are making a genuine mistake in asking questions like, "Why he can go?" The question we want to raise is this: how would children learn the correct hypothesis? Of course, negative feedback from parents would do the trick. Parents could simply inform children when they make ungrammatical utterances, and children could respond by changing their hypotheses. But, as we just saw, parents do not systematically provide this kind of feedback (and children do not respond to whatever feedback they are given). So, the question remains: how do children come to reject the erroneous hypothesis, in favor of the correct, adult rule? If they don't reject it, then the error would continue into adulthood. Having reached adulthood, then, there would be grown-ups still asking such questions, and asking them right in front of their children. Their children, then, would have good reason to form the same hypothesis, and ask the same questions, and would do so in front of their children, and this would continue on and on. In other words, the language would change. Languages do, of course, change over time. But, with respect to this particular structure, we know that this is not happening, because no native-speaker adult (that we know of) asks these ungrammatical questions. So, the fact that this does not happen calls for an explanation.

In some cases of linguistic knowledge in the absence of experience, we have argued that children are somehow prevented from making mistakes. We have seen that, at least in some cases, their hypotheses are sufficiently constrained by principles of Universal Grammar (such as structure dependence) to circumvent some kinds of errors that might otherwise occur. In the present case, however, we need to explain how children move from an apparent grammatical error to the correct adult form. One possibility is that there is a further innate constraint on grammar formation, in the form of a **Uniqueness Principle**, which would limit expressions to a unique form. In the case of questions, the following uniqueness principle would suffice: "Questions can be asked in only one way, unless there is positive evidence for other forms."

To see how this principle would serve as a substitute for negative reinforcement, consider the child who asks, "Why he can go?" The child would actually hear questions of a different form, namely, "Why are you still awake?" and so on. Upon hearing these questions, the child would note that she would have used a different word order to ask the same question. The child's word order would have "are" and "you" reversed: "Why you are still awake?" At this point, the Uniqueness Principle comes to the rescue. Since any question is asked in only one way, the child's way of forming the question must be in error. Therefore, the child amends her hypothesis about question formation to produce the correct (= adult) forms. This explanation relies on the presence of innate knowledge, in the form of the Uniqueness Principle. Such innate knowledge is not part of the Behaviorist theory. Behaviorists would be hard pressed to solve this problem in language acquisition.

2   Stimulus Generalization

In animal experiments it has been found that an animal conditioned to one sort of stimulus will respond to physically similar stimuli in a similar way, but they will not respond similarly to distinct stimuli. For example, a pigeon can be trained to respond in a certain way (say, pecking a key) to a yellow light, but not to a dark-colored light. Giving a differential response to different stimuli is called **discrimination**. Now, suppose the pigeon trained to peck when presented with a yellow light is presented with a novel-colored light. If the new light is orange or green, colors relatively close to yellow, the pigeon will **generalize**, and peck the key (although with less vigor). However, the pigeon will not peck (or will peck only slightly) when presented with red or blue lights, colors which are more distinct from yellow. This process is called **stimulus generalization**.

Notice how different language is. The response one gives to the sounds, "Please pass the salt," is usually one of passing the salt. But the same response may also be evoked by very different sequences of sounds, such as, "Could you possibly hand me the sodium chloride?" Also, our responses to physically similar sounds are often quite different, as the following pair of sentences illustrates:

(3) a. Bill and Hillary appeared to the crowd to be friendly.
    b. Bill and Hillary appealed to the crowd to be friendly.

In still other cases, there are TWO possible responses to the same stimulus, as when there is some ambiguity, such as in, "I'm going to sit on the bank" or, "Mary had a little lamb." These examples show that the properties of the physical stimulus are far less important than what the mind makes of them. The way we respond to sentences depends on how we interpret them, and it just happens that sentences which sound alike don't necessarily mean similar things, and sentences that are physically different don't necessarily mean different things.

To make matters worse, it seems clear that stimulus generalization would actually hinder, rather than help, language acquisition in many cases. To see this, let us consider once again the linguistic phenomenon of "wanna contraction." We observed earlier that in many instances, and most likely in the vast majority of cases, people pronounce the sequence of words "want" and "to" as "wanna." It is important to avoid generalizing, however, because the contraction of these words does not give the right result in certain cases:

(4) a.   Which Big East team do you want to beat the most?
    b.   Which Big East team do you wanna beat the most?
    c.   Which Big East team do you want to win the most games?
    d.   *Which Big East team do you wanna win the most games?
         (cf. I wanna win the most games.)

This is an example of a **partial syntactic generalization**. Clearly, the grammars we have internalized as children somehow preclude us from completing the paradigm, since we don't produce these ungrammatical sentences and we judge them to sound "odd." The point is that by laws of conditioning, in particular by stimulus generalization, we would expect just the opposite – that people would fill in the missing cell in the paradigm, on analogy with other data that they encounter. What prevents people from filling in the missing cell is knowledge of grammatical rules and principles, as we will see.[1] We will find that the same grammatical knowledge that prohibits contraction in (4d) also explains other facts, such as the loss of ambiguity in (5b).

(5) a. Which player did Coach Calhoun want to shoot at the end of the game?

     b. Which player did Coach Calhoun wanna shoot at the end of the game?

It is easy to find further examples of partial syntactic generalizations. In each case, a child who generalized from the "positive" examples from the speech around her would end up uttering an ungrammatical sentence – the "gap" in the paradigm. And, as noted in the discussion of reinforcement, the child would not have recourse to the kind of input that is needed in order to eradicate these sentences (negative feedback).

(6) a. Picasso took a picture of Bill.
     b. Picasso took my picture of Bill and tore it up.
     c. Picasso took a picture of himself.
     d. *Picasso took my picture of himself and tore it up.

(7) a. I'll have a strawberry margarita with salt.
     b. What did you say you will have a margarita with?
     c. I'll have a Dos Equis beer and pretzels.
     d. *What did you say you will have a beer and?

Let us add these partial syntactic generalizations to our arsenal of facts to be explained. We will have to leave them as puzzles for now, but we'll return to them in the course of examining the system of rules and principles that make up the theory of Universal Grammar.

Conclusion

The Behaviorists wanted to deal only in observables, including people's overt behavior and the observable world in which they operate. Their goal was to show that all human behavior was triggered by environmental events, which includes other people's behaviors. Under this theory, all behaviors are just *habits* or *associations* between environmental stimuli and behavioral responses. In dealing with language, Behaviorists started with the most trivial kinds of verbal behavior, and hoped that if enough of all those small pieces were put together they could result in complex verbal behavior – language. But, this was not in the cards. Even the most sophisticated talk of stimuli and responses can't account for many aspects of a person's verbal behavior – including her knowledge of the grammar of the language.

We believe that this conclusion also holds for more complex association or learning models of language development as well. Although new models may use principles different from those of Behaviorism, a learning-theoretic model of language development depends more heavily on the surface features of the environment rather than on innate characteristics of the child to attempt to account for language learning. Given the sorts of facts reviewed in this and the previous chapter, we believe that *any* model which does not include innate knowledge of specifically linguistic principles will not be able to account for the data. This being so, it is time now to turn to an alternative theory – Chomsky's theory of Universal Grammar. According to this theory humans have an internal mental grammar. The grammar is a system of rules and principles that allows us to mix and match our fund of words into an unlimited number of new and different sentences – not just chains of words. In learning a language, according to this theory, the learner internalizes a rich and complex system of rules for processing linguistic phenomena, which cannot be explained as simple automatic responses to stimuli.

Note

1   The same grammatical knowledge can account for a range of data. Here is another example of a partial syntactic generalization involving contraction, but the words that can and cannot be contracted are different ("get" and "to"), and the structure is not a question, but a declarative construction (called **Topicalization**).

> (i)   Michael Jordan, they've just got to see at the Civic Center.
> (ii)   Michael Jordan, they've just gotta see at the Civic Center.
> (iii) Michael Jackson, they've just got to sing at the Civic Center. (= hired)
> (iv)   *Michael Jackson, they've just gotta sing at the Civic Center.

Bibliographical Comments

The relation between behavior and reinforcement has been studied by many psychologists since Thorndike (1898) proposed the law of effect: roughly, that responses are determined by (positive or negative) reinforcement. We have already mentioned that Brown and Hanlon (1970) were among the first psycholinguists to show that positive and negative reinforcement cannot serve the purpose of leading children to learn language. Stimulus generalization in pigeons was studied by Guttman and Kalish (1956).

6 Universal Grammar and the Logical Problem of Language Acquisition

Introduction

This chapter summarizes the solution proposed by the theory of Universal Grammar to the "Logical Problem of Language Acquisition." This problem is the one we have been discussing all along: how is it that children acquire the complex system of language so quickly, given their limited experience? It has become increasingly apparent that the process by which children acquire language is quite remarkable. Not only do children achieve mastery of a rich and complex system of syntactic and semantic principles at a very young age, but the transition appears to be effortless; children take very few wrong turns in the course of development, they make rapid progress despite the latitude in environmental input within a linguistic community, and they proceed in the absence of certain kinds of evidence from the environment that would seem to be helpful in instructing learners about which kinds of hypotheses to pursue and which to avoid. To explain these basic observations, we will appeal to the theory of Universal Grammar. In this chapter, our focus will be the fundamental argument for the theory of Universal Grammar (UG), the argument from "the poverty of the stimulus."

 ## 1 The Argument from the Poverty of the Stimulus

We have now seen several examples of the problems which face a theory of the acquisition of language. The input to a child consists of sample sentences generated by the grammar. From these sample sentences, the child must deduce the rules of the grammar. However, if the child fails to generalize properly, she will not be able to generate all of the sentences of the language. On the other hand, if the child fails to constrain her generalizations, she will generate sentences not in the language. The input does not provide sufficient information to tell the child exactly what the correct hypotheses are. In other words, the "stimulus" (input) is too poor to provide all the information the child ends up knowing. The conclusion drawn by many linguists from this state of affairs is that certain linguistic knowledge must be innately given.

The situation just described is sometimes referred to as *Plato's problem*, because the Greek philosopher, Plato, was among the first scholars to argue from situations such as this that humans have innate knowledge. In Plato's dialogue, the *Meno*, he argued that humans had knowledge that could not have come from their experience. As in all of the dialogues by Plato, the main character is the philosopher, Socrates. In the *Meno*, Socrates attempts to demonstrate that a slave boy has innate knowledge of geometry. He shows that certain concepts are available to the boy even though he had never been taught them. Rather than geometry, in linguistics, the problem of concern is to explain how children come to know things about *language* without the requisite experience. The parallel with the situation Plato discussed is so clear that we can call it Plato's problem – and, we can accept Plato's conclusion.

We have seen examples of sentence forms and sentence meanings that are prohibited in adult English. Prohibitions such as these, against forms and meanings, are encoded in a grammar by certain statements, which we refer to as **constraints**. Constraints can be distinguished from other kinds of grammatical statements, such as rules. Notice that the addition of a rule to a grammar results in an increase in its generative power; sentences that could not be generated before now can be. In this sense, rules can be said to be **positive** statements. In contrast to rules, constraints are **negative** statements; the addition of a constraint results in an overall reduction in the language that would otherwise be generated (that is, if the constraint were absent from the grammar). Constraints are viewed as prescriptions for hypothesis formation within which children construct their grammars. Constraints circumscribe the set of hypotheses that children (unconsciously) entertain in response to their linguistic experience. How do children acquire knowledge of constraints? Proponents of the theory of Universal Grammar have argued that constraints must be innately specified.

There are three premises to the argument for innateness. The first premise is that constraints are negative statements – they are sanctions against certain ways of putting a message, or sanctions against assigning certain interpretations to sentences. Given that constraints are negative statements, the second premise in the argument for innateness is this: the only way a constraint could be learned is if learners have access to negative evidence, perhaps in the form of parental feedback. To take an example, children could acquire the constraint on **wanna contraction** if parents inform them whenever they illicitly contracted *want* and *to*. This sort of information is called negative evidence. The second premise, then, is that learning constraints requires negative evidence.

The third premise is that negative evidence is not available. Notice that negative evidence would have to be systematically available, as part of every learner's primary linguistic data, because every language learner abides by the constraint, at least by the time they reach the Final State. As far as we can ascertain, negative evidence, if it is available at all, is certainly not available in the quantity and with the consistency that would be needed to guarantee that every child achieves the Final State.

To summarize the argument: constraints are negative statements, and the only source of data by which they could be *learned*, negative evidence, is not available. Assuming that the premises are all true, the conclusion that follows is that constraints are not learned. Also by assumption, anything that is not learned is in some sense or other innately specified (perhaps requiring certain "trigger" experiences). Therefore, constraints are innately specified. This constitutes the argument from the poverty of the stimulus. The conclusion of the argument is that some aspects of linguistic knowledge, namely constraints, are innately specified.

2   The Language Acquisition Device

The knowledge that a child brings to the task of language acquisition is known as the Language Acquisition Device (LAD). The LAD is the means by which the child/learner analyzes the linguistic input (from parents and other caretakers). The linguistic input to the learner is called the Primary Linguistic Data (PLD). On the basis of these data, the LAD hypothesizes a series of grammars. The last grammar that is formulated is the adult grammar, or Final State. The process can be represented schematically as in (1):

(1)   **Input** (PLD) → **LAD** → **Final State** (Adult Grammar)

Before we proceed, a few further remarks may be helpful. We adopt the viewpoint, common to many linguists, that knowledge of language is inside our minds or brains; it is not a concrete object that can be pointed to or measured. Attempts to describe knowledge of language are made by postulating a theory of grammar. A grammar is a set of principles which characterizes all and only the sentences of the language that we as speakers are able to produce and understand. To learn a language, then, is to master the principles of a mental grammar.

3   Universal Grammar

As we have seen, the course of language acquisition is remarkable for its universality, uniformity, and rapidity. A simple learning theory cannot explain the ways in which we display knowledge of things for which we have had no evidence. The theory of Generative Grammar has set for itself the task of explaining this remarkable acquisition scenario. A distinguishing feature of this theory is that it postulates universal principles that are special to grammar formation, rather than attempting to characterize the acquisition of language in terms of some general principle of cognitive growth. Taken together, the specifically linguistic principles form Universal Grammar (UG) – a theory of the internal organization of the mind/brain of the language learner. It is important to notice that, since UG is taken to be a theory of our biological endowment, the principles of UG should be observed in every natural language. Just as we cannot help but grow fingers and toes, because they are part of our biological blueprint for body development, we are preprogrammed to adhere to certain constraints on our linguistic development, according to the theory of UG. Therefore, the concepts we will be discussing should be observed **universally** – hence the name "Universal Grammar."

A related observation is that the principles of UG should, *ceteris paribus*, emerge **early in the course** of development. Just like our hearts and livers, we would suppose that our mental capacities should be functioning at birth or should mature rapidly. Of course, children do not speak at birth, but there are several reasons for this that don't preclude the existence of UG. For one thing, children must learn the words of their language, and words are arbitrarily related to the things that they denote. Until words are mastered, however, it is pointless to look for principles of syntax that explain how words are combined, for instance. Once children begin to combine words into simple sentences, they should quickly show signs that the principles of UG are operative in them.

A third property of UG deserves comment. Another important prediction of a biological theory of language development is that children will evince mastery of linguistic principles on the basis of only minimal environmental input; since these principles are not learned, they can be acquired within a considerable latitude of experience, or **on the basis of no experience** at all in certain instances. Again, we have seen evidence of just this type of phenomenon.

We have stressed that properties of Universal Grammar should apply uniformly to all languages. Of course, we know that there is variation between languages, so UG cannot contain everything there is to know about any one language. To take a simple example, the words of languages differ, and children must learn the vocabulary of their language by exposure. Languages also differ, however, in systematic, limited ways. There are aspects of UG which specify the limits of variation allowed in certain parts of the grammar. These aspects of limited variation are captured by **parameters**. Parameters specify the possible choices which languages can make. Although not every language makes the same choices, parameters are still part of Universal Grammar, because they set out what the choices are. We will discuss one example of a parameter in some detail in chapter 9, when we discuss word order (and we will discuss other examples too later in the text). We will see that languages differ in word order, but the differences are not random. Rather, there are systematic differences between languages, but each language applies its canonical order to different kinds of phrases. This type of systematic, limited variation is the concern of parameters.

How do children determine which setting on a parameter is used by their language? UG provides the possibilities, but the child must have experience with the target language to zero in on the correct choice. That is, parameters must be "set" on the basis of experience. This means that some positive evidence must be available in the input for correct parameter setting. Thus, setting parameters is different from using the universal principles: principles are in place even in the absence of evidence, but parameters require some kind of evidence. Parameters are still different from a learning theory which requires all learning to be based on evidence, however. For one thing, the possible choices are set out – so that impossible choices will never be considered. Furthermore, parameters have consequences beyond the data used as evidence on which they are set. Because innate knowledge is involved, once a child sets a parameter – even if it is set on the basis of one type of evidence – she may reach more than one type of conclusion. Thus, parameters are a crucial part of the theory of UG.

4   Sentences and Meanings

Following Aristotle, we can view language as pairings of sound and meaning. In more current terms, a language can be thought of as a (psychological) mapping between sentences and their meanings. Learning a grammar, then, is learning which sentences are associated with which meanings. We will abbreviate this as in (2):

(2)   <sentence, meaning>

Now we can frame the following question: are there properties of the mapping between sentences and meanings for which there is no corresponding input? Let us look, first, at some property of the mapping that is provided by the

Primary Linguistic Data. Consider the knowledge of what the unambiguous utterance, "The former rock star sleeps in the park," means. Clearly, a learner might encounter sentences like this in relevant situations. It is conceivable (though the process is far from obvious) that the learner can figure out the meaning of the sentence from this situation. So, this <sentence, meaning> pair, and others like it, form part of the learners' experience (= Primary Linguistic Data). Let us represent this as in (3):

(3)   <sentence1, meaning1>
       <sentence2, meaning2>
       <sentence3, meaning3>

Although there are many examples of sentence and meaning pairs in the input, there are important kinds of knowledge which we have argued have not been learned on the basis of experience. For one thing, every speaker of English is somehow able to judge that sentences like the following are ambiguous (the alternative interpretations are indicated by the paraphrases):

(4)   a.   We fed her chicken McNuggets.
Cf.   b.   We fed her some. *versus* We fed it some.

(5)   a.   They seem to enjoy boiling champagne.
Cf.   b.   They enjoy doing it. *versus* They enjoy drinking it.

Speakers are able to recognize both meanings of these sentences even if they have not experienced both meanings. We can represent knowledge of ambiguity using the abbreviation in (6):

(6)   <sentence, <meaning1, meaning2>>

This is read: a single utterance is associated with two semantic interpretations, meaning1 and meaning2. The angle brackets simply provide an ordering for the meanings.

5   Constraints on Form

Extending our terminology, we can represent knowledge that certain sentences are ungrammatical (although they might still be meaningful). For example, the verbal elements "want" and "to" contract to form *wanna* in certain cases, but not others:

(7) a. *Who does Arnold wanna make breakfast?
     b.   Who does Arnold wanna make breakfast for?
     c.   Does Arnold wanna make breakfast for Maria?
     d.   Why does Arnold wanna make breakfast?
     e.   I don't wanna make breakfast for Arnold or Maria.

Knowledge of facts of this kind (i.e., about the kinds of sentence **forms** that cannot be used) can be represented as in (8):

(8) <*sentence, meaning>

The star (*) is attached to the **sentence**, not the meaning, because the fact is about what can**not** be said.

6   Constraints on Interpretation

Constraints on the meanings that can**not** be assigned to sentences are another matter, to which we turn now. Language users also exhibit knowledge that some sentences may not be interpreted in the expected fashion. To illustrate this, note that the pronoun "he" and the name "the Ninja Turtle" may pick out the same individual in sentence (9a), but must refer to different individuals in (9b). Sentence (9b) means that someone else danced while the Ninja Turtle ate pizza.

(9) a. While he danced, the Ninja Turtle ate pizza.
     b. He danced while the Ninja Turtle ate pizza.

Knowledge of what sentences cannot mean can be represented as in (10):

(10)   <sentence, *meaning>

Since the sentences in question are themselves well formed, we do not attach an asterisk to the sentence portion of the sentence/meaning pair. Rather, we are noting that some particular **meaning** cannot be assigned to the sentence. In the second sentence, the pronoun "he" cannot designate the Ninja Turtle – it must pick out some individual not mentioned in the sentence. Non-coreference facts such as this are attributed to a principle which rules out coreference between a pronoun and a name when they are in a certain structural relationship to each other. We will discuss children's knowledge of the relevant structural notions in chapter 15.

Conclusion

In short, the logical problem of language acquisition is that the data available underdetermine what the learner comes to know. The solution offered by proponents of Universal Grammar is that the phenomena are innately given, as part of the LAD itself. The argument from the poverty of the stimulus can be graphically depicted using the notation developed here. In this chapter, we have mentioned three linguistic phenomena which appear to be candidates for innate knowledge: knowledge about ambiguity, knowledge that certain linguistic forms are prohibited (as in the case of "wanna" contraction), and knowledge that certain meanings are prohibited (as in the case of disjoint reference). Each of these aspects of the Final State (= adult grammar) is such that it must be mastered in the absence of decisive evidence from the environment. In fact, the last two phenomena constitute negative facts in the sense that we discussed. We noted also that the only apparent source of data by which negative facts could be learned (i.e., negative evidence) is not available at all, as far as we know. This invites the inference that such facts are not learned, but are part of the human biological blueprint for language acquisition (i.e., the LAD). The situation confronting the language learner is depicted in the diagram in (11).

(11)   Input (PLD)   → LAD →   Final State
        <sentence, meaning>   <sentence, meaning>
                                          <sentence, *meaning>
                                          <*sentence, meaning>

We have presented a number of facts and a framework for applying the UG solution to this problem. However, it is still necessary for us to back up some of our statements, and to provide a detailed analysis of the constructions we used to support the UG hypothesis. This we will do in the coming parts. However, we will first end this part by considering the functioning of the LAD with relationship to other cognitive faculties. As we have implied, the mechanisms we appeal to for language acquisition and processing are quite distinct from those used for other cognitive domains. In the next chapter, we will spell out this point more explicitly.

Bibliographical Comments

Plato's problem, as discussed in the *Meno*, can be read in the translation by Allen (1984). A significant discussion of the problem and Chomsky's solution is found in chapter 1 of

Chomsky (1965). Discussions of the "logical problem of language acquisition" can be found in Baker and McCarthy (1981), Baker (1979), Dell (1981), Hornstein and Lightfoot (1981a), Lightfoot (1982), Matthews and Demopoulos (1989), Wexler and Culicover (1980), among others. The Principles and Parameters model of Universal Grammar as outlined here was developed in Chomsky (1981) and in many works since. The issue of parameter setting is discussed by Roeper and Williams (1987), and one of the early important examples of applying this theory to the analysis of child data was presented by Hyams (1986). Much of the research in language acquisition since the late 1980s assumes this approach. A detailed discussion of the criteria for innate knowledge is presented in Crain (1991).

7 The Modularity Hypothesis

Introduction

We have presented evidence for the hypothesis that certain aspects of linguistic knowledge are innately determined. We argued that general-purpose learning mechanisms would be insufficient to account for the properties of language acquisition, and that instead, a specialized linguistic faculty must be appealed to. In the following chapters we will bolster this argument with additional data from the structure and acquisition of language.

In this chapter we will present another hypothesis which accompanies our nativist view. Although the two issues are logically independent, many researchers who adopt the nativist viewpoint also consider that language functions as a cognitive **module**. This follows from a proposal about the functional architecture of the brain – the Modularity Hypothesis. According to the Modularity Hypothesis, linguistic knowledge is a *module*: it is kept in a form separate from other cognitive knowledge; it is processed independently from other cognitive processes; it has its own characteristics for acquisition, breakdown, timing, etc. In a word, language is *special*. Because, in some ways, all types of cognitive processing are independent (there is a sense in which knowledge of chess is different from knowledge of colors, for example), it is important for us to clarify this notion of a linguistic module, which we will now attempt to do.

The Modularity Hypothesis can be traced back to Franz Joseph Gall (1758–1828), who maintained that many brain functions are organized independently (i.e., there is a faculty, or module, for language, and one for music, and so on). Each of these faculties or modules is **autonomous**, according to Gall, in the sense that it is supported by specific brain structures. It was also Gall's view that each faculty operates according to principles that are specific to it and not shared by other faculties.

These ideas about the independence of certain cognitive functions have received some empirical backing in recent research. However, Gall's own claims about these matters were not confirmed. Gall's main empirical mistake was to suppose that the brain structures underlying the different faculties correspond to bumps on the head. This proposal developed into the "science" of "phrenology." The basic claim of phrenology was that one could tell whether someone had a special propensity for some cognitive domain – music, mathematics, or even criminal behavior – by examining the surface of his or her skull. The notion of "phrenology" was soon disproved. It was shown that people with bumps in similar areas as great composers or notorious criminals failed to exhibit the same tendencies as these people. Despite the demise of phrenology, however, it should be noted that Gall's basic idea – the modular organization of the brain – appears to have some merit, at least as it pertains to language.

1 The Modularity of Mind

If modularity as we currently take it does not correspond to phrenology, what exactly does it take for some type of processing to be modular? Recall that Gall claimed that *faculties* are supported by specific brain structures, and operate according to domain-specific principles. If language is modular, then, the principles by which it operates are specifically linguistic; one cannot use general cognitive processes such as analogy to account (in full) for linguistic knowledge. It should be clear to you that, according to this view, our innate mental model of Universal Grammar is a candidate for a modular system, whereas the simple Behaviorist model we discussed in chapters 4 and 5 is not a modular view of language. This is not just because we use terms (such as *phoneme*, *word*, or *clause*) in our description of language which would not be used in other cognitive domains. It is because we take those terms to have *psychological reality* for the processing of language, and not for other domains, that ours is a modular theory.

We can understand the Modularity Hypothesis more precisely by considering one detailed proposal regarding it. This proposal comes from Jerry Fodor's 1983 book, *The Modularity of Mind*. Here, the essential tenet concerns the locus of interaction between different cognitive systems. For Fodor, language processing is modular in the sense that it is sealed off from other systems, so that a person's beliefs and desires do not influence language processing *per se*, but exert their influence only after language processing. Fodor describes the autonomy of the language processor as "informationally encapsulated."

One source of evidence of the autonomy of grammar in this sense is the fact that peculiar, revolutionary, and false sentences are readily understood. This argument was first given by a psychologist named Forster. The point of the argument can be seen using sentences as simple as (1):

(1) Mice chase cats.

Suppose we were to try to assign a meaning to the words in (1) without attention to syntax, say by trying to combine their meanings in any way that appears to make sense according to our beliefs based on experience. If so, we would misunderstand it, taking it to mean that *cats chase mice*. The essential role of syntax in sentence processing, Forster concludes, is supported by the finding that we correctly understand sentences like this despite their *a priori* implausibility. Take another simple example: however unlikely it is that doctors are cured by patients, we can understand sentences like (2) should the occasion arise:

(2)   The doctor was cured by the patient.

The point of an autonomous syntax, on the modularity perspective, is that it allows us to describe the world no matter how unexpected things turn out to be in it. To underscore the point, Forster adds that the most advantageous way to construct a human brain would be to insulate syntax *as much as possible* from the influences of inference and beliefs about the real world – to keep it completely *encapsulated*, in Fodor's terms.

What other characteristics do modular systems have, as opposed to non-modular ones? One way to help you conceptualize the difference is to consider another example from Fodor's proposed set of modular systems. According to Fodor's criteria, visual processing is modular in the same way as language. We're not talking about the processing done by the eyes, or even the *primary* visual processing which takes the first steps in analyzing patterns of light and darkness. Fodor's proposal is that *secondary* visual processing, which interprets patterns into figures we understand and recognize, is modular. Why? Special structures apply in this phase of visual processing, as is well known from studies of the brains of animals and humans. Visual processing is carried out independently of other types of processing. It can also break down independently of other types of processing. Most importantly for our purposes is that visual processing is informationally encapsulated. As Fodor points out, it is easy to see why visual processing should be informationally encapsulated. Like language, we need to be able to understand what we see without any influence from what we might expect, or what is most plausible. If we don't expect to see a tiger in the living room, and so we don't actually see it when faced with one, the results could be disastrous.

On the other hand, cognitive functions such as problem-solving are not modular. Problem-solving requires general cognitive information and processing. It is highly influenced by beliefs and plausibility. There is no special brain localization for problem-solving; it does not break down nor is it acquired independently of other cognitive functions. Using Fodor's terms again, problem-solving and other general cognitive functions are "horizontal" faculties, which are used in performing many cognitive tasks; language and visual processing are examples of "vertical" faculties, i.e., modules that operate autonomously.

What kind of evidence is there that language constitutes a module? The arguments we have made that highly specific linguistic constraints are needed to explain language structure and acquisition are arguments for the modular view. Arguments for modularity can also come from an examination of language processing; if there is evidence that linguistic information is processed independently from general cognition, for example, this will support the Modularity Hypothesis. If language is represented by separate, specific brain structures, which can break down independently from other cognitive processors, this too would constitute support for the Modularity Hypothesis. We will not discuss evidence from these areas in this text, but merely point out that such evidence has been presented. Let us now consider the language module in more detail.

2   The Modularity of Language

An extension of the Modularity Hypothesis conceives of the language faculty as itself divided into autonomous subcomponents. Under this view, the lexicon, the phonology, the syntax, and the semantics, are modules within the language module – each uses its own principles, each operates separately, each doesn't affect the processing of the others (except in so far as certain components provide the input to others, as discussed immediately). Let us refer to these components as **structures**. In addition, there are **processors** that serve each of these subcomponents. The processors used for language include working memory and the syntactic parser. Several proposals have been advanced concerning the **interaction** of these component systems of the language apparatus during sentence processing. An early proposal, by Forster, was that language processing is composed of discrete stages, organized in a hierarchical, bottom-up fashion, as figure 7.1 illustrates.

Information flows upward within the language module, so that the semantics does not tell the syntax what to do – in fact, just the reverse is true. The flow of information is represented by the directionality of the arrows. Each level provides input to the next level up, but they do not otherwise influence each other.

3   Language Loss

Another source of evidence for the Modularity Hypothesis comes from studies of language breakdown, commonly referred to as **aphasia**. There is evidence that a lesion in circumscribed locations in the left cerebral hemisphere may selectively

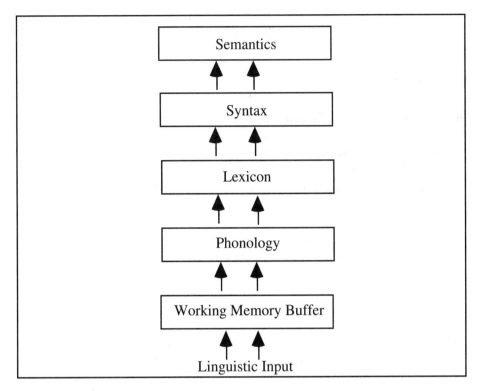

Figure 7.1   The Language Module

perturb language performance, leaving many other cognitive abilities relatively intact. It is important to keep several points in mind about the disruption of language resulting from brain damage. If a person suffers damage to a particular part of the brain, and then cannot perform some subsequent function, what can we infer? When the same symptoms appear in a number of patients who have suffered from injury to the same site in the brain, then it is usually inferred that the injured portion of the brain controlled, or was involved in the control of, the function that is lost. It is inferred that the damaged area of the brain serves the function that was lost, but the nature of the service is unclear.

We must also be cautious in making inferences about the normal brain based on evidence from the damaged brain. Care is needed because we don't ever know the full extent of the problems that brain damage brings. We have to assume that damage to a particular area causes problems in functions which that area serves, but we can't assume that this deficit is unconnected to secondary deficits. It could be that brain damage has caused a general memory deficit, for example, which influences language processing, and not that the brain damage has caused a particular language deficit itself.

With these caveats in mind, we will briefly sketch some findings from research on aphasia that are consistent with the Modularity Hypothesis.

Broca's Aphasia

In 1861, Paul Broca, a French doctor, had a patient who had suffered brain damage, and as a result lost the ability to use language. As Broca showed, the language loss was not due to paralysis of the vocal organs, or to a general cognitive deficit. Rather, the language ability in particular was impaired. Broca hypothesized that the particular area of the brain that was damaged in his patient was the area that subserved language. After the patient died, his brain was examined, and sure enough there was a lesion in a particular part of the left hemisphere. This part of the left hemisphere has come to be known as Broca's area, and the aphasia that results from damage to this area has come to be known as Broca's aphasia.

The area of the brain involved is near the part of the motor strip that controls facial movements. Note that it isn't particularly a problem with the facial muscles. (People who have such problems are said to suffer from *dysarthria*, not aphasia.) People with aphasia can move their mouths in appropriate speech movements, as shown when they are asked to blow out a candle, or whistle, or make other such noises. However, a person with Broca's aphasia has very stilted, slow, effortful speech, which contains mostly content words and is lacking in most of the grammatical morphemes. For example, a person with this kind of aphasia might say, "Dad .. er .. Paul .. and .. Dad .. hospital .. er .. two .. er .. doctor .. and .. er .. thirty minutes .. er .. yes .. er .. Thursday .. er .. doctor .."

The general characterization of Broca's aphasia is that the speech is effortful and slow, and it is often called "agrammatic." Broca's aphasics can understand speech to a much greater extent than they can produce it. They can appropriately respond to many kinds of commands or language tests. They also seem to have a good awareness of their problems, and of the fact that their speech is impaired.

For these reasons, Broca's aphasia is sometimes called "expressive" aphasia. The hypothesis that was held most generally until very recently is that the Broca's aphasic has trouble using his vocal apparatus to produce language. Since the effort to put words together is so intense, the Broca's aphasic eliminates the grammatical words, producing only the content words. However, since this hypothesis supposes that the understanding of grammatical words is not impaired, it predicts that the Broca's aphasic can understand complex sentences without much problem.

An alternative hypothesis emphasizes the "agrammatic" quality of Broca's aphasics' language, in both production and comprehension. That is, under this hypothesis, the Broca's aphasic has syntactic problems in comprehension as well as production. Since the Broca's aphasic does not produce the grammatical morphemes, this hypothesis supposes that she also will be insensitive to these morphemes in comprehension. For example, the difference between the meanings of the sentences, "The woman kissed the man," and, "The woman was kissed by the man," is signaled by the grammatical morphemes "was" and "by." In some tests, Broca's aphasics do not seem to do well on such "reversible passive" sentences, where both nouns can assume the semantic role of AGENT or PATIENT. Under the agrammatism hypothesis, this is because the Broca's aphasic is insensitive to the meaning of words like "was" and "by" in comprehension as well as production.

This issue is not yet resolved. Part of the problem in interpreting such fine points is that it is hard to find patients with small, well-defined lesions. For many patients, the brain damage includes Broca's area and also other areas of the left hemisphere. It is hard to know which functions to attribute to which areas of the brain in such cases.

Isolation Aphasia

Another type of aphasia bears even more directly on the Modularity Hypothesis. What do you suppose would happen if the areas of the brain responsible for language were all intact, but were cut off from the rest of the brain? One way this can happen is if a person suffers damage to large portions of the brain, but not to the language areas themselves. This results in an aphasia called "Isolation Aphasia." In cases of Isolation Aphasia, the patient is unable to transmit relevant information between the language centers and other domains of cognition, so the language centers function on their own. However, since information can flow into the language areas, and then out again, these patients can receive and repeat back verbal material, and this material can be processed by the intact levels of linguistic representation with the language centers. For example, the linguistic input is assigned a structure by the syntax.

An interesting example of Isolation Aphasia was reported by Haiganoosh Whitaker. The patient, who is referred to by the initials HCEM, suffered from presenile dementia. However, the patient did not suffer from motor or sensory deficits, and had excellent hearing and pronunciation. But, as Whitaker reports, she "could not follow even the simplest commands. She demonstrated echolalia [meaningless repetition of speech] and some perseveration and had no spontaneous speech" (p. 7). Able to name only two objects, *pencil* and *cup*, HCEM could repeat most numbers (e.g., three hundred and twenty five) and could count to nineteen (but not backwards). Despite the ability to repeat numerical expressions, HCEM was "unable to perform any mathematical calculations" (p. 20).

She was also unable to name colors, except for orange. In summary, Whitaker remarks that "the patient had very little comprehension . . . She did not carry out instructions given to her. . . . She failed the token test, matching pictures to objects, matching objects to objects, etc. The fact is that no one has been able to elicit by means of all the operational tests employed, any evidence of 'thinking' or cognitive behavior. . . . the data clearly demonstrate that cognition and creative language can be literally separated from the noncreative and automatic aspects of language" (p. 50).

Despite the loss of creative language, HCEM had certain remarkable linguistic abilities. For example, when presented with ill-formed sequences of words, HCEM would not repeat them back verbatim, but she would convert them to well-formed sentences. Some examples of such exchanges between Whitaker (WI) and HCEM are given in (3). By contrast, HCEM repeated verbatim sequences of words whose anomaly depended on general knowledge of the world, as the examples in (4) illustrate.

(3) Structural Repairs

WI: She likes eat.
HCEM: She likes to eat.

WI: Can you told the time?
HCEM: Can you tell the time?

WI: Is the money him?
HCEM: Is the money his?

WI: She wrote she mother a letter.
HCEM: She wrote her mother a letter.

WI: In a first place, read this.
HCEM: In the first place, read this.

WI: He shaved herself.
HCEM: He shaved hisself.

WI: Are you happy all a time?
HCEM: Are you happy all the time?

(4) Absence of Repairs for "Semantic" Anomalies

WI: The pencil smelled the flowers.
HCEM: The pencil smells the flowers.

WI: The pencil can't see very well.
HCEM: The pencil can't see very well.

WI: The door opened the woman.
HCEM: The door opened the woman.

WI: I had a building for breakfast.
HCEM: I had a building for breakfast.

We will conclude this chapter by returning to the arena of language development, where a similar phenomenon was demonstrated by Richard Cromer. Cromer
investigated an instance of what he dubbed the "chatterbox syndrome." The
patient, a young girl, was known as DH. According to Cromer, DH's "speech is
fluent, appropriate and not bizarre, is filled with complex syntactic forms, shows
the correct use of semantic constraints, an extensive vocabulary, and incorpo-
rates the use of normal pragmatic devices. But on a large variety of standardized
tests she performs at the severely retarded level and functions in everyday life at
the retarded level. She has been unable to learn to read and write in her late teenage years and cannot add or handle money." Like the patient HCEM, Cromer
goes on to report that "DH performed almost without error on grammaticality
judgments." Here is Cromer's conclusion: "language acquisition proceeds on a
different course, basically independent of general cognitive development."

Conclusion

The Modularity Hypothesis presents the case that the mental faculty which
subserves language is distinct from other cognitive processors. The arguments
for this view include logical considerations, evidence regarding the types of
mechanisms necessary to account for linguistic knowledge, on-line processing of
information, and evidence from language breakdown. We believe there is considerable evidence of a dissociation between language processing and other cognitive
functions. In our view, the evidence supports the kind of modular mental
architecture that we believe is characteristic of the human faculty for language.

Bibliographical Comments

The Modularity Hypothesis was presented clearly in Fodor (1983), and summarized
(with some humor) in Fodor (1985), which also contains reactions by prominent scientists who agree or disagree with the proposal, and Fodor's responses to them. Forster's
model discussed in the text was presented in Forster (1979). Other discussions of modularity
can be found in Mattingly and Studdert-Kennedy (1991) and Garfield (1989), as well as
many other sources. Gall's work is discussed in Hollander (1920).

Studies of aphasia constitute a whole field of research which contributes to our understanding of the brain's processing of language. For an overview of linguistic issues in aphasia, see Zurif (1995); Goodglass (1993) has a broader treatment of aphasia. Broca's famous patient is described in Broca (1861). The deficit of the patient HCEM was reported by Whitaker and Whitaker (1976). The "chatterbox syndrome" discussed by Cromer (1991) is also known as Williams' Syndrome. Another recent study of the linguistic abilities of children with Williams' Syndrome is presented by Bellugi, Bihrle, Neville, Doherty, and Jernigan (1992).

Part II   Constituent Structure

Introduction

Up to this point, our discussion has been limited to pointing out the sorts of linguistic facts that a theory of language and mind has to cope with. We argued that the general model and the specific mechanisms of Behaviorism cannot handle many of these facts. Instead, we will now argue for the following alternative theory of language and mind – the theory of Universal Grammar, which originated with Noam Chomsky. As we develop the theory in detail, it will soon become quite complex. This is inevitable, as should be clear by now. We saw that even complex principles of learning such as response chaining do not even begin to solve the linguistic puzzles we have before us. The theory of Universal Grammar, on the other hand, will enable us to understand our knowledge of these intricate linguistic phenomena – knowledge about which sentences are grammatical and which are not, which sentences have only one meaning, which sentences are ambiguous, and so on. In this part we will begin to present the mechanisms of the theory.

We begin with a brief overview of the entire system of rules that make up the theory. The system has several parts or components: the rules of syntax, the rules of semantic interpretation, the phonology, the lexicon, and more. The chapters of the book that follow will examine one component in some detail: the syntactic component. Our discussion of syntax will go into considerable detail because the rules of syntax are complicated. Our first topic in this part will be the rules that combine words into natural groups, called **phrases** or **constituents**. Together with our discussion of the technical aspects of the rules of phrase structure (or constituent structure), we will discuss children's knowledge of these rules. Then, in the next part, we turn to another type of syntactic mechanism, called a **transformation**, and the acquisition of the principles concerning transformational rules. As we go along, we will also stop to reconsider many of the linguistic phenomena we have already introduced, to see exactly how they are handled within the framework of the theory of Universal Grammar.

An Outline of the Grammar

The entire system of rules and principles that account for our linguistic behavior is called a **grammar**. A major goal of linguistics is to figure out the grammar that we use as speakers of a natural language such as English. But the grammar of a particular language, such as English, is not our main concern because our linguistic abilities enable us to learn the grammar of any language. Linguistics is concerned with the structure of language – the properties that all languages share. It is clear that grammars of different languages cannot vary without limit from one to another, or children would not find it easy to learn any language. In order to explain the uniformity of language acquisition, linguistic research as it is currently practiced focuses on the universal properties of language. In other words, linguistic research attempts to contribute to the theory of Universal Grammar. By separating out the aspects of a language which are universal, the task of learning what is left becomes more tractable.

The grammatical system of a language is multi-layered, consisting of several components. These include the following:

(a) *The Phonological Component*
     The rules which tell how the sounds of the language are put together to form the words. These rules are called the **phonological** rules, since "phone" means sound, just as in the word "telephone."

(b) *The Lexical Component*
     The rules which tell how words are put together out of smaller words (called **morphology**), and a list of all the words people know, called the **lexicon** or dictionary. The list of words in the lexicon gives each word's pronunciation and its meaning. This list is long, and new words can be added to it, but it is finite. This mental dictionary is not to be confused with the standard dictionaries we use, such as Webster's dictionary. For example, there is no reason to think that the dictionary inside a person's head lists words in alphabetical order. But it does list all the words a person knows, and their entries include information about their sounds and meanings.

(c) *The Syntactic Component*
     The rules that tell how the words are to be organized into sentences, and what the structures of these sentences are. These are called the rules of **syntax**. Notice that syntax and grammar are not the same. The syntactic component is only part of the grammar of a language.

(d) *The Semantic Component*
The rules that tell how to interpret the meaning of sentences, based on the meaning of the individual words and the way they are combined by the rules of syntax. These interpretive rules comprise the **semantic** component. We will begin by concentrating on the rules within the syntactic component. In later sections of the book, we will elaborate on the rules of the semantic component.

The different kinds of syntactic rules that we will discuss were originally developed by Noam Chomsky. Chomsky did not provide linguistics with all of the rules of the syntax of even a single language. But that was not his goal, as we have seen. Chomsky's goal was much more ambitious. He sought insight into the basic operating principles common to the syntax of all natural languages. It is important to appreciate that many changes have been made in the formulation of these operating principles since the 1960s. It is important to realize also that, despite the progress, there is still plenty of work remaining to be done. And, as this work proceeds, the operating principles themselves will sometimes have to be further revised. Linguistics is a dynamic field in which there are going to be constant revisions as linguists attempt to extend the coverage of the theory on two fronts: (a) working in greater depth on the details of individual languages; and (b) extending the theory to account for languages not previously studied.

The system of syntactic rules that we develop here will, we hope, be one that remains essentially compatible with all human languages, at some level of detail. The specific formulation of the theory will no doubt change as research proceeds, but we trust that the phenomena we are discussing are real, and that future linguistic theory will simply offer a deeper explanation of these phenomena, tying them to other phenomena whose relatedness was previously undetected.

As always, our interest is in principles of Universal Grammar. Because we have some idea about what is in Universal Grammar, we have some notions about what the possible rules for a language could be, and we also have some notion about what they could not be. This is not to say that the rules themselves will be identical from one language to the next. A distinction between **form** and **content** must be made. The content of the different types of rules will differ across languages, but the forms of rules that are available are universal. In addition, there appear to be universal constraints both on the form and on the content of rules. One constraint on the form a rule can take is structure dependence, which we have seen before. Constraints on content will be discussed later; one example is the prohibition on contracting "want" and "to" into "wanna" in certain cases. These considerations about the nature of language invite us to compare human language with other computational systems we could imagine – and this holds the promise of gaining new insight into the nature of the human mind.

8 Phrase Structure

Introduction

In chapter 4, we discussed the Behaviorist principle called response chaining. We argued that this could not be an operating principle made available by Universal Grammar. A Behaviorist system invoking response chaining would yield generalizations such as, "If X is the first word of a sentence, then Y can be the second word of a sentence, and Z can be the third word," and so on. Generalizations such as this are not viable descriptions of grammatical English sentences, as we saw. Any operating principle like response chaining, which adopts a "beads-on-a-string" model of sentences, gives only an approximation to English. It does not provide all and only the well-formed English sentences; it produces many ungrammatical sentences in addition to the well-formed ones it creates. The only kind of rule system that yields the right results must have the property of being structure-dependent: it must be capable of assigning abstract hierarchical structure to sentences. In this chapter, we begin to explain how structure is assigned to sentences in natural language.

1 Phrase Markers

To begin, we will rely on our intuitions that certain words in a sentence are grouped together. As we will see, the words that "go together" according to our intuitions turn out to belong together in the hierarchical structure that is formed by the application of the rules of Phrase Structure. The words themselves lie at the bottom of the structure. Above the words are labels indicating the syntactic categories that the words belong to, such as "noun" and "verb." You are probably familiar with some of these categories, but others will be unfamiliar. Don't worry, they will turn up often enough in the chapters that follow for you to remember them, and we will provide a summary list of categories in chapter 9.

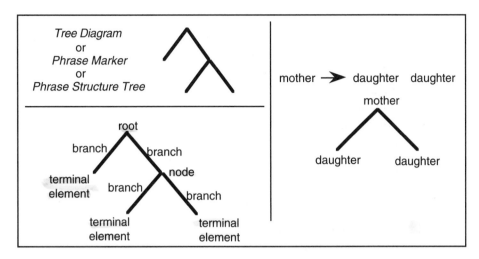

Figure 8.1 Phrase Structure terminology

How are individual words (and their category labels) grouped together in a hierarchical structure? The answer is that they are grouped into phrases, whence the term **Phrase Structure.** Phrases are higher-level groupings of words, called **noun phrase** and **verb phrase**, and so forth. The name given to a phrase usually indicates the one element of the phrase that cannot be eliminated without destroying the integrity of the entire phrase. It is also worth noting that phrases can be linked together, to form larger phrases; eventually, the hierarchical structure for an entire sentence is formed.

To illustrate the hierarchical structure for phrases and sentences, we will frequently use a diagram which is called a phrase structure **tree** – so called because it looks (somewhat) like an upside-down tree. It is also called a **phrase marker** (or "PM"), because it shows how phrases are organized. A schematic example of a phrase structure tree is given in figure 8.1. The tree diagram helps us to identify the structure of the phrase, and eventually of the whole sentence. In the diagram, the top is called the **root** of the tree. The lines are called **branches**. Points in the tree at which two branches come together (or even when one point is above only one other point) are **nodes**. The words at the bottom of each branch are **terminal elements**. We will often talk about which node **dominates** (is above) another node. We will also sometimes describe the relationships between different nodes in a phrase marker using kinship terms. It is common to call the domination relation a mother–daughter relation: a node which dominates another node is called a **mother**, and the dominated node is called a **daughter**. All the nodes which are daughters of the same mother are **sisters**.

Now let's consider the different sorts of phrases that we find. Look at the phrases in (1).

(1)   a.   *Mary*
          he
          milk
          men

      b.   a *man*
          some *milk*
          every *student*
          those *eyes*

      c.   Susan's *boyfriend*
          every student's *parents*
          the man up the street's *dog*

      d.   *pictures* of my friends
          nectar of the gods
          man up the street

      e.   these *rumors* that the President will resign
          the *fact* that my mother is uninsured
          Bill's *complaint* that the service was poor

Each of the phrases in (1) is called a Noun Phrase ("NP"). We give these phrases this label because they all have a noun (which is italicized). The noun (abbreviated "N") is the only part of the noun phrase which is absolutely essential. This can be seen in the examples in (a), such as the name "Mary" and the pronoun "he." In these examples, which contain a name or a pronoun, there is nothing in the noun phrase other than the noun. Additional information can precede the noun in certain noun phrases, as in the (b, c) examples, and certain information can follow the noun, as in the (d, e) examples. Some types of nouns, such as "boyfriend" and "student," never occur without other information; e.g., "your boyfriend," "no boyfriend," "every boyfriend," and so on. The additional information further specifies the individual(s) being described. Some noun phrases resist further specification; for example, it is odd to say "the he" or "Mary of my friends".

The examples in (1) indicate the kind of further information that can be included in a noun phrase. The examples in (1b) show that a noun can be preceded by "a," "some," "every," "those," etc. These words are called **Determiners** ("Det"). Determiners include the indefinite article "a," the definite article "the," and certain quantifiers (e.g., "every"). The examples in (1c) show that a noun can also be preceded by a **Possessive Phrase** ("PossP," such as "every student's," "Susan's"). A possessive phrase patterns like a determiner. The difference is that a possessive phrase has internal structure; it contains a noun phrase, plus the possessive marker "'s". For example, the possessor in "Susan's boy-friend" is made up of the NP "Susan" and the possessive marker "'s". The possessive "the man up the street's" is composed of the NP "the man up the street" and the possessive marker. Because determiners and possessive phrases pattern together, they are jointly called **specifiers** of the noun. Thus, noun phrases must contain a noun, and may optionally contain a specifier (abbreviated "Spec").

The examples in (1d, e) show that some linguistic expressions can also come after a noun. In the examples in (1d), what follows the noun is a **Prepositional Phrase** (PP). In the examples in (1e), what follows the noun is a whole sentence (preceded by the word "that"). Since both prepositional phrases and sentences (preceded by "that") occur in the same position inside noun phrases, after the noun, they are given a single cover term – they are called **complements** of the noun (abbreviated Compl).

The examples in (1e) show that a noun phrase can contain both a specifier and a complement, with the specifier occurring before the noun and the complement following it. This gives us the three main components of a noun phrase: a noun, which is obligatory; a specifier, which is optional; and a complement, which is also optional.

How do these three components of a noun phrase combine? There are a couple of possibilities. One possibility is that all three components have equal weight, and combine into a noun phrase without any additional structure. In (2), we have drawn a tree diagram to illustrate this possibility.

(2)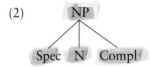

The phrase marker in (2) is one possible phrase marker for the syntactic category NP. However, there is evidence that NPs have more structure than is indicated in (2). Putting the point differently, there is evidence that phrases do not have the kind of "flat" structure illustrated in (2). In certain ways, the noun and its complement cooperate with one another, separately from the specifier. Therefore, we must add an intermediate layer of structure linking the N and the Compl, to indicate that they conspire together in certain ways. What label should we give to the additional layer of structure between the N and the NP? Linguists have decided to call it **N′** (pronounced "N-bar"). The N′ represents a category which is larger than a noun (i.e., it can contain both an N and a Compl), but smaller than a noun phrase (which includes both an N′ and a Spec). The actual structure of an NP can be drawn schematically as in (3):

(3)

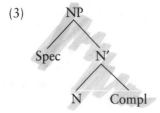

Figure (3) is a blueprint for the phrase structure of NPs, but like a blueprint, it is only schematic. We must fill in the actual contents of the Spec and Compl positions. We have seen that determiners (e.g., "a," "the," "some," "every") reside under the Spec position of an NP. Another possibility is that the Spec position is filled by a possessive phrase. Both possibilities are illustrated in (4). The determiner "the" occupies the Spec position of the lowest NP ("the man"). The possessive phrase "the man's" occupies the Spec position of the full NP.

(4)

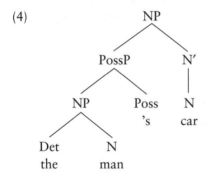

Besides the noun and the Spec, the remaining part of an NP is the (optional) Compl. As we saw, one kind of expression that can be in the Compl of a noun phrase is a prepositional phrase (see the examples in 1d). In (5), we illustrate a PP "up the street" as the complement of the N "lady". (The structure under the PP has been left unspecified for now.)

(5)

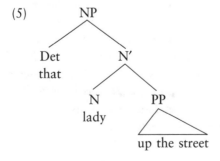

We have now a basic outline of the structure of NPs. However, we know that sentences contain more than just NPs. We need to see what other types of phrases can be found, so that eventually we will be able to diagram whole sentences. Consider the examples in (6).

(6)   a.   *sleep*
           run
           eat

      b.   *read* a book
           watch a video
           eat an apple

      c.   *put* the book on the table
           give a dollar to the man on the street
           show an example to the class

      d.   *think* that Al will win
           hope that the strikers will agree to play
           wait for Nina to report on the lawsuit

      e.   *tell* Mary that she will be there
           promise Dan that I would mow the lawn
           whisper to Stephanie that she can go

The examples in (6) are all **Verb Phrases** ("VP"), with the obligatory verbs ("V") italicized. As with NPs, the verb may be alone in the VP (6a), or it may occur with something else; this something else is the complement[1] of the verb. There are many different types of complements which can occur with verbs, as the examples in (6b–e) illustrate. In (6b), the complements are NPs. In (6c), two complements appear: an NP, and a PP. In (6d), what follows the verb is a complement sentence. Finally, in (6e), both an NP and a sentence appear. Remember, these syntactic categories are generated by the Phrase Structure rules. Their category label depends on their inner structure – there is no phrasal category "Compl." We use the term Compl to state a generalization; that is, certain kinds of phrases can occur with different categories.

These observations should lead you to conjecture that, similar to an NP, a VP can contain a V′ which contains a V plus a complement. Indeed, this is correct. What about a specifier? None of the examples in (6) shows a specifier of V. In fact, we will routinely omit specifiers of V. The arguments that a Spec of V exists are more advanced than we need to go into in order to appreciate how the Phrase Structure system works. Therefore, for our purposes, the structure of VP will be as in (7).

(7)   VP
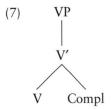

Since a Compl of V may be an NP, we can combine what we know about the structure of NP and the structure of VP to illustrate the structure of one of the examples in (6b), "eat an apple":

(8)

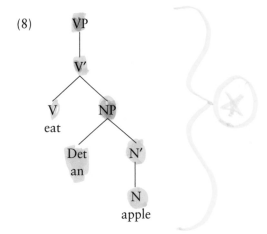

The VP consists of a V′, which consists of a V and a Compl. Since the Compl is an NP, we insert the category NP into the phrase marker; then, we expand the NP into its two components; in the example, these components are a specifier (Det) and the noun. In this instance, the NP within the VP does not contain a complement, so the N′ simply introduces an N.

What happens when a VP contains more than one complement? This is an important issue, about which we will have more to say later. For now, let us simply illustrate the structure of a VP with more than one complement, for concreteness, and we will put off discussing related issues until chapter 12.

In order to introduce more than one complement, we can make use of V′ as an intermediate category. V′ can dominate a complement, and another V′. The lower V′ can then be used to introduce another complement. Notice that the lower complement is the one that is closest to the verb, both hierarchically and linearly. An example of a phrase marker for a VP with both an NP and a PP complement is given in (9).

(9)

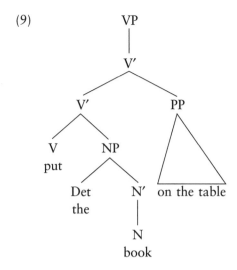

What other kind of phrasal structure do we need before we can tackle whole sentences? So far, we have seen several examples of **Prepositional Phrases**. As you should predict, and as the examples in (10) show, a PP must contain a preposition, and can optionally contain additional information.

(10) a. *in*
          out

      b. *over* the hill
          by car

      c. *over* the hill in Mansfield
          on the stage of the theater

      d. *in* over our heads
          out from under his control

As we found with VPs, PPs may consist of a P only, or a P with various complements. As with VPs, we will thus say that PP contains a P′, which can consist of a P and a Compl. We will ignore possible specifiers of P, for the same reason as before – to keep things as simple as possible.

(11)

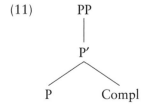

One complement of PP can be an NP. This yields PPs such as "on the roof."
The phrase marker associated with "on the roof" would be as follows:

(12)

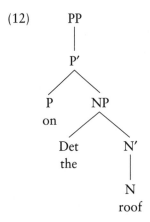

We are now in a position to fully diagram a complex verb phrase, as in (13).

(13)

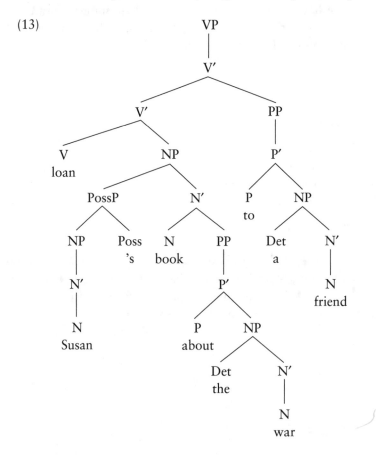

2   The Structure of Sentences: IP and CP

We still have not reached our goal of providing phrase markers for entire sentences. The tree diagram we gave for the VP in (13) represents the **predicate phrase** of a sentence, but as you know, a sentence needs a **subject phrase** as well as a predicate phrase. Subjects are usually NPs, and predicate phrases are VPs, in the system we are developing. We already know how to diagram the internal structure of an NP and a VP, but we still need to determine how NPs and VPs are combined. To help us decide the matter, let us first make the following observation. Suppose we add to the VP, "loan Susan's book about the war to a friend," the pronoun "He," so that the sentence has a subject NP – is the result a complete sentence? Not quite, as (14) indicates.

(14)   *He loan Susan's book about the war to a friend.

There is still something missing from the sentence in (14). The sentence needs some kind of tense marker: for example, the auxiliary verb "will" (making "He will loan . . .") or a tense marker "-s" or "-ed" on the verb (i.e., "He loans . . ." or "He loaned . . .").

As we figure out how to diagram what's missing in forming a sentence from an NP and a VP, we will make use of the generalizations we have developed so far. So, let's summarize them. In all of the phrases we have examined so far, NP, VP, and PP, there is one **obligatory element** – the N, V, or P, respectively. This obligatory element is called the **head** of the phrase. The head projects a phrasal category – NP, VP, PP, using an intermediate bar-level category – N', V', P'. If we want to combine a subject NP and a predicate VP into a sentence, what kind of phrasal category will the sentence be? In other words, what is the head of the sentence? The answer is that the head of the sentence is the element that's missing in (14): the tense marker. The tense marker is called **Inflection** (abbreviated "I"); thus, a sentence is called an **Inflection Phrase** ("IP").

In many (English) sentences, the inflection is attached to the verb. For example, in the sentence, "Susan walked to the office," the verb "walked" is marked with "-ed," for past tense. It is also possible for the inflection to be a separate word, such as "will," as in, "I will see the doctor tomorrow." These separate words, such as "will," and certain instances of "have" and "be," are called **auxiliary verbs,** or simply auxiliaries. In the sentence, "Every Monday I walk to the office," it might seem that there is no inflectional marking on the verb, "walk." However, it is clear from the interpretation of the sentence that the tense is non-past; that is, it is present tense. In this case, we say that there is an inflectional marker on the verb: it is a **zero morpheme** – a morpheme that is not pronounced. With this in mind, we can make the generalization that every sentence has an inflectional element: it might be an auxiliary, or a past tense marker, or even a zero morpheme. Whatever form it takes, however, the inflectional element can be considered to be the head of the sentence.

Where does inflection go in a tree diagram? Notice that an auxiliary comes before the verb, while the past tense marker goes after the verb. We will use the position of the auxiliary, which is a separate word, as the basic position for the inflectional element. We will assume that if the inflection is an affix (like the past tense marker), when the sentence is pronounced the affix "hops" onto the verb in order to make the appropriate verb form. The main requirement for affix-hopping is that the affix and the verb must be adjacent to each other. This "affix-hopping" operation will be discussed in more detail in chapter 16.

The complement of an IP is the predicate phrase, VP; its specifier is the subject NP. As in the previous examples, the head and the Compl combine together into a bar-level category (I′); then the I′ and the Spec combine to make IP (= sentence). An example of the structure of a full sentence can now be given in (15).

(15)

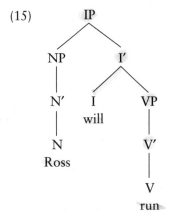

Using the terminology of phrase markers, we are now in a position to define structurally the notion **subject**: the subject is the NP which is immediately dominated by the IP. Similarly, an **object** is an NP dominated by VP.

Let's diagram another sentence:

(16)

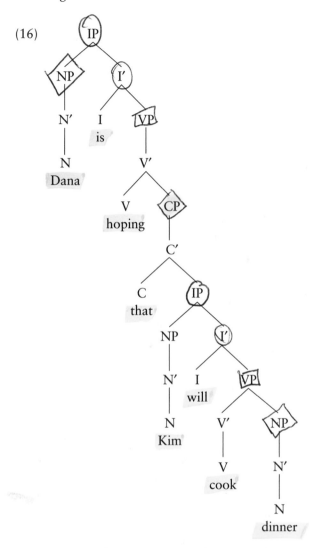

This phrase marker requires another new category. The new category is introduced because this sentence has a sentence inside of a sentence. This is the source of an important kind of productivity in natural language which we'll discuss in more detail in chapter 12. The inside sentence (called a **subordinate** or **embedded clause**) is called a **Complementizer Phrase** ("CP"). The CP, as expected, contains a **Complementizer** ("C") as its head. (Be careful not to confuse "complementizer" and "complement." These two similar words refer to different things.) A complementizer is a sentence-introducing word such as "that" or "for." CP can have a Spec, although it is not used in this example. In Part III, we will make use of the

Spec of CP. As expected, C′ dominates both C and the complement of C, which is the embedded sentence (**IP**).

Now, let us proceed to another example.

(17)

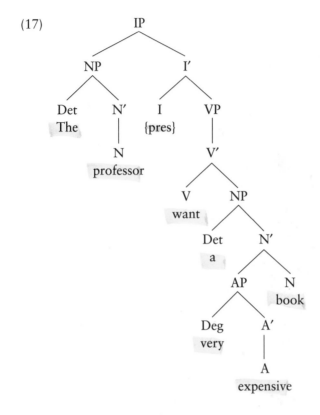

This phrase marker exemplifies several new concepts. First, we see a new category: AP (**Adjective Phrase**). The head of AP is, of course, A (Adjective). An AP may also contain a Degree word as its Spec: degree words in APs include "very," "quite," "more," etc. APs may also have complements, as in, "That book is very expensive for students."

APs themselves may be inside NPs, as example (17) shows. APs are unusual, because they appear under N′, but before the head N (unlike PP complements of N). It will become clear that they are under N′, rather than in the Spec of NP, in chapter 11.

Finally, notice that under the I node is written {pres}. This stands for the present tense inflectional marker that goes with the sentence, "The professor wants a very expensive book." In the phrase marker, the inflectional element is in its basic position, under I. When the sentence is pronounced, {pres} combines with "want" to make "wants." If the sentence were, "The professor wanted a very expensive book," then what is under the I node would be {past}.

Conclusion

Sentences have structure. In this chapter, we have begun to see how to express this structure, using the hierarchical relations of phrases in trees. So far, all we have done is to describe (some of) the kinds of phrases which occur. Using the mechanisms presented so far, you could diagram any number of sentences of English. However, we have not yet shown how the grammar represents this and generates all the structures of the language. We begin that task in the next chapter.

Note

1   We will call many different kinds of constituents that follow verbs "complements," even though there are important differences between true complements and other phrases which follow verbs, such as **adjuncts**. (Temporal and locative phrases, such as "yesterday" and "there," are frequently adjuncts.) Similarly, we will use only one type of constituent structure for them (the structure of a true complement). This is sufficient for our purposes, but in later courses you may find them distinguished.

Bibliographical Comments

The basic concepts of Phrase Structure introduced in the first part of the chapter are very common in modern linguistics, and even before. The generalization that categories of different types have basically the same structure, that of a head, a complement, and a specifier, was made by Chomsky (1970). Earlier models of sentence structure did not use I as the head of the sentence; rather, they suggested that the node S (for sentence) was different from other nodes in having three daughters (NP, Aux, VP), none of which is the head. Similarly, the label S′ was used for Comp(lementizer) + S. The IP and CP innovation was made in Chomsky (1986), and is now very common.

9   Phrase Structure Rules and X′-Theory

Introduction

As we saw in the last chapter, sentences have structure. That is, any sentence can be assigned a hierarchical representation in which certain groups of words are joined into phrases. By mapping out the structure of sentences, we begin to capture the regularities in language – the fact that groups of words in different sentences are organized in similar ways. In addition to this, these hierarchical representations account for our intuitions about which words combine to form phrases and which do not. It is important to note that these hierarchical representations are not just notations used by linguists. There is evidence that they are psychologically real – that they are in our heads as we learn and process language. We will be giving evidence for this claim later when we talk about children's knowledge of Phrase Structure.

We described the structure of sentences by diagramming them, using what we call a phrase marker or tree diagram. But, so far, we simply illustrated how these phrase markers represent the structure of the sentences. We haven't yet specified the rules for producing these representations of sentences. This is our next task: to show how phrase markers (tree diagrams) are derived by just a few rules and a finite stock of words. The rules for forming phrase markers are called **Phrase Structure Rules** (PS rules), and they will be the topic of this chapter. In later chapters we will present more evidence for the constituent structures proposed here, and we will put PS rules to further work. We will demonstrate how these rules can be used to explain several of the basic facts about language that we presented earlier. PS rules account for: (i) the *productivity* of language, (ii) the *ambiguity* of some sentences, and (iii) our *acquisition* of certain linguistic knowledge in the absence of experience (i.e., Plato's problem, or the problem of the poverty of the stimulus).

1   How to Derive Phrase Markers

Let us begin by looking at a simple phrase marker, such as (1). If we consider this phrase marker without the terminal elements (words), we can see that it shows the hierarchical structure which would fit many different sentences (for example, "The teacher should read the book;" or, "Those students will pass the exam"). It names the categories of the words in each sentence, and it represents the groups of words that go together.

(1)

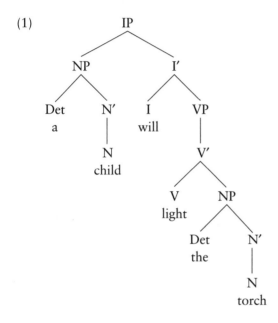

Now we can turn to the Phrase Structure rules that are used in creating this structure. Linguists have found that the same pieces of structure are found across many different sentences. Rules capture such generalizations about the structure of sentences. Like a phrase marker, Phrase Structure rules describe the structure of a tree diagram (or phrase marker). But PS rules describe the structure of sentences in a different format. To form a PS rule we start at the top node of the tree – the root – and work down, looking at each node of the tree below it. The topmost node is IP; thus, IP is the root node, and it dominates the nodes NP and I'. Phrase Structure rules reflect the domination relation; they categorize the nodes that dominate other nodes, until we reach the lowest nodes – the words. Here is the first PS rule:

(2)   IP → NP I'

This rule is read as follows: "IP is rewritten as NP followed by I'," or, "An IP consists of an NP and an I' in that order." This is really just another way of writing this portion of the tree:

(3)

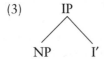

We can describe the nodes NP and I' in the same way. Let's look at NP first. It dominates Det and N', while N' dominates N. This can be stated in the PS rules in (4), which give us the tree in (5).

(4) NP → Det N'   (5)

N' → N

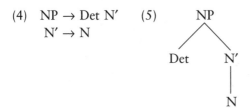

Combining the trees in (3) and (5), the result so far is (6).

(6)

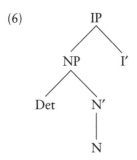

I' dominates I and VP. Thus, the next PS rule we need is (7), which gives us (8) in the tree.

(7) I' → I VP   (8)

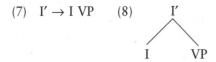

Now look at VP. It dominates V', which dominates V and NP. As you can now guess, we express these relations with the rules in (9), which produce the tree in (10).

(9) VP → V'   (10)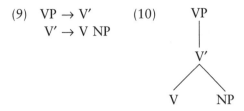
     V' → V NP

Combining everything we have so far results in the tree in (11).

(11)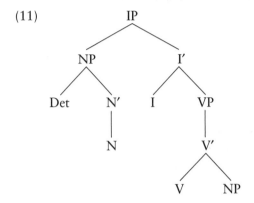

Now we must expand the final NP. This is accomplished by using the same PS rules we introduced before: NP → Det N', and N' → N. Since the same rules are used twice, this suggests that the phrases themselves should be interchangeable. This is often the case. For example, we can say, "The man watched the child" or, "The child watched the man."

It is very important to notice that order is strictly interpreted in PS rules. We write IP → NP I' to mean "IP is rewritten as NP followed by I' *in that order*." If we wrote IP → I' NP, this would correspond to a phrase marker which looks like (12). This is not one of the PS rules of English, although it could be a rule of another language.

(12)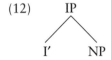

With the last NP in place, we have now accounted for all of the branches in the tree. The final step is to spell out the leaves of the tree, by indicating how words are introduced. We do this by looking in the mental dictionary (or lexicon) for words of the proper categories. Each word in the lexicon has information about its grammatical category (noun, verb, etc.), as well as its meaning and pronunciation. The lexicon also gives some information about which words go together – for example, whether a verb requires an object or not. For now, we will just refer to grammatical category information to find appropriate "leaves" for our trees. Some examples are given in (13).

(13)   N: tiger, teacher, president . . .
       V: chase, need . . .
       Det: the, a, one, two . . .

Summing up, what we have so far is the PS grammar in (14).

(14)   IP → NP I′
            I′ → I VP
          NP → Det N′
           N′ → N
          VP → V′
           V′ → V NP
           N: boy, tiger, president, teacher . . .
           V: chase, have, need, request . . .
           I: is, will, {pres} . . .
          Det: the, a . . .

The Phrase Structure rules permit us to generate the phrase markers for a host of English sentences, so they put us in a position to make generalizations about what types of phrase markers are most common in English. But first we must add to our rules. We can decide what rules to add by looking at other sentences. Consider next a very simple sentence:

(15)

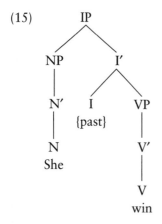

This phrase marker underlies the sentence, "She won." It illustrates one of the most basic concepts of Phrase Structure: each phrasal category must have a head. The head of NP is N; the head of VP is V, and the head of the sentence, IP, is I. Notice two things about I. First, the past tense marker {past} appears in the position that an auxiliary might take. As already noted, the past tense marker and the verb will combine when the sentence is pronounced. Second, look ahead to the combined V + I. We know that "win + {past}" is pronounced "won," not "winned." This irregularity is not illustrated in the phrase marker, because it has no effect on the phrase marker. We will use the past tense marker {past} as a shorthand for "past tense," whether or not the past tense is realized on the verb chosen according to the regular rules or by exception. Similarly, the abbreviation {pres} will be used for present tense, regardless.

Now let's consider a more complex example, such as (17). Notice that in this example the two NPs are interchangeable, just as we mentioned earlier. The sentence could just as well have been, "The broadcaster threatened the candidate on television." In addition, there is something that we haven't seen in our Phrase Structure rules yet, namely the prepositional phrase "on television." To generate this phrase, we need to add another option to the rule for expanding the V', making it as follows: V' → V' PP. We also need some rules for expanding prepositional phrases. These rules are listed in (16) below.

(16) V' → V' PP
      PP → P'
      P' → P NP

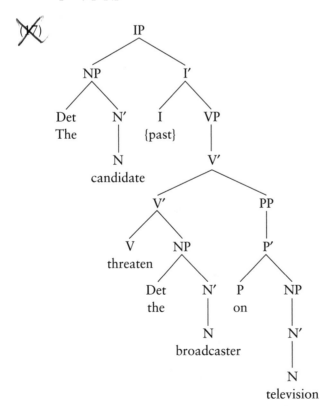

From chapter 8, we can add examples (19) and (20). In order to account for these examples, the new rules in (18) are needed:

(18)   V′ → V CP
        CP → C′
        C′ → C IP
        N′ → AP N
        AP → Deg A′
        A′ → A

(19)

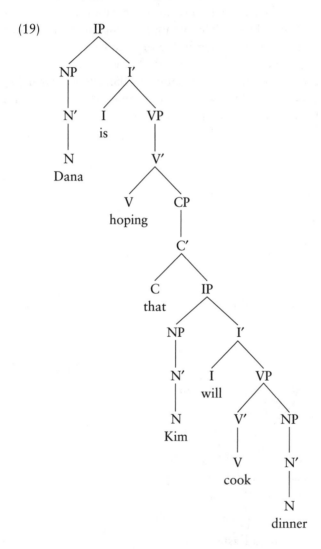

(20)

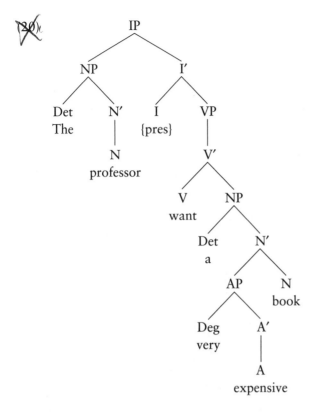

Embedded clauses are always introduced using CP. Many VPs can contain an embedded clause, and embedded clauses can also appear in a VP containing an NP or another category. For example, consider (21). It shows that we need rule (22).

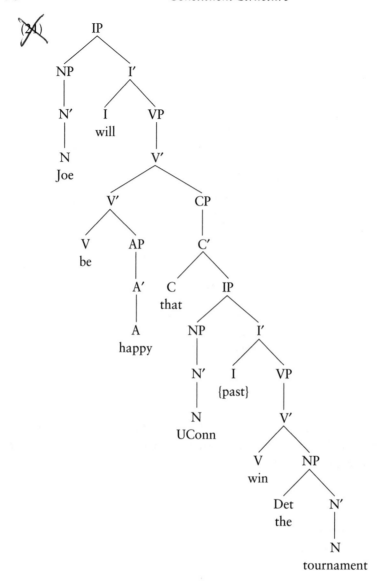

(22)   V′ → V AP

Notice that the material which follows a verb depends on the verb itself. Some verbs do not allow an embedded clause (e.g., "*John ran that Bill will pass"), while others allow one (e.g., "John knows Bill" or "John knows that Bill will pass") or require one (e.g., "John thinks that Bill will pass" and not "*John thinks Bill"). Some verbs take an NP object (e.g., "Mary saw Alice"), while others take an NP and a PP (e.g., "Mary put the book on the shelf").

Now we have enough rules in our grammar to form certain generalizations about English sentences. For different sentences, we see that the same parts of the description occur over and over again. For example, every sentence we have considered so far requires the rules IP → NP I' and I' → I VP. Rather than stating these rules over and over again for each sentence, we just list them once in the collection of Phrase Structure rules for English, and we use them over and over to expand IP any time IP comes up in different sentences (or even in the same sentence).

We will refer to the collection of Phrase Structure rules which generates some part of a language as a Phrase Structure Grammar (PSG) for that language fragment. Although we have only accounted for a fragment of English, it should be obvious that even a few PS rules can generate a wide variety of sentence types. Let's summarize the Phrase Structure Grammar for English (so far). (The parentheses in the PS rules indicate that the element is optional.)

(23)   *Phrase Structure Grammar*

CP → C'	VP → V'
C' → C IP	V' → V NP
IP → NP I'	V' → V AP
I' → I VP	V' → V PP
NP → (Det) N'	V' → V CP
N' → AP N	V' → V
N' → N PP	PP → P'
N' → N	P' → P NP
AP → (Deg) A'	
A' → A	

Abbreviations

C	= complementizer	CP	= complementizer phrase
I	= inflection	IP	= inflection phrase
V	= verb	VP	= verb phrase
N	= noun	NP	= noun phrase
P	= preposition	PP	= prepositional phrase
A	= adjective	AP	= adjective phrase
Det	= determiner	Deg	= degree word
Poss	= possessive	Conj	= conjunction

Clearly, the list of PS rules above does not exhaust the PS rules of English. But we can see already that, using this set of rules, we can generate many sentences that we haven't seen before.

2 X'-Theory

At this point, we have already seen enough about Phrase Structure to make some deeper generalizations. One goal of a scientific theory (including, of course, linguistic theory) is to recognize and capture in a meaningful way those properties which go together, even if they seem disparate on first glance. Within linguistic theory, this means that we attempt to find commonalities across different sentence types, and posit a more abstract generalization, principle, or constraint which can account for this commonality.

If we look now at what we have seen regarding different phrase types, we have learned that every phrasal category contains at least one element. Every VP must contain a V; every NP must contain an N; every PP must contain a P; and so on. As we have seen, these required elements (V, N, P) are called the **heads** of their phrases. We can now use a variable, just as variables are used in mathematics, to refer to any phrasal category and any category head. Using a variable, X, we may refer to any phrasal category as an XP, to indicate properties that pertain to any phrasal category (NP, VP, PP, and so forth). Similarly, the variable, X, is used to indicate properties that hold of any head (N, V, P). In this way, we can state generalizations such as (24):

(24) Every XP (i.e., phrasal category) must contain an X (a head).

What else does an XP contain? It can be broken down into two further components, a specifier and a complement. These elements are arranged in a hierarchical relationship. First, the phrasal category XP (NP, VP, etc.) consists of a Spec and an X'. At the next level down in the hierarchical relationship, the X' is cashed out – it consists of a head X and a Compl. All phrasal categories pattern in exactly the same way:

(25)

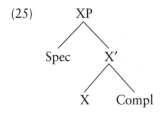

Now we can state two other generalizations:

(26) Every XP can contain a specifier,
        and must contain an intermediate level category, X';

(27)   X′ introduces X, and possibly a complement.

Now that we have Phrase Structure rules at our disposal, we can state these generalizations in more formal terms.

(28)   a.   XP → (Spec) X′
       b.   X′ → X (Compl)

The Phrase Structure schemata in (28) form the basis of what is known as **X′-Theory**. According to this theory, phrases typically have the structures given in (28). Consider what an advantage this makes for language acquisition. At the end of the previous section, we provided a partial list of the Phrase Structure rules of English. Without X′-theory, it would seem that children need to learn this entire list of rules (and the rules we did not yet introduce) in order to use the correct sentence structures of English. However, X′-theory allows for the possibility that children don't have to learn a long list of rules. The schemata given in (28) might be part of our innate endowment for language acquisition. How plausible is this suggestion?

Recall from chapter 2 that one of the properties that must be displayed by a principle to be part of the innate linguistic component is universality. That is, the principles of Universal Grammar are universal, in the sense that all languages must share these principles. In some cases, the universal principles are parameterized, which means that a very limited set of cross-linguistic variation is possible – and the variation is itself also given by the universal principle. Are the rules in (28) universal, given the possibility of parameterization?

It seems that the answer is yes. Across all languages, the word order found in basic sentence types can be characterized by these two simple rules. (We will see in later chapters that there are ways to modify basic sentence types.) There are differences between languages, for example, in the order of a head with respect to its complement. In some languages, like English, a head appears before its complement. In other languages, however, the complement appears first. For these languages, rule (28b′) would be used instead of (28b).

(28)   b′.   X′ → (Compl) X

In some languages, specifiers come after their heads, rather than before, as in English. Rule (28a) thus requires parameterization for order, just as does rule (28b). For specifier-final languages, rule (28a′) is needed.[1]

(28)   a′.   XP → X′ (Spec)

Languages that use rule (28b′) rather than rule (28b) include Japanese and Korean, among others. Languages that use rule (28a′) rather than rule (28a) include Palauan. Does a child learning Japanese or Palauan have to learn a long set of Phrase Structure rules different from those which a child learning English must acquire? According to X'-theory, no. Children learning English must learn that complements follow heads, while children learning Japanese must learn that heads follow complements. Since the word order displayed by almost every sentence will provide this information, it will not be difficult for children to master this. And that is all children will need to learn to command the word order found in all phrases for basic sentence types. In the next chapter, we turn to some evidence regarding how children determine which version of the X'-rules their language uses.

Conclusion

Phrase Structure rules generate phrase markers. The PS rules of a language can be generalized by the X'-schema set with the particular order used by that language. This simple pair of rules can then be used to generate many, many sentence types. Importantly, the claim being made here is not just that PS rules can be used to describe the set of sentences found in observing some language. Instead, the claim is that PS rules are part of a speaker's linguistic competence: the mental knowledge of grammar, which is psychologically real. Furthermore, we have seen that the X'-schema is part of Universal Grammar, which we have argued is part of the innate Language Acquisition Device. This means we might see evidence for it in young children's language. We turn to this topic next.

Note

1   We are oversimplifying somewhat here. It seems that in some languages, not all categories follow the same ordering for head and complement (or specifier and head). For example, a language might have V before its complements, but I following its complements. The range of possibilities has not been completely determined yet, but it seems to be rather restricted.

Bibliographical Comments

The concept of Phrase Structure rules presented in the text is essentially that developed by Chomsky, in particular Chomsky (1957) and Chomsky (1975) (written in 1955), as modified in Chomsky (1970). See also Jackendoff (1977), Lasnik and Kupin (1977), Stowell (1981) for several important modifications of Chomsky's theory of phrase markers. A few introductory textbooks which contain detailed discussions of PS rules and PS grammars are Akmajian and Heny (1975), Baker (1978), Cook and Newson (1996), Radford (1981), and Riemsdijk and Williams (1986).

10 Setting the X′-Parameters

Introduction

We propose that children acquire their native language using the principles and constraints of Universal Grammar. For the most part, we have stressed the theoretical rationale for this proposal. The observation that any child can learn any natural language invites us to pursue the idea that the principles and constraints of Universal Grammar are innately specified, as part of the human genetic endowment for language. It is time to find out how theory relates to data. This chapter explores the actual time course of early language development. We discuss some evidence regarding children's acquisition of the settings of the X′-parameters for the language they are learning. We will see that data from the laboratory are entirely consistent with our theoretical proposals, and show that children obtain the adult settings of these parameters at an early age.

1 Acquisition of Word Order: English

A child's earliest two-word combinations often consist of a limited number of formulaic utterances like those in (1).

(1) more cookie   no bed
     more read   no down
     more juice   no water
     other bib   light off
     other shoe   shirt off
     other milk   water off

These first word combinations have very limited productivity. Typically, the first word combinations consist of one of a very small set of words such as "more," "no," "off," etc., together with some word from a larger class (often names for familiar objects or actions). At this stage (usually around 18 months), the range of combinations produced by the child is very limited. However, it is noteworthy that even at this early stage there is usually a regular ordering between elements. For example, "more" or "no" usually come first in a two-word combination, while "off" or "there" come second. We cannot learn much about the child's emerging grammar until more productive combinations appear.

Shortly after the emergence of these formulaic utterances, children begin using much more productive combinations in two- and three-word "sentences." Some examples are given in (2).

(2) block broke   car coming
      I did it   doll eat
      Eve find it   doll eat celery
      Neil sit   man have it
      lie down stool   find it
      man taste it   Eve writing

You will notice that these examples are not fully adult-like. Elements are often missing, particularly inflections and determiners. However, if you pay attention to the order of the elements, you will see that they always follow the subject–verb–object–locative order used in adult English.

Although there might seem to be very little syntax required in putting two or three words together, it seems that from the very beginning children learning English do use the correct word order. Even if some constituents are missing, those that are expressed almost always follow the correct order for English. For example, to express the notion, "Adam pushed the ball," a 20-month-old child might say, "Adam push," "push ball," or "Adam ball," but she would not say, "push Adam." Following the syntactic rules we discussed in the previous chapter, we could diagram such children's utterances using complete adult-like phrase markers, with some elements missing. An example of one such phrase marker is given in (3). In this example, we have used parentheses to indicate potential missing elements.

(3)

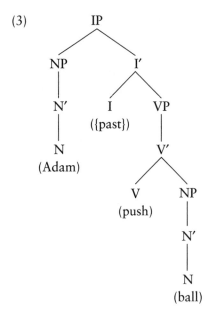

There has been considerable debate as to whether or not the child who says "push ball" really has all the structure given in (3). We will return to discuss this question a bit more in chapter 13. For now, let's assume that children have the syntactic structures of the X′-theory available from UG, and concentrate on how the child determines the settings of the X′-parameters for English.

Notice what the child's problem is. On the basis of grammatical adult input, the child needs to determine whether heads precede or follow their complements, and whether specifiers come before or after the rest of the phrase. For the child acquiring English, a great many of the input utterances supply evidence regarding the English settings. After all, the specifier–head–complement order is rarely altered in adult English (although we will see some examples of modifications in order). Thus, we might expect the English-learning child to quickly apprehend the adult order, set the parameters, and then use these settings in production and comprehension. Although occasional non-adult orders are found in English-learning children, the bulk of the evidence supports this scenario.

Many studies have debated how to account for those aspects of the child's earliest utterances which are non-adult-like, such as missing elements or lack of grammatical morphology. However, word order errors are virtually non-existent. In cases where English adult word order is strict, children almost invariably use the adult order. In those few cases where children's order shows variability, adults also have syntactic mechanisms allowing for variations in order.

We have presented evidence that young children learning English produce utterances with only those word orders that are permitted in the target language. One researcher who studied this phenomenon in the 1970s, Lois Bloom, stated that "the consistency with which the surface order corresponded to the inherent grammatical relation within the utterance was impressive." Even when considering the ordering of two elements we can observe adherence to particular ordering constraints. However, the degree of consistency in word order in children's sentences is even more impressive when we examine the three-word stage and beyond. With any three elements, there are logically six possible linear arrangements; with four elements, there are 24, and so on. The generalization is that there are **n**-factorial ways of ordering **n** elements. At the three-word stage, with six possible word orders, there is compelling evidence that children are **conservative**, postulating only a subset of the possible word orders.

There is, in fact, additional empirical evidence for our alternative hypothesis, in addition to the conceptual arguments advanced above and the evidence presented from English. This evidence includes cross-linguistic support for the UG model of word order acquisition, which we will discuss in the following section of this chapter. Additional evidence comes from children's early utterances, where the indications are that they make use of both syntactic categories and Phrase Structure; this evidence will be presented in chapter 13.

2   Word Order: Cross-Linguistic Evidence

Since English is a language with very limited grammatical word orders in the target language, when we find that young children consistently use a subject–verb–object ordering of the three main sentential elements, we can conclude that the order they choose is the correct one for the adult language, and that they are conservative in their word order acquisition. We can find even more telling information about children's word order choices and conservativity by examining the acquisition of languages other than English. First, we want to know if children acquiring other languages with limited word order variation (as in English) also quickly grasp the adult order. In addition, we can gain important information from considering languages which, unlike English, allow for a greater flexibility in order. We will discuss evidence of these two types in turn.

Mandarin Chinese is a strict subject–verb–object (SVO) language. Changes in surface word order are found even less often than in English. The psycholinguist Mary Erbaugh found that children use SVO from a very early age, and were very strict in their use of this order. Even in the cases which would allow order variations for the adult grammar (OV instead of VO), Erbaugh found that children maintained SVO order until around 3 years of age. Some examples of children's early Mandarin utterances are given in (4).

(4)   a.   wǒ chī
           "I eat"

      b.   wán zhège
           "Play [with] this"

      c.   huā hǎo piàoliang
           "The flower [is] very pretty"

We have seen, then, two examples of early acquisition of adult word order in languages which allow fairly limited variation in word order. However, what about languages which allow greater variation in the adult surface word order? For example, Japanese, Turkish, Korean, and Russian are languages with many more word order possibilities than English. Sometimes languages which allow variation in order are called "free word order languages." However, this name is misleading because no language is completely free to order words in any way. Rather, languages like these use rules (called transformations, to be discussed in much more detail in Part III) to re-order elements, and some languages tolerate more changes in order than English does. Thus, it is instructive to look at children learning Japanese and other freer word order languages, to see whether they, like children learning English, initially choose correct word orders, and whether they are also conservative (i.e., producing a subset of the word order possibilities).

In a review of studies of the acquisition of Japanese, Patricia Clancy says that children learning Japanese acquire both the unmarked "standard" order (SOV) and other orders which are allowed in particular contexts. She claims that children use the other orders appropriately from a young age. Similarly, Ayhan Aksu-Koç and Dan Slobin found that children learning Turkish acquired both the unmarked SOV order and other pragmatically conditioned orders very early. Hence, it appears that in some cases children acquiring languages permitting freer word order very quickly zero in on several adult options.

Different results have been reported for children learning Korean and Russian, however. One study of the acquisition of Korean was conducted by a researcher named Tschang-Zi Park, who reported on his daughter's acquisition of the language. Park's daughter avoided many of the possible combinations available in the parental input. Instead, she strongly favored a single word order, in which the subject, verb, and object appeared in that order.

Dan Slobin makes the same point reporting on a Russian child named Zhenya, who was studied by the Russian linguist Aleksandr Gvozdev. Word order is relatively free in Russian, but the dominant order used by adults is SVO. The child subject, Zhenya, did not initially adopt this order as his dominant word order, however. Neither did he allow words to be ordered freely. Rather, at first Zhenya produced sentences with SOV order for the most part, and later switched to SVO. Slobin concluded that the LAD compels learners to begin with word orders that do not necessarily match their experience.

We have seen, then, several possibilities for word order acquisition. In the cases of English, Mandarin, Japanese, and Turkish, the evidence has shown that some children quickly adopt the adult word order – whether it is relatively strict or relatively free. On the other hand, some children (the Korean and Russian cases) apparently use a more strict order even when the adult language allows variation. We believe that Slobin is correct in concluding that the LAD is responsible for the cases of conservativity in children learning free word order languages. In addition, we expect not to find children acquiring languages such as English or Chinese producing illicit word order variations, again, due to the LAD. Let's see why.

When the child quickly adopts the basic and alternative word orders made available by the adult language, there is no question of learnability. The only issue is to wonder how children come to have this knowledge so quickly! Clearly, the availability of such grammars in UG aids early and error-free acquisition.

On the other hand, what if the child does not quickly settle on the adult grammar? If the child exposed to Korean or Russian chooses only one possible order, there will be abundant evidence in the input to allow the child to switch the setting of the X'-parameters. There is no problem of learnability when there is abundant positive evidence. However, if the child exposed to a language such as English or Mandarin wrongly hypothesized that it was a "free" word order language like Korean or Russian, the child would produce word order combinations that were not grammatically well formed. Moreover, without evidence to abandon these incorrect forms, the child would continue to over-generate, i.e., produce incorrect forms, into adulthood. In the absence of negative evidence about which sentences are not part of the target language, the child would not be able to converge on the correct grammar. Obviously, this does not happen: there are no speakers of English or Mandarin who regularly produce word orders that are not exhibited by other speakers of these languages.

To explain how children acquire the correct word orders for their target language, there must be something innately specified within the LAD preventing them from generating word order possibilities that they will not encounter. By adhering to what we will call the **Subset Principle**, children will encounter positive evidence if they entertain the (erroneous) hypothesis that the target language has "fixed" rather than "flexible" word order.

The Subset Principle provides an ordering of hypotheses for language learning. According to this principle, when there are several options available to a child, the learner should initially hypothesize the "narrowest" possible language. Only when positive evidence reveals greater variation in word order will the child move to that hypothesis. This ensures that children do not have to backtrack from an over-inclusive hypothesis. Such backtracking requires negative

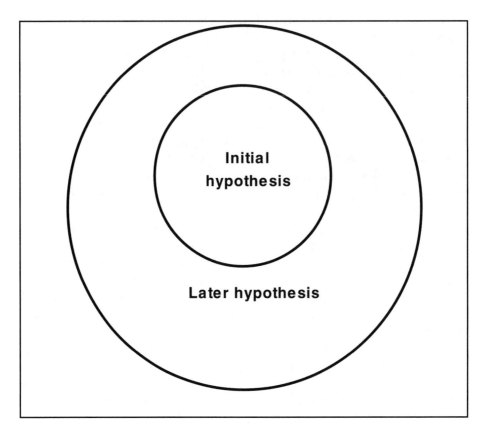

Figure 10.1   The Subset Principle

evidence, which we assume the child does not have access to. The working of the Subset Principle is diagrammed in figure 10.1.

The Subset Principle applies in cases in which UG allows one grammar to generate a set of sentences which is fully included in the set of sentences generated by another grammar. For example (simplifying), a language like English allows the order subject–verb–object (SVO), but not OSV, OVS, etc. Korean allows SVO as well as SOV, OSV, and OVS. Thus, the hypothesis that the target language allows only one word order results in a narrower class of sentences (a subset) compared to the hypothesis that the target allows multiple word orders (the superset). The Subset Principle instructs the child to choose the hypothesis which generates the narrower class of sentences first. Positive evidence (the existence of sentences with SOV, OSV, OVS orders) will be available to motivate the learner to change her hypothesis. On the other hand, if the learner initially chose the superset hypothesis, there would be no positive evidence to tell her that the hypothesis was incorrect. This would require negative evidence. Since we assume that negative evidence is not available, we must ensure that the child begins with the narrower hypothesis, to avoid a learnability problem.

The evidence of the conservativity of children learning English, Korean, and Russian which we just summarized supports the idea that the Subset Principle is at work in language acquisition. The initial hypothesis dictated by the Subset Principle is that children should choose one word order only. Gradually, as the child encounters evidence that other orders are available, she can change her hypothesis, until her grammar equals the adult's. We thus conclude that the Subset Principle is an important part of the Language Acquisition Device.

Conclusion

We have seen that much of the time, children quickly attain the adult setting of the X'-parameters. In fact, by the time children are combining two- and three-word utterances (around 2 years of age), they have been observed to home in on the correct adult word order, including possible variations in word order, in many cases. In some cases, we saw evidence that children seem to have a more restricted grammar than the target grammar. This kind of "error," however, does not pose a learnability problem, because positive evidence will be available in the environment to induce a grammar change. This is not the case if children were to make the other type of error – assuming that their language allowed more sentence types than it does. We proposed that the Subset Principle, a part of the Language Acquisition Device, prevents children from choosing superset grammars, correction of which would require negative evidence.

Bibliographical Comments

The first large-scale project on the acquisition of English syntax in the generative approach was published in Brown (1973). Much of the early work on the acquisition of English is summarized and reviewed in deVilliers and deVilliers (1985). Quotations in the text attributed to Lois Bloom are from Bloom (1970). Many studies on the acquisition of a variety of languages are reported in Slobin (1985), including those cited in this chapter by Erbaugh (1992), Clancy (1985), and Aksu-Koç and Slobin (1985). The study of Korean reported here is from Tschang-Zi Park (1970). Slobin (1966) summarizes the study by Gvozdev on the acquisition of Russian discussed here. The Subset Principle was discussed and named by Berwick (1985).

11   Phrasal Categories

Introduction

We have argued that sentences have structure – that the combination of words into sentences requires more than just a linear juxtaposition, but also a hierarchical arrangement. We have also shown that there are several sources of evidence for the psychological reality of the kind of phrase structures we have been assigning to sentences. First, we appealed to your intuitions about which words of a sentence group together, and which words do not. Phrase Structure explains these intuitions. Then, in the previous chapter we looked at some evidence from language acquisition, to show that children acquire the basic Phrase Structure schemata of their language at a very young age. In chapter 13, we will look at additional evidence regarding children's knowledge of the phrasal structure of sentences. There we will look in more detail at the internal structures which children employ.

In this chapter and the next, we will focus on another source of evidence for Phrase Structure. This is often referred to as **distributional evidence**, because the evidence consists of observations about which words distribute together in sentences. We will see that the categories we posit make sense of the way groups of words distribute in sentences.

There are two kinds of distributional evidence we will discuss in this chapter. The first concerns "movement" tests. Groups of words can sometimes be moved around in a sentence. The only groups that can move, however, are **constituents** – that is, words which all hang together under one node. The second type of distributional evidence concerns the fact that certain groups of words can be replaced by a single word. This phenomenon can also be used as a diagnostic for seeing whether or not a sequence of words forms a unit or constituent.

1   Movement Tests

One diagnostic for constituent structure asks which groups of words can appear together at the beginning of a sentence, as a topic. For instance, the sentence in (1a) can easily be changed to the one in (1b) or the one in (1c). However, the version in (1d) is ungrammatical.

(1) a.   Ashley parked her sports car in the garage.
     b.   Her sports car, Ashley parked in the garage.
     c.   In the garage, Ashley parked her sports car.
     d.   *Sports car in the garage, Ashley parked her.

Examples (1b, c) illustrate "topicalization" – putting the topic of the sentence at the very beginning. In (1b), the topic is the NP "her sports car." In (1c), the topic is the PP "in the garage." However, in example (1) the group of words "sports car in the garage" does not form a constituent – these words do not all hang from one node. The ungrammaticality of (1d) indicates that only a constituent can be topicalized.

Notice next that certain sequences of words, such as "up his drainpipe," may appear both at the end of a sentence, as in (2a), and, with only slight awkwardness, as the topic mentioned at the beginning of a sentence, as in (2b). Notice also that these two sentences mean the same thing.

(2) a.   John was looking up his drainpipe.
     b.   Up his drainpipe, John was looking.

By contrast, a similar sequence of words, "up his number," can appear as a sequence at the end of a sentence, as in (3a), but this phrase cannot be topicalized; that is, it may not appear at the beginning, as the ungrammaticality of (3b) shows.

(3) a.   John was looking up his number.
     b.   *Up his number, John was looking.

Example (3b) sounds much odder than its counterpart (2b). This might lead us to propose that the word "up" is used differently in "up his drainpipe" and "up his number." This turns out to be correct. We can explain the oddity of (3b) if we assume that "up" does not belong within the same phrase as "his number." The word "up" does belong within the same phrase as "his drainpipe," however. That is, in (2), the entire sequence of words, "up his drainpipe," is a PP, consisting of the P, "up," followed by the NP, "his drainpipe." In (3), however, "up his number" does not constitute a PP; instead, "up" is associated with the verb "look." This use of "up" is called a "verb + particle construction," to indicate that "up" belongs with the verb and not with the following NP. To explain the oddity of (3b), we need only recall that whole phrases, such as a PP, can be displaced to the beginnings of sentences, as we saw in (1). Since the expression "up his number" is not a phrase (because "up" does not reside with the NP under a PP), it cannot be displaced to the beginning of (3).

As further confirmation, compare (4a–b) and (5a–b).

(4) a.   John looked up his number.
     b.   John looked his number up.

(5) a.   John looked up his drainpipe.
     b.   ?John looked his drainpipe up.

The examples in (4) illustrate that the particle "up" can be displaced to the end of a sentence, without a corresponding change in meaning, whereas in (5) it is clear that this is not true of the preposition "up." The only way to interpret (5b) is to give it a quite specific meaning, suggesting that John is looking up which kind of drainpipe he has. We doubt that this meaning occurred to you when you read (5a).

By observing distributional properties such as these, we can begin to make claims about the special status of certain groups of words, as opposed to others. These distributional properties are used by linguists as constituency tests to decide whether or not some sequence of words forms a constituent. In addition to being evidence of phrasal structure, these linguistic tests of constituency provide new linguistic phenomena to be explained. By appealing to the notion of hierarchical structure, then, we are in a position to explain a broadening range of linguistic facts.

2   Substitution Tests

We can also find evidence for certain syntactic structures by using substitution tests. Some words in English can substitute for other words or phrases. A case in point is the substitution of pronouns, such as "you," "he," "she," "they," for entire noun phrases such as "the man with the Golden Gun." A pronoun can appear where a noun phrase can appear. Although pronouns are only single words, because they substitute for phrases they provide evidence for the existence of abstract phrasal structure in sentences. Consider some further examples.

(6) a. The woman left.
    b. She left.

(7) a. Two old friends arrived.
    b. They arrived.

In these examples, a pronoun agreeing in number (either singular or plural) is able to substitute for NPs with determiners or adjectives. There are also slightly more complex cases, as in (8–9).

(8) a. The woman in the red coat left.
    b. She left.

(9) a. A man and a boy in a baseball uniform arrived.
    b. They arrived.

These examples show that a single word, the pronouns "she" and "they," substitute for fuller noun phrases. In the first example, the singular pronoun "she" substitutes for a noun phrase that consists of a Det ("the") and an N ("woman") followed by a PP ("in the red coat"). This is evidence that all of these words and groups of words are joined to form a single constituent; it is this single constituent that the pronoun replaces. For convenience, we will sometimes represent the whole NP using a triangle, as in example (10). The triangle is used when the internal structure of a phrasal category is not of immediate concern. The phrasal node replaced by "she" is the NP dominating the triangle in the phrase marker; this is the subject NP, "the woman in the red coat."

(10)

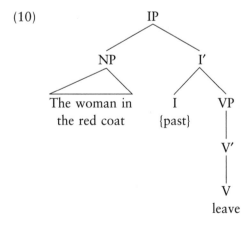

The second example (9) is even more compelling evidence of the formation of higher-level categories. In this example, the singular NPs "a boy" and "a man"

are conjoined (by "and") to form an NP that is plural. This is why the plural pronoun "they" replaces it, rather than a singular pronoun. Another use of this conjoined NP is illustrated in (11).

(11)

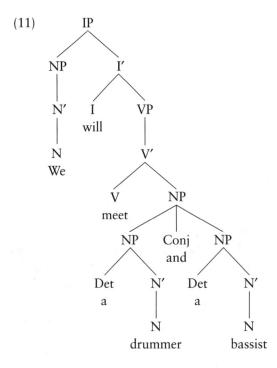

Noun phrases are not the only categories for which we can provide a constituency test. Verb phrases can be replaced by the word "did," as in the following examples:

(12) a. Barbara went to the museum, and Raisa went to the museum too.
      b. Barbara went to the museum, and Raisa did too.

(13) a. Marilyn studied in college, and Dan studied in college too.
      b. Marilyn studied in college, and Dan did too.

The seemingly simple auxiliary verb "did" has other uses as well. It is used in several types of sentences: for example, it provides emphasis, as in (14a), it is used with negatives, as in (14b), and it is used with questions, as in (14c). We learn more about "do" in chapter 18.

(14) a. Marilyn did study in college.
      b. Marilyn studied in college, but Dan didn't.
      c. Marilyn studied in college, but did Dan?

In these examples, the word "did" sometimes stands in place of a VP, and it sometimes appears as an auxiliary to a VP. It is important to observe, however, that when it substitutes for a VP, it substitutes for the whole thing – not just the verb, or some part of the VP. This can be seen in examples like the following. While (15a) is fine, it sounds odd (or funny) to say (15b):

(15) a. Marilyn studied hard every night in college, and Dan did too.
          (This means Dan studied hard every night in college.)

      b. ?Marilyn studied hard every night in college, and Dan did too,
          but only once a week.

3   "One"-Substitution

The substitution test of constituency can be applied to other syntactic categories besides NP and VP. We will now apply the substitution test to provide evidence for the category N'. Consider the following example:

(16)   Sarah wants to rent this big red house,
       but Janice wants to rent that other one.

The word "one" is another proform. What category does it substitute for? In the sentence above it can substitute for the phrase "big red house," which contains several adjectives as well as a head noun. What category is this phrase? It's not a full NP, because the word "this" precedes the phrase in the first half of the sentence, and the words "that other" precede the word "one" in the second half. The word "this" is a determiner, a part of the NP that seems to have been left behind in the example. On the other hand, the phrase being replaced is not just a single noun. Apparently, what is needed is a category smaller than an NP, but larger than a noun. This is the intermediate category N'. The basic generalization to be reached is that the proform "one" substitutes for an N'.

To see how this generalization is reached, let us consider the NP, "this big red house." This NP has the following structure:

(17)

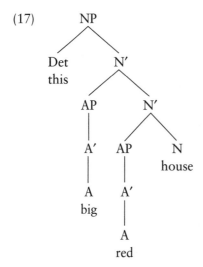

Notice that there are two possible N's for the word "one" to substitute for: the N' dominating "big red house," and the N' dominating only "red house." This prompts us to make the following prediction. In the example under consideration, "that other one" should be open to two interpretations: (i) that other big red house, and (ii) that other red house. What do you think?[1]

There is confirming evidence that the proform "one" may substitute for any occurrence of N'. Compare what "one" refers to in the following example:

(18)   Sarah wants to rent this big red house,
       but Janice wants to rent that small one.

In this example, "one" doesn't refer to the highest N' "big red house," since it is a contradiction to say that Janice wants to rent a big small house. This shows that "one" is substituting for the lower N' in the structure, "red house."

Further evidence for the internal structure of NPs can be obtained by examining examples such as (19).

(19)   James fell in love with this woman in a red coat,
       but Earl fell in love with that one.

As before, "one" substitutes for a phrase larger than an N, but smaller than an NP; viz., "woman in a red coat." The structure of the NP "this woman in a red coat" is given in (20).[2]

(20)

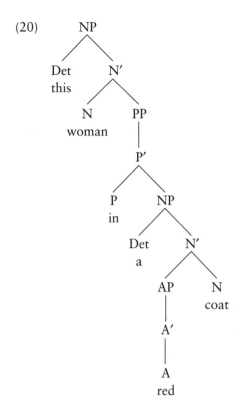

The phrase marker (20) could be expanded in several ways to produce new sentences. The N′ dominating "woman in a red coat" could be expanded with another, internal N′, which could introduce another PP or an AP. These possibilities are illustrated in (21):

(21)   a.   The woman in a red coat behind Barbara is extremely wealthy.
       b.   The rich woman in a red coat won the election.

As we expect, "one" can substitute for any of these N′s, as illustrated in (22):

(22)   a.   But the one behind Hillary is poor.
       b.   But the one in a mink paid for her campaign.

When we first introduced the notion of N′, you might have been dubious about its necessity. After all, the flat structure we rejected is certainly more simple than one with an N′. However, following this discussion of "one"-substitution, we expect that you are more convinced that the more complex hierarchical structure is necessary. Without N′, it would be very difficult indeed to account for the distribution of the proform "one."

In this chapter, we have seen that tests of constituency are useful in two ways. First, they can provide syntactic confirmation for some of the phrasal categories which we originally established just on the basis of our intuitions about sentences. Second, they even offer evidence for the existence of new syntactic categories, which we might not have thought of otherwise. In the next chapter, we turn to some additional facts which Phrase Structure helps to explain, regarding ambiguity and productivity. We mentioned these facts in the introductory part, when we brought them up as pieces of evidence which our theory of language would need to account for in order to be adequate. Now we will see how the Phrase Structure theory is able to do so.

Conclusion

It would be simpler to describe sentences without so much hierarchical structure. Therefore, it is important to show that the structure is needed for an accurate account of language. Movement and substitution tests provide such evidence for the existence of phrasal categories and constituency. Even the intermediate level of structure N′ has been motivated by considering such tests. These tests are a crucial part of linguistic data.

Notes

1   In many cases, it seems that "one" can also substitute for just the head noun, here leading to the interpretation: that other house. In these cases, the structure would be as in (i).

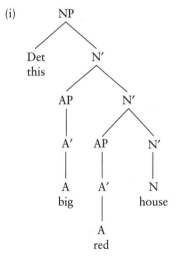

We will use the structure in (i) where needed to illustrate such interpretations, but otherwise will stick with the simpler structure in the text.

2 In this example, like the previous one, "one" can also substitute for "woman" or "coat," as illustrated in (i).

  (i) James fell in love with this woman in a red coat,
       but Earl fell in love with that one in a blue one.

Bibliographical Comments

The use of substitution tests for determining phrasal categories dates back to the work of classical grammarians in the American structuralist tradition. For example, Bloomfield (1933), Harris (1951), Hockett (1958), and Gleason (1961) all make use of tests such as pronominalization, distribution, and ellipsis, as well as other syntactic, morphological, and phonological criteria, to establish various categories of constituency. Many of these tests were adopted, with further modifications, in later work in transformational-generative grammar. Explicit use is made of the distribution of adverbs and the possibility of co-ordinate structures in Chomsky (1975). An introduction showing how a wide range of syntactic and non-syntactic evidence can be used to determine phrasal categories is given in Radford (1981). One-substitution is paid particular attention to in Baker (1978) and Hornstein and Lightfoot (1981b).

12 Ambiguity and Productivity

Introduction

The phrase markers (tree diagrams) we have presented show the hierarchical structure of sentences, and name each of the phrases and categories which are part of the structure. Although the specific examples we used are from English, these categories and phrases and the hierarchical structures that result from putting them together are part of Universal Grammar – all sentences in all languages are formed into these abstract units of structure. The order of the units can vary from one language to another, but all languages have these categories, and all languages group the categories hierarchically.

Every well-formed sentence has a phrase marker. Moreover, phrase markers reveal certain patterns of language. They show how languages mix and match words into sentences, in accordance with structural principles. These principles follow from certain rules of language that identify the building blocks of phrase markers, and spell out which ones occur together. By describing the language in terms of rules, the grammar of the language defines the well-formed phrase markers and distinguishes them from ill-formed ones, namely, the ones that the rules do not generate.

The rules of Phrase Structure put us in a position to explain several of the puzzles we noted earlier in this book. For instance, we will see in the present chapter how Phrase Structure (PS) rules account for two facts. First, the PS rules we introduced in chapter 9 can be invoked to explain, at least in part, why some sentences are ambiguous. Recall that sometimes the same sequence of words can be interpreted in more than one way; that is, these phrases are ambiguous. Some such cases of **ambiguity** can be explained by PS rules. These cases of ambiguity are explained in the sense that the PS rules are seen to provide different phrase markers for each of the meanings of these sentences. The different phrase markers correspond systematically to the different interpretations of the sentences. Of course, the PS rules don't themselves assign meanings to sentences. However, we will see later that in many cases (all the cases we consider here) syntactic ambiguity and semantic ambiguity go hand in hand. Therefore, the discovery that certain ambiguous sentences are associated with more than a single phrase marker is an important step towards understanding semantic ambiguity. All that remains is to show how the rules of the semantic component of the grammar assign different interpretations to the different phrase markers. We must postpone that step until Part V.

The second phenomenon that PS rules help to explain is the fact that we can produce and understand novel sentences and meanings. The grammar of any natural language must be finite, since it is part of the finite minds of human beings. However, it must be capable of generating an unlimited number of sentences. Any set of grammatical rules which is capable of producing an unlimited number of sentences is called a productive system of rules. The PS rules we have advanced allow for this kind of **productivity**, as we will also see in this chapter.

1 Ambiguity

As a preface to the discussion of PS rules and ambiguity, we wish to note again that the detection of ambiguity is part of the linguistic competence of all native speakers. Also, it seems unreasonable to suppose that this capacity is learned from one's experience. It is important to appreciate, therefore, that this knowledge falls out naturally from simply knowing the PS rules of a language. Of course, most ambiguities go unnoticed, except when they are pointed out to us. For instance, the following sentence is ambiguous, but is most likely new to many readers:

(1)   Bill read the letter to Bob.

It is difficult to believe that everyone (who notices an ambiguity) realizes that this sentence has two meanings on the basis of previous experience, or by analogy with other sentences. However, we will demonstrate that the ambiguity in sentences like this is an automatic consequence of the PS system that characterizes English. Even if a person had never encountered a single ambiguity before, he or she would be able to recognize that such sentences are ambiguous. This underscores the point that ambiguity is due to a kind of linguistic knowledge that can be gained without recourse to experience.

To begin, suppose that some person's linguistic experience consists of just the following UNambiguous sentence:

(2)   The letter to Bob put Bill in a bad mood.

The phrase marker for this sentence appears in (5). Focusing first on the subject NP, "the letter to Bob," this constituent requires the collection of PS rules given in (3). It is important to note that this is the only way to structure this phrase. In other words, the sequence of words "the-letter-to-Bob" is not ambiguous in the example we are discussing. We will also need the PS rules in (4) to assign structure to the VP, "put Bill in a bad mood."

(3) NP → (Det) N'   (4) VP → V'
     N' → N (PP)   V' → V' PP
     PP → P'   V' → V NP
     P' → P NP   N' → AP N
                           AP → (Deg) A'
                           A' → A

(5)

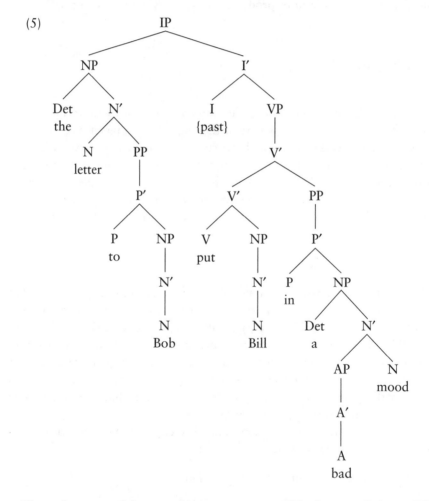

That takes care of the unambiguous sentence, "The letter to Bob put Bill in a bad mood." Now let us assign a phrase marker to the ambiguous sentence: "Bill read the letter to Bob." An ambiguity crops up in interpreting the sequence of words "the letter to Bob." One reading of these words is given by using the PS rules in (3), which were essential for generating the subject NP of the unambiguous sentence, "The letter to Bob put Bill in a bad mood." As in the unambiguous sentence, the meaning of the phrase "the letter to Bob" is a letter addressed to Bob, which Bill read (possibly to Hillary). In this case, the structure of the object "the letter to Bob" is the same as the structure used in the unambiguous sentence, as shown in (6).

(6)

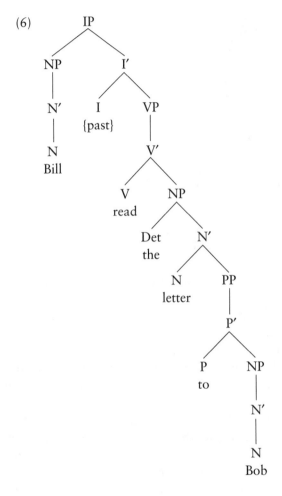

But there is another reading for the string of words at the bottom of the phrase marker in (6). It so happens that the PS rules in (4), needed for the phrase "put Bill in a bad mood," can be used to supply a different phrase marker for the words "read the letter to Bob," as (7) below illustrates. The meaning here is that Bill read to Bob some letter which may have been addressed to Al, or Bill, or somebody else. The important part is that Bob listened to Bill reading the letter (possibly addressed to Hillary).

(7)

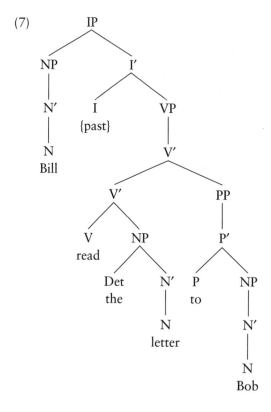

The basic ingredient for creating the ambiguity stems from the fact that the original unambiguous sentence (2) requires two ways of introducing a PP into a phrase marker, under an NP, and under a VP. These alternatives for inserting a PP give rise to ambiguity in some sentences. When the PP is introduced under the NP, then it tells more about that NP. Hence, "to Bob" modifies "the letter," when the PP is under the NP. When the PP is introduced under the VP, then it tells more about that VP. In this case, "to Bob" describes the reading event – not the letter.

This type of ambiguity is one which appears in numerous examples. It is important to keep in mind that the point at which each constituent attaches in the tree affects its interpretation. When a PP attaches to an NP, it modifies the noun – it tells more about the person or thing. When a PP attaches to a VP, it modifies the verb – it tells where or how the action took place. As practice, think of the two meanings for the sentence, "We discussed the man on TV," and try to draw the phrase marker that goes with each meaning. Then, look at figure 12.1.

Most ambiguities in language go unnoticed. This is because there is generally a favored reading that people consistently assign to ambiguities. This favored reading may come from processing strategies which people use as they comprehend utterances. Here we are simply accounting for the existence of more than

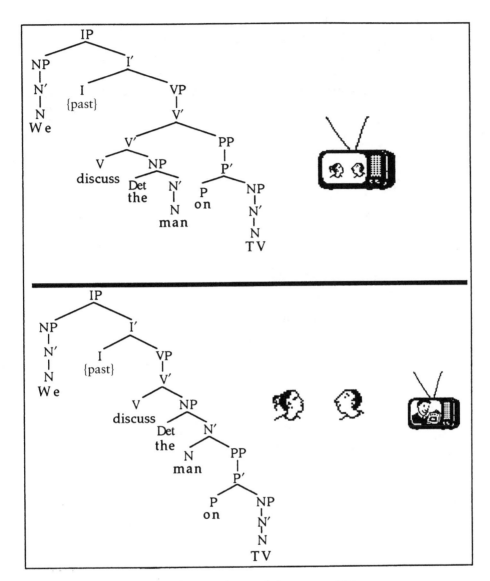

Figure 12.1 Phrase markers for "We discussed the man on TV"

a single interpretation for certain phrases and sentences. Consider the next example of an ambiguous sentence, in (8).

(8) The clown watched the dog jump through a hoop.

Under the most obvious interpretation, the dog's jumping is done through a hoop. The tree diagram for that interpretation is given in (9). In this interpretation, the clown watched something happen, namely the dog jumping through a hoop. This event is signified by the IP which is the complement of the verb. The event the clown watched was the dog jumping through a hoop. The prepositional phrase, "through a hoop," tells us how the dog jumped. Since this PP modifies the verb "jump," it is attached alongside the verb, beneath the VP which dominates it. That is, "jump through a hoop" forms a constituent on this analysis.

(9)

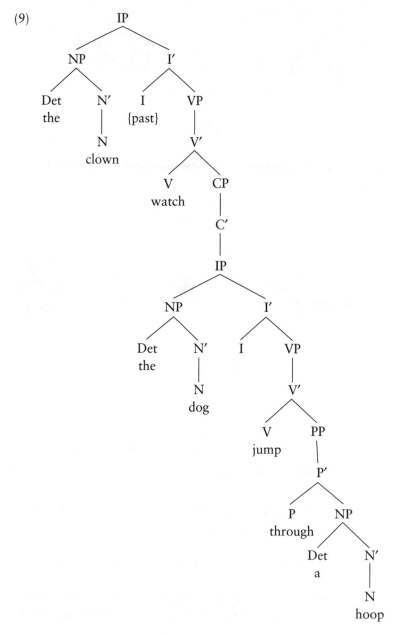

The other interpretation of this sentence is that the clown was looking through a hoop at a dog jumping (up and down, perhaps). The tree diagram corresponding to this interpretation is given in (10).

(10)

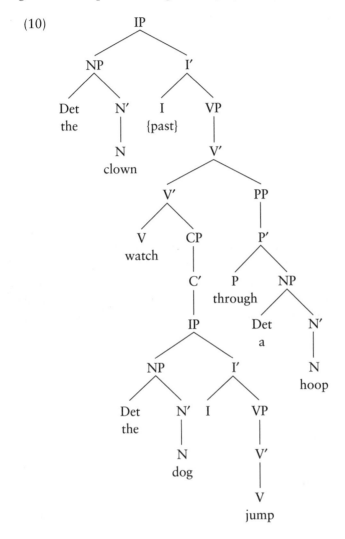

In this interpretation, "through a hoop" explains how the clown was watching. Therefore, it modifies the verb "watch," rather than the lower verb "jump"; so, the PP is attached under the matrix VP. Therefore, "jump through the hoop" does not form a constituent on this analysis.

Let us take another example of a case where the phrase markers show us the difference between two interpretations of a string of words. The phrase in question is: "fat cats and dogs." This phrase has two interpretations. In one, "fat" modifies just cats. This meaning is illustrated in (11):

(11)

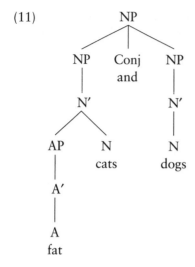

Notice how the constituent structure "mirrors" the meaning of this phrase. In both the semantic interpretation and in the phrase marker, the word "fat" modifies only "cats," being attached to the N' above the N dominating "cats."

You probably noticed already that there is also another interpretation of the phrase, according to which the adjective "fat" modifies both NPs, so both cats and dogs are fat. We represent this interpretation using the following diagram:

(12)

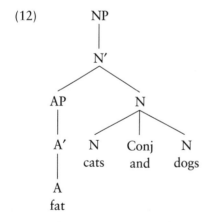

In this diagram, "fat" doesn't just modify "cats," but the entire phrase "cats and dogs." Consequently, this phrase marker is interpreted as picking out cats and dogs, all of which are fat. This is a further example, then, of how PS rules can account, in part, for different meanings of certain linguistic expressions.

So far in this chapter we have seen that PS rules not only provide the structure for unambiguous sentences, but can also be used to provide different structures for certain sentences. Moreover, we gave examples where these different structures resulted in different interpretations for the same sequence of words. That is, the Phrase Structure system explains why certain ambiguities arise. By now, it should be clear that PS rules are quite powerful. They enable us to generate phrase markers for a large number of English sentences. We now show that the PS rules which we have written allow us to generate an infinite number of English sentences.

2 Productivity

Recall that the (finite) set of PS rules must be able to generate an infinite number of sentences, since the number of sentences in English is infinite. We have already pointed out one reason to think that the grammar of English is productive: the fact that we can understand novel sentences. The productivity of language means that we can understand sentences we have never encountered before. It also means that we can understand an unlimited number of such sentences. There is an interesting proof that the grammar of natural language is infinite. What the proof shows is that there is no longest sentence. The proof amounts to the demonstration that for any given sentence, a longer one can be created. To take a simple example, consider the following sentence of English:

(13)   Your mother wears army boots.

This sentence can be made longer in the following way:

(14)   Your mother's uncle wears army boots.

Similarly:

(15)   Your mother's uncle's wife wears army boots.

And so on. As these examples illustrate, there is no limit to the number of insults that can be handed out by any speaker of English. After a while, sentences which go on like this would be very hard to understand, and very boring; we would run out of breath, or out of memory, or out of patience before they got too long. BUT – if you or some other speaker of English wanted to say such long sentences, the grammar would allow it.[1]

There are other ways that sentences can be extended. A slightly more complex case involves words such as "believe," "know," and "think," among others.

Note that the linguistic material that can follow one of these verbs is a sentence (a CP). So we can precede any sentence with "Someone thinks/knows/believes that . . .". Similarly, we can precede the sentence that results by the same thing, namely, "Someone thinks/knows/believes that . . ." This yields: "Someone thinks/ knows/believes that someone thinks/knows/believes that . . ." And so on. Here is a concrete example. To begin, let the sentence be "The mouse roared."

(16)   The mouse roared. → Terry thinks that the mouse roared.

Note, though, that the result of adding "Terry thinks . . ." to the sentence we began with is itself a sentence. This means that we can add "Everyone believes . . ." to THAT sentence:

(17)   Everyone believes that Terry thinks that the mouse roared.

And so it goes on, indefinitely:

(18)   Thomas knows that everyone believes that Terry thinks that the mouse roared.

It is important to bear in mind that we can't really go on indefinitely. No one can actually say all of the things that their grammar would permit, because of our limitations on memory, and so on. This is one place where we must again distinguish between our linguistic **performance** and our linguistic **competence**. Our linguistic performance will often be constrained and even marred by our limited capacities of memory and attention. Recall that it is not performance, but our linguistic competence, that we are attempting to explain by a theory of grammar. According to our linguistic competence, there can be no longest sentence, although because of our linguistic performance, we can only produce sentences of finite length.

Productivity and PS Rules

We will now show how Phrase Structure (PS) rules create an infinite number of English sentences from a finite set of rules. For now, it will suffice to note that the number of sentences that the grammar can generate is potentially infinite. But, since the grammar must be represented in a finite form, it cannot simply consist of a list of the possible sentences. Such a list might be a simple way of achieving the goal of generating all and only the sentences of the language – by listing all and only the sentences of the language – but we have just proven that this is impossible.

By definition, a set of PS rules is productive only if it is capable of generating an infinite number of sentences. To generate an infinite number of sentences, the set of rules must have the property of being **recursive**. Roughly, the idea is that a set of PS rules is recursive if it can apply to its own output, so that the rules can keep applying over and over. Not every imaginable set of PS rules is recursive. Notice that the following set of rules is not recursive: they can generate only a finite number of sentences of English.

(19)   IP → NP I′
        I′ → I VP
      NP → N′
       N′ → N
      VP → V′
       V′ → V

Since there are only a finite number of words, adding words will increase the number of sentences generated by these rules, but eventually we would reach the last of the sentences that can be produced by this PS grammar.[2] To make this set generate an infinite number of sentences, we have to add a particular type of rule: one that is recursive.

We already informally presented one example of a construction of English that requires the system of rules to be recursive. In arguing that there is no longest sentence of English, we noted that verbs such as "think," "believe," and "know," can be used to extend any sentence. That is, these verbs take sentences as their complements. What this means is that these verbs may be followed by a CP. An example is given in (20). This sentence illustrates again a PS rule which introduces embedded sentences: V′ → V CP. Notice what this rule says – that in the course of deriving a sentence, we can introduce another sentence as a constituent. But this means that in the course of forming the lower sentence, we are also free to create another sentence, or another embedded clause. The example in (21) illustrates how another level of structure can be created in just this way.

(20)

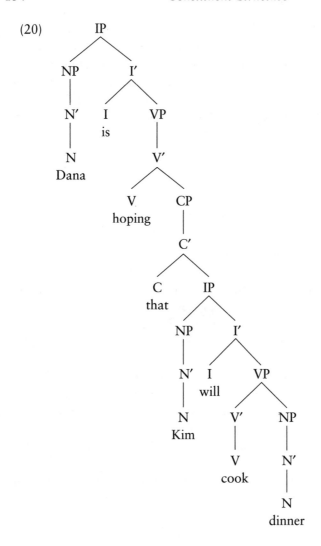

(21)

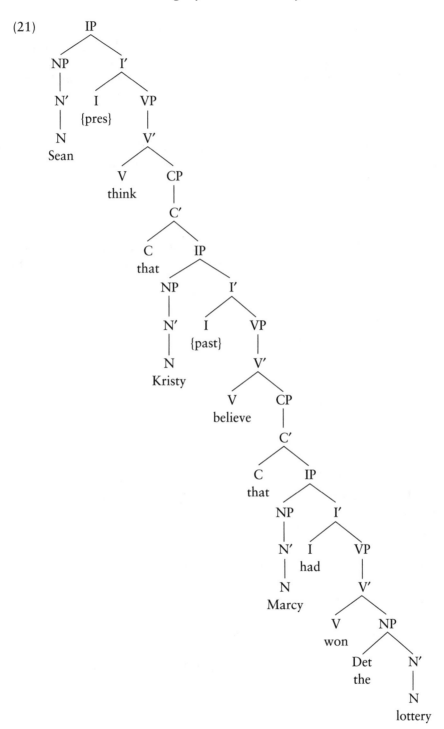

Whenever a set of rules creates the necessary conditions for its own reapplication, the system of rules is **recursive**. In some cases, a single rule creates a recursive loop. This property is graphically depicted by the following schematic form (where the (. . .) can be any category introduced by a PS rule, or it can be empty):

(22)   X → . . . X . . .

We need a rule like this to produce NPs with multiple modifying adjectives. For example, to show the structure of the phrase "big red house" (in chapter 11), we used a rule of the following form:

(23)   N′ → AP N′

This rule, together with the rule for introducing N′ into NPs (NP → Det N′), and the rule for cashing out N's (N′ → N), will produce the following structure:

(24)

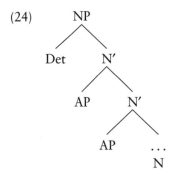

The ellipsis in (24) shows that any number of APs can be inserted in this structure. By applying this recursive rule, we can generate an infinite number of sentences of English. One example would be: "The large ugly dumb striped tiger."

Notice that the property of recursion is that each application of the rule produces an environment which allows another application of the rule to take place. That is what is special about a recursive rule; since it contains the same symbol on both sides of the arrow, it creates the context for its own reapplication. That is how recursive rules create an infinite number of sentences. If the grammar contains even just one recursive rule, it can be very simple, but it will define an infinite language. With this type of rule, we don't need more and more rules to get longer and longer sentences.

There is another way to achieve recursion. For example, consider the following rules:

(25)   NP → PossP N′
       PossP → NP Poss

No one rule in this pair is recursive in itself, but together they can form a recursive loop. Schematically, this can be represented in the following way:

(26) X → ... Y ...
      Y → ... X ...

This pair is recursive because when the first rule applies, it produces the situation for the second rule to apply, and applying the second rule creates the context for applying the first rule again. And this can go on forever. (See (13)–(15).) This recursive pair of rules produce phrase markers like the following:

(27)

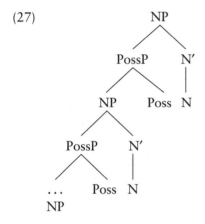

Notice that there is no limit to the number of possessive modifiers (e.g., "friend's") we can insert before a noun, as indicated again by the ellipsis. Recursion makes it possible to generate an infinite number of sentences using a finite number of rules.

This explains one aspect of what we called the productivity of language – its infinite character. Using grammatical constructions which allow recursion, we can generate an unbounded set of new sentences. Although many of these new sentences are not very useful (how often do we want to say, "Your mother's sister's neighbor's aunt wears combat boots"?), the productivity of language is quite remarkable, when we consider, for instance, other communication systems. We have seen that PS rules explain the systematic way in which words can be used over and over again to make up longer expressions of the same type – by recursion.

Conclusion

In conclusion, it should be noted that PS rules explain two aspects of human linguistic knowledge that are mastered in the absence of experience. First, PS rules explain how we can know that some sentences are ambiguous even if we have never encountered them, or ones like them, before. Recursion takes the language user beyond the data in a second way. Because of recursive PS rules, experience with a limited set of data allows the learner to generalize to a wider range of cases that had not been considered before, as the example in (28) illustrates.

(28)　Experience: John's sister

　　　Knowledge: John's sister; John's sister's friend; John's sister's friend's mother . . .

Notes

1　Another simple proof is the following. Here is a sentence of English: I have one brother. Another sentence of English is: I have two brothers. Another is: I have three brothers. And so on. Since the natural numbers are infinite, and we can substitute any natural number before the word "brothers" in this sentence, the number of possible sentences in English is infinite. Although this is a proof of the infinity of the number of sentences, it is a trivial sort of infinity, because the different sentences do not have different structures. The examples discussed in the text are more crucial for an explanation of the generative power of English.

2　As mentioned in the preceding note, the natural numbers are infinite, so one might suppose that our goal of an infinite number of sentences can be met without incorporating any recursive rule(s). We could simply utter sentences such as: "I have one brother," "I have two brothers," "I have three brothers," and so on indefinitely. There are two points to note in response to this argument. First, as we mentioned earlier, several constructions in natural language show that the number of possible sentences is infinite, and any adequate grammar must be able to account for these types of constructions. Second, returning to the example sentences, it should be noted that the infinite number of phrases representing the natural numbers arises by combining a finite number of words – and this is only possible by recursion.

Bibliographical Comments

The idea that the ambiguity of sentences can be explained by the Phrase Structure rules of a grammar is suggested in Chomsky (1957), Chomsky (1975), and Chomsky (1965). Akmajian and Heny (1975), Lasnik (1990), and Radford (1981) are among the textbooks which discuss structural ambiguity and recursion.

13 Children's Knowledge of Phrase Structure

Introduction

We have proposed that children acquire their native language using the principles and constraints of Universal Grammar. Fundamental to the organization of sentences is phrasal structure, and we showed some aspects of Phrase Structure which come from UG, such as X'-theory. Now that we have seen additional evidence for phrasal structure, it is time to consider the evidence regarding children's knowledge of categories and hierarchies. Do very young children have tacit knowledge of trees like the ones we have argued for? In this chapter, we will first discuss two different views on the principles underlying young children's early utterances. We will then see evidence that children do indeed have the kind of phrasal categories we have presented for the adult grammar. This is the conclusion which is expected under the Universal Grammar theory we have espoused.

1 Are Children's Early Grammars Semantically Based or Syntactically Based?

In chapter 10 we saw some examples of children's early two-word utterances. These simple utterances convey a large variety of semantic (meaning) relationships. Some of the most common relationships include: agent–action–patient; modifier–head; object–location; possessor–possessed. Some examples of children's early utterances with such semantic descriptions are given in (1).

(1) Doggie bite   agent–action
    push car   action–object
    Adam ball   agent–object
    more juice   modifier–head

cup table   object–location
Daddy pipe   possessor–possessed

In the 1960s and 1970s, researchers debated whether these simple sentences were best described in terms of semantic relations, as in (1), or in syntactic terms, as in the type of description we gave in chapter 10. On the syntactic analysis, children make use of tree structures to express meanings such as those in (1). On the semantic analysis, children simply use rules of semantic relations to structure their utterances, with no syntactic knowledge assumed. Many researchers thought that children should not be "credited" with knowledge of syntactic rules when their early utterances could be simply described using a relatively short list of semantic relations. How do we know whether children have such categories as "subject" or even "noun" if they do not utter complex enough sentences to prove it?

As an alternative to the syntactic analysis, many researchers thought that children deduced ordering rules such as "agent–action" or "action–object." However, the number and type of semantic organizing principles proposed was not well defined. What one researcher called "X + Locative," another called "Action + Locative," another called "Locative action," and another called "Place." The semantic relations are not any clearer *a priori* than the syntactic notions they are being used to replace. The semantically based hypothesis rests on the assumption that notions like "agent" are in some way simpler than notions like "subject," but there is no evidence for this assumption.

Furthermore, the arguments we presented in the previous chapters (and many to come) show that it is necessary to describe adult linguistic knowledge using syntactic concepts such as "subject" and "noun," as well as Phrase Structure and X′-theory. Thus, even if we supposed that such concepts were beyond the ken of young children, we would still have to identify some point in development at which they were acquired. But what would be the evidence for these concepts? If semantic relations are sufficient to describe and generate the first word combinations that children produce, what would compel them to abandon this kind of grammar for a syntactically based grammar? How (and when) would such a radical change take place? This question has been greatly debated in the literature on children's early grammars. One researcher, Lila Gleitman of the University of Pennsylvania, suggested that children at this time period would have to go through a maturationally induced "tadpole to frog" conversion, so radical is the change that such a view necessitates. Other than a biological change (like the biologically timed changes that bring on puberty), we find no convincing explanation for the semantic-to-syntactic transition that this hypothesis requires.

Our alternative hypothesis emerges from the model of Universal Grammar we motivated at the beginning of this book. According to this model, certain concepts of grammar are innately given. If the notions "subject" and "noun" are part of UG, then there is no reason to suppose that children's early grammars are semantically based instead of syntactically based. We can assume that children go into the language acquisition task prepared to find "nouns" and "subjects" in their input. They must learn which words (patterns of sounds) are nouns in the language they are acquiring, and they must learn how that language orders subjects *vis-à-vis* other constituents (i.e., they must determine the settings which their language uses on the head/complement parameter). They can determine these things based on the positive evidence in their input, and thus even their earliest grammars can make use of them.

2   Children's Command of PS Rules and Categories

In addition to the theoretical debate, we can bring some empirical evidence to bear on the question of children's early grammars. We used distributional evidence to argue for the existence of phrasal categories in the adult grammar. Is the same type of evidence available from child language?

Virginia Valian, now at the CUNY Graduate Center, is one of many researchers who have studied young children's knowledge of phrasal categories and Phrase Structure rules. She cites numerous examples that show English-speaking children have a good command of Phrase Structure, based on regularities in children's speech which mirror those of the adult language. Her own study focused on the categories determiner, adjective, noun, noun phrase, preposition, and prepositional phrase. She wanted to see whether there were regularities in children's language which also hold of the adult grammar. She reasoned that if the distribution of children's productions overlapped with those of adults, then it would be correct to infer that the same syntactic representations attributed to adults were responsible for children's utterances as well.

Valian studied six children between the ages of 2 and $2\frac{1}{2}$ (MLU 2.93–4.14). She used information from substitution tests (such as the pronoun substitution tests described in chapter 11), subcategory information, and the ways and orders in which elements can combine to determine category membership.

Valian found that all the children she studied showed knowledge of the rules governing use and placement of determiners. The determiners which they used most often included "the," "a/an," "my," and "this/that." When they appeared, they were always in the right place. No child placed determiners after an adjective or a noun, and no child used a determiner alone. With some apparent counterexamples to be discussed immediately, children also did not use two determiners in sequence. The apparent counterexamples consisted of utterances like the following:

(2) This the boy   [Child A; age 2;0]
      This one a baby   [Child A; age 2;0]
      This two   [Child A; age 2;0]

These examples seem to be violations of the PS rules which allow only one determiner per NP. However, in these examples "this" and "that" seem to be functioning as NPs and not as determiners. Valian raised the possibility that children were simply omitting the verb "is" in utterances with the intended meaning, "This is the boy," etc. To corroborate this, she points to evidence like the following self-correction by another child:

(3) This a elepha– this is a elephant   [Child E; age 2;5]

With this explanation for the apparent counterexamples, Valian concludes that all of the children she studied passed her criteria for showing knowledge of the category determiner.

Valian also gives data on children's use of adjectives. Det–Adj–N sequences were fairly common in the children she studied. When both determiners and adjectives were present, children correctly put the adjectives after the determiners. This reveals that they distinguished between adjectives and determiners, and that they knew they must be placed in order. No child ever placed an adjective after a noun or before a determiner.

Four of the six children produced two or more adjectives in a row. Examples of adjective combinations which the children produced are given in (4):

(4) big long tall   [Child D; age 2;3]
      big big   [Child D; age 2;3]
      little tiny   [Child E; age 2;5]

Children also showed command of other PS rules involving NPs. All six children knew that "a" went with singular nouns only. All children used nouns ending in "-s" and all had at least one singular and one plural form of the same noun. The children's awareness of the category noun seemed rich. Children used determiners with nouns, but never with a pronoun (e.g., "*the she"), despite the fact that the two are otherwise found in similar environments.

All children displayed further knowledge of NPs. For example, they used "it" to substitute for an NP that had been introduced earlier. All six children substituted "it" for an NP, as the following examples show.

(5)   I ride the bike. Ride, ride it.   [Child A; age 2;0]

    A wagon go boom. It zoom, zoom, zoom.   [Child A; age 2;0]

    See there's a brown car.
        That's the tires and wheels are on it.   [Child N; age 2;0]

    I'm gonna get the birthday cake.
        Gonna sit down and eat it.   [Child D; age 2;3]

    I have got my telephone.
        Look at it hang there.   [Child I; age 2;5]

    That's a sweater. I need that sweater.
        I needa put it on (me).   [Child S; age 2;5]

    Open it. Open your hand. Open it up.   [Child E; age 2;5]

We saw earlier that substitution tests are good evidence of constituent structure. Children were found never to substitute "it" for plural NPs. Two of the children substituted a form of "they" for plural NPs.

NPs appeared in all the major places where they are syntactically licensed to appear. These positions, and the children's productions of NPs in those positions, are summarized in (6).

(6)   Pre-verbal NPs   43% total
     Post-verbal NPs   43.6% total
     Post-prepositional NPs   13.4% total

Finally, the children also showed command of the rules governing the use of prepositions and PPs. Valian states that the children overall produced 58 examples of V–N–PP or V–Adj–PP, and no examples of V–PP–NP – evidence that children always correctly ordered a PP relative to an NP or an Adj. She also cites that children never inflected prepositions for tense, and verbal complements never appeared after a P. Children did use the correct sequences for prepositions and determiners in constructions such as "in the room," whereas they never put together determiners in a sequence such as "the that room." This is evidence for a distinction between prepositions and determiners. Also, children infrequently failed to use a preposition when needed, whereas they frequently failed to use a determiner, more evidence for the distinction between them.

In sum, the evidence presented by Valian indicates that children do have and make use of knowledge of syntactic categories and Phrase Structure rules including Det, Adj, N, NP, P, and PP. This supports our argument that even children's earliest grammars are syntactically based, not semantically based.

Conclusion

If a child uses an element or structure in an adult-like way, is it safe to assume that the child does so for the same reason as the adult – that is, that the child has the adult grammar in the relevant respects? To some researchers, simply observing that children behave like adults is not enough to prove that they have the same grammar. However, we take a different view. Since we know that the child must eventually attain an adult grammar, and we are convinced that Universal Grammar is necessary for this accomplishment, there is no reason to think that children's behavior has a different source from that of adults even when they pattern the same. In fact, we take it to be the default assumption that children's grammars are like adults' – and we require some clear proof to make the opposite conclusion. When children are different from adults, some reasonable explanation for the difference is necessary, and this is just as important in building a theory as accounting for the child's behavior on its own. Throughout the text, we will see more cases in which the child's behavior is similar to adults', and in such cases we will attribute adult-like knowledge to them. When the child's behavior is non-adult, we will offer suggestions as to how the child eventually comes to have an adult grammar.

Bibliographical Comments

Some of the debate between proponents of semantically based and syntactically based children's grammars is summarized in deVilliers and deVilliers (1985). Brown (1973) and Bloom (1970) are among the early syntactically based writers, while Bowerman (1973) was one of the early adherents to the semantically based approach. Lila Gleitman's observation was made in Gleitman and Wanner (1982). The study described here by Valian was published in Valian (1986).

14 Constraints on Reference

Introduction

In Part I, we introduced the notion of linguistic **constraints**. The tools we have developed so far allow us to generate an unlimited number of sentences, and we will see in the next part ways to generate yet additional sentence types. However, not every string of words is a grammatical sentence, and we want our generative grammar to correctly rule out the ungrammatical strings. One type of sentence which we can already rule out would be sentences which do not follow the Phrase Structure rules for a particular language. For example, in English, we cannot generate sentences in which the specifier follows the head, because this does not follow the English version of the PS rules. However, other strings of words are not grammatical sentences even though they do adhere to the PS rules. Some of these examples must be ruled out as non-sentences by the use of constraints. Constraints tell us ways in which otherwise general rules cannot operate. For example, the constraint we will examine in this chapter puts a restriction on the interpretation of pronouns. Without a constraint, it would be very difficult to explain the range of possible referents which pronouns can take without allowing in the impossible interpretations. The constraint allows us to make a relatively simple generalization.

1 The Interpretation of Pronouns

Pronouns can be interpreted as picking out, or **referring** to, people (or animals, things, etc.) in a particular context. The referent of a pronoun is sometimes mentioned in a sentence before the one in which the pronoun occurs, sometimes in the same sentence. These possibilities are illustrated in (1).

(1) a. *She* did it! (pointing to a female in the situation)
    b. I saw *Mike* yesterday. *He* failed the exam.
    c. *Bill* thought *he* wouldn't get caught.

In (1a), the pronoun "she" refers to the woman in the situation, but there is no NP in the discourse to identify her. In (1b), the pronoun "he" can refer to the NP "Mike" in the previous sentence – this is probably the preferred interpretation. There could be some context, however, in which "he" might refer to someone other than Mike (for example, suppose Mike told you the results of the exam – then "he" might refer to someone in the context whose fate was under discussion). In (1c), the pronoun "he" can refer to the NP "Bill" earlier in the same sentence, or again it might refer to someone not mentioned in the sentence (such as Bill's friend Vernon). The NP to which a pronoun refers is called its **antecedent**.

From the examples in (1) only, we might think that pronouns can freely pick out an antecedent from outside the sentence, from another sentence, or from the same sentence. For the most part, we will not be interested in the interpretations in which a pronoun refers to someone not mentioned in the discourse, although this is usually a potential interpretation. When a pronoun refers to an unmentioned antecedent, we say that it receives a "deictic" interpretation or, equivalently, that it is "free." For the present discussion, we are mainly interested in the cases in which a pronoun refers to an antecedent in the same sentence. However, there are constraints dictating that a pronoun cannot refer to an NP in the same sentence in certain instances. In these cases, the pronoun is free; that is, it has a deictic interpretation.

We now show how to distinguish, by means of a constraint, between the NPs which can and cannot be the antecedents of a pronoun in the same sentence. Consider the examples in (2).

(2) a. *Sajak* thinks *he* should get a free spin of the wheel.
     b. **He* thinks *Sajak* should get a free spin of the wheel.

The first example (2a) could mean that Sajak thinks that he, himself, should get a free spin. In this case, we say that "Sajak" and "he" are **coreferential** – they pick out the same person. This is another way of saying that "Sajak" is the antecedent of the pronoun "he." This may not be the preferred interpretation in this situation, but it is clearly permissible. In the second example, however, this interpretation is impossible. Example (2b) simply can NOT be interpreted with the name "Sajak" and the pronoun "he" referring to one and the same person, Pat Sajak. In this case, "Sajak" and "he" must be **non-coreferential**. In (2b), then, the pronoun must be given a deictic interpretation.

One possible explanation for the difference in interpretive possibilities between (2a) and (2b) concerns the order of the NP and the pronoun. Note that in all the cases discussed so far, the NP precedes the pronoun in the permissible cases of coreference, and the pronoun is first when coreference is not allowed. However, we can easily see that this explanation will not work by considering examples like (3):

(3)   When *he* is bored, *Sajak* likes to spin the wheel.

In (3), "he" may refer to "Sajak," even though the pronoun is first. The relationship between a pronoun and its antecedent is sometimes called **anaphora;** when the pronoun comes before the antecedent, as in (3), the relationship is called **backwards anaphora.**

The next examples are included to demonstrate that the constraint in question is not specific to names, but applies more generally between pronouns and other NPs.

(4)   a.   *The girl* forgot that *she* was poor.
      b.   **She* forgot that *the girl* was poor.
      c.   As *she* worked, *the girl* hummed.

As the examples indicate, the restriction on coreference also holds between the **definite description** "the girl" and the pronoun "she." In (4a) and (4c), but not in (4b), the definite description can be interpreted as coreferential with the pronoun.

The constraint which prohibits the coreferential interpretation in (2b) and (4b) but not in (2a), (3), and (4a, c) must be structural. In order to understand how the constraint works, we need to examine the structures of these sentences, and we will need to introduce some technical machinery.

2   C-Command

First, let's concentrate on the examples in which the pronoun precedes the NP. The structure of examples like (2b) and (4b) should be familiar to you: they involve an embedded clause. A schematic representation of the structure of these examples is given in (5).

(5)

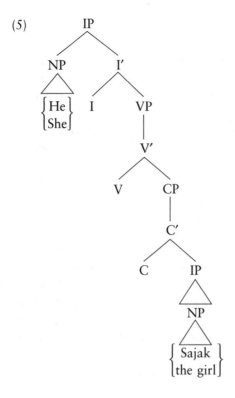

Notice that in these examples, the pronoun is much higher in the tree than the NP. This will play a role in the constraint to be developed.

Next, in (6) we present a schematic representation of the structure underlying examples like (3) and (4c). We have not previously demonstrated the structure of such examples, which involve a phrase (beginning with "when" or "as") called an "adjunct." This kind of modifying phrase attaches to the main clause, as shown in (6) where the modifying phrase is assumed to be a PP.

(6)

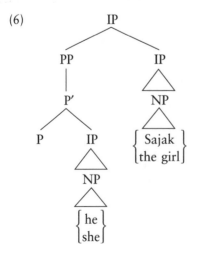

In these examples, the pronoun is not higher in the tree than the NP. It is this difference in height which is crucial for defining the constraint we need. By examining a number of examples with various structures, linguists have come to define more precisely the notion of height we have illustrated here.

The structural relation we need is called **c(onstituent)-command**. Although there is some controversy regarding some details, the following definition will do for our purposes.

(7) Constituent A c-commands another constituent B if the constituent immediately dominating A also dominates B.

To illustrate, consider the tree in (8).

(8)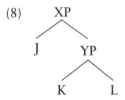

In (8), J (constituent A) c-commands K and L (constituents B). This is because the constituent immediately dominating J (XP) also dominates K and L. K c-commands L; but K does not c-command J, because the constituent immediately dominating K (YP) does not dominate J.

Now let's see how this definition works in our trees. Tree (5) is repeated here as (9), with identification of the relevant constituents for c-command.

(9)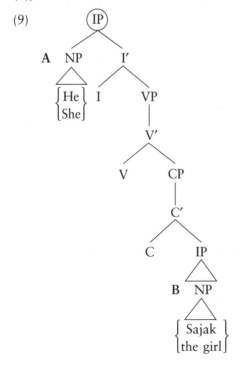

In tree (9), the pronouns are marked as "A" and the NPs as "B." The constituent immediately dominating A is the IP, which is circled. This constituent also dominates B. Thus, A c-commands B; the pronouns c-command the NPs.

Turn to tree (6), repeated here as (10) for consideration of the c-command relations.

(10)

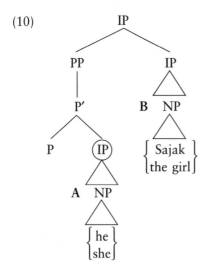

In tree (10), again the pronouns are marked as "A" and the NPs as "B." However, in this example the constituent which immediately dominates A (the circled IP) does NOT dominate B; the pronouns do *not* c-command the NPs.

C-command is a structural notion which helps to identify the relationships between elements in a tree. You can ask of any two constituents in a tree whether or not one c-commands the other. It is more complex than the structural relationship of domination, although it uses domination in its definition. It is also clearly more complex to speak of c-command than simply of linear order. We wouldn't want to use such a complex notion if we could explain all language facts without it. However, it is just the thing we need to account for the coreference constraint, to which we now turn.

3   Principle C

With the definition of c-command under our belts, we can state the principle which constrains coreference as in (11).

(11)   **Principle C (Coreference Constraint)**
       A pronoun cannot be coreferential with an NP which it c-commands.

To understand this definition, it may be helpful to think of c-command as a relationship between family members. Coreference is ruled out if the mother of a pronoun phrase has the NP as a descendant, possibly a daughter, but perhaps a granddaughter or great granddaughter, or even a more distant relative. In all of these cases, if the abstract structural relation of *c-command* holds between a pronoun and an NP, then they can NOT be coreferential.

It is important to keep the positives and negatives straight, but with some effort, this should be possible. The notion of *c-command* plays such a prominent role in the theory of Universal Grammar that it is worth the effort it takes to master it. Let us call the constraint on coreference Principle C. This term will serve both to remind you that "C"-*command* is involved, and that the constraint is used to rule out "C"oreference relations.[1]

As always, examples will help, so let us return to our examples. In (2b) and (4b), illustrated in (5) and (9), the pronoun "he" or "she" does c-command the NP "Sajak" or "the girl." Following the constraint in (11), the pronoun and the NP cannot be coreferential. On the other hand, in (3) and (4c), illustrated in (6) and (10), the pronoun does NOT c-command the NP. In this case, they CAN be coreferential.

Now let us consider one more pair of examples, to be sure that this complex machinery has been mastered. Look at the examples in (12).

(12)   a.   As *it* barked, *the dog* jumped through the hoop.
       b.   *It* feared that *the dog* was lost.

The structure of (12a) is similar to that in (6, 10). The pronoun "it" does not c-command the NP "the dog." Hence, they can be coreferential. The structure of (12b), however, is similar to that in (5, 9). In this case the pronoun does c-command the NP. Hence, they cannot be coreferential.

Conclusion

We can see that the coreference constraint stated in (11) accounts for the facts laid out at the beginning of this chapter. It also accounts for a range of similar facts with slightly different sentences involving pronouns and NPs in various structural relationships. Furthermore, we will see in chapter 25 that it applies in yet another kind of structure, this time concerning the interpretation of pronouns in WH-questions. Hence, this negative constraint is a prime candidate for a principle of UG. We expect constraints to be part of UG since they aren't learnable. As a UG constraint, we expect Principle C to display all of the hallmarks of innateness. We – correctly – expect it to be universal. We also expect it to appear early in the course of language acquisition. In the next chapter, we consider in detail the hallmark of early emergence, by looking at what we know about children's knowledge of Principle C.

Note

1   Actually, the constraint is called Principle C in Chomsky's theory because it is the third of the principles governing the coreference or "binding" relations among different kinds of NPs. The other two principles are called Principle A and Principle B.

Bibliographical Comments

Early proposals on the treatment of non-coreference facts include Lasnik (1976), Postal (1966), Reinhart (1976), and Wasow (1972). The three principles (A, B, and C) governing coreference among NPs were developed in Chomsky (1981), into what has come to be known as Binding Theory. The notion of c-command referred to in the text is that of Reinhart (1976). Introductory chapters on Binding Theory, including non-coreference facts, are found in Lasnik and Uriagereka (1988), and Riemsdijk and Williams (1986).

15 Children's Knowledge of Constraints: Backwards Anaphora

Introduction

This chapter will examine children's knowledge of the constraint that was introduced in the last chapter, Principle C. Based on the assumptions we have made about the course of language development, young children are expected to demonstrate adherence to Principle C as soon as they can be tested. To put this expectation to an empirical test, we cannot simply observe children's spontaneous productions. It might be several years before any given child is confronted with a situation that draws upon their knowledge of Principle C in a way that can be measured unequivocally. This is one factor that makes it difficult to assess children's knowledge. Furthermore, in order to demonstrate adherence to Principle C, it is necessary to show not only that children allow coreference where they should, but also that they do prohibit coreference when this is dictated by Principle C. Finally, we would like to demonstrate children's interpretation of pronouns in various structural positions. The only way to accomplish all of these goals is to devise experiments that assess children's tolerance and intolerance of several different types of sentence meanings. In this chapter we show how one experimental technique, known as the Truth-Value Judgment task, has been successful in illuminating children's grammatical knowledge of constraints on meaning – and for comparison, we will also mention some methodologies which have proven less successful. In short, this chapter will be instructive as to children's knowledge of Principle C, and it will describe the kinds of experiments that can and cannot assess children's linguistic competence.

1 Knowledge of Principle C: Previous Research

There is a large body of research on children's knowledge of coreference relations between pronouns and NPs. Since we concluded that knowledge of Principle C must be innate, we predicted that children will show adherence to it from an early age. However, the findings of the initial studies of children's knowledge of Principle C were somewhat disconcerting. Some researchers were led to conclude that, at least initially, children did not use Principle C in restricting their interpretation of pronouns. Instead, these researchers claimed that children use different mechanisms to interpret pronouns.

Let us consider the hypothesis that was made, and the reason for it, in more detail. We will see that there are some problems with the evidence used for drawing this conclusion. This is good, because there are also serious theoretical problems with the hypothesis. After we see why the first hypothesis was, after all, not supported, we will look at evidence in favor of the view that children do adhere to Principle C from early on.

The investigations which led to the first hypothesis were carried out by psycholinguists Lawrence Solan and Susan Tavakolian. The studies employed "act-out" tasks with 3- to 8-year-old children. In this task, children are presented with toy figures and other props placed in the experimental workspace in front of them. Then, the experimenter gives a sentence, and the child is invited to act out the meaning of the sentence using the toys. One pair of sentences from one of the studies is given in (1).

(1)   a.   For *him* to kiss the lion would make *the duck* happy.
      b.   That *he* kissed the lion made *the duck* happy.

Let's consider how these sentences measure up to Principle C. To remind you, the statement of Principle C given in chapter 14 is reproduced here in (2), and the definition of c-command is repeated in (3).

(2)   **Principle C (Coreference Constraint)**
      A pronoun cannot be coreferential with an NP which it c-commands.

(3)   Constituent A c-commands another constituent B if the constituent immediately dominating A also dominates B.

A schematic diagram of the structure of the sentences in (1) is given in (4).

(4)

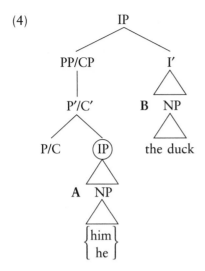

In both (1a) and (1b), the pronoun ("him" or "he") is dominated by the IP node which is circled. This IP is dominated by several other nodes (projections of the preposition "for" in (1a), and the complementizer "that" in (1b)) before the root of the sentence is reached. The NP "the duck" is clearly not dominated by the constituent immediately dominating the pronoun (i.e., the circled IP). So, since the pronoun does not c-command the NP, according to Principle C they can be coreferential. We hope this is consistent with your own intuitions – in the sentences in (1), the pronoun can refer to the duck.

However, as we know, the pronoun in (1) can also refer to some other character not mentioned in the sentence – for example, a pig (these are stories for children). And it turns out that this is the interpretation that the children in this study most frequently gave to these sentences. If the props in front of the children when this sentence was given included a lion, a duck, and a pig, the children used the pig to kiss the lion two-thirds of the time. Fourteen of the 24 subjects consistently acted out these sentences in this fashion.

This led the researchers to conclude that children ruled out the interpretation allowed by Principle C. Recall from chapter 14 that we originally entertained the possibility that a pronoun cannot take an NP as its antecedent when the pronoun precedes the NP. This hypothesis was raised in our consideration of how to prohibit coreference between the pronoun and the NP in sentences like (5) (= example (2b) in chapter 14).

(5)   *He* thinks *Sajak* should get a free spin of the wheel.

However, we quickly saw that this explanation did not work. We saw that co-reference is allowed in some cases in which the pronoun comes first, such as the example in (6) (= example (3) in chapter 14).

(6)   When *he* is bored, *Sajak* likes to spin the wheel.

The comparison of these sentence types led us, eventually, to Principle C.

On the basis of the experiment just described, previous researchers claimed that children entertain the hypothesis which we rejected – that a pronoun which precedes an NP cannot take that NP to be its antecedent. Clearly, this is a structure-independent hypothesis – it is based on the linear order of the words, not their structure. As Solan claimed, "children use direction rather than structural principles in restricting anaphora."

In fact, this hypothesis is more restrictive than Principle C, disallowing coreference in more situations than Principle C does. In this case, then, it might be possible for children to recover from this error, since there would be positive evidence in the form of sentences in which coreference is permitted. However, it would be necessary for children to determine exactly which situations allow coreference, and which do not – and this might be a daunting task for a 4-year-old. Furthermore, we expect that children know that language operates in a structure-dependent way. If children initially adopt a structure-dependent hypothesis regarding the interpretation of pronouns, this will considerably restrict the hypotheses they must entertain, helping to solve the logical problem of language acquisition. Thus, we should hesitate to adopt a theory which proposes an initial structure-independent hypothesis.

Even putting learnability aside for the moment, the conclusion that children employ a strictly linear prohibition on backwards anaphora is still unwarranted, for several reasons. First of all, one-third of the subjects' responses indicated acceptance of coreference between the pronoun and the NP in examples like (1). So the statement that children never allow backwards anaphora is too strong. But suppose every child had chosen an unnamed referent on every opportunity. Even still, this would not constitute proof that children ruled out coreference in this situation. At most, this would be evidence of a strong preference for interpreting the pronoun as referring to an entity outside the sentence over backwards anaphora.[1] What is really needed to test the prediction that children adhere to Principle C is an experiment which shows that, at least sometimes, they do allow coreference in backwards anaphora, AND that they reject it in the appropriate circumstances. We turn now to such an experiment.

2   When They Should, Children Accept Backwards Anaphora

The question of children's knowledge of the constraint on backwards anaphora was pursued in a new comprehension experiment conducted by Stephen Crain and

Cecile McKee. The experimental procedure used in this study is the **Truth-Value Judgment task**. As the name of the experimental technique suggests, this task requires subjects to judge the truth or falsity of a sentence, according to its fit to the context. In the Truth-Value Judgment task, there are two experimenters. One experimenter uses toys and props to act out a situation corresponding to one interpretation of the target sentence. A second experimenter manipulates a puppet, Kermit the Frog. Following each situation, Kermit the Frog says what he thought happened on that trial. If Kermit says the right thing, the child feeds Kermit one of his favored treats, like a cookie. But sometimes Kermit isn't paying close attention and says the wrong thing. When this happens the child asks Kermit to eat something "yukky," like a rag or a cockroach, or to do push-ups, to remind him to pay closer attention on the next trial.

These procedures make it fun for children to reward or punish Kermit. Without the rag ploy children are reluctant to say that Kermit has said anything wrong. Also, if the experimenter, rather than a puppet, produces the target sentences, children often assent to sentences that they judge to be false, because they are reluctant to correct an adult. However, with Kermit and the special treatment, children much more freely give their true reactions to the experimental sentences. To make it easier for children to give negative judgments, we make it clear to children that Kermit sometimes fails to pay attention to the events that unfold in the stories, and consequently makes assertions that are not accurate descriptions of these events. Using this method of assessment, the experimenter controls both the test sentences and the acted-out events. This allows unparalleled experimental control and at the same time reduces extraneous processing demands that are present in comprehension tasks in which children are required to act out the events themselves. This makes the Truth-Value Judgment task a better method for finding out which interpretations of sentences children accept and which ones they reject.

In the experiment, children encountered sentences like (7) in circumstances appropriate to both the extra-sentential (= deictic) and the backwards anaphoric interpretations of the pronoun.

(7) a. While *he* was dancing, *the Ninja Turtle* ate pizza.
     b. *He* was dancing while *the Ninja Turtle* ate pizza.

For ambiguous sentences such as (7a), the same sentence was presented on two separate occasions, in two contexts. In one context for (7a), the Ninja Turtle was dancing and eating pizza; in the other, someone else was dancing while the Ninja Turtle was eating pizza. Kermit uttered the same sentence following both situations. Thus, sentences like (7a) were used to test children's acceptance of backwards anaphora. To test children's knowledge of Principle C, sentences like (7b) were presented in situations corresponding to the meaning that is ruled out by Principle C. For example, (7b) would be uttered in a situation in which the Ninja Turtle was dancing and eating pizza, but some other character, such as Darth Vader, was not dancing.

The results of this study were that children correctly accepted the backwards anaphoric reading in sentences like (7a) about two-thirds of the time. They also correctly accepted the extra-sentential reading (given on different trials), only slightly more often. Only one of the 62 children interviewed in this way consistently rejected backwards anaphora when it was allowed. In addition, sentences like (7b) were correctly judged to be false almost nine-tenths of the time in the contexts displaying coreference.

These findings show that even 2- and 3-year-olds prohibit backwards anaphora only when structural conditions (involving c-command) dictate that they should. Additional evidence from both production and comprehension investigations confirm this fact. It is important to appreciate that the evidence we have reported supports the view that children do not rely on their linguistic experience in making judgments about the appropriate mappings of sentences with their meanings. Since there is nothing in children's experience to tell them that certain sentence/meaning pairs are NOT allowed, there is no way to learn the structural constraint prohibiting coreference, Principle C. It must be part of UG.

3   Research Design

The Truth-Value Judgment task makes two meanings available for each test sentence. One of these meanings is true in the context, and one is false; the subject responds "yes" or "no" depending on whether they judge the sentence to be true or not. Researchers working within the generative framework typically assume as their experimental hypothesis, designated H_1 in the literature, that children have the UG principle in question. The experimental hypothesis is contrasted with another possibility, namely that children lack the relevant principle of UG. This is referred to as the null hypothesis, designated H_0. Positive findings lead us to reject the null hypothesis but, in an important sense, positive findings cannot be said to confirm the experimental hypothesis. The reason for this is that positive findings could have resulted from factors other than those assumed by the experimenter; the most an experimenter can hope to accomplish, then, is to reject the null hypothesis. This would leave open the possibility that the experimental hypothesis is true.

The design features of an experiment are measures that are taken to ensure that the most **conservative** possible test of H_1 is conducted. A feature of design is conservative to the extent that it aids in reducing the chance of a **Type I error**.

A Type I error is a fallacious rejection of the null hypothesis. For example, in order to provide a conservative test of children's linguistic knowledge, care must be taken to avoid tasks in which child subjects are credited with "correct" answers when they should not have been.

One way to commit a Type I error in a task that requires a yes/no judgment is to have the "yes" answer correspond to the experimental hypothesis. It is well established that subjects have a tendency to say "yes" if they do not understand a sentence. To circumvent this bias, the experimental hypothesis should be associated with the "no" response. Then whenever child subjects misunderstand a test sentence, they will say "yes," and the response will count against the experimental hypothesis rather than for it, thereby avoiding the commission of a Type I error.

To aid our discussion of experimental methodology, let us run through an example of an experimental trial that was used in the Crain and McKee experiment. Recall that one of the test sentences presented to children was (8). We will use this sentence to illustrate how the context which preceded this sentence was constructed.

(8) He was dancing while the Ninja Turtle ate pizza.

By Principle C, sentence (8) cannot be paired with the meaning that the Ninja Turtle was dancing and eating pizza. As we saw, the context should be such that this meaning is associated with a "yes" response. Let us call this Meaning1. If children lack Principle C, they should be able to access Meaning1, in addition to the meaning that *is* permitted by Principle C, the adult interpretation. Let us call the adult interpretation, which is not filtered out by Principle C, Meaning2. With or without Principle C in children's arsenal of constraints, they should have access to Meaning2. In short, children who lack Principle C will find sentence (8) *ambiguous*, but children whose grammars contain Principle C will find (8) *unambiguous*, just as adults do. In short, the experimental hypothesis and the null hypothesis predict different results. These features of the study are summarized in (9).

(9) Null Hypothesis H_0: Children lack Principle C.
Expected results: Children permit both Meaning1 and Meaning2.

Experimental Hypothesis H_1: Children know Principle C.
Expected results: Children permit Meaning2, but not Meaning1.

Condition of falsification

Since the experimental hypothesis is that children will access Meaning2, but not Meaning1, the context in which (8) is presented should make Meaning2 false.

If Meaning2 is false, then it will evoke "no" responses from children. As noted, this feature of experimental design is implemented in order to avoid Type I errors.

We will now describe how to implement this feature of the study. We call it the **condition of falsification**. To satisfy the condition of falsification the context must be such that the test sentence (8) is false on Meaning2. There is another way to look at it; the context must be such that the *negation* of the test sentence is *true*. The negation of sentence (8) is (10).

(10)   He was not dancing while the Ninja Turtle ate pizza.

In order for (10) to be true, there must be someone in the context other than the Ninja Turtle, for example, Darth Vader. In addition, the context is constructed so that Darth Vader does not dance while the Ninja Turtle eats pizza. This aspect of the context makes (10) true and, therefore, makes (8) false, the desired result.

The context surrounding Meaning1 is more straightforward. As noted earlier, this meaning will be permitted if children lack Principle C, so that the context should make the test sentence true if children access Meaning1. Given the test sentence (8), *He was dancing while the Ninja Turtle ate pizza*, therefore, the context must be such that the Ninja Turtle dances and eats pizza. If children lack Principle C, they will accept (8) on this reading, and will respond by saying "yes." If children do not understand the task, or the test sentence, they will also tend to say "yes."

Summarizing the discussion so far, the following graphic should be helpful, where the asterisk simply indicates that Meaning1 is *disallowed* by the adult grammar.

Test sentence: *He was dancing while the Ninja Turtle ate pizza.*

Meaning1: He (= Ninja Turtle) was dancing while the Ninja Turtle ate pizza.
   Context: The Ninja Turtle dances and eats pizza.
   Meaning1 = True = "Yes"

Meaning2: He (= Darth Vader) was dancing while the Ninja Turtle ate pizza.
   Context: Darth Vader does not dance while the Ninja Turtle eats pizza.
   Meaning2 = False = "No"

To avoid Type I errors, the events of the story should be ordered so that those aspects of the context associated with Meaning1 are presented last, following those aspects related to Meaning2. This maneuver will heighten the availability of Meaning1, if children lack Principle C. If those aspects of the context associated with Meaning2 come last, then children may access Meaning2 despite the availability of Meaning1 in their grammars, thereby inflating the occurrence of responses that conform to the experimental hypothesis.

Condition of plausible dissent

In the context for sentence (8), *He was dancing while the Ninja Turtle ate pizza*, we have established that the context should be such that Darth Vader does not dance while the Ninja Turtle ate pizza. This fact, stated in (10), must be made clear to the child subjects. There are several ways to accomplish this. One way would be to have Darth Vader dance while someone other than the Ninja Turtle eats pizza, for example, Robocop. The necessary ingredients for an appropriate context are getting pretty complicated. To simplify them, it will be useful to partition the experimental context corresponding to Meaning2 into four components: the **background**, the **assertion**, the **actual outcome**, and the **possible outcome**. These components of the context we are constructing for (8), on Meaning2, are summarized in (11). We postpone discussion of the possible outcome for the moment.

(11) Context for Meaning2: *He was dancing while the Ninja Turtle ate pizza*

    (a) Background: Darth Vader dances while *so-and-so* eats pizza

    (b) Assertion: Darth Vader dances while *the Ninja Turtle* eats pizza

    (c) Actual outcome: Darth Vader dances while *Robocop* eats pizza

The **background** makes it clear that Darth Vader will dance while someone eats pizza; the question is who. Following the story, Kermit makes the **assertion** that Darth Vader danced while the Ninja Turtle ate pizza. The **actual outcome** makes it clear to children (whose grammars contain Principle C) why the test sentence is false on Meaning2. Although Darth Vader did dance while someone ate pizza, the someone in question was Robocop, not the Ninja Turtle.

The one remaining ingredient is the **possible outcome**. At some point during the story, the assertion made by the puppet should have been a possible outcome. By this we mean that the events that transpired might have taken a different turn, and if they had taken this turn, then Kermit's utterance (8) would have been true. In the present example, it should be clear to child subjects that Darth Vader might have danced while the Ninja Turtle ate pizza. That possible outcome should come under consideration at some point in the story, but some turn of events prevented this from happening (e.g., Darth Vader preferred to dance while Robocop ate pizza, because his favorite song was being played then).

We call this component of the design of the experiment **the condition of plausible dissent**. This condition is summarized as follows.

(11)   Context for Meaning2: *He was dancing while the Ninja Turtle ate pizza*

(d)   Plausible dissent: the assertion was a possible outcome.

The condition of plausible dissent is a felicity condition for asking someone to judge whether sentences are true or false. If there was no way for (8) to have turned out to be true on the interpretation that is licensed by children's grammar (i.e., Meaning2, according to the experimental hypothesis), then it is odd to ask children to judge whether the sentence is true or false. To make Kermit's utterance of (8) felicitous, the assertion should be a possible outcome.

In a paper in 1948, the British philosopher Bertrand Russell made a related observation. He pointed out that the denial of a proposition is felicitous only if the proposition is under consideration. Russell remarked that "perception only gives rise to a negative judgment when the correlative positive judgment has already been made or considered." Similarly, it is appropriate to ask children for a (possibly) negative judgment of a sentence only if the corresponding positive judgment has been under consideration. In the context for sentence (8), this is accomplished if the referent of the pronoun "he," Darth Vader, entertains the possibility of dancing while the Ninja Turtle eats pizza. Ultimately, he declines, and ends up dancing while Robocop eats pizza.

What happens if the condition of plausible dissent is not satisfied? In our experience, children who do not see the relevance of providing a (possibly) negative judgment are often confused by the task, and they often end up making affirmative responses. Although these responses do not result in Type I errors, the failure to satisfy felicity conditions imposes an unnecessary impediment to our understanding of children's linguistic competence.

Conclusion

It should be clear that the construction of a good experiment is far from trivial. There are many critical features of design that must be attended to in any test of children's linguistic competence. The justification for many of the additional design features also appeals to the adage: avoid Type I errors, by stacking the cards against the experimental hypothesis, as far as possible.

Note

1   Indeed, such a preference is expected, as a result of children's limited memory capacity. In other studies, similar effects of working memory have been revealed on other linguistic constructions, including restrictive relative clauses and temporal adverbial clauses. Thus, children's extra-sentential interpretation of pronouns is not by itself convincing evidence that they disallow all cases of backwards anaphora.

Bibliographical Comments

The early studies on backwards anaphora reported here were conducted by Solan (1983) and Tavakolian (1978). A critique of these studies is presented in Lasnik and Crain (1985). Effects of children's limitations on memory capacity for other structures is presented in Crain, Shankweiler, Macaruso, and Bar-Shalom (1990). The Truth-Value Judgment task was developed and used to test children's knowledge of backwards anaphora by Crain and McKee (1986). For a detailed discussion of issues relating to experimental design, see Crain and Thornton (1998).

Part III   Transformational Syntax

Introduction

Phrase Structure rules provide a formal procedure for constructing tree diagrams (phrase markers). This kind of rule can take us some distance towards our goal, which is to account for the full range of linguistic knowledge. We have seen that PS rules form the basis of an explanation for two important linguistic facts: ambiguity and productivity. PS rules also provide an explanation for our knowledge of these linguistic facts in the absence of experience. However, we will soon see that PS rules do not go far enough. In addition to PS rules, Chomsky introduced another type of syntactic rule, called a **transformational rule**. This type of rule is the technical innovation that Chomsky is most famous for. He brought it to prominence in his book, *Syntactic Structures*, which started the intellectual revolution in linguistics.

We saw that with PS rules alone, it is possible to generate an infinite number of sentences. But even if we had all of the PS rules for English, we could not generate all and only the grammatical sentences of English – we need transformational rules as well. As we will see, the interaction of PS rules with transformational rules gets pretty complicated. It's not the sort of thing you'd dream up unless there was good evidence for it, so we will consider several types of evidence in favor of transformational rules. But first, let us sketch out how the syntactic component consisting of PS rules and transformational rules operates. Then, we can look in more detail at how transformations work. To motivate the use of transformational rules, we will look at several types of sentences which cannot be generated by PS rules. We will show how transformational rules manage to generate them. Then we will see how, like PS rules, transformational rules help explain several interesting linguistic phenomena.

Transformational rules apply to phrase markers, changing (transforming) one into another. To give an example, one transformation shows the relationship between declarative sentences and yes/no questions (the rule of Subject–Auxiliary Inversion, discussed in chapter 16.) This means that before a transformation applies, a phrase marker must be generated. In other words, the input to the **transformational component** (= the set of transformational rules) is a phrase marker. So, to give this component its input, we proceed just as before, using PS rules to build up a phrase marker. Once a phrase marker is derived, we can apply transformational rules to it. These rules transform the first phrase marker into another one. Sometimes the resulting phrase marker (that was the output of the transformational rule) can be transformed again (by another, different rule, or by the same rule applying in another way). In other words, there are a number of transformational rules, which may be applied in turn, each one operating on the output of the last. Each transformational rule changes the previous phrase marker into a slightly different one. The entire process is called the **derivation** of a sentence.

The initial phrase marker, which is derived from the PS rules, is called the **Deep Structure**. Another way of saying it is this: Deep Structures are the output of the PS rules. Each time we use a transformational rule, we create a **derived** or **intermediate** phrase marker. When we get to the last one, we call it the **Surface Structure** of the sentence. The Surface Structure corresponds to the sequence of words that is actually pronounced.

Here is a schematic diagram of the derivation of a structure:

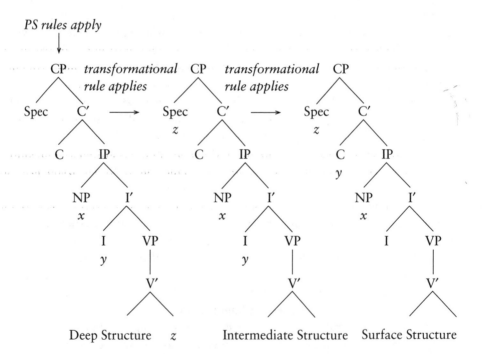

PS rules apply

Deep Structure   *z*   Intermediate Structure   Surface Structure

Remember, Deep Structures are generated by the PS rules, so PS rules begin the entire process. Transformational rules only begin to apply once we have a Deep Structure – the initial phrase marker. It is also important to recognize that the Deep Structure does not necessarily indicate the order in which the words will actually be spoken. The Deep Structure is derived from the PS rules, and then transformed to produce the Surface Structure. The Surface Structure corresponds to the string that is actually pronounced.

Why should we complicate the grammar by adding transformational rules? As we saw, PS rules are adequate for a great many sentences – they establish a core of sentences whose structure is more-or-less straightforward. As a matter of historical note, sentences formed by PS rules alone were called *kernel* sentences by Chomsky in his earliest works, although this term has gone out of fashion. However, there are many other sentences which PS rules cannot cope with. These are variations from the kernel sentences of the language. In the following chapters, we will consider several types of sentences that are problematic for PS rules, and which require transformational rules.

As we discuss the operation of one particular transformation rule in some detail (the rule of WH-Movement), we will see that transformations are subject to *constraints*. We introduced constraints in chapter 14, where we saw that our interpretation of pronouns is constrained by Principle C. Transformational operations are also governed by constraints, including Principle C. As before, the technical machinery becomes somewhat complicated, but we will see that it accounts for a curious distribution of facts which alternative theories cannot handle.

In addition to the syntactic evidence for transformational rules and constraints, in this part we will present evidence that children understand the transformation of WH-Movement and obey the constraints in their productions of long-distance questions. First, we will investigate children's ability to produce basic matrix WH-questions. Then we will turn to long-distance questions. We will show that although young children do not produce many long-distance WH-questions in spontaneous production, such questions can be elicited in experimental settings, and they do show that children adhere to the constraints of UG.

In these chapters our conclusions rely heavily on the results of recent experimental studies using the technique of elicited production. This methodology is a particularly useful tool to address current linguistic issues in the acquisition of complex syntax. Much of the work summarized so far on language acquisition used analysis of children's spontaneous productions. This kind of data is useful for certain types of investigations, especially those with very young children. Children who are <u>less than</u> 3 years old usually do not have the cognitive maturity for complex linguistic experiments. Various methods for testing their production and comprehension can be used, but they are generally variations on the theme of naturally occurring productions. For investigating such phenomena as basic word order, for example, such methods are adequate, since every utterance the child makes will contribute relevant data.

However, in order to investigate children's knowledge of constraints on long-distance questions, or other complex syntactic phenomena, observation of spontaneous production is not adequate. Children do not produce long-distance questions very often in natural discourse. The experimenter might have to wait many months, even years, before the relevant sentence type is uttered! Further-more, by the age of 3 years, children can participate in experimental studies. Various methods for studying both production and comprehension of complex syntax have been developed, with quite notable success. Thus, such methods are to be preferred for studies of complex syntax. They allow the experimenter to pinpoint specific structures of interest, and provide much more reliable informa-tion than spontaneous production would in this domain.

16 A Transformation Generating Yes/No Questions

Introduction

Phrase Structure rules alone can generate an infinite number of sentences, but they are not sufficient to generate all the sentence types found in English or any other natural language. In particular, we find that sometimes a relationship, or **dependency**, exists between elements in disparate parts of a sentence. For example, an element which is normally found following the subject (such as a modal) may be found preceding the subject in certain sentence types (such as yes/no questions). Dependencies are best captured by the use of **transformational rules**. In this chapter we begin our discussion of transformations. You will see that the concept of a transformation is relatively straightforward, although the implementation may become somewhat complex, especially when constraints on transformations are considered. It is worth going into this complexity as it helps to make the strongest case for innate knowledge.

1 Yes/No Questions

Consider the declarative statement in (1), which can be diagrammed using the tree in (2).

(1) Hillary will go.

(2)

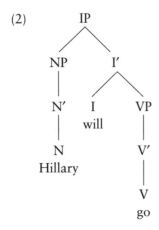

This tree should be very familiar to you.

Now, consider the yes/no question in (3). (The question in (3) is called a "yes/no" question because the expected answer is either "yes" or "no.") Can this question be derived by our Phrase Structure rules?

(3)   Will Hillary go?

The X'-theory as we have implemented it in English cannot generate a sentence in which the subject comes after the element in I. It is possible to imagine ways in which to change our assumptions in order to generate this sentence using PS rules alone. For example, we could generate "will" higher in the structure, for example, in C, rather than in I. Or, we could generate the subject in the specifier of VP. However, there are reasons to take a different approach. Considering the similarities between the declarative in (1) and the question in (3), the grammar should capture the relationship between these sentences. Furthermore, we will see that the same kind of relationship exists between declaratives and other kinds of questions. In order to capture the generalizations these relationships exhibit, a different type of linguistic rule is used in addition to PS rules to generate questions such as that in (3). These are *transformational rules*.

A transformation begins with a well-formed **Deep Structure**. A Deep Structure is simply a phrase marker which is derived using the PS rules. It should always be compatible with these rules. The Deep Structure is the input to the transformation; the transformation then affects the Deep Structure in some way, producing a **Surface Structure** as its output. In this example (and in the example we turn to in chapter 18), the transformation moves an element from one position to another.

What is the Deep Structure for the sentence in (3)? It is essentially the structure of (1), but with one modification, anticipating the application of the transformation. The Deep Structure is given in (4).

(4)

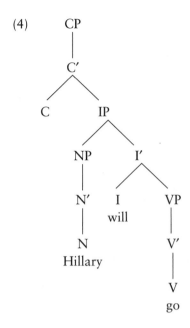

This phrase marker is very similar to the one in (2), and it is easy to see that it does follow the PS rules we have already presented (refer to chapter 8 if you have forgotten about CP). One special feature of this phrase marker is that the node C is present, but it has nothing beneath it. The node itself is not new: C was needed earlier in generating sentences such as "Dana is hoping that Kim will cook dinner." The word "that" which begins the subordinate clause, "that Kim will cook dinner," is dominated by the category C. Usually, we do not leave an empty node position in a tree (e.g., we routinely leave off the Spec of VP and PP). However, because we will use this tree as the Deep Structure for a transformation which will need the C position, we included it here. From now on, when an empty node is needed later in a derivation, it will be inserted at Deep Structure. In any case, it is clear that the phrase marker in (2) can be seen to follow from the usual set of PS rules within X'-theory.

How does a transformation transform the Deep Structure in (4) to the Surface Structure which goes with the yes/no question in (3)? The transformation, which we will call "Subject–Auxiliary Inversion" (or "SAI"), moves the contents of I to the position of C, resulting in the Surface Structure given in (5). (This transformation is also sometimes called "I-to-C movement," for obvious reasons.)

(5)

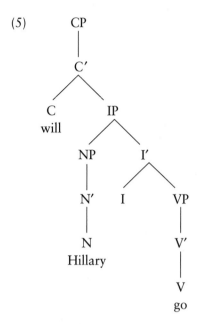

It is important to remember that the structure in (4) is the *Deep Structure* of the question in (3), because it follows the PS rules, and the structure in (5) gives the *Surface Structure*, which has the words in their appropriate places. Notice as well that (2) is the Deep Structure and the Surface Structure for the declarative in (1). That is, any sentence for which no transformation applies has the same Deep and Surface Structures.

Let's try another example. How is the question in (7) related to the declarative in (6)?

(6)   Al is speaking.

(7)   Is Al speaking?

The answer is diagrammed in figure 16.1.

Thus, we have discovered how to derive a "yes/no question." First, a Deep Structure is generated using the usual PS rules. Next, the transformation of SAI applies, moving the contents of I to C, resulting in the Surface Structure.

2   Affix-Hopping and Do-Support

Let's now consider what happens to create a yes/no question from a declarative like the one in (8).

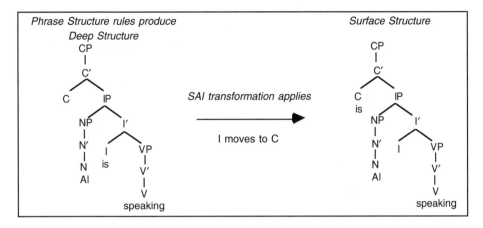

Figure 16.1   The derivation of a question

(8)   Bill left.

As you can tell by your intuition, the corresponding yes/no question is (9).

(9)   Did Bill leave?

Notice that in (8), the verb is marked for past tense, but it isn't in (9). Also, notice that (9) has the word "did," but (8) doesn't. You have probably deduced that these two facts are related.

First, consider the phrase marker for (8), given in (10).

(10)

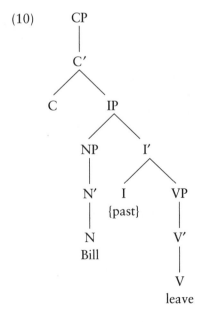

As we saw in chapter 8, in a declarative sentence the inflectional affix hops onto the verb. In this case, {past} joins with "leave" to make "left," as in (8). However, suppose {past} moves to C by I-to-C movement in order to create a yes/no question. This results in the Surface Structure given in (11).

(11)

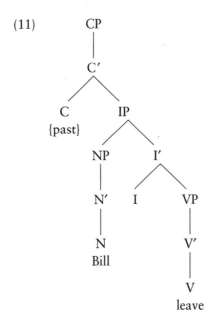

The restriction on affix-hopping which we noticed in chapter 8 was that the affix must be *adjacent* to the verb. This is true in (10), but not in (11) – in (11) the subject "Bill" comes between {past} and the verb.

In English, we save the structure in (11) by using an operation known as "Do-support." The dummy verb "do" is inserted as a host for the {past} affix in C, and of course "do" + {past} = "did." This gives us the desired surface form (9).

Do-support is only used as a last resort operation. It applies to save a stranded tense affix in questions and in a few other situations. Always apply all other transformations first. If the tense affix ends up next to the verb, then apply affix-hopping. However, if the tense marker is stranded, then apply Do-support.

Do-support in negative sentences

Additional evidence for the operation of Do-support as a last resort comes from negative sentences. Consider the examples in (12)–(13).

(12) a. Sandy will leave.
       b. Sandy will not leave.

(13) a.   Sandy left.
      b.   *Sandy not left.
      c.   Sandy did not leave.

The examples in (12) show us that a negative sentence looks like a positive sentence with the word "not" before the verb. However, (13) shows that the negative element "not" cannot appear before a tensed verb. Apparently, the tense affix cannot adjoin to the verb by affix-hopping in negative sentences, as (13b) shows. This means the affix will be left stranded. Just as in questions, to save the stranded affix, Do-support must apply.

Let's take a moment to see how this works. First, assume that a negative element such as "not" is the head of a new phrasal category, which we'll call "NegP." NegP follows the X'-schema we saw in chapter 9, and it comes between IP and VP. This means that the structure of (13c) will be that in (14).

(14)

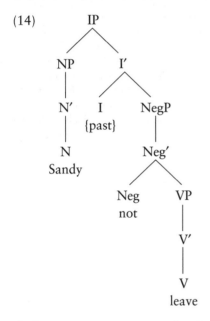

With this tree, it is easy to see that {past} cannot affix-hop onto "leave" because they are not adjacent – the negative "not" intervenes. Thus, Do-support must apply to host the stranded tense affix in I.

Conclusion

Let's step back for a moment, and consider the properties of the mental grammar. It consists of a finite set of PS rules, which generate phrase markers (Deep

Structures), as well as transformational rules which are relatively simple, for converting phrase markers into still other phrase markers. The output of the transformational component is a Surface Structure. Together, the combination of rules is able to generate an infinite array of Surface Structures for a language. Transformational rules are needed in addition to PS rules because sentences of natural language sometimes exhibit dependencies between constituents that are distant from each other (on the surface). These dependencies are characteristic of transformational rules, but not of PS rules.

Bibliographical Comments

We have cited Chomsky's early works in our discussion of Phrase Structure, but it was his development of the transformation which served as a vital new tool for analyzing language. As we have mentioned earlier, it was his reorientation of the goals of linguistics which truly revolutionized the field. These early works, which gave detailed transformational analyses of English, as well as discussions of the limitations of Phrase Structure grammars, include Chomsky (1975) (first distributed in 1955), Chomsky (1957), and Chomsky (1965). The terms Deep Structure and Surface Structure were first introduced in Chomsky (1965), where the notions are discussed in detail. Good introductory textbooks on the transformational approach to grammar described here include Akmajian Demers, Farmer, and Harnish (1995), Baker (1978), Cook and Newson (1996), Radford, (1981), and Riemsdijk and Williams (1986).

17 Children's Adherence to Structure Dependence

Introduction

We observed earlier that the principles of Universal Grammar should emerge early in the course of development, all other things being equal. A fundamental constraint of this kind is **structure dependence**. According to the theory of Universal Grammar, children's hypotheses are concerned with the abstract structural properties of sentences. They should never postulate purely structure-independent rules which treat sentences just as strings of words. In this chapter, we report the findings of an experiment that was designed to test this claim. The experimental technique is to elicit sentences from children; the sentences that are elicited in the experiment are ones that can unveil children's use of structure-independent and/or structure-dependent operations. In this way, the experiment is designed to tell us whether or not children follow the guidelines of UG in opting for structure-dependent rules at a time when structure-independent rules would do just as well. A positive result would support the solution to Plato's problem which is proposed by Universal Grammar – that children are genetically endowed with knowledge of certain linguistic principles.

1 Structure Dependence and Yes/No Questions

It is a basic tenet of the theory of Universal Grammar that grammatical operations are structure-dependent. Based on this tenet of the theory, the expectation is that children invariably formulate structure-dependent hypotheses in the course of language acquisition, even if their linguistic experience is limited such that it is also consistent with structure-independent hypotheses. As a reminder, a linguistic hypothesis is structure-dependent if it applies to abstract properties of sentences, such as constituent structure. A structure-independent hypothesis, on the other hand, operates on sentences construed as strings of words, rather than on their structural representations. Because structure-independent hypotheses apply to ordered strings, they involve linear relations such as "first," "leftmost," and so on.

In the last chapter, we introduced the formation of yes/no questions using the Subject–Auxiliary Inversion transformation. We formulated this transformation in a purely structure-dependent way: move I to C. However, it is possible to state the relationship between simple declaratives and their yes/no counterparts using either structure-dependent or structure-independent operations. Only more complex yes/no questions show that the structure-dependent formulation of the rule is required. This makes yes/no questions a good testing ground for the claim that children invariably hypothesize structure-dependent operations.

We begin by considering how simple yes/no questions could be formed by a structure-independent operation. Consider the examples given in (1).

(1)   *Declarative*   *Yes/no question*
    a. The man is tall.   → Is the man tall?
    b. Geraldo can sing well.   → Can Geraldo sing well?
    c. Your father will come home.   → Will your father come home?
    d. The lady can dance and sing.   → Can the lady dance and sing?

What kind of simple, structure-independent operation would suffice to account for the examples in (1)? One possibility is the following:

(2) In forming yes/no questions, move the first "is" (or "can," "will," etc.) of a declarative sentence to the front.

The strategy in (2) produces the correct question forms for many simple yes/no questions. We often say that a structure-independent hypothesis such as (2) treats sentences as if the words were combined like beads on a string, without regard to hierarchical structure. According to such a "beads-on-a-string" model of language, the structure-independent operation is quite simple. To form a yes/no question, each word from the corresponding declarative sentence is checked in turn. As soon as a word from a short list ("is," "can," "will," ...) is encountered, it is moved to the front of the sentence. The result is the desired yes/no question. Figure 17.1 depicts the formation of the yes/no question, "Can the lady dance and sing?" under the structure-independent hypothesis.

In contrast to the simplicity of the structure-independent way of producing yes/no questions, the structure-dependent rule of SAI seems quite complex. As we saw, it analyzes sentences using abstract notions such as "subject noun phrase" and categories such as I and C. These notions refer to the abstract phrase structure of the sentence. Figure 17.2 depicts the formation of the yes/no question, "Can the lady dance and sing?" under the structure-dependent hypo-

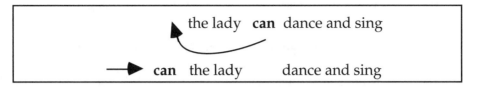

Figure 17.1   Structure-independent yes/no question formation

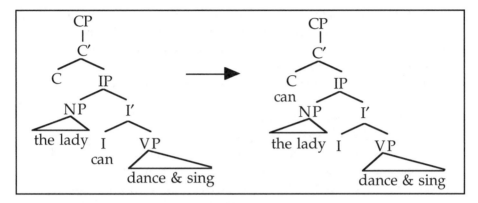

Figure 17.2   Structure-dependent yes/no question formation

thesis. This analysis is abstract in the sense that there is nothing corresponding to these notions in the stream of speech that bombards our ears when someone asks us a yes/no question. Unlike written sentences, spoken sentences do not even have discernible boundaries between words in most cases.

What is so striking about the constraint of structure dependence is that it rules out hypotheses like the one stated in (2), even though they appear to be computationally simpler than structure-dependent rules such as the Subject–Auxiliary Inversion transformation. Given the reasonable assumption that children encounter simple sentences first, at least some children might be expected to adopt the structure-independent hypothesis were it not precluded by Universal Grammar. However, children who opted for a structure-independent hypothesis such as (2) would be in trouble later in the course of language development, when they began to ask more complex questions.

We can see that the more complex structure-dependent operation is required by the adult grammar by considering questions that contain a complex subject, such as a relative clause. Consider sentence (3a). The subject noun phrase of this declarative sentence is, "The only girl who can do a triple vault." Notice that the subject noun phrase contains the relative clause, "who can do a triple vault." Applying the structure-independent rule to (3a) results in the ungrammatical question (3b). The correct question form is (3c).

(3)   a.   The only girl who *can* do a triple vault *is* too young for the team.

             →

NOT   b.   *Can the only girl who ____ do a triple vault is too young for the team?

BUT   c.   Is the only girl who can do a triple vault ____ too young for the team?

Example (3) uncovers the basic problem with the structure-independent hypothesis. Because it ignores constituent structure, it works only in cases where the first "is," or "can," etc. in the sentence is in the main clause; when the first "is" or "can" is part of a relative clause, as in (3), the structure-independent hypothesis yields the wrong yes/no question form, as in (3b). The structure-independent rule moves the first "can" in the linear string to the front, regardless. Clearly, this is not how language works in complex sentences.

What is needed is the structure-dependent transformational rule of Subject–Auxiliary Inversion, which yields the correct yes/no question forms in all cases, both simple and complex. In the example (3a), the entire phrase "the only girl who can do a triple vault" is the subject NP. The "is" after this entire phrase is the auxiliary verb of the main clause. It is this "is" that moves. The occurrence of "can" within the subject noun phrase is simply ignored by the transformational rule.

According to the constraint on structure dependence, children should produce well-formed yes/no questions corresponding to any declarative sentence. Therefore, they should not be misled by sentences with simple NPs into thinking that yes/no questions can be formed using structure-independent operations such as (2). We will present the findings of an experiment that tests this prediction in the next section of this chapter. Following that, we discuss another expectation that is based on the assumption that children invariably utilize structure-dependent rules. A consequence of this is the expectation that children should not be tempted to form generalizations about yes/no questions based on the semantic properties of sentences. This is the topic of the last section of this chapter.

2   Children's Complex Yes/No Questions

Several experiments have been designed to see whether children produce structure-dependent questions such as (3c) above, or structure-independent yes/no questions such as (3b) when they first begin to ask complex questions (i.e., ones with relative clauses).

The first study we report was conducted by Stephen Crain and Mineharu Nakayama. It is a simple experimental procedure developed to elicit yes/no questions from children. The original experiment tested thirty 3- to 5-year-old children, who were interviewed individually. The instructions to the child were quite simple. The experimenter had a toy figure of Jabba the Hutt (from Star Wars), and some pictures. The experimenter asked each child to pose questions to Jabba, using the phrase, "Ask Jabba if . . ." Following each question, Jabba was shown a picture and would respond "Yes" or "No." Various types of declarative sentences were inserted into the carrier phrase, "Ask Jabba if . . ." One example is (4). Notice that the experimenter's request in (4) demands a yes/no question which corresponds to the declarative sentence, "The man who is beating a donkey is mean."

(4) Ask Jabba if the man who is beating a donkey is mean.

The purpose of the first experiment we will discuss was to see whether or not children apply structure-independent operations when they begin to produce complex yes/no questions with a relative clause. If they do, then children should sometimes produce questions that conform to the structure-independent hypothesis, such as, "*Is the man who beating a donkey is mean?" If children obey the structure dependence constraint, then questions of this form should never appear.

The outcome was as predicted by the theory of UG. Children never produced incorrect sentences like (3b). This is not to say that they made no errors. If they made no errors at all, we might be afraid that they were too linguistically mature to test the hypothesis (although, given their ages, this in itself would also be evidence for the UG hypothesis!). However, the errors they made did not indicate that they had adopted the incorrect, structure-independent hypothesis. Rather, they indicated that the relatively complex sentences introduced a heavier processing load on the children.

Thus, a structure-independent strategy was not adopted in spite of its simplicity and in spite of the fact that it produces correct question forms in many instances. The findings of this study, then, lend support to one of the central claims of UG, that the initial state of the language faculty contains structure dependence as an inherent property. Even when a structure-independent strategy was consistent with the input children receive, this route was never taken. This conclusion supports the view that children's linguistic hypotheses are restricted to ones that take into account the structural properties of sentences.

It is worth underscoring that system-internal constraints such as structure dependence help children avoid wrong turns that they might otherwise take. These constraints obviate the need for detailed corrective feedback that would otherwise be required to inform children of their grammatical errors. We have seen that so-called "negative data" is not systematically available to children. But in its absence it is hard to see how children who err in grammar construction might unlearn the incorrect hypothesis and realign their grammars so as to converge on a system that is equivalent to that of adult members of the linguistic community. Since everyone in the same linguistic community reaches an equivalent Final State, it seems reasonable to infer that they do not fall prey to false grammatical hypotheses. This is the "poverty of the stimulus" argument advanced in Part I. It is reassuring to find that experimental studies of young children back up this argument.

3   Structure Dependence: Syntax or Semantics?

Although the innateness hypothesis is widely accepted among linguists, many researchers in other fields remain unconvinced. Few alternative proposals have been advanced, however. Fortunately, the linguistic phenomenon of structure dependence proved to be an exception. In the remainder of the chapter, we consider an alternative proposal which has been advanced – that children's ability to form yes/no questions is guided by a semantic generalization rather than by their adherence to structure dependence.

According to this account, advanced by Nathan Stemmer, children do not appeal to an abstract notion of subject noun phrase in forming yes/no questions; rather, they notice that certain sequences of words pick out the actors of the events they witness. Then they experience a number of simple questions in which words like "is" and "will" precede the word strings which refer to actors. Eventually, experience leads children to form the generalization that words like "is" and "will" appear before such expressions in yes/no questions, but after them in statements.

On this account, the children's semantically based hypothesis is learned from simple data; but it produces the right question forms for complex sentences, like the ones with relative clauses that were used in Experiment 1. For example, notice that the first auxiliary, "can," in (3a) follows the sequence "the only girl who"; since this sequence of words does not refer to the actor of an event, it does not fall within the scope of the child's generalization. The second auxiliary, "is," does follow a referential word string, "the only girl who can do a triple vault"; so this "is" can appear in the yes/no question corresponding to (3a).

The semantically based account of children's yes/no questions can be contrasted with the structure-dependent account. On the structure-dependent account, children should be able to form a yes/no question corresponding to any declarative sentence, regardless of the semantic properties of the subject noun phrase. By contrast, if yes/no question formation is based on the semantic properties of sentences, children would not form yes/no questions corresponding to all noun phrases. Instead, their initial yes/no questions should be limited to ones that conform to the semantic generalization. Assuming that children initially make the semantic generalization that yes/no questions are formed only for sequences of words that refer to the actor(s) of an event, this is the subset of the yes/no questions (of the target grammar) that children allow.

On a semantic-based account, then, children should initially undergenerate yes/no questions. On the acquisition scenario according to which children form yes/no questions only with word strings that refer to actors, questions such as (5) would not be produced.

(5) a. Is running dangerous?
     b. Is his thinking correct?

The undergeneration of yes/no questions poses no learnability problem, however, because there would be plenty of counterexamples in the input to children to extend their semantic generalization beyond its current coverage. Questions like those in (5) are produced by adults, so children will encounter them at some point in their lives. These adult questions will serve as the requisite counterexamples to the child's hypothesis, because they do not contain word strings with the prototypical semantic attribute, reference to a particular object. The presence of such questions in the child's input would lead them to abandon their original hypothesis in favor of one that produced both questions like (5) and ones like (3c). In this fashion, children would ultimately achieve the adult grammar.

4   Experiment 2: A Test of the Semantic Account

An experiment was designed to evaluate the possibility that children form semantically based hypotheses in the acquisition of yes/no questions. On any such account, the early stages in the development of yes/no questions should be semantically constrained. In particular, children should be able to form interrogatives only for certain constructions, for example, if the words preceding "is" and "can" refer to a particular object. In other circumstances, the child should fail to invert the subject NP and the auxiliary verb, for example, if the initial words in an assertion refer to an action or to an abstract object (as in (5) above). If the syntactic account is correct, then the subject NP and the auxiliary verb will be inverted in all yes/no questions, regardless of the semantic properties of the words they contain.

To test the competing accounts, children responded to an experimenter's assertions, using the procedures described in Experiment 1. Fourteen children participated in the experiment. They ranged in age from just under 3 to almost 5, with an average age of $3^3/4$.

The experimenter used a variety of assertions to fill in the carrier phrase, "Ask Jabba if ..." Included among them were examples like those in (6), with "it" and "there." These are called "expletives." Expletives are semantically empty, dummy subjects, without inherent reference. They do not refer to anything. It seems clear that questions corresponding to the assertions in (6) would not be produced early in the course of language development according to the semantic account of yes/no question formation.

(6)   *Declarative*   *Yes/no question*
      It is raining in this picture.   → Is it raining in this picture?
      It is easy to see the little ghost. → Is it easy to see the little ghost?
      There is a snake in this picture.   → Is there a snake in this picture?

Other test sentences referred to an action and an abstraction, respectively:

(7)   *Declarative*   *Yes/no question*
      Running is fun.   → Is running fun?
      Love is good or bad.   → Is love good or bad?

Finally, there were control sentences, with referential NPs, like those in the first experiment.

The results of the test sentences clearly go against the semantically based account of how children learn yes/no questions. Children uniformly deployed a structure-dependent rule across the board, rather than one based on the semantic properties of the declarative sentences they encountered. In response to sentences such as (7), children produced 92 percent correct yes/no questions, and they produced 88 percent correct questions in response to assertions with expletive subject noun phrases, as in (6). Their responses to the referential NP control sentences were correct 93 percent of the time. In other words, children were impervious to the semantic features of the subject noun phrases which served as context terms in their yes/no question transformations. Expletives, abstract/action noun phrases, and referential noun phrases are all integrated into the grammars of young children, under the syntactic category of subject NP, as predicted by the theory of Universal Grammar.

Conclusion

We have seen that children adhere to structure-dependent rules at a time when their linguistic experience is extremely limited and, therefore, compatible with both structure-dependent and structure-independent rules. The finding that children do not violate the constraint on structure-dependence when they begin to ask complex yes/no questions constitutes evidence that structure dependence sets a boundary condition on the hypotheses children can formulate in response to their linguistic input. In addition, we saw that this conclusion could withstand the challenge of an alternative, semantically based explanation of how yes/no questions are learned. Finally, the discussion in this chapter points out the importance of experimentation in testing competing hypotheses about the nature of language development.

Bibliographical Comments

Chomsky has often cited the formation of yes/no questions as an example of the principle of structure dependence. The experiments described here were conducted by Crain and Nakayama (1987). A follow-up study was presented by Nakayama (1987). The alternative, semantic, account was proposed by Stemmer (1981).

18 WH-Movement

Introduction

We have seen that Phrase Structure rules alone cannot generate all the sentences of English, and rules of another kind are also needed. These transformational rules take Deep Structures generated by PS rules as their input, affect these structures in some way, and produce Surface Structures as their output. The transformational rule we have already discussed, Subject–Auxiliary Inversion, affects the DS by *moving* an element from one location to another. The next transformation we will present is also a movement rule, called WH-Movement. After introducing the basics of this rule in this chapter, we will continue to discuss structures affected by WH-Movement for the rest of this part. We concentrate on WH-Movement because of the variety of structures and constraints which are relevant to it.

1   Indirect Questions

The WH-Movement transformation involves words (or phrases) called WH-words. These are question words such as "who," "what," "where," and so on, which in English generally start with the letters "WH." Even though their equivalents in other languages do not start with the letters "WH," they have come to be known as "WH"-words generally. WH-words are used in WH-questions (as well as some other structures), which come in several types. We begin by discussing **indirect questions**.

Consider the following sentence:

(1)   Bill wondered who Al spoke to.

This kind of sentence is called an indirect question because the whole sentence isn't a question (the listener isn't expected to reply), but it has something resembling a question embedded in it, namely, "who Al spoke to." The presence of the question fragment "who Al spoke to" as an embedded (= subordinate) clause identifies an indirect question.

Upon short reflection we will see that it is not possible to generate this indirect question with PS rules alone. Assuming that the WH-phrase "who" is an NP, and that the proper name "Al" is another NP, then it appears that the PS component would require the addition of a PS rule that introduces two NPs at the beginning of the embedded clause, to license the appearance of both "who" and "Al" following the verb "wondered" in (1). Yet another rule would also be needed to generate (1). In ordinary declarative sentences, we find that the verb "spoke" is followed either by an NP (e.g., "Hussein spoke Arabic"), or by an adverb (e.g., "Vanna spoke softly"), or by a full PP (e.g., "Hussein spoke to Vanna"). However, it would be grammatically deviant to lop off the NP after the P in ordinary declarative sentences (e.g., "Hussein spoke to"). But in the indirect question under consideration, there is a PP following "spoke" without an NP. Therefore, we would need to add a rule permitting a P to be left with no NP following it.

Unfortunately, the addition of these two new rules causes certain unwanted consequences. By adding these rules to the PS component, we would add new options for expanding IP and PP, allowing ungrammatical sentences to be produced. For example, it is not correct to leave off the NP in the PP following the verb "spoke" in an ordinary declarative, as (2) shows.

(2) *Bill thought Al spoke to.
    (Cf. Bill wondered who Al spoke to.)

And, in fact, the converse is true. If we choose the option of including an NP in the PP in the indirect question under consideration, the result is also ungrammatical:

(3) *Bill wondered who Al spoke to Fred.

The point here is that the two "new" rules form a tandem, and cannot work alone. If one applies, the other must also be applied. But if one does not apply, the other also must not. In other words, there can be a "missing" NP in a PP if and only if an "extra" NP appears elsewhere. This relationship is called a **dependency**: the missing NP is dependent on the extra NP.

The problem with the potential PS rules under consideration is that there is no way to guarantee that PS rules are applied in a dependent way, such as under a condition stating: rule X if and only if rule Y. At any point in a derivation any PS rule can apply. There is no means at present for keeping track of the other PS rules that might have been applied elsewhere in a phrase marker. This means that "dependent" PS rules like this must be avoided. If either rule is added to our PS system, there would be ungrammatical consequences. This discussion points out the need for another kind of rule, one that relates the presence or absence of an NP in a PP to the presence or absence of an NP at the front of the embedded clause in the indirect question.

Now we shall show how to capture this kind of dependency using the transformational rule of WH-Movement. Again, our target is the sentence "Bill wondered who Al spoke to." This sentence corresponds to the Surface Structure, remember, because this is how the sentence is actually pronounced. First, we need to uncover its Deep Structure. This, we said, was a function of the PS rules. Of course, these PS rules do not include the potential rules we discussed above, since it was argued that these rules were too costly. Instead, the usual PS rules will have to suffice. These can be employed in coming up with a Deep Structure that can be transformed appropriately by the WH-Movement rule. We propose the phrase marker in (4) as the Deep Structure.

(4)

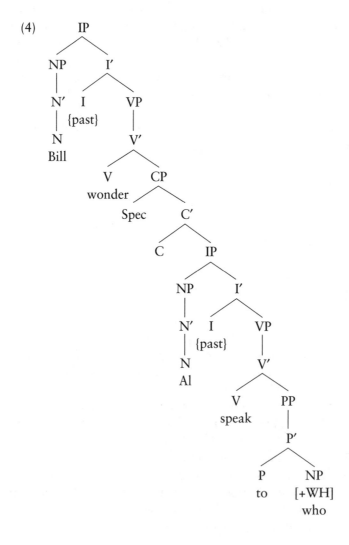

Notice that as with the yes/no questions discussed in chapter 16, this Deep Structure contains empty nodes: both C and the specifier of CP have nothing beneath them at the level of Deep Structure. As before, we include these nodes here in anticipation of needing them later. Although we noted the existence of the specifier position of CP, we have not yet seen which elements go in it. Now the time has come to use this position. In (4), the empty Spec of CP position is used to create an open slot. This slot has no words in it at Deep Structure, but it is filled with "who" in the Surface Structure of the sentence. To obtain the desired result, the Spec of CP node is left empty at the level of Deep Structure.

So we have created a Deep Structure in which every clause has a verb, there are no "extra" noun phrases, and the PP has an NP. It is important to see that this is the Deep Structure of the sentence, because it follows the PS rules, but it cannot be the Surface Structure, because the words are not in their appropriate places. If we uttered the words in the order given at Deep Structure, the result would be the ungrammatical sentence, "*Bill wondered Al spoke to who." This means that the transformation that is needed is obligatory.

It is the task of the WH-Movement transformation to convert the Deep Structure into another phrase marker, a Surface Structure, which does exhibit the proper order relation among the words. The WH-Movement transformation moves an NP with so-called "WH-features" into an empty Spec of CP at the beginning of a clause. In the present example, the transformation moves the NP "who" (which is marked [+WH] in the tree, to identify it as bearing WH-features) to the appropriate position. Now we can see why there is an extra NP at the beginning of the clause: this NP, at Surface Structure, corresponds to the NP at the end of the clause, at Deep Structure. Notice that this explains the fact that we understand "who" as the object of "speak to." The question is asking who was spoken to (by Al). We understand the sentence in relation to the Deep Structure position of the WH-word.

What will the Surface Structure look like? First, we know that the WH-word occupies the Spec of CP position in the Surface Structure. There are two possibilities to consider regarding the structure of the phrase marker following WH-Movement, with respect to the position from which the WH-word is moved. One possibility is that the position that the WH-phrase moves from is completely eliminated. This would result in the phrase marker in (5) for the present example.

(5)

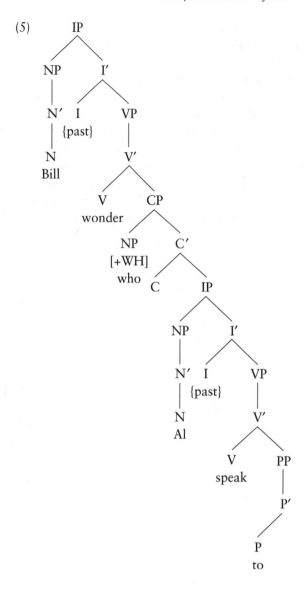

A second possibility, known as the **trace theory of movement,** is that a marker of the WH-phrase that previously occupied this position is left behind following WH-Movement. On this analysis, the Surface Structure phrase marker keeps a record of the Deep Structure position of the moved WH-phrase. This record takes the form of a **trace,** abbreviated *t,* as illustrated in the phrase marker in (6). The theoretical and empirical motivation for leaving behind a trace of any moved constituent is discussed in later chapters. For now, we will follow the convention of leaving a trace from WH-Movement. However, to keep the trees from becoming too complex, we will not mark the trace of Subject–Auxiliary Inversion. It will become clearer in later chapters why we make this distinction between these two operations. Trace Theory has wide consequences within the theory of Universal Grammar.

(6)

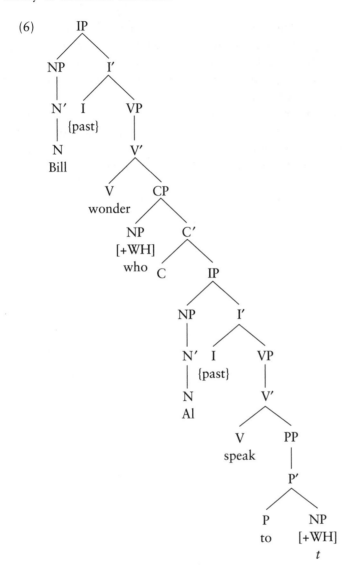

2   WH-Movement in Direct Questions

We now turn to consideration of WH-Movement in **direct questions**, that is, those which the listener is expected to answer. To begin, compare the indirect question in (7a) with the direct question in (7b).

(7) a.   Bill wonders who Al will speak to.
     b.   Who will Al speak to?

As before, our target is the Surface Structure of (7b), the result of applying the
WH-Movement transformation. But we must see how this transformation applies
for direct questions. We begin by deciding what is the Deep Structure underlying
the Surface Structure. The Deep Structure must be derived from our system of
PS rules. Then, the WH-Movement transformation is applied. This converts
the Deep Structure into the Surface Structure, namely, one with the words in the
right order at the bottom of the phrase marker. Let us call the words at the
bottom of a phrase marker the "terminal string." Our goal is to proceed through
these steps in order to derive a phrase marker with the terminal string, "Who
will Al speak to?"

   The first step is to use the PS rules to generate the Deep Structure. Check for
yourself that (8) is a well-formed Deep Structure.

(8)

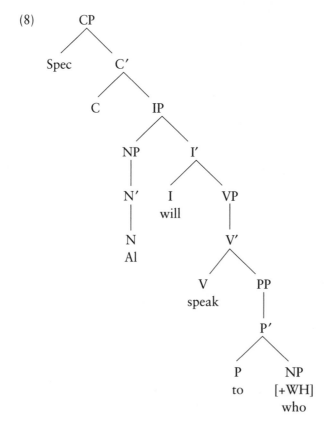

This time, the Deep Structure begins with CP as the topmost node (root) of the
phrase marker. Thus, the first PS rule that is used will be: CP → Spec C′. Note

that, as with an indirect question, the Spec and head C nodes are empty. It is a special property of CP that its specifier (and head) can appear empty at the level of Deep Structure. Although empty initially, the specifier serves as a "landing site" for the WH-phrase to move into at Surface Structure. Also note that this example contains the auxiliary verb "will" in I.

Having constructed the Deep Structure, we are in position to apply the WH-Movement transformation. In the present example, this rule must move the NP "who" (which bears the [+WH] feature) to the Spec of CP position at the beginning of the sentence. The result is given in (9).

(9)

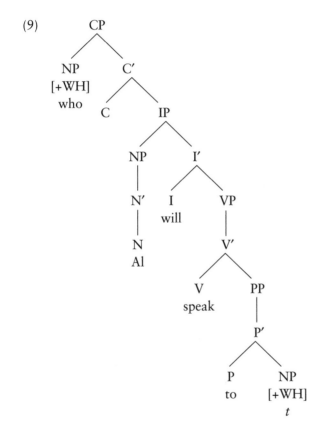

This phrase marker is not yet the desired result. Notice that the words "Al" and "will" are in the wrong order. If the CP in (9) followed the verb "wonder" in an indirect question, as in "Bill wondered who Al will speak to," the words "Al" and "will" would be in the correct order. But, this is a difference between indirect questions and direct questions. An additional transformation is needed to obtain the correct Surface Structure for matrix (main clause) WH-questions. Since more than one transformation has to apply, we will call the structure

above, which was derived on the way from the Deep Structure to the Surface
Structure, an **Intermediate Structure**.

What is the additional transformation that is needed? The additional transformation must change the order of the subject noun phrase (Al) and the auxiliary
verb (will). That is, the additional transformation is Subject–Auxiliary Inversion,
which we discussed in chapter 16. As we saw there, SAI moves the element in I
to the head of CP (i.e., C). The result will be the structure given in (10). (As
mentioned earlier, we will not include the trace left by I-to-C movement in our
diagrams. Under current linguistic theory, it has a different status from the trace
left by WH-Movement.)

(10)

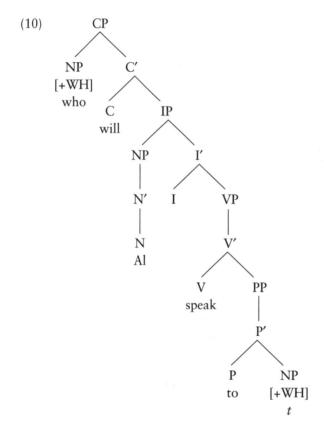

This is the correct Surface Structure, because the terminal string of words is in
the correct order for pronunciation.

When does the rule of SAI need to apply? So far, we have seen that it applies
in direct questions, but it does not apply in indirect questions. If you think of
more examples, you will see that this is always the case. What would happen if
SAI applied in an indirect question? To find out, let's consider the indirect question given in (11).

(11)   Bill wonders who Al will speak to.

The relevant difference between this sentence and the sentence diagrammed in the previous section ("Bill wondered who Al spoke to") is that this sentence uses the auxiliary "will." In (11), there is a subject NP (Al) in the embedded clause, and an auxiliary (will) in the embedded clause which could invert with the subject. But, if we try applying the rule of SAI, the result would be (12).

(12)   *Bill wonders who will Al speak to.

Since (12) is ungrammatical, we know that SAI does not apply in indirect questions. We are just going to stipulate that SAI applies in direct WH-questions, but not in indirect questions. You will always be able to tell if SAI has applied, simply by looking at the subject and the auxiliary in the Surface Structure. If the subject is first, SAI has not applied. If the auxiliary is first, SAI has applied.

Subject questions

If you look back at all the examples of WH-Movement we have given so far, you will see that in every case the constituent that has moved has been an object – in fact, the object of a preposition. It is important to point out that objects are not the only constituents which can be affected by WH-Movement. Adjuncts undergo WH-Movement in much the same way as objects. Subjects can also be questioned. However, when subjects are questioned there are interesting consequences, especially for SAI. Let's look at an example to see how this is.

First, consider the following subject question:

(13)   Who walked Socks?

This is a subject question, because it is the subject – the person who took Socks for a walk – which is being questioned. What is the Deep Structure for this question? If you try to construct the Deep Structure by using the PS rules, the structure in (14) will be the result.

(14)

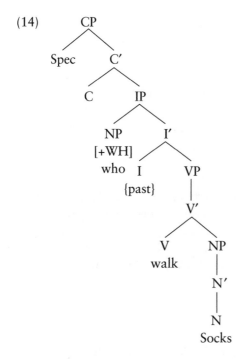

Notice that the subject "who" is in the subject position, not in the Spec of CP (yet). Now, to move the [+WH] phrase to Spec of CP, we use the WH-Movement transformation. The result is given in (15).

(15)

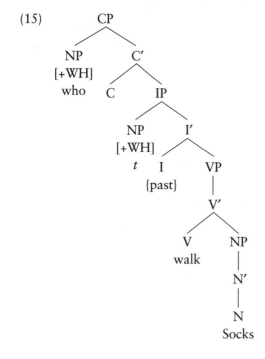

You have probably noticed that this change in the structure does not affect the way the sentence is pronounced. The WH-word "who" was first in the Deep Structure, and it is still first in the Surface Structure. However, we will still claim that the subject WH-word moves to Spec of CP. There are two reasons for this. First, we will consider another type of question, long-distance questions, later in this part, and there we will see that subject WH-elements do move, so to maintain our generalization we will say that matrix subject WH-phrases are not an exception, but move like all other WH-phrases. Second, the interpretation of all WH-questions involves a notion called **scope**. Scope tells us whether the question is direct or indirect, for example. The most straightforward way to define scope uses CP: a WH-phrase has scope over the clause in which it appears in CP. Thus, subject questions must have a WH-word in CP for the correct scope. (We will discuss scope further in chapter 19.)

Now, consider whether SAI should apply in the derivation of subject questions. Tree (15) shows the structure after WH-Movement has applied, but SAI has not applied. What happens if SAI applies in the derivation of subject questions? The result is shown in (16).

(16)

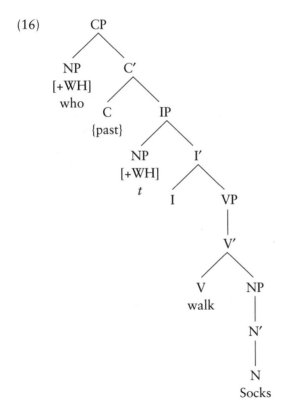

How is (16) to be pronounced? Notice that the affix {past} in C must have a host. Can it combine with "walk" in V by affix-hopping? Not if we maintain the constraint on affix-hopping which requires an affix to be adjacent to the verb. In (16), the WH-trace comes between the affix {past} and the verb. Even though they are not pronounced, WH-traces do block certain phonological processes. In chapter 23 we will see a clear example of this. So, we will assume here that the WH-trace blocks affix-hopping. In this case, Do-support must be applied. If we apply Do-support, however, we do not derive the correct question ("Who walked Socks?"). Instead, we derive (17).

(17)   *Who did walk Socks?

Do-support is not allowed in subject questions unless the "do" is emphatic. This tells us that SAI must not apply in subject questions. This means that tree (15) represents the Surface Structure of the question. All that is needed is for {past} to hop onto the verb, and the correct question will result.

Conclusion

In this chapter, we have seen the application of WH-Movement in direct and indirect questions. WH-Movement moves a WH-element to Spec of CP, leaving behind a trace. In direct WH-questions (except matrix subject questions), SAI also applies. So far, we have only discussed relatively simple WH-questions. We will continue to concentrate on simple (one-clause) WH-questions for now, turning to examine some of the cross-linguistic aspects of the structure and acquisition of simple WH-questions. Later in this part, however, we will turn to examine more complex WH-questions, which serve to illustrate several constraints of UG.

Bibliographical Comments

WH-Movement has been, and continues to be, one of the most extensively researched areas of syntax. The two specific transformations discussed in this chapter, WH-Movement and Subject Auxiliary–Inversion, were first proposed in Chomsky (1957) and Chomsky (1975). Other early analyses of WH-questions are proposed in Bach (1971), Baker (1970), Klima (1964), and Ross (1967). More introductory discussions of these two transformations are given in Baker (1978), Radford (1981), and Emonds (1976). For early discussion of trace theory see Chomsky (1976), Fiengo (1977), and Wasow (1972).

19 Cross-Linguistic Aspects of WH-Questions

Introduction

We have seen several properties of WH-questions in English, including the application of WH-Movement and Subject–Auxiliary Inversion. In later chapters, we will see how constraints apply to restrict the operation of WH-Movement, and how children perform with respect to these constraints. First, however, we will step back for a moment and ask which aspects of our current treatment of WH-questions are part of UG, and which are particular to English. If WH-Movement and SAI are universal, then they can be part of the innate component of grammar, and we can expect to see evidence of them in very young children. On the other hand, if there are aspects which require learning or parameter setting, these may be acquired later.

1 Cross-Linguistic Variation in WH-Movement

In our discussion of English, we have seen that WH-Movement moves a WH-phrase to the specifier of CP position, which is at the beginning of the clause. After studying a large number of languages, many linguists believe that these two aspects of WH-questions are universal:

(1) WH-Movement universally moves a WH-phrase to Spec CP
     Spec CP is universally on the left

This claim would reasonably lead you to believe that WH-phrases appear at the beginning of the clause in all languages. This, however, is not true.

All languages have WH-questions. However, not all languages show WH-Movement in the surface order of questions. For example, in numerous languages, including Japanese (an SOV language), and Chinese (which is SVO),

WH-words can remain in their Deep Structure position, as illustrated in (2)–(3). When a WH-word remains in this position on the surface, it is said to be *in situ*.

(2) *Japanese*
John-ga   **dare-ni**   sono hon-o   age-ta   no
John-NOM who-DAT that book-ACC give-PST Q
"Who did John give that book to?"

(3) *Chinese*
ni   kanjian-le **shei**
you see-ASP   who
"Who did you see?"

In yet other languages, WH-phrases can either remain in their Deep Structure position, or optionally move to the topmost specifier of CP. One example of a language of this type is French, in which a WH-phrase may move or remain in its Deep Structure position only in matrix clauses. Examples are shown in (4a) and (4b) respectively.

(4) a. **qui** as-tu   vu
       who have-you seen
       "Who did you see?"

    b. tu   as   vu   **qui**
       you have seen who
       "Who did you see?"

Do these facts require us to reject the claim that the phenomena in (1) are universal? No, these differences in the surface form of WH-questions can be accounted for by considering a further level of the grammar which we have not yet discussed. We have seen so far two levels of syntax: Deep Structure and Surface Structure. We also know that the Surface Structure gives us the order of the words as they are actually pronounced. The component of the grammar which takes care of the pronunciation is called the **Phonetic Form**. So far, then, the model of the grammar which we have discussed can be illustrated as in figure 19.1.

However, the model as given is incomplete. There is an additional component needed, which is called **Logical Form**. This is the representation which gives important information for the semantics, or meaning, of the utterance. A diagram of the model including the relationship between Logical Form and the other levels is given in figure 19.2.

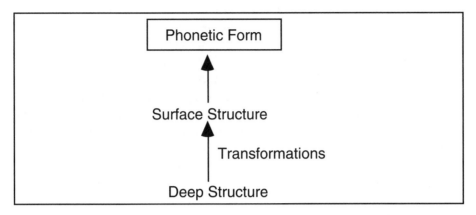

Figure 19.1   The model of the grammar so far

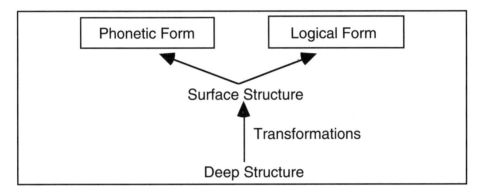

Figure 19.2   The revised model of the grammar

What purpose does Logical Form (or LF) serve? Just as Phonetic Form can be considered as an interface between language and pronunciation, Logical Form is the interface between language and thought. One important function of language is to communicate thought. To do this, some concept must be translated into language, and transmitted by the movements of our vocal organs (or hands and body, in the case of signed languages). Logical Form connects the language component to the concept component, and Phonetic Form connects it to the pronunciation component.

The operations which transform Surface Structures into structures of Logical Form are very similar to the operations in the syntax (the mapping from Deep Structure to Surface Structure). In fact, it has been proposed that one of the ways in which languages may differ from each other is that some operations may apply in the mapping from Deep Structure to Surface Structure in some languages, but in the mapping from Surface Structure to Logical Form in others. WH-Movement is one such operation.

A linguist named James Huang argued that the difference between languages such as English and languages such as Japanese or Chinese was not whether or not WH-Movement applies, but the level at which it applies. He claimed that at the level of LF, all WH-phrases occupy the clause-initial position. Thus, in Japanese and Chinese, WH-Movement applies between Surface Structure and LF – hence the movement is **covert**, or not reflected in the pronunciation, which is read off the Surface Structure, before the WH-Movement applies. On the other hand, in English WH-Movement applies between Deep Structure and Surface Structure, so it is **overt** – we pronounce the words in the moved order.

Huang reasoned as follows. As we mentioned before, in English the position of a WH-element aids in the interpretation of its "scope" – that is, whether it is in a direct or an indirect question. A WH-element in the matrix specifier of CP position signals a direct question, while a WH-element in an embedded specifier of CP position signals an indirect question. Examples of these two kinds of questions in English are given in (5).

(5) a. **Who** does Mary believe bought books?
     b. I wonder **who** Mary saw.

Huang pointed out that Chinese has direct and indirect questions too. However, in Chinese, the WH-element is pronounced in the Deep Structure position, in both direct and indirect questions. Some examples are given in (6).

(6) a. Zhangsan xiangxin **shei** mai-le shu?
         Zhangsan believe   who bought books
         "Who does Zhangsan believe bought books?"

     b. wo xiang-zhidao Lisi mai-le **sheme**
         I   wonder   Lisi bought what
         "I wonder what Lisi bought."

What indicates in Chinese whether the question is a direct or an indirect question? Huang suggested that the same signal is used in both languages: direct questions have a WH-word in the matrix specifier of CP, while indirect questions have a WH-word in an embedded specifier of CP – but in Chinese, only the Logical Form shows this distinction (while in English, both the Surface Structure and the Logical Form show it). The "invisible" movement of the WH-word on the way to Logical Form in Chinese results in the same scope information as in other languages at the level of Logical Form.

This, then, is another example of parametric differences allowed by Universal Grammar. UG permits languages to use the transformation WH-Movement to create WH-questions. UG requires that WH-elements be in their "scope" positions at Logical Form (the representation that is relevant to meaning). But UG allows some languages to employ WH-Movement between Deep Structure and Surface Structure, while others employ it between Surface Structure and Logical Form. Thus, the parametric variation between languages such as English, Japanese or Chinese, and French, is in what level WH-Movement applies at, not whether it applies at all.

There is another reason to believe that in some languages WH-Movement applies in the mapping from Surface Structure to LF, and this has to do with **multiple questions**. Consider the English examples in (7).

(7) a. **Who** bought **what**?
     b. *__Who what__ bought?

The question in (7a) is about both "who" and "what" – this is why it is called a "multiple question." The expected answer to (7) is a paired list, such as that in (8).

(8) John bought chips,
     Alice bought salsa,
     and Kim bought soda.

In other words, if we consider the scope of the question in (7a), we would say that both "who" and "what" have matrix scope – the respondent is expected to answer both questions. But we have seen that a WH-phrase should be in the specifier of the matrix CP if it has matrix scope (compare this to the Chinese examples). Thus, even in English, WH-Movement sometimes applies in the mapping from Surface Structure to LF. In particular, English allows only one WH-phrase to move to each Spec of CP overtly (we know this because (7b) is ungrammatical), so in multiple questions the other(s) must move covertly, that is, after Surface Structure.

Further evidence for the claim that all WH-elements move to the specifier of the CP at which they take scope comes by looking at multiple questions in Slavic languages such as Bulgarian and Romanian. In these and other languages, more than one WH-phrase can move overtly, as illustrated in (9)–(10).

(9) *Bulgarian*
     Koj kogo vižda?
     who whom sees
     "Who sees whom?"

(10) *Romanian*
     Cine cu ce   merge?
     who with what goes
     "Who goes by what (i.e. means of transportation)?"

These languages show us that every WH-element can be in Spec of CP at Surface Structure. Then, just as we argued that in Chinese, WH-Movement applies from Surface Structure to LF, we can see that the same is true for English. The difference is that in English, one WH-element must move overtly, so covert movement is used only for multiple questions, while in Chinese, all WH-elements move covertly.

2 Cross-Linguistic Variation in I-to-C Movement

We have seen that WH-Movement is a universal operation, although languages may differ in the level at which it applies. What about SAI, the other operation we associate with WH-questions in English?

We showed that SAI is I-to-C movement. This makes it an example of a more general kind of operation known as Head Movement. Notice that both I – the thing moving – and C – the landing site – are *heads*, as we defined them in our discussion of Phrase Structure. This points to an important property of movement operations: heads move to head positions, while XPs move to XP positions. This general restriction on movement keeps the structure from changing too radically.

As the foregoing discussion indicates, Head Movement is a general operation made available in UG. So, children do not have to learn how Head Movement operates (for example, they do not need to learn that heads only move to heads). However, the particular instance of Head Movement we have been calling SAI is NOT a universal aspect of WH- or yes/no questions. Some languages are like English in having inversion, but others are not. For example, Russian does not use inversion in the formation of either yes/no or WH-questions, as illustrated in (11).

(11) *Russian*
    a. A   Ivan sdal   ekzamen?
         PRT Ivan passed exam
         "Did Ivan pass the exam?"

    b. čto Maša kupila v magazine?
         what Masha bought in store
         "What did Masha buy in the store?"

Furthermore, some languages raise all verbs to C, not just auxiliary verbs, as in English. For example, in French and Spanish questions (illustrated in (12)–(13)) the inflected verb appears in C.

(12) *French*

a. Où   vas-tu?
where go-you
"Where are you going?"

b. Veux-tu   un café?
want-you a   coffee
"Do you want a coffee?"

(13) *Spanish*

a. A dónde va   Juan?
where   goes Juan
"Where is Juan going?"

b. Trabaja María hoy?
works   Maria today
"Does Maria work today?"

In yet other languages, verbs move to C in questions and in declaratives. German, illustrated in (14), is a well-known example. In yes/no questions (14a), the verb appears first. In WH-questions (14b), the WH-element appears first (in Spec of CP), and the inflected verb is next (in C). In declaratives (14c, d), something must precede the verb, but it is generally assumed that the verb is in C, since the verb must always be "second," whatever element (subject or object or adjunct) is first.

(14) *German*

a. *Kauft* Karl das Buch?
buys Karl the book
"Does Karl buy the book?"

b. **Was** *kauft* Karl?
what buys   Karl
"What does Karl buy?"

c. Dieses Buch *kaufte* Karl gestern.
this   book bought Karl yesterday
"This book Karl bought yesterday."

d. Gestern   *kaufte* Karl dieses Buch.
yesterday bought Karl this   book
"Yesterday Karl bought this book."

In languages with verbs in C, inversion can be thought of as involving V-to-I (head) movement as well as I-to-C (head) movement. However, unlike WH-Movement, there is no reason to think that inversion applies in the mapping from Surface Structure to Logical Form. No interpretive considerations require such movement. Hence, the application of SAI in questions is something that children must learn on the basis of experience with their target language.

One further comment about what is universal and what is language-particular in the syntax of questions. English is almost unique in its rule of Do-support. Of course, the word "do" is English-particular, so there can be no rule "Do-support" in UG. But even more abstractly, the use of a dummy verb to support a stranded affix as a last resort is not common. Hence, English-learning children will have to deduce the properties of this operation on the basis of their input, without much help from UG.

Conclusion

We have seen that there are both universal and language-particular aspects of WH- and yes/no questions. WH-Movement is a universal operation, made available by UG. The level at which it applies: from Deep Structure to Surface Structure, or from Surface Structure to Logical Form, does vary from language to language. In fact, some languages have both overt and covert WH-Movement (such as French, which allows either overt or covert movement for all matrix questions, and English, which requires only one WH-element to move overtly, and thus has covert movement for multiple questions). Children must learn which kind of language is being spoken around them, but exposure to a few basic WH-questions should inform them about the correct parameter setting. On the other hand, the application of inversion is much more varied. The existence of Head Movement is allowed by UG, but its application in questions is subject to much more learning. Therefore, we might expect to see a difference between children's acquisition of WH-Movement and their acquisition of inversion. This is the topic to which we turn in the next chapter.

Bibliographical Comments

The existence of a level of Logical Form is argued for by May (1977, 1985), and an overview of the properties of LF under current theory is found in Hornstein (1995). An introduction to many of the properties of LF representations, including the interpretation of WH-questions, is found in Riemsdijk and Williams (1986). Huang (1982) is the classic work on LF WH-Movement in Chinese and English. Lasnik and Uriagereka (1988) provides a lucid introduction to the main issues found in Huang's thesis. For technical discussion of LF movement of WH-phrases in English multiple questions, see Aoun, Hornstein, and Sportiche (1980). For discussion of multiple questions in Slavic languages, see Rudin (1988).

20 The Acquisition of WH-Questions

Introduction

Chapter 19 illustrated one of the ways in which languages across the world may differ. Language variation occurs at the level at which WH-Movement takes place. In English, WH-Movement occurs between Deep Structure and Surface Structure; in Chinese and Japanese, WH-Movement takes place at Logical Form. Across all languages, WH-elements must be in their scope positions at Logical Form. Thus, WH-Movement is an area in which we see the influence of both a universal principle (WH-Movement moves WH-elements to the specifier of the CP over which they have scope by the level of Logical Form) and a parameter (WH-Movement may take place between Deep and Surface Structure, or after Surface Structure, at Logical Form). On the other hand, we saw that the application of Subject–Auxiliary Inversion requires language-particular knowledge. Not every language uses inversion in question formation, and some of the details of inversion in English (such as Do-support) must be learned by experience. The question we ask in the present chapter is how children acquire the correct forms of questions in English and other languages.

1 Parameter Setting: WH-Movement

Children's earliest WH-questions in the acquisition of English include examples such as those in (1).

(1) a. What doing?
     b. What dat?
     c. Where Daddy?
     d. Dat?

Children produce simplified questions like these around the age of 2 years. However, note that some of children's earliest questions seem to be *formulaic*.

That is, a child might ask questions like those in (1), but her repertoire may well be limited to only one or two questions. Before the questions show evidence of productivity, they may not necessarily represent the application of the WH-Movement transformation, but simply an unanalyzed string.

Notice also that the WH-question in (1d) is missing a WH-word. Some children at this age do sometimes leave out the WH-word, but their utterance can be interpreted as a question by its intonation or the context of use. Examples with no WH-word, although existent, are relatively rare.

By the age of $2\frac{1}{2}$, on the average, children produce WH-questions like those in (2).

(2)　a.　Who make that?
　　　b.　What Mommy eating?
　　　c.　Where Daddy's going?

Subject and object WH-questions, such as those in (2a) and (2b) respectively, appear at about the same time. Both of these tend to be earlier than adjunct WH-questions, such as that in (2c).

Despite the "errors" in children's questions, it is important to notice that in all of the examples above, the WH-element appears at the beginning of the utterance, as it should be in English. There is no evidence that children learning English go through a stage at which they leave the WH-element in its Deep Structure position. If there were, we would see examples such as those in (3) in young children's productions. Such productions are not attested, however.

(3)　*Not observed:*
　　　a.　Mommy eating what?
　　　b.　Daddy's going where?
　　　c.　You do that why?

Instead of non-moved WH-elements like those in (3), children's utterances display proper WH-Movement from the very beginning. This would seem to be striking evidence of early, accurate parameter setting. Evidence from children learning other languages with overt WH-Movement also shows that this is acquired early. Some examples of early German questions also displaying WH-Movement are given in (4).

(4)　a.　**wo**　Björn wohnt?
　　　　　where Björn lives
　　　　　"Where does Björn live?"

　　　b.　**was**　macht　Birgit?
　　　　　what making Birgit
　　　　　"What is Birgit building?"

In no language has it been reported that children erroneously initially leave the WH-element *in situ* systematically. In fact, although adult French allows both WH-Movement and WH-*in-situ* (as observed in chapter 19), it has been reported that children learning French initially use only moved WH-elements.

An alternative hypothesis to the proposal that young English-speaking children (as well as German-speaking, French-speaking, etc.) have correctly set the WH-Movement parameter is that the English setting might be the default: the setting which is assumed before the evidence is considered. In this case, the fact that young English-learners use the correct position for WH-elements would be attributed to an innate unmarked setting which happens to be the correct one – not to early, accurate consideration of the data.

On this hypothesis, we would expect to see children who are acquiring languages like Japanese and Chinese pass through a stage at which they erroneously apply WH-Movement by Surface Structure. If so, children at this stage would not leave the WH-element in its Deep Structure position. However, this too is not attested in the literature. Children learning covert WH-Movement languages correctly leave the WH-element in its Deep Structure position. Some examples of young Japanese-speaking children's early WH-questions are given in (5).

(5) a. kore wa **nani?**
         this TOP what
         "What is this?"

     b. Papa wa **doko** ni   i-ru?
         Daddy TOP where LOC be-NONPAST
         "Where is Daddy?"

     c. akachan wa **nani** shi-teru   no?
         baby   TOP what do-PRES.PROG PART
         "What is the baby doing?"

Apparently, positioning of the WH-element is acquired very early. To sum up, the available evidence is consistent with early, accurate parameter setting.

2 WH-Movement and SAI

Unlike the early, accurate parameter setting observed for WH-Movement, it has been observed that children sometimes fail to apply SAI in their questions. Examples such as those in (6) are sometimes cited.

(6)   a.   I ride train?
      b.   You want eat?
      c.   I have it?
      d.   We can go now?

Many researchers have claimed that children's earliest yes/no questions are signaled only by intonation, without inversion, as in (6). However, other researchers have found that children who produce non-inverted questions such as (6) may also produce yes/no questions with inversion, as in (7), at the same time.

(7)   a.   Are we talking?
      b.   Is this your baby?
      c.   Does lions walk?
      d.   Are you want one?

A similar discrepancy has been observed regarding inversion in WH-questions. While children produce correctly inverted yes/no questions, they may also produce WH-questions without inversion, such as those in (8).

(8)   a.   What she can drink?
      b.   Why the motorcycle guy is upside down?
      c.   Where the pig could hide?

But at the same time, WH-questions with inversion may also be found, such as those in (9).

(9)   a.   What can you see?
      b.   What will we eat?
      c.   What can he ride in?

How can the range of question types illustrated in (6)–(9) be accounted for?

Since children at an early age do use SAI in some yes/no and WH-questions, it would clearly not be appropriate to attribute the lack of inversion in (6) and (8) to an absence of I-to-C movement. That is, it would not be correct to say that young children do not know the SAI transformation. Instead, the problem seems to be that the transformation is not always applied when it should be.

In the mid-1960s, a researcher named Ursula Bellugi observed that children produce uninverted WH-questions like those in (8) at the same time as inverted yes/no questions like those in (7). Many researchers believed that this represented a stage of language development in which only one transformation could apply at a time. Such a *computational bottleneck* would account for the pattern in (7)–(8) by claiming that children could apply SAI only, in yes/no questions, or

WH-Movement only, in WH-questions, but not both of them together – presumably because of the kind of processing limitation we observed in children's earliest word combinations.

Although a computational bottleneck might be part of the reason for utterances like (8), there is now additional evidence from other types of questions that encourages us to look beyond this explanation. The additional information includes the following observations. First, at the same time that children ask WH-questions without inversion, they may also produce questions with inversion, as shown in (8)–(9). There is no observable period in development during which a child systematically fails to invert in all WH-questions. Second, it has recently been noticed that failure to invert occurs most commonly in adjunct questions, such as the "why" and "where" questions in (8), and not as often in object questions, as in (9). Third, in addition to a few examples like those in (8), it turns out that most of children's non-inverted WH-questions are ones in which Do-support would need to apply, such as those in (10).

(10) a. What you maked?
      b. What Papa have?
      c. Where Mommy go?

If children produce some inverted structures at an early age, what does this say about their grammatical knowledge? Let us separate knowledge of the universal properties of an operation such as SAI from its language-particular aspects. As we have seen, not every language employs a rule like SAI in the formation of questions. Unlike WH-Movement, there is no universal principle requiring an auxiliary in C. However, there are universal constraints on the application of transformations, and these principles will require that if an auxiliary verb (or a tensed main verb, in some languages) does front, it will appear in the C position. Thus, the child acquiring English must learn that English does employ SAI in yes/no and WH-questions; also, the child must learn which lexical elements appear in I (tense, modals, auxiliary "be"), and what happens when an affix such as tense gets separated from the verb (Do-support). Thus, we may expect to find some errors in whether or not SAI is used, and in the form of the auxiliary system, and in the application of Do-support, but not in *how* SAI is applied.

The fact that children do use inversion in examples like those in (7) and (9) indicates that they are employing the universal availability of a rule for moving a verbal element from I to C, from a young age.

Consistent with this is the observation that children learning other languages (such as German) which also use rules moving elements from I to C in questions also may apply the rules at an early age. However, as in English, early German does not seem to systematically show inversion; rather, both inverted and non-inverted questions are found, as illustrated in (11).

(11) *German*
   a. Henning, **wo**   gehst du, Henning?
       Henning where goes you, Henning
       "Where are you going, Henning?"

   b. **Wo**   ich sitzen?
       where I   sit
       "Where do I sit?"

Hence, it is appropriate to analyze children's occasional failure to invert as indicating problems with language-particular aspects of the auxiliary system (including Do-support) rather than as a lack of knowledge of the existence or mechanics of the operation. Another observation consistent with this hypothesis is that young children speaking English sometimes make similar errors in their declaratives, as in the examples in (12), which show auxiliary omission.

(12) a. She eating cracker.
      b. That a doggie.

And the errors they make with auxiliaries in questions go beyond lack of inversion: they also may make errors of auxiliary selection, or doubled auxiliaries, as in the examples in (13).

(13) a. Where can you go? (for *Where did you go?*)
      b. Are you want one?
      c. Why is he will stop?
      d. Why does he doesn't like that?

This pattern tells us that our separation between language-universal and language-particular is appropriate. Children do not show evidence that their knowledge of Subject–Auxiliary Inversion is incorrect. Rather, their knowledge of the English-particular inflectional system takes some time to develop. This is what the Principles and Parameters theory predicts. Further evidence for this position will be brought up in the following chapters.

Conclusion

We have seen evidence for the UG theory in considering children's early WH-question formation. However, even stronger evidence can be found by considering constraints that UG imposes on the application of WH-Movement. These constraints distinguish between cases in which WH-Movement is allowed and those in which it is prohibited. In effect, constraints rule out certain sentences as ill formed – sentences which would otherwise be expected to be well formed. Hence, they provide an excellent source of evidence for innate knowledge. Without innate knowledge of constraints, children would be expected to make mistakes which violate them, and in fact they would not be able to acquire the knowledge that certain strings are ungrammatical without negative evidence. Thus, in the next several chapters we will discuss the nature of the constraints that apply in the adult language, and evidence of children's adherence to these universal principles. This discussion will provide evidence supporting the theory of Universal Grammar.

Bibliographical Comments

The earliest work on the acquisition of WH-questions using Transformational Grammar was Bellugi (1965). This report and others of the time by Bellugi and her colleagues give her observations on children's questions and her computational bottleneck hypothesis. Many studies since have examined the acquisition of simple WH-questions in English, particularly paying attention to inversion. A good summary of previous works with an extensive review of spontaneous production data on the acquisition of auxiliaries is Stromswold (1990). The data on the acquisition of Japanese are from Clancy (1985), and the data on German came from Wode (1971).

21   Successive Cyclic Movement

Introduction

Chapter 18 introduced indirect questions and single-clause direct questions. We now turn to another kind of question, called **long-distance questions**. In these questions, the WH-word moves long distance – out of an embedded clause. Its final resting place is the matrix CP. We will see that there are constraints on the application of WH-Movement in the derivation of long-distance questions. The next chapter describes children's knowledge of these constraints on WH-Movement.

1   Long-Distance Dependencies

Compare the indirect question in (1a) with the long-distance question in (1b).

(1)   a.   Bill wonders who Al will speak to.
       b.   Who will Bill say Al spoke to?

Since the long-distance question in (1b) has a WH-word in initial position, and a preposition at the end, it is safe to assume that this kind of question is derived by WH-Movement. To illustrate the derivation, let us first look at the Deep Structure for the long-distance question in (1b), given in (2). As with single-clause matrix questions, the Deep Structure begins with an empty Spec of CP node, which comes from the PS rule CP → Spec C′.

(2)

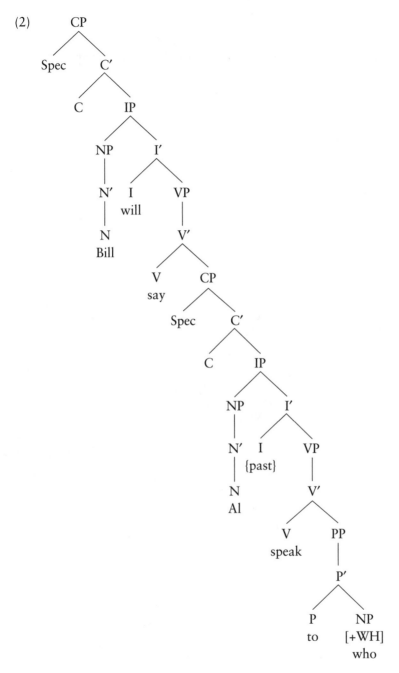

Having constructed the Deep Structure, we are ready to apply the WH-Movement transformation. In the present example, this rule must move the NP "who" (which bears the [+WH] feature) to the CP position at the initial position of the phrase marker. The empty Spec of CP at the beginning of the embedded clause is used as a temporary landing site for the movement of the WH-word "who." As the WH-word moves through this empty Spec, it leaves behind a trace. Finally, it continues its journey until it reaches the matrix Spec of CP. The result of this long-distance movement is given in (3).

(3)

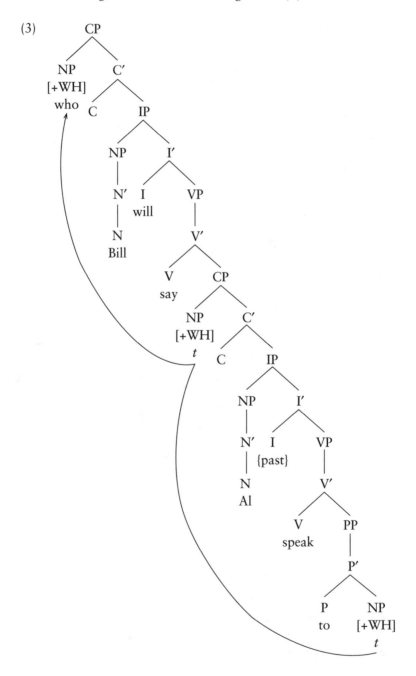

Since the target sentence is a direct long-distance question (rather than an indirect question), an additional transformation is still needed. The Subject–Auxiliary Inversion transformation (SAI) must apply to (3) because it is ill-formed as it stands. By SAI, the subject "Bill" and the auxiliary "will" are inverted. The phrase marker that results is the target Surface Structure, which yields a well-formed sentence, diagrammed in (4). Notice that the terminal string of words in (4) is now in the correct order for pronunciation.

(4)

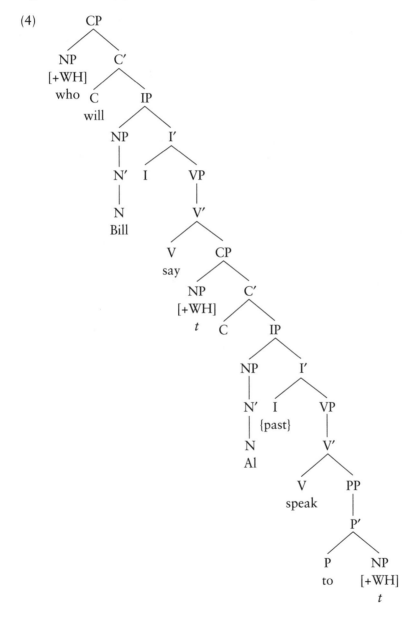

2   What Long-Distance Movement Explains

Now let us extend the WH-Movement transformation still further, to move a WH-phrase that is three clauses away from its landing site at its origin, at Deep Structure. We will use this example to show two things. First, we show that WH-Movement can move a WH-phrase a very long distance. In fact, as long as the constraints on WH-Movement (some of which are discussed in this chapter) are not violated, WH-Movement is unbounded – there is no limit to how far the WH-phrase can move. We have also thrown another wrinkle into the example. In the examples below, the sentence-initial WH-phrase agrees in number with the verb two clauses away. This kind of "long-distance dependency" was discussed in chapter 4, as a problem for Behaviorism. Subject–verb agreement is usually local: the verb agrees with the subject of its clause, which usually comes right before it. However, in the examples below the subject appears far from the verb. We will now show that this linguistic phenomenon poses no problem for Transformational Grammar.

The sentences we are concerned with are given in (5).

(5)   a.   Which country did Bill say Hussein thinks has/*have oil?
      b.   Which countries did Bill say Hussein thinks have/*has oil?

First, we need to establish the Deep Structures for these sentences. We will use the notation [+WH, +SING] to stand for the singular WH-phrase "which country," and [+WH, +PL] will stand for the plural WH-phrase "which countries." The Deep Structure is given in (6).

(6)

```
        CP
       /  \
    Spec   C'
          /  \
         C    IP
            /    \
          NP      I'
          |      /  \
          N'    I    VP
          |   {past}  |
          N          V'
         Bill       /  \
               V     CP
              say  /    \
                 Spec    C'
                        /  \
                       C    IP
                          /    \
                        NP      I'
                        |      /  \
                        N'    I    VP
                        |  {pres}   |
                        N          V'
                     Hussein      /  \
                              V     CP
                            think  /   \
                                Spec    C'
                                       /  \
                                      C    IP
                                         /    \
                                       NP      I'
                                       |      /  \
                                       |     I    VP
                                       |  {pres}   |
                                       |          V'
                                       |         /  \
                                       |        V    NP
                                   {+WH }      has    |
                                   {+SING}            N'
                                                      |
                                   {+WH}     have     N
                                   {+PL}             oil
```

The explanation for the apparent long-distance agreement is as follows. The WH-phrase that appears at the front of these questions originates next to the agreeing verb, right before "have" or "has," at Deep Structure. At Deep Structure, the process of agreement takes place. The WH-phrase, marked [+SING] or [+PL], calls for a verb-form of the same type ([+SING] or [+PL]). This happens before WH-Movement, making agreement between the subject and verb in any clause a strictly local affair. So, agreement in long-distance questions is just as straightforward as it is in simple sentences like those in (7).

(7) a. Iraq has/*have oil.
    b. Iraq and Kuwait have/*has oil.

In long-distance WH-questions, agreement is settled at the level of Deep Structure, before movement of the WH-phrase takes place. After the WH-phrase is moved, at Surface Structure there is still agreement, but only at a distance. The Surface Structure corresponding to the Deep Structure in (6) is given in (8).

(8)

```
                    CP
          ┌──────────┴──────┐
     { +WH  }             C'
     { +SING }      ┌──────┴──────┐
                    C            IP
          ┌─────────┴──────┐
     { +WH }   NP          I'
     { +PL  }   |     ┌────┴────┐
                N'    I        VP
                |              |
                N   {past}     V'
                |         ┌────┴────┐
               Bill       V        CP
                         say   ┌───┴────┐
                               NP       C'
                              [+WH] ┌───┴───┐
                                t   C      IP
                              ┌─────┴────┐
                              NP         I'
                              |     ┌────┴────┐
                              N'    I        VP
                              |              |
                              N   {pres}     V'
                              |         ┌────┴────┐
                           Hussein      V        CP
                                      think  ┌───┴────┐
                                             NP       C'
                                            [+WH] ┌───┴───┐
                                              t   C      IP
                                                ┌─────┴────┐
                                                NP         I'
                                               [+WH] ┌─────┴────┐
                                                 t   I         VP
                                                  {pres}       V'
                                                        ┌──────┴──────┐
                                                        V            NP
                                                    { has }          N'
                                                    { have }          |
                                                                      N
                                                                     oil
```

In sum, we have seen that long-distance WH-Movement can be "unbounded," and yet there can be long-distance dependencies between a WH-element in one part of a sentence and another element indefinitely far away. There are, however, certain constraints on long-distance WH-Movement that we need to discuss. These constraints are good examples of the kind of constraint we have argued must be part of UG: they account for the ungrammaticality of certain examples which might otherwise be expected to be grammatical; and it turns out that they are also universal. Hence, we expect that children will show early adherence to constraints on long-distance movement. In the next sections of this chapter, we will discuss two constraints on WH-Movement, and in the next chapter we will present evidence that children do indeed respect them at an early age.

3   Successive Cyclic Movement

We have seen that long-distance WH-questions are formed, in part, by moving the WH-phrase through an embedded CP. In examples with two embedded clauses, the WH-phrase passes through both embedded CP positions. In order for a WH-phrase to reach the matrix CP, it is *required* to pass through each intervening CP in succession, no matter how many there are. This type of movement is called "Successive Cyclic WH-Movement." Each embedded clause constitutes a "cycle" within which transformations apply. Thus, movement of a WH-word from an object position, say, to the first CP up, is movement within one cycle. Then, movement from the first CP to the next CP up is made at the next cycle up. Hence, movement through each embedded CP will be successive cyclic – one cycle after another, in succession.

Why must WH-Movement occur in successive cycles? Why not just have a WH-word move to its final CP in one fell swoop? The proposal that WH-Movement occurs in successive cycles is necessary to explain certain facts about WH-questions. These facts concern ungrammatical sentences which would be generated if such a constraint were absent from UG. To see this, first consider the indirect question given in (9).

(9)   Bill knows which program Newt will vote against.

In this type of sentence, WH-Movement applies, but the result is not a direct question, which the listener is supposed to answer. Rather, the WH-phrase only moves to the beginning of the embedded clause, and no answer is expected. Now, suppose the Deep Structure of this sentence has "who" instead of "Newt" in the embedded subject position. This would be the case if the speaker wanted to know which candidate Bill knows about. This Deep Structure string is given in (10).

(10)   [DS]   Bill {pres} know who will vote against which program.

If "which program" undergoes WH-Movement to the Spec of the embedded CP, the following Intermediate Structure would be derived.[1]

(11)   [IS]   Bill {pres} know which program who will vote against *t*.

If WH-Movement applied to "who" in this Intermediate Structure to make a direct WH-question, it would have to move the "who" over the "which program" in the specifier of the embedded CP. The result would not be a grammatical sentence of English, as (12) illustrates. (To help keep track of the multiple traces, we number each trace and its antecedent (e.g., who$_1$ goes with t_1; which program$_2$ goes with t_2), and as usual we leave out traces of SAI.)

(12)   *Who$_1$ {pres} Bill know which program$_2$ t_1 will vote against t_2?

The derivation of this ungrammatical string is given in (13).

(13)

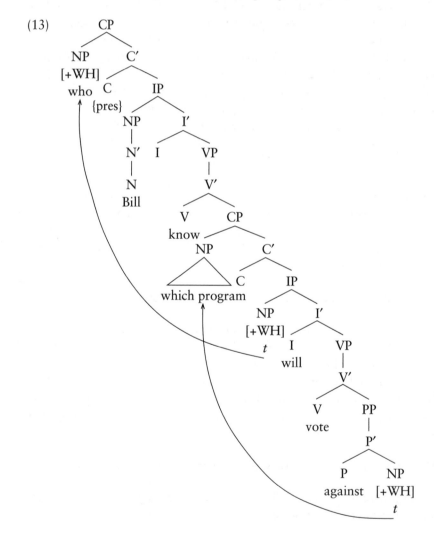

The problem with (13) is that "who" must move from its position in the embedded clause to the matrix specifier of CP without stopping in the embedded specifier of CP, since it is already filled. Example (13) shows us that WH-Movement must go successive cyclically, through each specifier of CP. When this type of movement is blocked, the WH-question cannot be formed (i.e., the sentence is ungrammatical).

Because a WH-element cannot move out of an indirect question, such a structure is sometimes called an "island" for movement. That is, the embedded clause with its Spec of CP filled becomes an island prohibiting any other WH-element from moving off it. Other structures are also islands for movement, and the "island constraints" are an important part of Universal Grammar.

Successive Cyclic Movement is a core part of the operation of WH-Movement. There are numerous other types of examples which show that movement of a WH-element must proceed one clause at a time. However, this is not the only constraint on WH-Movement. We will turn now to another constraint, known as the Empty Category Principle. Although this is rather technical, we will see in the next chapter that very young children are (tacitly) aware of it.

4   The Empty Category Principle

There is a constraint that pertains to the trace left behind by movement. This constraint is called the **Empty Category Principle** (ECP). Like other constraints, the ECP is used to rule out ungrammatical sentences; hence, it must be innate, and is predicted to hold universally. In the case of the ECP, however, there are some parametric differences in the ways that it is applied cross-linguistically. This makes it more complex, and it makes the acquisition story more complicated as well.

However, it is useful to see that even cross-linguistic variation can be accounted for within the theory of Principles and Parameters of Universal Grammar, and that complicated facts can be accounted for in an elegant theory. To the extent that parametric differences among languages are innately specified, the problems of language acquisition in the absence of negative evidence are reduced.

The *that–trace effect*

We have seen that WH-Movement out of an embedded clause must take place through the embedded specifier of CP. It is important to point out that movement must go through the *specifier* of CP. An element in the CP *head* need not block long-distance WH-extraction. Consider the sentences in (14)–(17).

(14) a. I think   Sarah will hire Bob.
      b. I think that Sarah will hire Bob.

(15) a. Who do you think   Sarah will hire *t*?
      b. Who do you think that Sarah will hire *t*?

(16) a. I think   Bill will win.
      b. I think that Bill will win.

(17) a.   Who do you think   *t* will win?
      b. *Who do you think that *t* will win?

In (14) and (16), we see that the complementizer "that" is optional in (such) declarative sentences. In (15), we see that the complementizer clearly does not block movement, since it can be present in a WH-question. "That" does not block movement because it is a head – it occupies the C position. WH-Movement goes through the specifier of CP, so an element in the head position need not block movement. In (15), the WH-phrase "who" begins as the object of the embedded verb. It moves through the embedded specifier of CP, and lands in the matrix specifier of CP. Since there is nothing in the embedded specifier of CP to block movement, these questions satisfy Successive Cyclic Movement, and grammatical WH-questions result.

However, the long-distance subject questions in (17) are different. In (17b), the presence of the complementizer "that" appears to make the sentence ungrammatical, compared to the grammatical (17a) without the complementizer. From what we have seen so far, we would expect that these sentences would both be fine. The WH-element "who" begins in the embedded subject position. It moves through the embedded specifier of CP (which is not occupied), and lands in the matrix specifier of CP. Why then is (17b) ungrammatical?

Let us examine the similarities and differences between the sentences in (14)–(17) carefully to see exactly what the problem is. The examples in (14) and (16) seem to show us that the complementizer is always optional in declarative sentences. The WH-questions in (15) show that it is possible to have a complementizer in some WH-questions. The major difference between the sentences in (15) and those in (17) is that the questions in (15) are *object* questions – the trace is in object position; while the questions in (17) are *subject* questions – the trace is in subject position. It seems that the complementizer is optional when extraction is from the *object* position of an embedded clause, but it is not allowed when extraction takes place from the embedded *subject* position.

The observation that sentences of the type in (17b) are ungrammatical has come to be known as the *that–trace effect. Roughly, (17b) is ungrammatical because "that" is followed by a trace. Such sequences are apparently ruled out.

We could simply say that the sequence "that–trace" is ungrammatical: *that–trace. However, we want to account for this effect in more general terms, terms that refer to structure, and terms that will apply to languages other than English. We turn now to this more abstract principle.

The Empty Category Principle

The difference in grammaticality between subject extraction and object extraction WH-questions, sometimes referred to as a subject/object asymmetry, has been a topic of much linguistic investigation since the 1980s. The principle that excludes the sentence in (17b) is called the Empty Category Principle. The Empty Category Principle (ECP) constrains the appearance of WH-traces. Traces are called "empty" categories, since they have no phonetic content – that is, you cannot hear them. The ECP requires that traces must be licensed.

> (18)   **The Empty Category Principle (ECP)**
>   A trace must be licensed.

In order to understand how the ECP works, we must explain "licensing." By "licensing," we mean that the trace must have a particular kind of licenser, and that its licenser must be in a particular structural configuration. For our purposes, it will be sufficient to use the configuration known as **c-command**, which we introduced in chapter 14, as the relevant configuration. To remind you, the example in (19) illustrates.

(19)

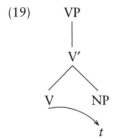

Notice the following characteristics of the diagram in (19). First, V is the head of VP. NP is the complement of VP. The trace is in NP. In this configuration, we say that the V c-commands the trace. The definition of c-command given in chapter 14 is repeated in (20).

> (20)   Constituent A c-commands another constituent B if the constituent immediately dominating A also dominates B.

In (19), we consider V to be the constituent (A) which c-commands the trace (B), since the node that immediately dominates V (V') also dominates the trace. Thus, the verb is in the correct structural configuration to license the object trace. The licensing is indicated by the arrow.

What about the relationship between a complementizer and a subject? This structure is illustrated in (21).

(21)

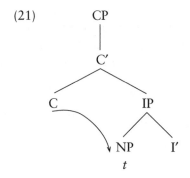

If we follow the definition of c-command given in (20), we will see that C (constituent A) does c-command the trace (constituent B), since the node that immediately dominates C (C') also dominates the trace.

So, verbs are in the correct configuration to license their objects, and complementizers are in the correct configuration to license subjects. However, there are certain restrictions on which elements qualify as licensers. Verbs are always able to license their objects. In addition, certain complementizers count as licensers, but only those which are called "agreeing complementizers." Other, non-agreeing complementizers are not able to be licensers.

Why is it said that only "agreeing" complementizers can be licensers? This can best be seen by considering the form of complementizers used in questions in French. In French, the regular complementizer "que" appears only in object questions, when the verb licenses the trace. However, in subject questions, in which the complementizer must license the trace, a special form of the complementizer is used: "qui" (which is also the same as the word for the WH-element "who"). French questions using "que" and "qui" are illustrated in (22).

(22)   a.   Que crois-tu   **que** Jean aime?
            what think-you that John likes
            "What$_1$ do you think John likes t$_1$?"

       b.   Que crois-tu   **qui** est arrivé?
            what think-you that has happened
            "What$_1$ do you think t$_1$ happened?"

In (22a), which is an object question, the verb licenses the trace of the WH-word ("que" = what), so the regular complementizer ("que" = that) is used. However, in (22b), a subject question, the complementizer must license the trace, and the form "qui" must be used. This observation tells us that a special form of the complementizer may be needed when it is required to license a trace: this special form is called an "agreeing" complementizer.

Now let us see how the ECP applies to various questions in English. We will concentrate on long-distance questions, since that is where the interesting contrasts are found.

First, consider the questions in (15), repeated here as (23). In these questions, the embedded verb "hire" licenses the trace. This is illustrated in (24).

(23) a. Who do you think   Sarah will hire *t*?
      b. Who do you think that Sarah will hire *t*?

(24)

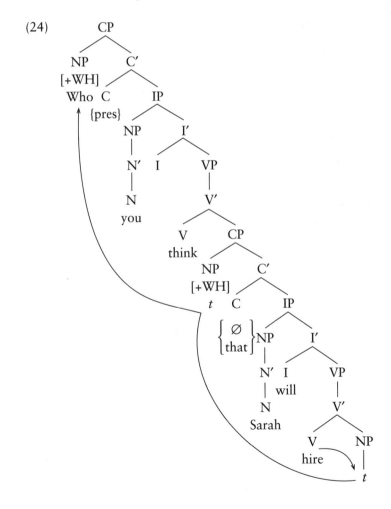

The arrow going from the verb to the trace indicates licensing. We saw earlier that a verb is able to be a licenser, and is in the correct configuration to license its object. Since all the licensing goes on much below the complementizer position, it doesn't matter whether or not the complementizer "that" is present. Notice also that the movement is successive cyclic.

However, consider the long-distance subject questions in (17), repeated in (25). (25b) is illustrated in (26).

(25) a.   Who do you think   *t* will win?
      b.   *Who do you think that *t* will win?

(26)

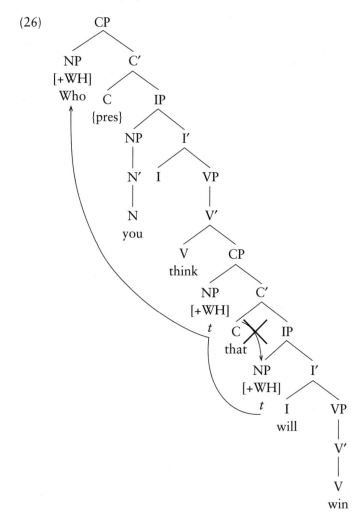

The derivation shown in (26) does use Successive Cyclic Movement. However, the fact that (25b) is ungrammatical leads us to conclude that the complementizer "that" is not an "agreeing" complementizer, so it does not count as a licenser, and hence cannot license the trace in the subject position. No other element is in the right position to license this trace, and so it violates the ECP. Hence, the derivation is ungrammatical.

On the other hand, the question in (25a) is grammatical. How can this be? Look at the derivation in (27).

(27)

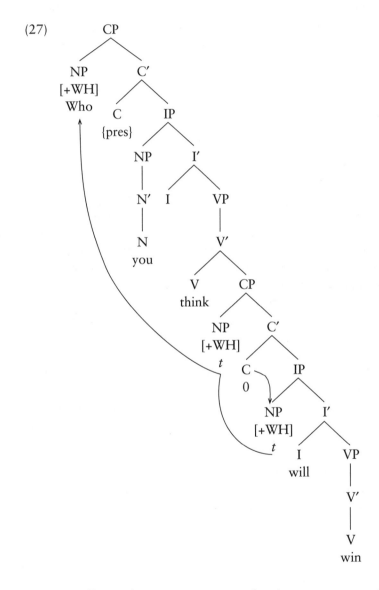

In (27), a **null** complementizer (i.e., one that is not pronounced) occupies the head C position in the embedded clause. Since (25a) is grammatical, we know that a null complementizer must be able to license a trace. In technical terms, we say that in English the null complementizer is agreeing.[2]

To summarize, in the examples in (25), it is the embedded subject that moves. Subjects cannot be licensed by verbs. In examples like (25), the embedded subject must be licensed by some element in C. Not just any C will do, however. The C must be "agreeing." In English, the overt complementizer "that" is not agreeing. Therefore, nothing licenses the trace in (25b), and the sentence is ungrammatical. On the other hand, a null C is agreeing in English. When the null complementizer is used instead of the overt word "that," the embedded subject trace is licensed, and the sentence (25a) is grammatical.

Conclusion

This chapter showed how long-distance WH-questions are derived. Their derivation involves Successive Cyclic WH-Movement. We also observed a constraint on WH-Movement, the Empty Category Principle. Although explaining this constraint requires some complex machinery, the machinery is not something a child has to construct without instructions. The instructions are provided by the theory of Universal Grammar. It follows that the Empty Category Principle (ECP) is a likely candidate to be a linguistic universal. If the ECP is part of the child's innate Language Acquisition Device, it will automatically be invoked by children to rule out ungrammatical sentences like (17b). If the ECP were not part of UG, a child who heard (17a) might think that (17b) is also grammatical, based on similar sentences such as (15a) and (15b). In this case, the child would encounter difficulty learning the grammar of her linguistic community. No positive evidence would be available to compel the child to add the ECP to her grammar. Therefore, the child would continue to violate the ECP as an adult. Since this does not happen, we are led to consider another acquisition scenario, according to which children know the ECP in advance of experience. In other words, the ECP is a property of UG. On this scenario, convergence to the adult grammar is no longer a problem.

There is one aspect of the ECP which does require learning. In French, as we saw, an overt complementizer can license a trace, as long as it shows agreement features. In English, an overt complementizer cannot license a trace; only a null complementizer counts as "agreeing." Thus, children must learn which elements count as licensers (that is, which elements show agreement) in the language they are learning. It is possible that children will make mistakes in this area. However, it will be possible for them to recover from such mistakes, with other principles of UG to guide them through the acquisition process. We will see an example of exactly this course of language development in the next chapter.

Notes

1 Notice that "who" is the subject of the embedded clause – at this point, it is in Spec of IP, not Spec of CP.
2 The agreement features are passed onto the null complementizer by the WH-element passing through the specifier of CP.

Bibliographical Comments

For detailed technical arguments for the successive cyclic nature of WH-Movement, as well as discussion of its other properties, see Chomsky (1973, 1977). Ross (1967) coined the term "island" to indicate structures which are inaccessible to certain rules, although he did not use it for the case discussed here. The ECP has received considerable attention, especially in the 1980s. See, among others, Aoun, Hornstein, and Sportiche (1980), Chomsky and Lasnik (1977), Chomsky (1981), Lasnik and Saito (1984), Lasnik and Uriagereka (1988), Lasnik and Saito (1992), Pesetsky (1982), Rizzi (1990). These are all primary sources, and the textbooks cited in earlier chapters are good places for the beginner to start.

22 Successful Cyclic Movement

Introduction

The present chapter examines children's ability to produce long-distance WH-questions. We focus on how children's long-distance WH-questions are subject to constraints on WH-Movement. Our concern will be with questions involving extraction from tensed embedded clauses; such questions allow us to assess children's adherence to the Empty Category Principle. We begin by reviewing the application of the ECP in English and a few other languages. Then we will discuss a study which used an imaginative technique to see how young children produce long-distance WH-questions. The study will lead to a better understanding of one of the universal principles of grammar.

1 Successive Cyclic Movement and the ECP

In chapter 21, it was argued that WH-Movement must take place *successive-cyclically*, that is, WH-phrases must move in cycles, passing through any CP in the path to the highest CP. We also saw that traces that result from movement of a WH-phrase are subject to a constraint, the *Empty Category Principle* (ECP). The ECP is repeated in (1).

(1) **The Empty Category Principle (ECP)**
     A trace must be licensed.

To review, the ECP governs the traces that appear in object and subject questions in English, as illustrated in (2)–(3) respectively.

(2) a. Who do you think   Sarah will hire *t*?
     b. Who do you think that Sarah will hire *t*?

(3) a.   Who do you think   *t* will win?
     b.   *Who do you think that *t* will win?

As we saw in the last chapter, the verb is an eligible licenser, and in the proper configuration to license its object. Hence, both of the examples in (2) are grammatical. On the other hand, we found that although complementizers are in the correct position to license subjects, only an *agreeing* complementizer can be a licenser. In English, the overt complementizer "that" is not agreeing – only a null complementizer can license a subject trace.

The notion of agreeing complementizer was supported by data from French. We saw that in French, the overt complementizer used with subject and object questions differed. The complementizer "qui" is the agreeing complementizer used with subject questions. The examples we considered in chapter 21 are repeated here in (4).

(4) a.   Que crois-tu   **que** Jean aime?
          what think-you that John likes
          "What$_1$ do you think John likes t_1?"

     b.   Que crois-tu   **qui** est arrivé?
          what think-you that has happened
          "What$_1$ do you think t_1 happened?"

The data from French support the proposals of the ECP. In other languages, still more evidence can be found for Successive Cyclic Movement and the ECP. For example, in some dialects of German, an overt "copy" of the WH-phrase is left in the intermediate CP. This is illustrated in (5).

(5) **Wer**$_i$ glaubst du **wer**$_i$ nach Hause geht?
     who think   you who to   home   goes
     "Who$_1$ do you think t_1 goes home?"

As (5) shows, in some languages the intermediate CP may be filled by a WH-element. One possibility is that like the French "qui," this WH-element is an agreeing complementizer. It allows the embedded subject trace to satisfy the ECP.

By examining data from several languages, researchers have postulated that the ECP is a universal linguistic constraint; therefore we assume that it is part of UG. However, different languages use different forms of "agreeing" complementizers, which children must learn on the basis of exposure to their native language. Thus, examination of children's long-distance questions provides us with a good opportunity to see the interaction of universal principles (ECP) and language-particular learning (which elements count for licensing of traces). We expect that children will show adherence to the ECP from the earliest times they can be tested. On the other hand, they may make mistakes regarding just which elements are used as agreeing complementizers in the language they are learning. Let us see what has recently been found regarding the acquisition of long-distance questions in English.

2   Children's Knowledge of the ECP

In order to test whether children learning English show adherence to the ECP, an experiment was designed to elicit children's productions of both long-distance subject and object questions. Both kinds of extraction are crucial. First, it must be established that children are aware of the possibility of including a complementizer in the intermediate CP position in long-distance object questions. Then, it should be shown that children do *not* include a complementizer in long-distance subject questions. To ascertain this, the study attempts to elicit object extraction questions as well as subject extraction questions. Then the frequency with which children include complementizers in object extraction questions – where the grammar allows them – is contrasted with the frequency with which complementizers are present in children's subject extraction questions (if any). In the case of subject extraction, of course, complementizers should not appear at all if children are adhering to the ECP.

To elicit long-distance WH-questions, a researcher named Rosalind Thornton used a technique called *elicited production*. In the experiment, situations were devised to evoke WH-questions with the relevant structural properties from children. Two experimenters were needed to elicit the relevant WH-questions. One experimenter interacted with the child; the second manipulated a puppet called "Ratty," who was too timid to talk to grown-ups, but enjoyed talking to children. The first experimenter solicited the child's help in finding out information from Ratty. The children enjoyed this ruse and were eager to pose questions of Ratty. By carefully manipulating the protocols, the experimenter could set up the situation so that the only appropriate response for the child was to ask the target long-distance question.

For this experiment, Ratty was asked by the child to make a series of guesses; for example, about what pigs like to eat, what Cookie Monster likes to eat, what the child had hidden in a box, and so forth. Protocols such as the one given below were used to elicit both subject and object extraction questions.

Protocol for the Empty Category Experiment

Experimenter: In this game Ratty has to guess what Cookie Monster eats, and what is in the box, OK? But before we let Ratty guess, let's make

	sure we know the answers ourselves. (Experimenter whispers to the child, pretending that Ratty can't hear) Cookie Monster eats . . .
Child:	COOKIES
Experimenter:	Right, and in the box there are . . .
Child:	MARBLES
Experimenter:	Good. Let's ask about Cookie Monster first. We know that Cookie Monster eats cookies, right? Ask Ratty what he thinks.
Child:	WHAT DO YOU THINK COOKIE MONSTER EATS?
Ratty:	I think Cookie Monster eats ants.
Experimenter:	Ants! That's a silly rat! Well, let's see what Ratty says about the next one. Let's ask about the box. We know that there are marbles in the box, right? Ask Ratty what he thinks.
Child:	WHAT DO YOU THINK'S IN THE BOX?
Ratty:	A watermelon?

Notice that the experimenter's lead-in ("We know that Cookie Monster eats cookies. Ask Ratty what he thinks") contains several clues about the question that is being targeted, including several words that could be used by the children in their attempts to form an appropriate question. Despite these clues, the experimenter's lead-in is not itself a long-distance question; therefore it does not inform the child about the properties of such questions. This must come from the children themselves, by consulting their grammatical knowledge.

The task was quite successful in eliciting long-distance WH-questions. Questions with extraction from both subject and object position were elicited from 19 of the 21 child subjects (mean age = 4 years; 3 months). Some examples of the children's productions are given in (6). This in itself is a good indication of children's knowledge of grammar. Children of this age rarely produce such long-distance questions in natural situations of spontaneous production. However, by eliciting these questions we can see that this is not because of any grammar limitation.

(6) a. Who do you think is in the box?
    b. Who does he think has a hat?
    c. What way do you think the fireman put out the fire?

Unfortunately for the study of the ECP, the majority of children in this study produced WH-questions without any complementizers, regardless of the type of construction. This is, of course, perfectly consistent with the grammar, but not particularly revealing of adherence to the ECP, because for such evidence a contrast between subject and object questions needs to be found. Presumably, children's tendency to use null complementizers in both subject and object questions is due to a strong preference to use the most reduced form they could get away with. Therefore, their knowledge of the contrast between sentences like (7a) and (7b) could not be clearly ascertained. (Notice that this is not to say that children produced the ungrammatical long-distance subject question with a complementizer. However, if they did not produce even object questions with a complementizer, there is no evidence about whether or not they know the difference between the two structures.)

(7) a.   What do you think (*that) *t* eats pigs?
     b.   What do you think (that) pigs eat *t*?

A number of the child subjects did not exhibit a similar tendency to use reduced forms, however. The productions of these children were quite unexpected. Their productions contained an "extra" WH-phrase, in addition to the WH-phrase in sentence-initial CP position. The extra WH-phrase appeared in the intermediate Spec of CP position. These "medial WH-questions" occurred with extractions from both subject and object position within the embedded clause, as the examples in (8) show.

(8) What do you think what Cookie Monster eats?   (age 5;0)
     Who do you think who Grover wants to hug?   (age 4;9)
     What do you think what the baby drinks?   (age 3;3)
     What do you think what's in that box?   (age 3;3)
     What do you think really what's in that can?   (age 3;9)

The error of inserting an "extra" WH-phrase had not been reported previously in the literature. This is hardly surprising, however, given how infrequently long-distance WH-questions appear in the transcripts of children's spontaneous speech. Nevertheless, the medial-WH was quite systematic in the speech of those children who generated it. This is evidence that it is truly the product of their grammars, and not the product of a limitation in processing capacity, for example.

Questions with a medial-WH indicate that the phrase structure children assign to long-distance questions includes the intermediate CP position, because this position is "filled" by the extra WH-phrase. This fortuitous error therefore demonstrates children's successive cyclic movement of WH-phrases in long-distance questions. Thornton argues that medial WH-questions of English-speaking children are the consequence of adopting grammatical representations that underlie similar questions in other languages, such as German WH-questions that have a "copy" of the WH-word in the intermediate Spec of CP, as illustrated in (5) above. Let us turn to further discussion of children's "medial WH-questions."

3   Medial WH-Questions and the ECP

On the face of it, the children learning English who insert an "extra" WH-phrase in the intermediate CP in their long-distance questions might appear to be violating the ECP. Recall the contrast between subject and object extraction as illustrated in (9a–b).

(9)   a.   What do you think t eats pigs?
      b.   *What do you think that t eats pigs?

The difference between (9a) and (9b) is that the embedded C position is filled with "that," a non-agreeing complementizer, in (9b). The embedded C is also filled in children's medial WH-questions, even in subject questions, as illustrated in (10).

(10)   What do you think what's in that box?   (3;11)
       Who did they say who had ants in their pants?   (5;9)

These question forms are not part of adult English, but we have seen similar forms both in French and in dialects of German. It was proposed that in these languages, a WH-element serves as an "agreeing" C which is used to license embedded subject traces. Under this interpretation, it is not surprising that some children learning English might hypothesize that a WH-element can serve as an "agreeing" complementizer. Supporting this interpretation of the data is the fact that children who produced medial WH-questions put in the "extra" WH-phrase consistently, whereas other children exhibited a strong tendency to leave out the complementizer. We will assume, therefore, that medial WH-questions are not violations of the ECP, but are actually attempts by children to satisfy it. Let's compare the children's medial WH-questions with the German example given earlier, repeated in (11).

(11)   **Wer**$_i$ glaubst du **wer**$_i$ nach Hause geht?
       who think   you who to   home goes
       "Who$_1$ do you think t_1 goes home?"

As (11) shows, Universal Grammar must provide an option in which the WH-element appears twice in a sentence: once in the sentence-initial specifier of CP, and once in a medial position at the beginning of the embedded clause. Thus, it seems that children learning English may go through a stage in which they have selected a parameter setting which is used in German, but not in English. Further support for this idea comes from looking in more detail at the kinds of "medial" WH-questions which are produced. Under such an analysis, we find that the restrictions on children's medial WH-questions make them look even more like long-distance questions in German. For example, neither grammar allows full WH-phrases (such as "which Smurf") in both the sentence-initial and medial positions, as in (12).

(12)   *Which Smurf do you think which Smurf has roller skates on?

Instead of (12), children produce examples such as those in (13).

(13)   a.   Which Smurf do you think who has roller skates on?
        b.   What do you think which Smurf has roller skates on?

Thus, since children who produce non-English medial questions obey the same constraints on such questions that are found in other (adult) languages, this is good evidence that their errors in this case arise from a grammatical parameter missetting. But, even though the parameter is set to a value not used by English, it is important to point out that it is a setting made available by UG, and taken by other languages. This finding supports the parameter-setting theory of language acquisition, which predicts that when children's grammars appear to be different from adults', they will still be strictly within the bounds allowed by UG.

Conclusion

This chapter reported the findings of two experiments. Unfortunately, the first experiment was stymied by a property of the language processing system – the tendency to reduce forms. In that experiment, the tendency to reduce forms caused subjects to omit complementizers, making it difficult to evaluate their knowledge of the ECP. The first elicitation experiment did reveal a fascinating, and unexpected, finding, however. It turned out that a subset of the children who were interviewed produced a medial-WH in their productions of long-distance questions. The goal of experimental research then changed – to see the range of structures in which the non-adult questions appear, and why. This investigation led to the conclusion that children learning English sometimes adopt linguistic structures that are made available by UG, but not attested in the primary linguistic data. This kind of phenomenon indicates that children's hypotheses about linguistic structure are not strictly based on their experience; they may pursue other grammatical options, as long as these options are compatible with the theory of Universal Grammar.

Bibliographical Comments

The experiment described here is discussed in detail in Thornton (1990), Thornton and Crain (1994), and Thornton (1995). Additional discussion regarding children's medial WH-questions and their similarity to such questions in German can be found in McDaniel, Chiu, and Maxfield (1995).

23 A Constraint on Contraction

Introduction

This chapter examines a constraint that applies to certain WH-questions. This is not a constraint on the application of WH-Movement itself, but its effects can be most clearly seen in WH-questions. Sentences illustrating this constraint involve the phenomenon we called "wanna contraction" in chapter 2. In many places "want" and "to" can be contracted together to form "wanna," but in certain cases contraction is not possible. The illegalities of contraction will be seen to follow from a constraint on contraction across the trace of WH-Movement.

The constraint discussed in this chapter has a very specific application: it concerns the possibility of contracting the two elements "want" and "to." However, it is a useful illustration of the effects of constraints, and a further demonstration of the psychological reality of traces. Furthermore, data from children learning English are available to support the conclusion that young children know the proposed constraint, and this has implications for our understanding of the acquisition of WH-Movement more generally.

Wanna Contraction

One of the interesting linguistic phenomena mentioned earlier concerns "wanna contraction." There were several facts to explain. One fact was that "want" and "to" can sometimes be contracted to form "wanna," but sometimes not, as illustrated in (1).

(1) a. Who do you *want to* beat during the basketball season?
     b. Who do you *wanna* beat during the basketball season?
     c. Who do you *want to* win the game?
     d. *Who do you *wanna* win the game?

Another fact was that the contracted form "wanna" sometimes limits the range of interpretations that a sentence can be given. In support of this point, it was shown that the first of the following sentences has two meanings, but that the second sentence has only one.

(2) a. Who did Calhoun want to shoot at the buzzer?
    b. Who did Calhoun wanna shoot at the buzzer?

How can we explain these data? First, observe that the sentences that allow both "want to" and "wanna" are ones in which the embedded clause contains a transitive verb (a verb that takes a direct object). For a concrete example, examine the Deep Structure given in (3) which underlies the sentences, "Who do you want to beat?" and, "Who do you wanna beat?"

(3)

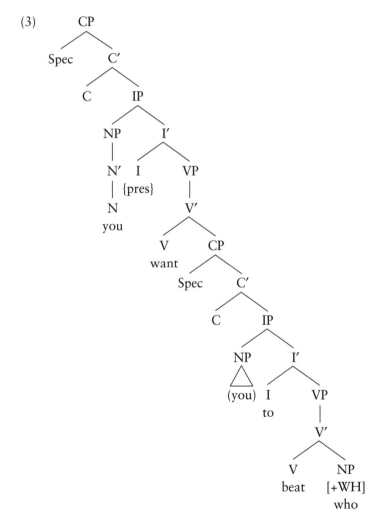

There are two properties of this phrase marker that deserve comment. First, it contains an I with the infinitival element "to." As the term suggests, an infinitival clause (in this case, the complement of the verb in the main clause) is one which contains a nonfinite verb (= infinitive).[1]

The second unfamiliar feature in the phrase marker is that the subject of the infinitival clause is superficially empty. Notice that the subject of the main clause is the "understood" subject of the embedded clause. This is not peculiar to embedded clauses with transitive verbs such as "beat," but also occurs with intransitive verbs such as "sleep," as in "Reagan likes to sleep." Again, the meaning is that Reagan likes for himself to sleep – the subject of the main clause is understood to be the subject of the embedded clause. We will indicate these understood subjects by putting them in parentheses in the structure.

Now consider what happens when we apply the WH-Movement transformation and Subject–Auxiliary Inversion to this Deep Structure. The result is given in (4).

(4)

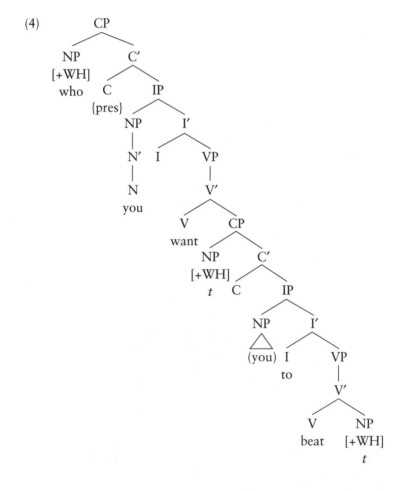

In this phrase marker, the original trace of the moved WH-phrase is in the object position of the embedded clause, after the verb "beat."[2] Another way of showing the position of the original trace is given in (5).

(5) Who do you *want to* beat t?

As (6) shows, contraction is permitted in structures like (5).

(6) Who do you *wanna* beat?

The next step is to examine the Deep Structure of a sentence that does not permit wanna contraction. Consider the example in (7). The Deep Structure of this example, given in (8a), is converted into an appropriate Surface Structure as shown in (8b) by (a) WH-Movement and (b) Subject–Auxiliary Inversion. Observe the position of the original trace of WH-Movement.

(7) Who do you want to win?

(8) a.

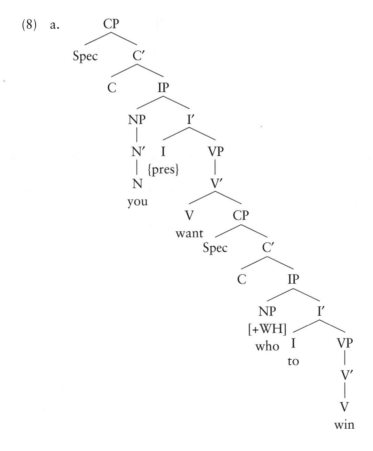

b.

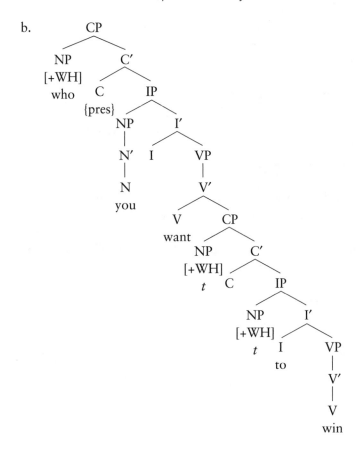

In the Surface Structure phrase marker, the position of the original trace is the subject of the embedded clause, between "want" and "to."[3] However, since the original trace intervenes between "want" and "to," contraction is impossible. The presence of the unpronounced trace blocks contraction just as surely as the presence of an overtly realized NP, such as a name, as shown in (9).

(9) a. I *want* Bill *to* sleep.   Cf. *I wanna Bill sleep. *I wan Bill -na sleep.
    b. I *want to* sleep.   Cf. I wanna sleep.

Note that the trace in the embedded specifier of CP does not block contraction as the trace in the embedded subject position does. Does this argue against the psychological reality of the trace in the embedded specifier of CP? We think it does not, because of the independent evidence for the intermediate trace. It is simply necessary to consider the constraint on wanna contraction in terms of the original trace, or an "argument" trace (the trace of an argument, which is a subject or an object).

Now we can also understand why the question in (10) is unambiguous.

(10)   Who did Calhoun wanna shoot at the buzzer?

Question (10) can only mean that Calhoun wants to shoot someone – it cannot mean that Calhoun wants someone to shoot (the basketball). The example turns on the ambiguity of the verb "shoot," which may be either transitive (= the "gun" interpretation) or intransitive (= the "basketball" interpretation). The order of the elements in the Deep Structure of the transitive interpretation is given in (11).

(11)   [DS]   Calhoun {past} want to shoot who at the buzzer.

After WH-Movement and SAI, the Surface Structure given in (12) will result.

(12)

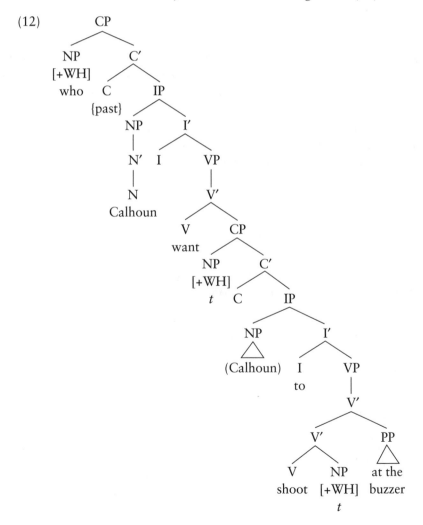

In this structure, the original trace does not intervene between "want" and "to," so contraction is allowed. On the other hand, in the intransitive interpretation, the original trace does intervene between "want" and "to," as can be seen from the order of elements in the Deep Structure given in (13).

(13) [DS] Calhoun {past} want who to shoot at the buzzer.

Contraction is not allowed in the Surface Structure which would be derived from (13). Hence, we as hearers interpret the question with contraction in (10) only to mean that Calhoun wants to shoot one of his players.

Conclusion

The constraint on wanna contraction is really much more general than it sounds. It is a constraint against applying certain phonological processes which require adjacency when a WH-trace intervenes. As we saw in chapter 18, this constraint also prohibits affix-hopping across a subject trace. These two effects of the presence of a WH-trace lend considerable credence to its psychological existence. Is this constraint part of UG? If so, we would expect to see early adherence to it in children's production of WH-questions with "want + to." We turn to this in the next chapter.

Notes

1 In English, finite verb forms are marked (= inflected) for number (e.g., he goes, they go) and tense (e.g., depart, departed, departing). The root or uninflected form of the verb is called the infinitive or nonfinite form.
2 An intermediate trace has also been left in the embedded specifier of CP. We will see that there are different effects of the original trace and the intermediate trace.
3 Again, there is an intermediate trace in the embedded specifier of CP.

Bibliographical Comments

An early discussion of wanna contraction, first noted in Lakoff (1970), is Selkirk (1972). Specific proposals are also made in Chomsky (1977), Chomsky and Lasnik (1977), Jaeggli (1980), and Postal and Pullum (1982), among numerous others. More extensive discussion of this phenomenon and its implications for the trace theory of movement is found in Riemsdijk and Williams (1986), and Lasnik and Uriagereka (1988).

24 Acquisition of Wanna Contraction

Introduction

In this chapter, we examine children's adherence to the constraint on "wanna contraction." By studying children's production of sentences with "want" + "to," we can find evidence that they understand the complex structure of these sentences, that they apply the WH-Movement transformation correctly, and that they leave a psychologically real trace in the position of movement, as shown by their respect for the constraint against contraction across a trace. As in chapter 22, an elicited production experiment was used to induce children to produce many utterances of the relevant type.

1 Wanna Contraction

As we saw in the previous chapter, one constraint which interacts with long-distance WH-questions is the prohibition against wanna contraction in certain questions. This constrains the contraction of the verbal elements "want" and "to" to form "wanna." This contraction can happen in simple declarative sentences, such as (1a–b), as well as in some WH-questions, such as (1c–d).

(1) a. I *want to* speak to Bill.
    b. I *wanna* speak to Bill.
    c. Who do you *want to* speak to?
    d. Who do you *wanna* speak to?

An exception to this pattern occurs when the WH-phrase is extracted from between "want" and "to," as in (2).

(2) a. Who do you *want to* speak to Bill?
    b. *Who do you *wanna* speak to Bill?

Example (2) shows that when the WH-phrase is extracted from the subject position of an infinitival complement clause (i.e., from between "want" and "to") the result is an odd-sounding question. To explain why contraction is blocked in subject extraction questions, linguists working within the framework of Generative Grammar have argued that the trace of a WH-phrase blocks contraction. Although the trace isn't overt – we don't pronounce it – the claim is that the trace left behind by movement is real; it does influence how we pronounce the words that surround it.

It is important to ask when children come to appreciate this observation about the WH-trace blocking contraction. The logic of the situation would suggest they must know it innately. Otherwise, they might err into making the wrong generalization – that contraction is permitted generally. This would be an easy mistake to make, since contraction is possible, even preferred, in so many different kinds of sentences. Subject extraction WH-questions are definitely the exception to the generalization. But suppose that children formed a full generalization and permitted contraction in sentences like (2b). We have seen that corrective feedback is not available to children, so children who made this false generalization would not be informed of their mistake. These children would presumably not attain the adult grammar. Since this doesn't happen (i.e., since every child achieves the correct Final State), it seems that the only logical conjecture is that children never make this error in the first place. The only way this could be possible, given the absence of relevant experience, is if children were born knowing that WH-trace blocks contraction. This question was the focus of a recent experiment by Rosalind Thornton.

2   Experiment on Wanna Contraction

This experiment used the technique of elicited production to see if children obey the constraint on wanna contraction. In the experiment, situations were devised to evoke WH-questions with the relevant structural properties from children. It was hypothesized that children would exhibit a preference for contraction of "want" and "to" whenever this was consistent with their grammars. In the present case, a preference for reduced forms would be revealed by looking at the proportion of contracted forms that children produced in their questions involving extraction from the object position of an infinitival clause. This result could then be compared with the proportion of contracted forms in extracting from the subject position. If children know the constraint against contracting across a WH-trace, then they should produce few, if any, contracted forms in the subject extraction condition. The object extraction condition served as a control condition to establish the baseline level of contracted forms that children produce when this is consistent with their grammars.

As in the elicited production study described in chapter 22, two experimenters participated in the study; the first described the stories, and the second manipulated a puppet called "Ratty."

One set of protocols was designed to evoke object extraction questions, and another set required children to ask subject extraction questions. Examples of the protocols are given below.

Protocol for Eliciting Object Extraction Questions

Experimenter: Ratty looks hungry. I bet he wants to eat something. Ask Ratty what he wants.
Child: WHAT DO YOU WANNA EAT?
Ratty: Some cheese would be good.

Even using protocols as simple as this one, the task often proved successful in eliciting "full" long-distance WH-questions from children. Notice, however, that a felicitous response in the protocol above would also be a "partial" question such as "What do you want?" Indeed, some children chose to give this simplified response. Because this response lacks information relevant to the issue of children's knowledge of the constraint on wanna contraction, more complex protocols were constructed to eliminate, or at least reduce the likelihood of, partial WH-questions. The pragmatics of the complex protocols demand a full WH-question, that is, one with an embedded clause. An example of such a protocol, designed to elicit subject extraction questions, is given below. Similar protocols were constructed to elicit object extraction questions.

Complex Protocol: Subject Extraction Questions

Experimenter: There are three guys in this story: Cookie Monster, a dog, and this baby. One of them gets to take a walk, one gets to take a nap, and one gets to eat a cookie. And the rat gets to choose who does each thing. So, one gets to take a walk, right? Ask Ratty who he wants.
Child: WHO DO YOU WANT TO TAKE A WALK?
Ratty: I want the dog to take a walk.

Using this technique, both subject and object extraction questions were elicited from 21 children (mean age = 4;3). The results were clearly in accord with the theoretical hypothesis based on learnability considerations. Nineteen of the 21 children successfully produced full WH-questions. In the object extraction questions of these children, 59 percent contained "wanna" in its contracted form. By contrast, in posing subject extraction questions to Ratty, only one child's utterances contained any contracted forms. In short, the data provide compelling evidence of children's adherence to the constraint which prohibits contraction across a WH-trace.

3 Long-Distance Movement in Children's Spontaneous Speech

One might ask whether the kinds of experimental procedures we described in this chapter and chapter 22 are really needed in order to obtain data relevant to the issue of children's knowledge of long-distance questions. Isn't it possible to address the issue simply by examining transcripts of children's spontaneous productions? The fact is that the available data from children's spontaneous speech concerning the development of long-distance questions is remarkably sparse. For instance, search of a large corpus of the spontaneous productions of a child named Adam revealed only 16 long-distance WH-Movement questions over a time span covering three and a half years. Some of the examples found in this search follow:

(3) a. What you think this looks like   (3 years; 2 months)
     b. What chu like to have   (3;2)
     c. What he went to play with   (3;6)
     d. What d'you think I am, a can't tell boy   (4;0)
     e. What do you think the grain is going to taste like   (4;9)
     f. What do you think the pajamas are for   (4;9)

What should we infer from the paucity of long-distance WH-questions in children's spontaneous speech? Based on these data, along with evidence from experimental studies, several researchers have reached the conclusion that long-distance movement is unavailable in early child grammar. Adopting this vantage point, these researchers have speculated as to why long-distance movement is unavailable. Several suggestions have been proposed. The proposals aim to establish which feature of the operation of WH-Movement is absent from the grammars of young children. One suggestion is that children are unable to project WH-traces; another suggestion is that children do not project the intermediate complementizer position needed to perform Successive Cyclic Movement. Still other possibilities have been advanced.

The common thread in all of these accounts is the view that the late emergence of a construction in children's spontaneous productions should be taken at face value – as evidence that these constructions are "missing" from early child grammar. But, as the results of the studies reported in this chapter and chapter 22 make clear, the absence of a construction in the transcripts of children's spontaneous speech should not be taken as evidence of its absence in their grammars. It may well turn out that the situations that are critical for someone to produce a certain construction may occur only rarely, perhaps because they are uniquely appropriate only in special contexts where a number of critical ingredients are present at the same time. In all but these special contexts, children probably use simpler forms of expression. No doubt the same is true of adults.

The alternative direction is to accept as the Null Hypothesis the view that all the relevant aspects of WH-Movement are innately specified. If the Null Hypothesis is correct, we are led to expect children to have command of long-distance WH-questions from a very early age. Before we reject the Null Hypothesis, then, it pays to investigate children's knowledge in experimental settings, where the complexity of situations can be carefully controlled and easily manipulated.

Conclusion

Without thinking about it, most adults probably think "wanna" is used by children indiscriminately. We suspect most adults are not even aware of the restrictions on the use of "wanna" their own grammars demonstrate. Yet, the experiment described here shows that children do obey the constraints on "wanna" contraction in their productions at a very early age. Since there would be no way for children to retreat from a mistake if they tried to (over-)generalize the application of "wanna" contraction to all surface sequences of "want" + "to," this constraint is a prime candidate for universal, innate knowledge.

Bibliographical Comments

The experiment summarized here is described in detail in Thornton (1990) and Thornton and Crain (1994). The suggestion that the paucity of long-distance WH-questions in children's early spontaneous productions indicates lack of a grammatical process was made by Roeper and his colleagues (deVilliers, Roeper, and Vainikka, 1990; Roeper, Rooth, Mallish, and Akiyama, 1984; and Roeper and deVilliers, 1991).

25 Principle C in WH-Questions

Introduction

This chapter continues our investigation of constraints on WH-questions. The kind of constraint we will now discuss applies to the meanings of sentences, and not to the form of the sentences themselves. In fact, the constraint we will discuss in this chapter is the one we discussed in chapter 14: Principle C, which restricts the interpretation of pronouns in certain declarative sentences as well as sentences with WH-Movement. We will first remind you of how Principle C applies in declaratives, and then we will show in more detail its application in WH-questions. In chapter 26, we will turn to considering children's knowledge of Principle C in WH-questions.

1 Principle C in Declaratives

In chapter 14, we discussed certain restrictions on the interpretation of pronouns. We found that whether or not a pronoun can be coreferential with another NP in the same sentence depended (in part) on the structural configuration of the sentence, and the relationship between the pronoun and the other NP. To refresh your memory, consider example (1).

(1) a.   *Sajak* thinks *he* should get a free spin of the wheel.
    b.   *He thinks *Sajak* should get a free spin of the wheel.
    c.   When *he* is bored, *Sajak* likes to spin the wheel.

In (1a), "he" can be coreferential with "Sajak" (and it can, of course, refer to someone outside the sentence; we will systematically concentrate on the possibility for intra-sentential coreference). In (1b), of course, "he" and "Sajak" cannot be coreferential. The example in (1c) shows us that the restriction in (1b) is not simply due to the linear order of the pronoun and the name, since a pronoun *can* be coreferential with a name which follows it (so-called "backwards anaphora"). Rather, we found that the constraint on interpretation of a pronoun refers to the structural notion of c-command. The constraint, Principle C, is given in (2), and the definition of c-command is given in (3).

(2) **Principle C (Coreference Constraint)**
A pronoun cannot be coreferential with an NP which it c-commands.

(3) Constituent A c-commands another constituent B if the constituent immediately dominating A also dominates B.

In examples (1a) and (1c), the pronoun "he" does not c-command the name "Sajak." Hence, they can corefer. On the other hand, in (1b), the pronoun does c-command the name, and they cannot corefer. (We encourage you to refer to chapter 14 if you want to see trees and more extensive discussion of this phenomenon.)

2 Strong Crossover

Principle C also applies in WH-questions. It has been used to explain certain restrictions on their interpretations. Here are some examples:

(4) a. Who thinks he has a big nose?
b. *Who* thinks *he* has a big nose?
c. Who does he think has a big nose?
d. **Who* does *he* think has a big nose?

In the first question (4a), the WH-phrase "who" can be used to ask about someone distinct from the person picked out by the pronoun "he," say, Steve Martin. In other words, this can be a question about which person thinks Steve Martin has a big nose. This same question can also be used when the WH-phrase and the pronoun are picking out the same person. That is, the speaker might be asking which person(s) thinks that he, himself, has a big nose. This interpretation is indicated by italicizing the WH-word and the pronoun in (4b).[1]

The same range of interpretations is not possible for the second question. In (4c), the "who" and the "he" must refer to different people. (4c) cannot be used to mean someone thinks he himself has a big nose. This is why we indicate that the "bound" reading is not possible, by marking (4d) ungrammatical. Take a moment to think about what these sentences mean to be sure you agree.

   To explain the facts that coreference is allowed in (4a), but non-coreference is required in (4c), it might be expected that we should focus on the relationship between the WH-phrase and the pronoun. Consider where the WH-phrase and the pronoun are in the trees representing these examples. Upon consideration, it should be clear to you that there is no difference between these examples in the c-command relationship of the WH-phrase and the pronoun. In both cases, the WH-phrase is in Spec of CP, and the pronoun is lower in the tree. The constituent immediately dominating the pronoun in both examples does not dominate Spec of CP, which is very high in the tree.

   As an alternative, let's consider the relationship between the pronoun and the *trace* of the WH-phrase. (Here and throughout, when we discuss the *trace* of WH-Movement, we have in mind the original trace, not the intermediate trace in an embedded Spec of CP.) Example (4a) is a subject question. The WH-phrase "who" starts in the Spec of IP position at Deep Structure, so that is where the trace is. The pronoun "he," in Spec of the embedded IP, does not c-command the trace of the WH-phrase in (4a), since the constituent immediately dominating the pronoun is the embedded IP, and this constituent does not dominate the matrix IP. In this example, coreference is allowed.

   Now, consider the trace of the WH-phrase in (4c). The WH-phrase "who" in (4c) originates in the *embedded* Spec of IP – it is a question about the person that has a big nose. The WH-phrase must move long-distance (through the embedded Spec of CP) to the matrix Spec of CP, leaving its trace in the embedded Spec of IP. The pronoun "he" in (4c) is in the *matrix* Spec of IP. The constituent immediately dominating "he" is the matrix IP. This constituent DOES dominate the trace of the WH-phrase – and in this example, coreference is not allowed.

   It is now clear that the way to appropriately restrict the interpretations of the questions in (4) is to apply Principle C to the relationship between a pronoun and the trace of a WH-element. In other words, the trace of a WH-element counts as an NP. The WH-phrase cannot ask about the same person as a pronoun if the pronoun c-commands the *trace* of the WH-phrase.

   It may prove useful to state the facts in different terms. Another way of looking at the situation is this: if a WH-phrase "crosses over" a pronoun as it moves from its Deep Structure position to its Surface Structure position, then the pronoun and the WH-phrase must be disjoint in reference. For this reason, Principle C in WH-questions is sometimes called the *Strong Crossover* constraint. Consider the Deep Structure of (4c), before the WH-phrase has moved, given in (5). Applying WH-Movement, the WH-phrase crosses over the pronoun, on its way to the Spec of the topmost (matrix) CP. The result is the Intermediate Structure given in (6).

(5)
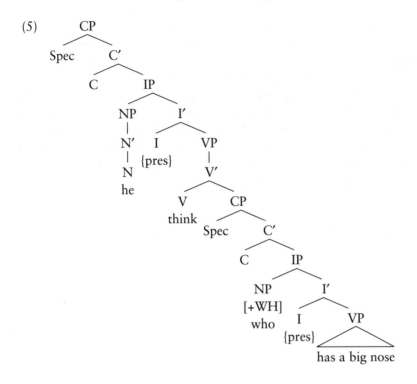

(6)
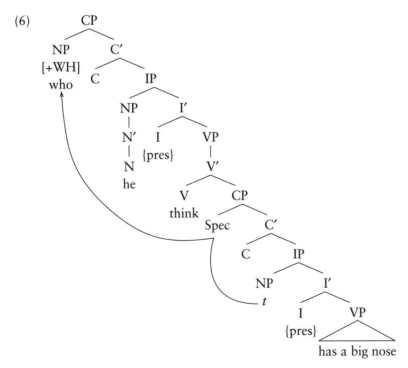

Of course, Subject–Auxiliary Inversion and Do-support are still needed to get a well-formed Surface Structure, but we will not illustrate the result of these familiar operations.

As we can clearly see from the tree, the WH-phrase "crosses over" the pronoun "he" on its way to the matrix Spec of CP. This reminds us that the interpretation of the Surface Structure of (4c) must be restricted by Principle C, as we have seen. The pronoun and the WH-phrase must be about distinct individuals. Of course, the question is fully grammatical, on the extra-sentential reading of the pronoun. Principle C is a constraint on interpretation. It only specifies how the question can and cannot be interpreted, but does not mark the sentence as ungrammatical.

Now consider example (4a), "Who thinks he has a big nose?", in which coreference IS permitted. Look first at its Deep Structure, given in (7).

(7)

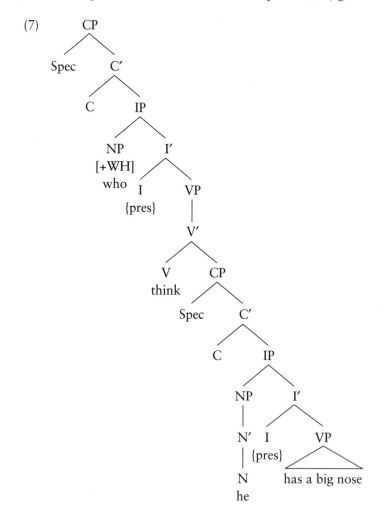

Applying WH-Movement, we derive the Surface Structure:

(8)

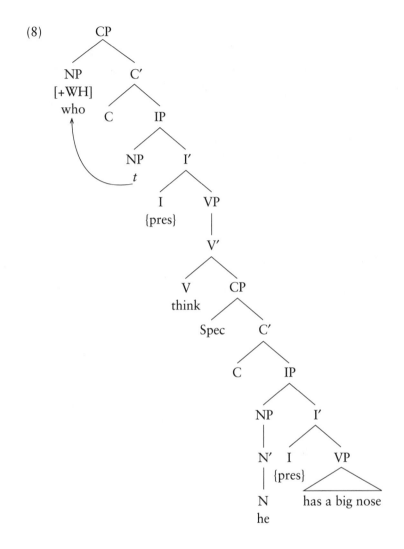

Since this is a subject question, moving the WH-phrase doesn't change much. What should be observed, though, is the position of the *trace* relative to the pronoun. The WH-phrase and the pronoun are roughly in the same alignment in this example as they were in the previous, Strong Crossover example. But the relation between the pronoun and the *trace* is quite different. The constituent immediately dominating the pronoun, the embedded IP, doesn't dominate the trace, hence the pronoun doesn't c-command the *trace*. Therefore, Principle C does not apply, and coreference is allowed between the WH-phrase and the pronoun. This is the desired result.

Conclusion

The same principle we discussed in chapter 14, Principle C, constrains the interpretation of pronouns in both declaratives and WH-questions. This should not be surprising, since the principle is about how pronouns are to be interpreted. The difference between the declarative cases we examined and WH-questions is that the element with which the pronoun interacts is an ordinary NP in declaratives, and a trace in WH-questions. Again, the application of the principle provides support for the psychological reality of traces.

Note

1   This is similar to our use of italic to indicate coreference in chapters 14 and 15. Strictly speaking, WH-phrases cannot corefer, because they do not refer (they are asking about a referent, not picking one out). When the question is asking about the same person a pronoun picks out, the pronoun is said to be "bound," so we will call such examples "bound pronoun" examples.

Bibliographical Comments

The phenomenon of Strong Crossover was first discussed by Postal (1971). Wasow (1972) first discussed the constraint in terms of trace theory. The Principle C account used here is roughly that of Chomsky (1981).

26 Children's Knowledge of Strong Crossover

Introduction

In the last chapter, we discussed how Principle C governs the interpretation of certain WH-questions. As with other constraints, it is reasonable to infer that Principle C is contained in Universal Grammar, that is, it is part of the human biological blueprint for language acquisition. Support for this conclusion was presented in chapter 15, where we reported experimental findings demonstrating children's early adherence to Principle C in declarative sentences. The present chapter examines the results of experimental attempts to assess children's adherence to Principle C in WH-questions.

1 Multiple Reference Interpretation

As we saw in the previous chapter, Principle C constrains the interpretation of WH-questions. Example (1a) can be a question about who thinks that he himself has a big nose, but example (1b) cannot. In (1b), the WH-phrase "crosses over" the pronoun on its way to Spec of CP, so it is subject to the restriction on interpretation called **Strong Crossover**.

(1) a. Who thinks he has a big nose?
    b. Who does he think has a big nose?

We can use a quasi-logical notation to indicate the differences in interpretation permitted for the sentences in (1). Example (1a) can be interpreted in two ways. First, it can have the interpretation in which "he" picks out a salient male individual in the conversational context, say Steve Martin. On this interpretation, the person asking the question is interested in the listener's opinion of the size of Steve Martin's nose. This interpretation is paraphrased in (2). Note that the pronoun "he" is not linked to the variable **x** in (2). Therefore, this occurrence of the pronoun is free; it has a deictic interpretation.

(2)   which person **x** is such that **x** thinks he (Steve Martin) has a big nose

Question (1a) can also have the interpretation in which the WH-word refers to whoever is doing the thinking. This interpretation is paraphrased in (3). The interpretation in (3) is the bound pronoun interpretation, because the pronoun is "bound" (restricted) by the WH-phrase.

(3)   which person **x** is such that **x** thinks he (**x**) has a big nose

We observed earlier that the bound pronoun interpretation of (3) is not available for crossover questions like (1b). The only possible interpretation of (1b) is one which presupposes that the person doing the thinking, say Dean Martin, and the person whose nose Dean Martin is asking about are distinct. This is paraphrased in (4). Again, the pronoun has a deictic interpretation, which we have filled in using Dean Martin.

(4)   which person **x** is such that he (Dean Martin) thinks **x** has a big nose

There is one final difference between questions (1a) and (1b) which will prove important in the experiments we discuss in this chapter. Notice that the "he" in question (1a) with the bound pronoun interpretation (3) can refer to more than one person. The speaker can say, without contradiction, "I know who thinks he has a big nose. Steve Martin (thinks he has a big nose), Dean Martin (thinks he has a big nose), and Martin Short (thinks he has a big nose)." Despite the singular form of the pronoun, there can be a **multiple reference** interpretation of the bound pronoun question (1a). Another way of putting this is that the variable **x** in (3) is a placeholder for more than one person: each person in the context that thinks he, himself, has a big nose.

The multiple reference interpretation of the pronoun is clearly not permitted in crossover questions. In question (1b), the pronoun cannot be interpreted as referring to several people; this question cannot be interpreted to mean that several people think they have big noses. This is because the multiple reference interpretation is only allowed with a bound pronoun, as in (3). This difference between the possible interpretations of questions like (1a) and (1b) has been exploited in several experiments with children.

Before we turn to the experiments, it will be useful to summarize the predicted outcomes that will be under discussion. The experimental hypothesis is that children adhere to the constraints on interpretation in just the same ways as adults do.

Experimental Hypothesis H_1: Children know Principle C.
  Bound pronoun questions: *Who thinks he has a big nose?*
  Expected results: Children permit both interpretations of the pronoun
          (a) the deictic interpretation
    and   (b) the bound pronoun interpretation

  Crossover questions: *Who does he think has a big nose?*
  Expected results: Children will permit only one interpretation of the pronoun
          (a) the deictic interpretation

The experimental hypothesis contrasts with the null hypothesis, that children lack Principle C:

Null Hypothesis H_0: Children lack Principle C.
  Expected results: Children permit both interpretations for both types of
          questions

There is another way to view the expected results according to the alternative hypotheses. On the experimental hypothesis, H_1, children are expected to find bound pronoun questions to be **ambiguous**, but they should find crossover questions to be **unambiguous**. According to the null hypothesis, by contrast, children should interpret both questions as **ambiguous**; children should be able to assign the same range of meanings to both questions.

2   Previous Research

There have been two previous studies investigating children's knowledge of the constraint on interpreting crossover questions. These studies focused on the contrast between crossover questions, where a singular pronoun cannot refer to more than a single individual, as in (5), and bound pronoun questions, where the pronoun can have multiple referents, as in (6).

(5)   Who does he think has a hat?

(6)   Who thinks he has a hat?

The findings of the first study, by Roeper, Rooth, Mallish, and Akiyama, were interpreted as evidence in favor of accepting the null hypothesis. In this study, it is claimed, children incorrectly accepted the bound pronoun interpretation of crossover questions like (5). On the basis of this response, the authors of this study concluded that children interpret crossover questions and bound pronoun questions in the same way. In both, they claimed, children interpret the pronoun as bound by the WH-phrase. As we have seen, this interpretation is not allowed by the adult grammar in the case of questions like (5). In fact, few children responded in the non-adult fashion, even in this study. To examine this claim further, and to redress a methodological flaw in the earlier task, a subsequent study was conducted by McDaniel and McKee.

In the McDaniel and McKee study, children's comprehension of crossover and bound pronoun questions was investigated using a different experimental technique. This study had children judge the appropriateness of particular answers to both kinds of questions. On each trial, one experimenter acted out a story with toys while two puppets (played by a second experimenter) and the child looked on. After the story, the first puppet posed a question to the second puppet about what had happened. The reply by the second puppet was always true. However, sometimes the second puppet's reply was appropriate to the question, and other times it was not. The child's task was to judge whether or not the reply was appropriate. The critical contrast in the experiment was children's responses to the following types of question/answer pairs:

(7) **Bound Pronoun**
     Question: Who said he was under the blanket?
     Answer: He did and he did.

(8) **Crossover**
     Question: Who did he say was under the blanket?
     *Answer: He did and he did.

In the example in (7), the bound pronoun interpretation is allowed, as indicated by the appropriateness of the multiple reference answer: He$_i$ did and he$_k$ did.[1] The puppet pointed to different referents as it produced each "he." In short, the puppet responded by saying something that was both true and appropriate as an answer to the question in (7). Consider the question in (8), by contrast. The bound pronoun interpretation is not allowed for (8), as we have indicated by an asterisk on the answer given by the puppet. This answer is not tolerated, as we saw, because the pronoun in a crossover question cannot be bound by the WH-word.

The goal of the McDaniel and McKee study was to determine whether children show Strong Crossover effects, that is, whether they follow adults in rejecting the bound pronoun interpretation of the crossover questions. If children lack the relevant constraint, they would be expected to permit a bound pronoun, hence a multiple referent answer, to both question types. Children had the opportunity to demonstrate knowledge of the constraint by rejecting the multiple referent answer ("He$_i$ did and he$_k$ did") as inappropriate for crossover questions, but accepting it as appropriate for bound pronoun questions.

To summarize the main finding of this study, the mean level of performance for children was 56 percent correct responses to crossover questions. A control group of adults performed slightly worse than this. The two groups accepted the bound pronoun interpretation for sentences like (8) more than half of the time. That is, both groups "overaccepted," permitting an answer to crossover questions that is illicit, according to linguistic theory. Despite the high error rates by both groups, the authors claim that the findings demonstrate that both children and adults know the constraint on Strong Crossover. The reason is that both groups accepted the multiple reference answer more often for the bound pronoun questions than for the crossover questions. The authors of this study argued that incorrect responses for both groups should be attributed to performance factors, and should not be taken as an indication of a lack of grammatical competence. As long as children and adults perform with the same degree of success, whatever the level of correct performance, we should infer that children have the same grammatical competence as adults.

However, we disagree with their interpretation of the results. On the model of UG that we assume, children (and adults) with knowledge of a grammatical principle will perform almost perfectly, at least if the experiment is constructed properly. Clearly, there was something about the task in this experiment that prevented subjects from displaying their full grammatical competence. This follows from that fact that even adults performed poorly, often accepting the ungrammatical crossover responses. For this reason, we will present the findings from another experiment on crossover questions. In this case, the results are more in line with the predictions of the UG model.

3   A New Experiment on Strong Crossover

Like previous research, the present experiment, by Crain and Thornton, investigated children's knowledge of the constraint on Strong Crossover questions. The experiment was conducted using a variant of the Truth-Value Judgment task, which was described in chapter 15. Each child was tested individually, with two experimenters. The first experimenter acted out an event with toys and props. The second experimenter manipulated a puppet: Kermit the Frog. Following each event Kermit said what he thought had happened. The child's task was to indicate whether or not the sentence uttered by Kermit accurately described the event that had taken place. In this case, this was done by feeding Kermit a piece of pizza, his favorite food, if he said the right thing – but feeding him one of his less favorite foods, or making him do push-ups, if he said the wrong thing. The child administered the "negative reinforcement" to help Kermit pay closer attention on subsequent trials.

The materials for this experiment included examples like those we have seen, with bound pronoun and crossover questions. Because the two-clause crossover examples we have seen so far might be more difficult for young children to process, this experiment also included one-clause crossover sentences, like those in (9). This permitted the investigators to see whether the constraint on Strong Crossover might emerge first on simpler sentences. As indicated, the sentences were presented twice, once with a singular pronoun, and once with a plural pronoun.

(9) a. I know who he/they washed
     b. I know who he/they dressed
     c. I know who she/they scratched

The stories for these sentences all had certain features in common. The storylines for sentences with a plural pronoun, for example, all involved five characters who have some kind of adventure. The story ends with one character needing help. This "helpless" character is aided by two of the other characters who are "merciful" in disposition. The remaining two characters in the party are "self-reliant," and take care of their own needs. In fact, the self-reliant tell the merciful characters they don't need their help. In this way, the merciful characters are made prominent and are the natural referents for the pronoun in the test question. Figure 26.1 illustrates a typical situation. This particular protocol was used in testing example (9c), with the plural pronoun.

The story tells of a group of friends who go for a hike in the woods and get bitten by mosquitoes. Big Bird needs help scratching all his bites. Robocop and Batman come to his rescue, while Bert and Huckleberry Hound refuse help and scratch their own bites. Principle C dictates that the target sentence is an inappropriate description of a situation in which Bert and Huckleberry Hound scratched themselves but were not scratched by someone else. Of course, this is precisely the situation that Kermit describes, as illustrated in the following protocol.

Protocol for One-Clause Strong Crossover

Experimenter: This is a story with Big Bird, Bert, and Huckleberry Hound. In this story they take a walk with Robocop and Batman just before dark. The problem is that mosquitoes came out at dark, and bit everyone except for Robocop and Batman because they

Figure 26.1   Situation for one-clause crossover

are wearing special suits. Big Bird got the most bites, and is having trouble scratching them. Robocop and Batman say, "We'll help you. We don't have any bites." They scratch Big Bird's bites. Then Bert says, "I don't need Robocop and Batman to help me. I can reach my bites." And Huckleberry Hound says, "Me neither. I don't need Robocop and Batman to help me."

Kermit: I know who they scratched. Bert and Huckleberry Hound.
Child: NO. Big Bird.
Kermit: No? What about Bert and Huckleberry Hound?

Child: THEY ARE SCRATCHING THEIRSELF.
Kermit: OK, then, I guess I'll do five push-ups, to wake up. Then I'll
                      pay closer attention to the next story.

The child's response above represents the expectations of the experimental
hypothesis, according to which children know Principle C. Children who lack
Principle C should also be able to give an affirmative "yes" response.

The predictions of the null hypothesis and the experimental hypothesis were
provided earlier. In the study under consideration, every effort was made to
avoid Type I errors, by stacking the cards against the experimental hypothesis.
One way this was done was by having the final event in each scenario be the
reflexive actions of the two characters that are named by Kermit, in this case
Bert and Huckleberry Hound. This put the pragmatic focus on these characters,
to make the incorrect bound pronoun interpretation more accessible to children
if it was consistent with a child's grammar. As another precaution against Type
I errors, there were many other trials on which Kermit said the right thing and
ones on which he said the wrong thing, to guard against any bias children might
develop to hand out positive or negative reinforcement to Kermit.

We discussed several other features of experimental design in chapter 15. It
was pointed out that the Truth-Value Judgment task involves four components:
the **background**, the **assertion**, the **actual outcome**, and the **possible outcome**. In
the present study, these four parts of each trial are given in (10).

(10) **Test sentence:** *I know who they scratched. Bert and Huckleberry Hound.*
      Background: I know who they scratched. So-and-so and so-and-so.
      Assertion: They scratched Bert and Huckleberry Hound.
      Actual outcome: They scratched themselves.
      Plausible dissent: The assertion is a possible outcome at some point in
         the story.

Notice how plausible dissent is built into the story, by having Robocop and
Batman say to Bert and Huckleberry Hound: "We'll help you. We don't have
any bites." In this way, the assertion was a possible outcome. Events transpired,
however, which prevent this from being the actual outcome. What happened
was that Bert and Huckleberry Hound refused the offers of assistance. Notice,
also, that the events make it clear to the child subject *why* Kermit is wrong in
saying, "I know who they scratched. Bert and Huckleberry Hound." If the
child's grammar has Principle C, the referents of the plural pronoun *they* must
be Robocop and Batman, and they scratched someone else, Big Bird.

Finally, it is worth pointing out that the protocols were designed to be biased
towards the incorrect "multiple reference" interpretation of the crossover question. If children lacked Principle C, and could interpret "I know who they

scratched" as "I know who scratched themselves," then they should have been able to judge the sentence/answer pairs as true descriptions of the stories, since the two characters named by Kermit, Bert and Huckleberry Hound, had indeed scratched themselves. The only thing to stop children from interpreting the question/answer pairs in this way is knowledge of Principle C. Therefore, children's correct rejections of the test sentences are compelling evidence of their knowledge of Principle C. The question is whether children's knowledge of Principle C causes them to override all of the pragmatic biases towards the multiple reference interpretation, such that they do indeed reject this interpretation.

There were also two-clause crossover questions testing the Strong Crossover constraint, as illustrated in (11). Only the singular pronoun was used, but the examples appeared with different verbs, as indicated.

(11) a. I know who he said/thinks has the best food.
      b. I know who he said/thinks is the best flier.
      c. I know who he said/thinks is the best color.
      d. I know who he said/thinks has the best smile.

The stories for two-clause crossover were also alike in many respects. Each story depicted some kind of competition. There were four characters: a judge and three contestants. The judge checks all the contestants, openly rejecting two of them and settling on a "winner." The would-be winners dispute the judge's decision by pointing out to him that they would have been a better choice, and he's mistaken. In this way the judge is made salient as the referent for "he" in the crossover question. In the typical protocol that follows, the judge, the Joker, decides which contestant has the best smile.

Protocol for Two-Clause Strong Crossover

Experimenter: Last year's winner of the best smile contest was the Joker. That makes him this year's judge of the best smile. Here are the three people in the contest: Grover, one of the Teenage Mutant Ninja Turtles, and Yogi Bear. The Joker walks over to each contestant in turn. To Grover, he says, "Pretty good, big mouth." To Yogi Bear, he says, "Not the best." Then, he looks at the Ninja Turtle and says, "Look at those teeth. You've definitely got the best smile." But Grover says, "Joker, you're wrong. I have the best smile. Look at how big my mouth is." And Yogi Bear says, "No, I have the best smile."

Kermit: I know who he said has the best smile. Grover and Yogi Bear.

Child: NO.

Experimenter: What really happened?

Figure 26.2   Situation for two-clause crossover

Child: **HE** (the Joker) SAID THAT **HE** (the Ninja Turtle) HAD THE
                     BEST SMILE.

As in the one-clause crossover stories, the condition of plausible dissent is
satisfied in the protocol given above. That is, the child has good reason to deny
that the Joker said that Grover and Yogi Bear have the best smiles, because it is
clear from the story that he chose the Ninja Turtle as having the best smile. The
protocol also parallels the one-clause protocol in its bias for a multiple reference
interpretation. The story ends with the action that corresponds to the incorrect
interpretation of the question, the two would-be winners of the contest, Grover
and Yogi Bear, both disputing the Joker's judgment about who has the best
smile. If the child understood "I know who he said has the best smile" to mean
"I know who said he has the best smile," then the answer "Grover and Yogi
Bear" would have been correct. Figure 26.2 illustrates the situation corresponding to example (11d), with the verb "said."

    The participants in this study were twelve children from a daycare center.
These children ranged in age from 3;7 to 4;8 with an average age of 4;2. The
main findings of this test of children's knowledge of the Strong Crossover constraint are as follows. Children in this study were steadfast in their adherence to
Principle C, in both one-clause and two-clause crossover questions. For one-
clause crossover questions, children correctly rejected the multiple reference
interpretation over 95 percent of the time, for both singular and plural pronouns. In two-clause questions, the multiple reference interpretation was re-

jected over 92 percent of the time. Collapsing the results, we find that children rejected the multiple reference response on 131 out of 138 opportunities, giving an overall rate of well over 90 percent correct rejections. In sum, the early acquisition of the constraint on Strong Crossover is confirmed.

Conclusion

Over the last chapters, we have presented evidence regarding whether or not children demonstrate knowledge of certain constraints that have been proposed within Universal Grammar. We have seen examples of children's adherence to constraints both in their production and in their comprehension of utterances subject to constraints. On the assumption that children only encounter possible sentence/meaning pairs, and do not have access to negative evidence, the existence of constraints on production and on comprehension raise a learnability dilemma. Children cannot learn constraint on the basis of positive evidence alone; negative evidence would be needed. Therefore, they would have to be very conservative in order to avoid making potential mistakes. However, we know that children are not over-conservative in their grammatical hypotheses; they make generalizations on the basis of limited data, exactly when these generalizations are allowed. Therefore, constraints – statements to the effect that certain meanings cannot be assigned to sentences or that certain utterances are ill-formed – must be a part of UG.

On other acquisition scenarios, children are seen to obey learning procedures such as generalization based on analogy, and so on. According to such scenarios, however, children could make errors. But this would resurrect the learnability dilemma – how could children recover from these errors so as to converge on the adult grammar, in the absence of negative evidence? Instead of invoking learning procedures such as analogy or stimulus generalization, the theory of Universal Grammar circumvents the problem of learnability in the absence of negative evidence by postulating that the knowledge contained in constraints is not learned, but is part of the human genetic blueprint for language growth. The results of testing young children conform to this prediction. The findings underscore the contention of the theory of Universal Grammar that linguistic constraints are not something children learn; rather, they are innately given.

Note

1 NPs with distinct indices (subscripts) are interpreted as picking out distinct referents.

Bibliographical Comments

The first experiment described in this chapter was conducted by Roeper et al. (1984) and deVilliers et al. (1990). The second experiment was by McDaniel and McKee (1992). The revised experiment is reported in Crain and Thornton (1991). For more detailed discussion of experimental design, see Crain and Thornton (1998).

Part IV   Universal Grammar in the Visual Modality

Introduction

In this part we examine cross-linguistic evidence for the Universal Grammar hypothesis. In particular, we look at the acquisition of American Sign Language (ASL), the visual/manual language used by deaf people in the United States. We find that ASL displays the same properties as spoken languages, supporting the conclusion that it is governed by the same Universal Grammar which holds for spoken languages – and thus, that its acquisition should be guided by UG as well. Our study of the acquisition of ASL by deaf children with deaf, signing parents shows that this conclusion is well founded. This cross-linguistic, cross-modality evidence is strong support for the UG hypothesis.

27 The Structure of American Sign Language

Introduction

We have illustrated the theory of Universal Grammar mainly by using data from English. However, we have made the claim that this UG is part of the innate endowment of all children – hence, the principles of UG will apply cross-linguistically. We will now make an even stronger claim, which is that the principles of UG also apply across **modalities**. "Modality" refers to the channel which is used to convey language. For English, this is the vocal-auditory channel. However, despite the fact that the contrary belief was held as recently as the early 1970s, it has now been determined that the vocal-auditory channel is *not* the only available modality for language. There exist languages which use the manual-visual channel: natural sign languages used by the deaf. Our claim that UG applies across modalities is a claim that the principles and parameters of UG are also relevant to these sign languages. We will support this claim using evidence from American Sign Language (also called ASL).

1 American Sign Language

First let's consider what kind of a language ASL is, and clear up some misconceptions that people frequently have about it. ASL is a visual-gestural language used by many deaf people in the United States and some parts of Canada. There are several common misconceptions about ASL, and signed languages in general. Some people believe that ASL is a variant of English, but it is not. Neither is it a manual representation of English, although systems which are manual representations of English are used in some schools for the deaf. ASL is its own language with a different structure from English. As we will see, in some structures ASL is more like Chinese than like English – and it has similarities with various other spoken languages as well. ASL uses handshapes, locations, and movements as the basic elements for **signs**. These signs in turn are the basic elements of phrases and sentences.

Another mistaken supposition people sometimes have is that the signs of ASL are *iconic*, or picture-like gestures, rather than arbitrary, complex combinations of visual gestures produced by rules. On this view, the signs of ASL are simply "hand drawings" of whatever is being referred to. This is not true. ASL is not simply drawing in the air. Of course, there are some iconic signs, in which the shape of the hands calls to mind a picture of the referent. For example, in the sign for "tree" the arm is extended upwards, representing the tree trunk, and the fingers extend outwards representing branches and leaves. Note that this sign is good for any tree, not just trees with long trunks and leaves at the top. It's also not a universal sign for "tree." In other sign languages, even when the sign for "tree" is also iconically based it's not made the same way. In the Danish sign for "tree," the shape and movement of the hands outline first a circle for the branches and leaves, and then move downward for a long trunk. This sign is also iconic, but the form of the sign itself is different from the ASL sign. This is what we mean by saying that some signs are iconically based.

It is important to recognize several facts about iconicity in ASL. First, although some signs might be iconically based, the majority of signs are *abstract* – that is, the relationship between the sign and the meaning is fully arbitrary. Second, those signs which are iconically based can be compared to the "onomatopoeic" words in spoken language, in which the sound of the word calls to mind the sound of the referent (such as "bow-wow" or "meow"). So spoken languages also have words which are "iconically based." The most important point is that despite the iconic basis of some signs, these signs are treated like linguistic units, both in the rules of the language, and in language acquisition, as we will see in the next chapter. When the rules of the language affect the iconic signs, they do not preserve the iconicity, but act like a regular linguistic rule. Hence, despite a possible iconic base for some signs, we should consider all signs as natural linguistic units which obey the properties of UG.

Another common misconception about ASL is that it is not a "natural" human language. Many people believe that ASL lacks the kind of rich and complex grammatical rules that characterize natural languages. This, too, is incorrect. The truth of the matter is that the "words" (signs) of ASL are organized into phrases and sentences according to a grammar that is every bit as complex as any other natural language grammar. A great deal of research in recent years confirms that ASL has all the properties of a natural human language. As noted above, however, the grammar of ASL is in many ways quite different from the grammar of English. It has unique grammatical rules, but it does have rules, and the type of rules it has are well within the range of natural human languages.

For example, we claimed that one of the universals for human language was Phrase Structure, and ASL has Phrase Structure which can be described using the same X'-schema we found for spoken languages. The PS rules are recursive in ASL, as they are in spoken languages, so they can generate an unbounded number of utterances. Another universal we proposed is transformational rules, and ASL has transformational rules. More importantly, ASL observes the *constraints* on the application of transformational rules which we have attributed to Universal Grammar. For example, the transformational rules of ASL are structure-dependent. A transformation affects the phrasal structure, not single words. We will discuss adherence to UG constraints in ASL in more detail in chapter 29.

Another misconception that people often have is that there is only one sign language – i.e., that deaf people in the United States use the same sign language as deaf people in China, or Italy (etc.). In fact, the sign language used by deaf people in the United States is not even the same as the sign language used by deaf people in Britain. So when we say that ASL obeys the principles of Universal Grammar, this is not the same as saying that there is a Universal Sign Language, any more than it is saying that a spoken language which obeys the principles of UG is universal.

This brings us to the differences between ASL and spoken languages such as English. Some of the differences are superficial, reflecting the different modalities that are used. ASL is visual, not auditory, so the processing mechanisms which exist for the perception of auditory speech won't be invoked for the perception of visual signs. Since ASL is signed, not spoken, the articulatory apparatus which must be developed for producing speech is not the same as the articulatory apparatus which must be developed for producing signs. In chapter 31, we will discuss the relevance of these modality effects for our theory of language.

In other ways, there are structural differences between a particular signed language, such as ASL, and a particular spoken language, such as English. However, these are the kind of differences which can be explained by the theory of Universal Grammar, using the same mechanisms that explain how spoken languages differ – for example, how English differs from Chinese. As we have seen, differences between languages in a limited range of variation are captured by parameters. We will discuss one such parameter in detail in chapter 30.

Now that we have given an overview of the nature of American Sign Language, we will turn to describe it in more detail in the next section.

2   Aspects of the Grammar of ASL

As we claimed above, ASL has rules at all levels of the grammar. Here we will summarize some aspects of the grammar of ASL to make this claim more concrete.

Phonology

We have not discussed phonology (sound patterns) in this text, so our mention of it here will be brief. Let us consider phonology more abstractly to be the study of the ways in which the smallest, non-meaningful units of language combine. Since the units are smaller than a lexical item (a word), they are called "sub-lexical" units. For spoken languages, these units are bits of sound. For signed languages, the units are described in different terms. Although it might seem that "phonology" would be the area in which differences between signed and spoken languages are the greatest, it is important to point out that there are remarkable similarities when abstract rules for organization and phonological processes are considered.

The smallest, non-meaningful units of signed languages can be described along three main dimensions. First is **handshape**. Although there are a great many ways in which you can configure your fingers, only a limited set of them are linguistic units in ASL. Many potential hand configurations are used in other signed languages, but not in ASL. This is akin to the units of spoken languages, which come from a limited universal set. No one spoken language uses all of the units. Furthermore, languages do not use all of the sounds which the human vocal tract can produce. Also like spoken languages, there can be slight differences in the way that similar handshapes are "pronounced" in different signed languages. For example, a closed fist is used as a handshape in many signed languages, but there are differences in the way the fingers touch the palm (curved or straight?) and in the way the thumb touches the side of the index finger (straight up and down? curved out or in?). Pronouncing a sign with this hand configuration in a non-standard way results in an "accent," just as the slight difference between the way that English-speakers and Spanish-speakers pronounce "d" is noticeable.

Signs are made with a particular handshape which undergoes some kind of **movement** in some **location**, the two other main dimensions of sub-lexical units. The locations used in ASL include locations in the space in front of the signer's body, as well as locations on the trunk, arms, head, and neck. In all three dimensions, but perhaps most notably in location, the permissible units of ASL are much narrower than those used in gesture or mime. Obviously, signers would not use the area behind them as a location for a sign, since the listener would not be able to see signs made in that location. But physical accessibility is not the organizing principle for which locations are used and which are not. Rather, this comes from the linguistic component: the language places restrictions on signs.

The movements of signs are similarly constrained linguistically. One interesting constraint is that signs do require some kind of movement. There is always movement to and from the locations used in signs, but it is conceivable that some signs would have no movement at all: just a particular handshape in a particular location. However, basic signs all have some kind of movement, either movement along some path or movement of the fingers.[1]

Morphology

The processes by which words are formed from meaningful units is morphology. In English, verb agreement and plural formation are examples of morphological processes, but all in all, English has relatively little productive morphology. ASL, on the other hand, is a language with complex morphological processes.

One of the interesting areas of morphology in ASL is verb agreement. Subject and object agreement morphology are indicated by adjusting the movement used in signing the verbs. To illustrate this, we first need to discuss how reference to different people is made, because some of the same mechanisms are used in verb agreement.

The pronoun signs for "ME"[2] and "YOU" involve directing an index finger to a point in space: to the signer for "ME," to the addressee for "YOU." These points in space are used as the end points for the movement of verbs marked with agreement. Usually, the verb moves from the location of the subject to the location of the object. For comparison, the uninflected form of the sign moves without specifying any particular subject or object. Let's take the sign "GIVE" as an example. To inflect the sign to mean "I give to you," the sign moves from me to you. We will notate these changes in movement by putting a subscript before the verb to indicate the beginning position of the movement, and another subscript after the verb to indicate the ending position. The numbers "1" and "2" will indicate first and second person, respectively. Thus, moving from me to you will be written as "$_1\text{GIVE}_2$." To inflect the sign to mean "You give to me," the sign moves from you to me: "$_2\text{GIVE}_1$." As you can see, if you produce this movement yourself (use a hand closed as if it is holding a piece of paper), the form of this inflected sign is iconically based: it almost looks like you giving to me.

The same principles of agreement work for other persons, and other verbs, obscuring the iconic base. In order to say, for example, that "Mom kissed Dad," first two locations have to be established to stand for Mom and Dad. Suppose a locus to the signer's left is chosen to represent Mom (we'll call that locus "a"), and a locus to the signer's right represents Dad (called locus "b"). We can use these loci in space for pronouns which pick out Mom and Dad. We refer to "her" (Mom) by pointing to locus "a," and we refer to "him" (Dad) by pointing to locus "b." Then, the sign for "KISS" can move from the signer's left to the right, or from point a to point b, to show agreement with Mom as the subject and Dad as the object: $_a\text{KISS}_b$.

One interesting fact about ASL, however, is that not all verbs mark agreement for subject and object in the way that we discussed. Some verbs do not mark agreement at all. For example, although the verb "HATE" does mark agreement, the verb "LOVE" does not. To say what the subject and object of a verb like "LOVE" are, the signer must name the persons, or use pronouns pointing to the locations in space established for these persons. The verb, however, does not change.

Several other morphological processes in ASL also involve changes in movement. For example, aspect marking, which indicates certain temporal properties of an action (such as ongoing, over a long period of time, quick, etc.), is conveyed by changing the movement of the verb. Other morphological processes involve changing the handshape: for example, it is possible to indicate the instrument used in an action by changing the handshape on the verb.

As you can see, there are many morphological processes involving verbs in ASL, which are quite distinct from the morphological processes found in English. Although the use of space (and certain consequences of using space) is unique to signed languages, there are spoken languages which have morphological processes of subject and object agreement, for example, or aspect marking or instrument incorporation. None of the morphological processes found in ASL are absent from spoken languages.

Syntax

As already mentioned, ASL uses Phrase Structure rules like those we described for English. As in English, in ASL the verb usually goes in the middle of the sentence, between the subject and object NPs – that is, ASL has specifiers before heads, and complements after. However, in ASL, unlike English, adjectives often go after the noun they modify, not before. This happens in many spoken languages, such as Spanish. An example of ASL basic word order is given in (1).

(1) BOY EAT ICE-CREAM
    "The boy ate an ice-cream."

The order of elements in ASL is frequently altered from the basic SVO, however. For example, ASL employs "topicalization" – a process we illustrated in chapter 11 when we showed that certain sequences of words formed constituents for movement operations. English uses topicalization, but much less frequently than ASL. ASL sentences frequently have some element topicalized, such as a direct object or a location. In ASL, when a constituent is topicalized, there is a grammatical marker of this process. However, the marker is not made with the hands, as described above for basic signs. Instead, the marker is non-manual;

that is, it is indicated by a particular facial expression and head position. For topicalization, the eyebrows are raised, and the head is tilted forward. This non-manual marker is indicated by a line over the elements with which it co-occurs, and the letter "t" to indicate the topicalization marker. An example of topic-alization is given in (2).

_____t

(2) ICE-CREAM, BOY EAT.
  "An ice-cream, the boy ate."

Other grammatical processes in ASL are also marked non-manually (and a similar notation is used for them). For example, relative clauses, conditionals, negation, and questions all employ different non-manual markers. They may or may not have manual markers in addition to the non-manual markers. For example, it is possible to express negation in ASL with a manual sign (such as NOT), together with a non-manual marker, as illustrated in (3a). As (3b) shows, it is also possible to use only the non-manual marker – even without the manual sign, the sentence is negated.

_____neg

(3) a. CHRIS NOT PASS TEST.

_____neg

  b. CHRIS PASS TEST.
    "Chris didn't pass the test."

One other aspect of ASL syntax deserves mention here, and will be referred to again. Often, some element from a sentence may be repeated at the end of the sentence, where it receives a "focused" interpretation (this includes emphasis or specifying one particular possibility). Negative elements, modals, quantifiers, and WH-elements are among those which can participate in this process. Some examples of such "doubling" structures are given in (4).

_____neg

(4) a. CHRIS NOT PASS TEST NOT.
    "Chris really didn't pass the test."

  b. BOY EAT THREE ICE-CREAM THREE.
    "The boy ate THREE ice-creams!"

  c. ME CAN READ PHYSICS CAN.
    "I surely CAN read physics!"

We will discuss the double structures in more detail in chapter 29, where we deal with WH-questions in ASL.

Conclusion

We have seen that the principles of linguistic structure apply in American Sign Language as well as in spoken languages. Here we have not had the opportunity to provide detailed evidence for this claim, but we have illustrated some of the basic aspects of the structure of ASL. More evidence of the principles of UG in ASL structure will be presented in chapters 29 and 30. In the meantime, we turn next to sketch the overall process of language acquisition in deaf children who are exposed to ASL by their deaf parents.

Notes

1 We say "basic" signs because some morphological processes involve no movement.
2 It is common practice to notate ASL by using uppercase English glosses.

Bibliographical Comments

One of the earliest works arguing for the linguistic status of ASL is Stokoe, Casterline, and Croneberg (1965), a dictionary which provided the first analysis of signs in terms of sub-lexical units. A summary of a number of early studies on the structure and processing of ASL is given in Klima and Bellugi (1979), a very readable book. A more thorough description of linguistic studies of ASL is given in Wilbur (1987). A more recent introduction to the linguistic study of ASL will be presented in Sandler and Lillo-Martin (in preparation).

28 The Acquisition of American Sign Language

Introduction

We have seen that children learning their native language are guided by innate principles of Universal Grammar. This explains why they go through the same sequence of stages in the language acquisition process, independently of the particular language they are learning. It also explains why children, everywhere, respect the universal constraints on language structure, such as structure dependence and Principle C.

This chapter looks at language acquisition in deaf children. As in earlier chapters, the goal of this chapter is to evaluate the innateness hypothesis. Looking at deaf children would seem to be a good way of helping us towards our goal. Since deaf children do not hear language spoken around them, it might be expected that their language acquisition would be rather different from the acquisition of speech which we have discussed. However, we will see that by focusing on deaf children's acquisition of sign language we find relatively few differences in the overall path of acquisition. Since the language which they are learning is *visual* rather than *auditory*, we might expect to see a number of differences based on the language *modality*. However, it would be particularly interesting if it turned out that language acquisition is the *same* in important respects for both deaf children and children with normal hearing.

We will focus primarily on a special population of deaf children: children whose parents are also deaf and so use American Sign Language (ASL) as their primary means of communication. For these children ASL becomes their native language, and their primary form of communication. It is important to note that this represents only a small percentage of the deaf population. Only 5 to 10 percent of deaf children have deaf parents. They are an important group to study, however, because they encounter a visual language, ASL, from birth, in much the same way that hearing parents use spoken language with their hearing children from birth. We will see that because these deaf children are exposed to a natural language input from birth (albeit a visual language), they acquire language in much the same way as hearing children. These deaf children learn

ASL as a native language in the same way that children hearing English learn it as a native language.[1]

We will also briefly discuss language acquisition by deaf children who do not receive input in ASL at an early age. We will see that the Language Acquisition Device is so powerful that its effects are found even in the absence of systematic linguistic input.

1 The Acquisition of ASL by Deaf Children with Early ASL Input

Several properties of ASL were discussed in the previous chapter, where we claimed that ASL falls under the principles and parameters of Universal Grammar. Accepting ASL as a natural language, with some potentially interesting characteristics, we now turn to its acquisition.

If a deaf child is born to deaf adults who use sign language, then he or she will have exposure to a natural language from birth – just as a hearing child born to hearing parents has exposure to a natural language from birth. Furthermore, we can assume that the parents don't *teach* ASL any more than hearing parents *teach* spoken language to their children. How, then, does sign language develop in such children?

Studies on the acquisition of sign language in deaf children have been carried out in much the same way as the studies of the acquisition of speech in hearing children. In fact, some of the same psychologists who did important studies in the acquisition of speech have done research on the acquisition of sign language. The same two kinds of approaches are used in studies of the acquisition of ASL as we found in studies of the acquisition of English. On one approach, the researcher visits the child in his or her home and videotapes many hours of natural interactions between the child and the parents, deaf siblings, or other deaf signers. The researcher then goes back to the laboratory and transcribes all of the signing that went on, analyzing the tapes in order to extract the particular patterns of language development. The second approach is usually carried out in conjunction with the first. This approach is to play specially designed language games with the child, to test the child's comprehension of particular kinds of sentences, or to elicit specific structures from the child. Both kinds of studies have provided the findings we now summarize.

Babbling

Deaf children with deaf parents do go through a stage of *vocal* babbling, as we have mentioned in chapter 3, but only for a few months. Interestingly, deaf children also seem to go through a stage of *manual* babbling, in which they produce different kinds of handshapes at different locations on the body, using different kinds of movements. As it is with hearing children, this babbling is not meaningful, but a kind of exercise in preparation for language.

First signs

When do the first real signs of sign language appear? Some early studies suggested that deaf children begin to use individual signs around 6 to 8 months of age. This is much earlier than the appearance of first words in children learning spoken languages. Why might deaf children make their first signs earlier than hearing children make their first words?

One suggestion that has been made is that this is because children develop the fine muscular coordination of their hands and arms which is needed for producing signs earlier than they develop the fine muscular coordination of their tongue and vocal organs which is needed for producing words. If this is true, then it would indicate the influence of the modality on the timing of language acquisition. One problem with this explanation is in the large difference in timing between first words and apparent first signs. It is not clear that the difference in development of the articulators is really this large.

However, more recent studies of the development of ASL would have us question the conclusion that first signs come several months before first words. The problem is that both deaf and hearing children make meaningful gestures during the period under consideration, but researchers studying the development of spoken language don't consider those gestures to be the first *words* in hearing children. Only when hearing children produce spoken words are they considered to begin vocabulary development. By contrast, some investigators looking at the development of ASL have counted some of the gestures of deaf children as their first signs, or words.

Should early gestures be counted as a child's first words, or not? According to some researchers, they shouldn't. They argue that, although gestures may be meaningful, they are not *words*. Of course, the argument hinges on what counts as a *word*. In natural language, words can be assigned a constant meaning despite the various circumstances in which they appear. However, the gestures that the children produce (both deaf and hearing) during this period before one year of age don't show this kind of consistency. Rather, a single form, such as stretching the arms out and opening and closing the fist, will be interpreted as "give-me," "up," "down," "milk," "hug," "want," and "what," depending on the circumstances. A single meaning, furthermore, might be interpreted from several gestures. Parents might interpret as "give-me," such gestures as holding out the arms and opening and closing the fist, or hitting oneself on the chest, or banging on the high-chair. When the circumstances, but not the form of the gesture, determines the meaning, then the gesture is not a word. Furthermore, these same natural gestures are used by children in a variety of language environments, including deaf families, and hearing families in which sign language is not used. Thus, it can be concluded that these are not the first signs.

Around the age of 11 months to one year, deaf children with deaf parents begin producing their first real signs. These signs, unlike the earlier gestures, display a consistent form–meaning relationship, and they are signs from the language, not natural gestures. Certainly there may be formational (phonological) errors in these sign productions, but they can be seen as real attempts towards a target sign which is in the adult language. As with hearing children, the first word-signs that deaf children produce have to do with things in their environment, like MOMMY, DADDY, and MILK. Some researchers conclude then that deaf and hearing children produce their first words at around the same age, because this is when the biological timetable is set for the first words. It seems that there may well be an advantage for sign, but only of about one month – not the four to six months previously claimed. If true, this could easily be accounted for by the difference in physical control mentioned earlier. Although this debate is not yet settled, this seems to be an area in which the modality doesn't have a strong special effect, and the effect which is possibly there is a delay in the production of speech *vis-à-vis* sign, not the other way around.

First word combinations

Around the age of $1\frac{1}{2}$, deaf children put together signs into two-sign sentences. They use signs without any of the grammatical morphology which ASL has, such as verb agreement. In addition to the kinds of morphology discussed in the previous chapter, ASL also uses special morphological markers to distinguish related sets of nouns and verbs (cf. English per'mit and permit'). During the two-word stage, deaf children don't use this grammatical morphology either. Rather, they put together sentences like "DADDY GIVE," or "DRINK JUICE," in a similar manner to the acquisition of English discussed earlier.

The order of elements in early ASL utterances is of interest in comparison with the acquisition of word order in other "flexible" word order languages, as discussed in chapter 10. We saw there that in some cases, children learning

languages with more variations on basic word order nevertheless were conservative, adopting one order and not using the variations available. In other cases, it
was reported that children from early on used the variety of orders available to
them, in the correct way. What about the acquisition of ASL?

One study reported that children rather consistently use the SVO basic order
of ASL, without adopting the variations in order allowed by the adult grammar.
However, a more recent study found that children do use variations in basic
order, largely in the correct situations (as well as could be determined). This
study found that two-word utterances including a verb and a subject had pre-
dominantly subject–verb order, but two-word utterances including a verb and its
object had both verb–object and object–verb orders. Of course, the object–verb
order could be derived by topicalization, as discussed in the previous chapter.
One difference between the children's use of object–verb order and adult
topicalization, however, is that the children frequently failed to produce the non-
manual marker of topicalization. We will see in chapter 29 that a similar finding
has been reported regarding the use of the non-manual marker for WH-
questions. In addition to topicalization, there are other conditions under which
object–verb order is permitted by the adult grammar, having to do with the type
of verb used. In this study, it was found that the majority of children's object–
verb utterances were produced with verbs which permit the object–verb order in
the adult grammar.

Hence, it seems that the acquisition of ASL is more like the cases in which
children use adult-like variations in word order from an early age, rather than
the more conservative strategy of only using one possible order. It is also possible that these differences reported in various studies actually reflect differences
in the way that individual children acquire their native language, more than
differences in the acquisition patterns found for different languages. More research is needed on the acquisition of such languages to settle this issue.

Acquisition of grammatical morphology

Around the age of 2 years, deaf children put together two- and three-sign
sentences expressing the meaning of a single clause. Meanwhile their vocabulary
is growing rapidly. Recall that we said children learning English begin to gradually
acquire grammatical morphemes beginning at around $2\frac{1}{2}$ years. This is also the
age at which deaf children begin to acquire some of the grammatical morphology
of ASL.

The grammatical morphology being acquired at this time includes the verb
agreement morphology. This is relevant for us in two ways. First, it is another
area in which we can check for the influence of iconicity in sign language

development. Second, it will be relevant to our discussion of how children set parameters, which will be presented in chapter 30.

It seems that signing children first use agreement morphology when the referents they are talking about are present in the situation. Recall that the locations used for agreement are the locations of the referents themselves, if they are present. Thus, the location for first person reference ("me") is the signer's own location; the locations for addressee or third persons who are physically present are their own physical locations. Children begin to use verb agreement with these locations around $2\frac{1}{2}$ to 3 years of age.

Children are later, however, in the use of verb agreement with non-present referents. If a referent is not present, then an abstract location in space is associated with the referent. This location is used for pronouns and verb agreement in the same way as for present referents. For children to acquire this system, however, they need to understand how to associate an abstract location in space with a referent, and they need to remember the locations associated with each referent. Studies of children's spontaneous and elicited signing indicate that this is not accomplished until relatively later in acquisition, 4 to 5 years of age.

As we said above, the verb agreement morphology in ASL is iconically based. For example, the sign for "You give me" involves moving the GIVE sign from you to me – as if you are giving me something. Does this iconic base ease the language acquisition burden? Deaf children learning ASL do not begin to use this verb agreement system until around $2\frac{1}{2}$ to 3 years of age. This is *not* earlier than hearing children learning English begin to use verb agreement morphology; in fact, it is *later* than hearing children learning some languages, such as Italian, use their verb agreement morphology. So the iconicity of the system does not seem to have an effect. Rather, the timing of the acquisition of verb agreement morphology in Italian, English, and ASL can be related to other linguistic aspects of the form and use of agreement.

Acquisition of pronouns

Let's look at another area in which the modality might make itself felt. As we said previously, some signs have an iconic base. Does this picture image help the child in language acquisition?

Let's take as an example the signs for "ME" and "YOU." The signs are the same as the gestures that hearing people use for these meanings – pointing to the person referred to: clearly very iconically based. For some hearing children learning a spoken language, it is found that for a short period in early language development, the terms "me" and "you" get mixed up: the child uses "me" to refer to "you," or "you" to refer to "me." We can see why they might do this, since the referent for "me" or "you" changes depending on who is doing the talking. The child has to learn this peculiarity of these terms, and some children go through a stage of mixing them up. But for the deaf child, since the forms used for "ME" and "YOU" are so transparent, it might be expected that no such errors would ever turn up.

One experimenter looked at whether this pronoun confusion would ever happen in deaf children's signing. To her surprise, she found that it did! One deaf girl that she was studying went through a period of a few months consistently signing "YOU" when she clearly meant "ME." In fact, sometimes her mother would try to correct her by turning her hand around so that her finger was pointing in the opposite direction, but, as you might expect, this did not have an effect. After a few months, the child corrected her mistake on her own, though in the meantime the experimenter did some tests with the child and found that she was quite consistent in making the mistake. After this study, the same result has also been found with other deaf children.

So, although it would seem that the iconicity in the visual modality would have a helpful effect on the process of language acquisition, we find that children are not attuned to the iconic aspects of signs. They are treating signs as abstract words, and thus they are not facilitated by iconicity or other aspects of the modality. They are simply moving according to the biological timetable for language.

Complex syntax

What do we know of the acquisition of complex syntax and adherence to constraints in ASL? Some issues relating to syntax acquisition will be discussed at more length in chapters 29 and 30. More work is needed in this area, but the research which has been done shows that, as expected, deaf children do obey the principles of UG.

As you can see, the picture looks remarkably like the one we have seen for the development of spoken language in hearing children. Studies of the acquisition of ASL in a number of deaf children have indeed come to this conclusion – that the natural acquisition of ASL is quite parallel to the natural acquisition of speech. We could go through all the stages we have seen for the acquisition of speech, and make the same claims for the acquisition of sign language as have been made for the acquisition of spoken languages. In the end, it seems that the basics of ASL are acquired by deaf children by around the age of 5 years, just as in the acquisition of speech.

Although it might seem very logical, this finding is quite important. For many years people thought that sound and sound patterning was a vital part of language, and that there could be no natural human language that did not rely on sound. The arguments for the linguistic status of American Sign Language are strongly supported by the finding that it is acquired in a natural means, parallel to the acquisition of spoken language. This finding also supports our idea of an innate component for language acquisition. As long as these innate principles are stated abstractly enough, so that they do not crucially rely on sound, then they ought to apply to the acquisition of a signed language. The finding that they do apply can be strong support for this hypothesis.

2 Gestural Communication by Deaf Children without ASL Input

Some parents of deaf children choose not to expose their children to signed languages, in the hope that they will successfully learn a spoken language. However, with a severe hearing impairment children do not acquire a spoken language in the usual way, and they often fail to become successful speakers and lipreaders. Thus, there may be a period of several years before these children can make use of spoken language, or before they are eventually exposed to a conventional signed language. In the meantime, they are not totally non-communicative. In the absence of sign language input, it should be expected that these deaf children would not acquire a signed language. This, of course, is true. However, it has been found that deaf children who are not exposed to a sign language nevertheless do gesture to communicate, and studies of these gesture systems have found that they have a relatively complex structure.

The gesture systems developed by deaf children who are not exposed to a signed language are called "home sign." The nature of home sign has been examined in some detail by psychologist Susan Goldin-Meadow and her colleagues. They have found that home sign systems, while far from being fully developed language, nevertheless have complexity which could not come from the input, because there simply is no input. For example, deaf children develop "signs" to express actions and objects, and they combine these signs in systematic ways. The signs are not mimes – although they are iconically based, they are much more stylized, use a confined area of space, and systematic. For example, one child used a sign involving tapping with the right index finger on the palm of the left hand to indicate "give."

The sign combinations created by these children rarely go beyond two or three elements. However, they are systematic in order: they most frequently take the order agent–object–action, or SOV. The same result has been found for several children in completely different environments, none of whom interacts with the others. Remember, these children do not receive input in a conventional sign language such as ASL. Their parents are trying to teach them to speak and lipread English, but of course since English basic word order is SVO they are not using English to structure their signed system. Rather, it would seem that the innate knowledge from Universal Grammar drives these children to create a language, even in the complete absence of primary linguistic data.

We do not know whether home sign has successive cyclic movement or respects the ECP, since the utterances produced by the children developing these systems never become complex enough to tell. Nevertheless, we find the systematic creation of a language-like system even when there is no input compelling evidence for the theory of innate linguistic knowledge.

Conclusion

Children who are exposed to ASL by their deaf, signing parents acquire it in much the same way that hearing children acquire their native language. Although fewer studies have been done with signed languages other than ASL, it is clear that the same is true for other signed languages. The Language Acquisition Device kicks in to guide the child in the process of language acquisition whether the language the child is exposed to is spoken or signed. In fact, when hearing children are born to deaf parents, they usually grow up bilingual: they acquire ASL from their parents, and they acquire English from other relatives and friends. Their language acquisition is much like that of other bilingual children, despite the difference in modality. These facts indicate that the principles of UG must be abstract enough to apply across modalities. Furthermore, these principles are so strong that even children who are not exposed to usable linguistic input seem to use them to create a rudimentary structured communication system. We don't know just how far the LAD can take a child with no accessible input, but the "resilience" of language (in Goldin-Meadow's terms) is a remarkable phenomenon.

Note

1   The process of language acquisition for deaf children with hearing parents depends on their linguistic input, which is quite varied. In some cases it might be a signed version of English, or in others, American Sign Language, or in many cases, spoken language input only (at least for the first several years of the child's life). Although there are many interesting properties of language acquisition in these differing sets of circumstances, we cannot go into them here.

Bibliographical Comments

For overviews of studies of the acquisition of ASL by deaf children see Newport and Meier (1985) and Lillo-Martin (in press). Petitto and Marentette (1991) report on the manual babbling of deaf children exposed to signed languages. An overview of the controversy regarding first signs is found in Meier and Newport (1990). The recent study on word order acquisition summarized in the text is by Chen (1998). Classic dissertations on the acquisition of verbal morphology and pronouns by children learning ASL are Meier (1982) and Petitto (1983). Extensive studies on home sign have been conducted by Goldin-Meadow and her colleagues; many of these studies are summarized in Goldin-Meadow and Mylander (1990).

29 The Structure and Acquisition of WH-Questions in American Sign Language

Introduction

In our discussion of syntax in spoken languages, we found that WH-questions have both universal and language-particular aspects. For example, we claimed that universally WH-Movement moves a WH-element to the specifier of CP, but that languages may differ in whether such movement applies overtly, between Deep Structure and Surface Structure, or covertly, between Surface Structure and LF. We also saw that Subject–Auxiliary Inversion is a particular aspect of WH-questions in English, but not universally. And we saw that constraints on WH-Movement, such as the requirement that long-distance movement be successive cyclic, and the ECP, are universals. In this chapter we will discuss some aspects of WH-questions in ASL, to see whether the proposed universals also apply in the visual modality. As always, we will also inquire into children's acquisition of this construction, to further test the theory of innateness.

1 WH-Questions in ASL

Let's consider how the WH-Movement transformation applies in ASL. WH-Movement can apply in the derivation of WH-questions in ASL, but SAI does not. Thus, some typical WH-questions in ASL are given in (1).

$$\overline{\text{WHO SEE BILL YESTERDAY?}}^{\text{whq}}$$

(1) a. WHO SEE BILL YESTERDAY?
         "Who saw Bill yesterday?"

<u>   whq</u>
b.   WHO BILL SEE YESTERDAY?
     "Who did Bill see yesterday?"

<u>   whq</u>
c.   WHERE YOU BUY COFFEE?
     "Where did you buy coffee?"

As we saw in chapter 27, the line above the ASL glosses shows that a specific non-manual marker was used during the signs. This marker, noted "whq," signifies a WH-question. It involves a facial expression with furrowed brows, and the head tilted back. You can think of the non-manual marker as something like the WH-question intonation in English.

ASL is unlike English, however, in that a WH-phrase can stay in its Deep Structure position: WH-Movement does not need to apply to derive the Surface Structure. As we saw in chapter 19, other languages, such as French, also optionally allow the WH-word to stay in its Deep Structure position; still others, such as Chinese, always leave the WH-word in its Deep Structure position at Surface Structure, not moving until LF. Examples of leaving the WH-word in its Deep Structure position (*in situ*) in ASL are given in (2).

<u>   whq</u>
(2) a.   BILL SEE WHO YESTERDAY?
          "Who did Bill see yesterday?"

<u>   whq</u>
     b.   JOHN BUY WHAT?
          "What did John buy?"

There is another way in which WH-questions in ASL are different from those in English. WH-questions are frequently made with the WH-element in two places in the sentence: both sentence-initial and sentence-final. Some examples are given in (3).

<u>   whq</u>
(3) a.   WHO SEE ANN WHO?
          "WHO saw Ann?"

<u>   whq</u>
     b.   WHICH COMPUTER PHIL BUY WHICH?
          "Which computer was it that Phil bought?"

<u>   whq</u>
     c.   WHY I FAIL TEST WHY?
          "WHY did I fail the test?"

"Double" constructions such as these were mentioned in chapter 27. There we pointed out that various elements of a sentence, including negative elements, modals, quantifiers, and WH-elements can appear in both their regular position and in the sentence-final position. We said that in such cases, the doubled element receives a "focused" interpretation. How can we account for these facts?

One account which has been proposed claims that in ASL, the C projection behaves unlike the other projections in that its head is final (while Spec is still initial). According to this proposal, the Surface Structure of a doubled WH-question is as given in (4).

(4)

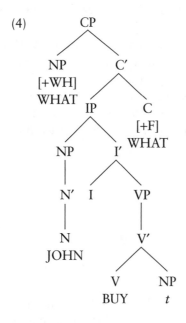

In (4), the WH-element "WHAT" has moved to Spec of CP, leaving a trace, as usual. In addition, another "WHAT" appears in C (it is generated there). The C is marked [+F] for "focus." A WH-element can be focused in C; so can a modal, negative, or quantifier.

What, then, does the child acquiring ASL have to learn about WH-questions? First, that WH-Movement may apply overtly, but it may also apply covertly. This is something that varies from language to language, as we have seen. Second, the child must learn the non-manual marker that accompanies questions (we have not shown how it is represented in the tree structure). Third, the child must learn about doubling constructions in general, and in particular that WH-elements can be doubled. We now turn to review the results of two studies of children's production of WH-questions in ASL.

2   The Acquisition of WH-Questions in ASL

A few studies have been conducted to investigate the acquisition of WH-questions in ASL, although more work is needed. We will report here the results of one study which examined naturalistic, spontaneous production as well as elicited questions, and one study of elicited production exclusively. The former study was particularly focused on the acquisition of the WH-question non-manual marker, while the latter study was interested in both placement of WH-elements and non-manual markers. Where they overlapped, the two methods supplied similar kinds of data.

The elicited production study included children from 4 to 7 years old, but here we will focus on the results from the 4- and 5-year-olds. The children were all deaf children with deaf parents and had had exposure to ASL from birth (as described in chapter 28). The method used was similar to that of the elicited production studies described in chapters 22 and 24, with some modifications.

Two experimenters, both deaf native signers of ASL, interacted with each child individually. One manipulated toys and told stories with them. The other was dressed as a cat, who was shy to talk with adults but eagerly interacted with children. The cat ploy was used instead of a puppet, since it is very awkward to manipulate a puppet while signing. The storyteller described the cat as very knowledgeable about animals, and started with a story about some new animals at the zoo, using a toy lion and a toy giraffe. They were hungry, but the story-teller didn't know which of the plastic foods in the experiment each liked. The story ended with the following prompt.

Protocol for the ASL WH-Question Elicitation Experiment

Experimenter: LION EAT SOMETHING . . . I DON'T-KNOW WHAT. $_2$ASK$_a$
$_a$CAT.
"The lion eats something, but I don't know what. You ask the cat."

Child: WHAT LION EAT?
"What does the lion eat?"

Using this method, subject, object, and adjunct questions were elicited from the children. The results showed that even the youngest children (4 years old) were able to use the variety of WH-question structures available. They used moved WH-elements, WH-*in-situ*, and doubled WH-elements. Some examples of the children's productions are given in (5)–(7).

(5) WH-Movement

    a. WHAT LION EAT
        "What does the lion eat?"

    b. WHY HE (Cookie Monster) MAKE CAKE BRING HERE HE (CM)
        "Why did he (Cookie Monster) make a cake and bring it here?"

(6) WH-*in-situ*

                        _____whq
    a. YOU FEEL WHAT
        "What do you think?"

    b. WHO WILL DRIVE
        "Who will drive?"

(7) WH-double

    a. WHO WILL DRIVE WHO
        "WHO will drive?"

                        _____whq
    b. WHAT YOU FEEL YOU WHAT
        "What do you really think?"

    c. HE (lion) WHERE SLEEP WHERE
        "WHERE does he (lion) sleep?"

We see, then, that at the earliest age tested these children had learned the ASL-specific aspects of WH-questions, including the options for movement and for doubled questions. Furthermore, there is no evidence that when they apply WH-Movement, children attempt to move the WH-element to some place other than Spec CP. Thus, children show evidence for the universal aspects of WH-questions.

However, there is one way in which the children's utterances were clearly non-adult. This concerns their use of the non-manual WH-question marker. As you can see from inspection of the examples in (5)–(7), the non-manual marker was not consistently used. In fact, it was not used very frequently, even by the oldest children. When it was used, it was used correctly, co-occurring with all of the signs in the question, but it should have been used in every question.

The spontaneous production study with younger children had a similar result. In this study, too, it was found that children did not consistently use the WH-question non-manual marker. It was appropriate in scope when it was used (that is, it correctly appeared with all of the signs in the question, not just a few), but it was frequently missing.

Apparently, the ASL-particular use of the WH-question non-manual marker, like the English-particular application of SAI, is one aspect of language which is not learned early. This makes the early appearance of the other features of WH-questions, in contrast, that much more impressive.

3 Long-Distance Questions in ASL

Even though ASL has the option of leaving a WH-word in its Deep Structure position, if the WH-word moves it is subject to the same constraints as WH-Movement in English and universally. For example, the requirement that movement be successive cyclic applies in ASL.[1] We can use the examples in (8) to illustrate.

(8) a. I DON'T-KNOW WHAT MOTHER LIKE.
        "I don't know what mother likes."

         _____ whq
     b. *WHO YOU DON'T-KNOW WHAT LIKE?
        "*Who don't you know what likes?"

     c. I DON'T-KNOW WHO LIKE CHOCOLATE.
        "I don't know who likes chocolate."

         _____ whq
     d. ?*WHAT YOU DON'T-KNOW WHO LIKE?
        ?"*What don't you know who likes?"

The ASL examples in (8a) and (8c) are grammatical indirect questions. As in English, in ASL an indirect question has a WH-word at the beginning of an embedded clause. Also as in English, the indirect question makes an "island" for further WH-Movement: a WH-phrase cannot be extracted from within the WH-island. Recall from chapter 21 that this is because such movement would violate Successive Cyclic Movement. Movement of a WH-phrase from within the embedded clause cannot go through the embedded specifier of CP, because it is filled by another WH-phrase. This accounts for the ungrammaticality of (8b) and (8d).

There is also evidence that ASL adheres to the Strong Crossover constraint (discussed in chapter 25), and that children are also sensitive to it. The study we will mention here used examples with topicalization rather than WH-Movement, but the same kind of considerations apply. As we have seen, in topicalization, an NP is moved to the beginning of the sentence, and highlighted as the *topic* of the sentence. The process that moves the topic to the beginning of the sentence is very similar to WH-Movement, and subject to the same constraints, including Strong Crossover.

Along with the constraints we have already described, in order to present this study we need to introduce a new concept: **resumptive pronouns**. In some languages, it is possible to have a pronoun in the position from which the WH-phrase moved, "saving" a constraint violation. This pronoun is called a *resumptive pronoun*. In English, the use of resumptive pronouns is somewhat marginal, but the following examples will show how a string violating some constraint on movement is rectified with a resumptive pronoun.

> (9) a.   **This candidate, he* wants everyone to vote for *t*.
>   b.   *This candidate, he* wants everyone to vote for *him*.

In (9a), the NP "this candidate" is topicalized, moving over the pronoun "he." If these two NPs are intended to be coreferential (as indicated by the italics), such movement would violate Principle C, or the Strong Crossover constraint, and so the sentence is ungrammatical on this reading. On the other hand, if the pronoun "him" appears in place of the trace, the coreferential reading is possible.

In ASL, as in English, a pronoun in the extraction site will "save" a sentence from being a Strong Crossover violation. In fact, in ASL, resumptive pronouns are used freely to avoid violating constraints. The study we report here used this fact to investigate children's adherence to the Strong Crossover constraint in ASL.

In this study, 3- to 5-year-old deaf children produced sentences with topicalization, including potential Strong Crossover violations. In all the crucial examples, deaf children used resumptive pronouns to avoid a Strong Crossover violation. When it was grammatical to leave off the resumptive pronoun, the children often omitted it – but they never omitted it when this would produce an ungrammatical sentence. An example is given in (10).

> (10) a. $\overline{t}$
> $_a$BABY, $_a$HE FEEL $_b$NURSE LOVE $_a$HE.
>   "As for *baby*, *he* feels the nurse loves *him*."
>
>   b. $\overline{t}$
>   *$_a$BABY, $_a$HE FEEL $_b$NURSE LOVE ____.
>   "*As for *baby*, *he* feels the nurse loves *t*."

In (10a), BABY has been topicalized. As long as both pronouns are overt, the sentence does not violate Strong Crossover. On the other hand, (10b) violates Strong Crossover because the NP "BABY" has moved from the object position to the beginning of the sentence, crossing over the coreferential pronoun, "$_a$HE."

In this study, the children produced sentences like (10a). They also produced other sentences with or without resumptive pronouns, when the resumptive pronouns were optional. However, they never left off the resumptive pronoun when it would produce an ungrammatical sentence like (10b). This is good evidence that the constraint is part of their mental grammar.

Conclusion

This quick overview shows that ASL has both universal and language-particular aspects to WH-questions and constraints on movement. This provides strong support for the universality of such principles, and their biological givenness as part of UG. Study of signed languages can thus help in the evaluation of linguistic theory. Furthermore, the study of signed languages can help in our understanding of the ways in which languages can differ. Since ASL is not equivalent to English or any other spoken language, there will be some ways in which it is different from these languages. We saw some examples of this in the language-particular aspects of WH-questions. We turn now to see how to account for some other differences between languages, within the theory of UG.

Note

1 We will not be able to show it here, but the ECP also applies in ASL.

Bibliographical Comments

The analysis of WH-questions in ASL summarized here was presented in Petronio and Lillo-Martin (1997). See Neidle et al. (1997) for an alternative proposal, involving rightward WH-Movement. The studies with children reported here are discussed in Reilly and McIntire (1991), Lillo-Martin, Boster, Matsuoka, and Nohara (1996), and Lillo-Martin (1992).

30 Parameter Setting

Introduction

We have seen that ASL adheres to the principles of Universal Grammar. This is important, because we have argued that language is not learnable solely on the basis of the evidence in the environment – innate knowledge is needed as well. Surely, if signed languages have the same kind of structure as spoken languages in general, the same argument would apply, so innate knowledge would be necessary for the acquisition of signed languages as well as spoken languages. Furthermore, we would not expect different innate knowledge for signed and spoken languages. Rather, we expect the same Language Acquisition Device to be responsible for the acquisition of languages in either modality.

ASL is not identical to English or any other spoken language, however. Some of the differences between languages (spoken or signed) must be learned. Others, however, are captured by **parameters**. Parameters allow for limited variation between languages within the realm of UG. By studying the ways in which languages differ parametrically, as well as the similarities between languages, we are better able to understand the extent of the properties of UG. In this chapter, we investigate one well-studied parameter, and how children determine which setting of it their language uses.

1 Parameters

Many aspects of language variation are explained as the consequence of *parameters*. A parameter is like a switch that can be set in two ways. Depending on the setting that is chosen, the language will exhibit certain grammatical properties. Of course, languages are not free to vary in just *any* respect, or they could not be learned. But, within the constraints on grammar imposed by the principles of

UG, there are a number of ways in which the grammars of different languages may vary. Some of these differences are captured by parameters.

One example of how languages can differ parametrically comes from studies of word order possibilities. As we have seen in chapter 10, not all logical combinations of basic word orders are found in the world's languages. Such limited choices are determined by parameters, which children must set on the basis of their linguistic experience. In other words, parameters establish the limits on the different directions that languages may take. As the term suggests, a parameter sets out the options that languages have available to them. Some languages may choose one option where other languages "set" the parameter in another way. Of course, it is really children, not languages, that fix the parameter settings of their language, but it is crucial for communication that all children in the same linguistic community choose the same settings.

We will turn now to look in some detail at an example of a parameter which has been proposed as part of Universal Grammar. The parameter we will discuss here is called the "Null Argument Parameter" (NAP), and we will see data from English and Italian, as well as American Sign Language, that bears on how this parameter is set. Then, we will look at data from language acquisition to see how children determine the setting used by their language for this parameter.

2 The Null Argument Parameter

First, let's see what the Null Argument Parameter is all about. In Italian, unlike English, it is possible to produce a sentence in which the subject is not overtly stated. For example, the following sentence is grammatical in Italian:

(1)   Mangia   una mela
      eat(3-sg) an   apple
      "(He/she) eats an apple."

In Italian, the ending on the verb (the verb agreement morphology) provides the information that the subject is third person singular, but there is no word in the subject position. Does this mean that Italian allows the Phrase Structure rule IP → VP? We think not. There are good reasons to believe that there is something in subject position, but it is silent. This silent subject is called *pro*. It is a *null subject*. In English, null subjects are not allowed, so the English example corresponding to (1) is ungrammatical. However, null subjects are allowed in

Italian and in a number of other languages. In fact, in some languages (although not Italian), objects are also allowed to be null.

This difference between English and Italian can be captured by a parameter in Universal Grammar, the Null Argument Parameter. (Since both subjects and objects are *arguments* of the verb, this name is more general than the "Null Subject Parameter.") Since parameters can be pictured as switches, we will talk about parameter values in terms of [+] and [–] settings. The Null Argument Parameter can thus be seen as having three possible settings. [–NA] is the setting under which no null arguments are allowed and is the setting used by English. [+NS] is the setting under which null subjects, but not null objects, are allowed; this is the setting used by Italian. [+NA] is the setting under which all null arguments are allowed. In fact, ASL is one of those languages in which both subjects and objects are allowed to be null, so the setting for ASL is [+NA].

As in Italian, the presence of null arguments in ASL can be tied to the presence of verb agreement morphology. We saw in chapter 27 how verb agreement works in ASL; subject and object agreement morphology are indicated by adjusting the movement used in signing the verbs. Usually, the verb moves from the location associated with the subject, to the location associated with the object. However, some verbs do not mark agreement: the movement is unaltered for different combinations of subject and object. This is what ties the presence of null arguments in ASL to the presence of verb agreement morphology: if a verb marks agreement, its arguments can be null, but if a verb does not mark agreement, its arguments cannot be null. We can think of the agreement as "identifying" the null arguments: when the agreement is there, the referent of the null argument is clear from that agreement, but if there is no agreement, the identity could be lost. Thus, ASL requires identification of null arguments.[1]

The notion of identification also helps us to understand the parametric difference between English and Italian. In Italian, verb agreement shows clearly the identity of the subject, just as in ASL: hence, null subjects are allowed. However, in English, verb agreement is too "weak" to identify the subject. If we say just "eat," the subject might be "me," or "you," or "we," or "they." Hence, in English, null subjects are not allowed.

To summarize, we have seen three types of languages with respect to the Null Argument Parameter. These are listed below.

Setting	Language
[–NA]	English
[+NS]	Italian
[+NA]	ASL

When children are exposed to these languages, they will have to figure out what setting their language takes, on the basis of their Primary Linguistic Data. We will discuss this process next.

3   Determining the Settings on Parameters

There are three settings on the NAP. In English, null arguments are not allowed, so children must learn to produce a subject for every sentence. In Italian, the setting of the NAP is [+NS], so children can use null subjects. In ASL, null subjects and null objects are allowed. It is important to recall that in ASL, the presence of null arguments is very directly tied to the presence of verb agreement morphology: if a verb marks agreement, its arguments can be null, but if a verb does not mark agreement, its arguments cannot be null. Thus, in order to use the null argument system correctly, children must understand the verb agreement system correctly.

Now, let us consider how children choose the correct setting on the Null Argument Parameter. Researchers have looked at children's early utterances, and as we have pointed out before, they have found that young English-speaking children utter sentences without subjects. Here are some examples.

(2)   Read bear book
      Ride truck
      Want look a man

Young children (about age $1\frac{1}{2}$ to 2 years) speaking English thus produce sentences that look like Italian: they have null subjects. Should we consider this as part of the results of the computational bottleneck that we discussed before? If children can put together only a limited number of words at a time, maybe that is why they are leaving out subjects.

This is a possible explanation for the pattern we have seen. However, we must bear in mind certain other facts. First, children leave out subjects, but they do not consistently leave out objects. If a simple computational bottleneck was causing children to leave out words, they ought to leave out objects just as often as they leave out subjects. However, this is not so. Secondly, at the same age at which children produce subjectless sentences like those in (2) above, they also produce sentences with subjects, as in (3).

(3)   I want take this off
      You read this book
      Fraser sit down

Thus, if children's subjectless sentences are due to some processing limitation, these facts would need to be accounted for. The model of children's processing limitation would need to be able to explain these facts as well as simple subject omission. Although such a model has been proposed, for our purposes we will consider children's early subjectless sentences as arising from a mis-set parameter. That is, we will make the hypothesis that English-speaking children begin with the assumption that English is like Italian – that is, [+NS].

Around the age of $2\frac{1}{2}$ to 3 years, English-speaking children cease producing subjectless sentences. At this time, their sentences always contain subjects, whether those subjects are meaningful or not. Some examples are given in (4).

(4) I see Kathryn in mirror
Mama take a nap
It's not cold outside
There's no money

Thus, at this point, the children have obtained the correct [−NA] setting.

What about Italian-speaking children? According to our understanding of Universal Grammar, there is one setting for each parameter that children always try first. From the evidence of English-speaking children, it appears that the initial setting for the NAP is [+NS]. If this is true, then Italian-speaking children should use subjectless sentences from an early age, and they should continue producing them since they are allowed in the adult grammar. This has also been found, as illustrated in (5).

(5) a. Taglio
"cut" (= I cut)

Giorgio le taglia
"Giorgio them-cuts" (= Giorgio cuts them)

b. E mia palla
"Is my ball" (= it is my ball)

Questo e mio papa
"This is my daddy"

Thus, Italian-speaking children use null subjects from an early age. Note that they also use verb agreement at an early age, so that their null subjects are "identified."

4   The Acquisition of Null Arguments in ASL

So far, we have evidence from English and Italian that the initial setting on the NAP is [+NS], and that children learning a [−NA] language such as English will change their grammars from [+NS] to [−NA] at around $2\frac{1}{2}$ years of age. Children learning a [+NS] language such as Italian will produce null subjects from an early age, and will continue producing such sentences since they are allowed in the adult grammar. What happens with deaf children learning ASL?

A study of the signing of deaf children beginning at just under 2 years was conducted to see how their use of null arguments developed. As expected, the youngest children, those under 3 years, produced sentences with null subjects, much like the sentences cited above for English-speaking children. Some examples are given in (6).

(6) (Steve: 2;3)
GIVE BALLOON
HOLD LET-GO
ₐPRONOUN HAVE BALLOON

Notice that this child produced sentences without subjects, and sentences with subjects. However, none of the verbs that the children of this age produced was marked for verb agreement. Recall from chapter 28 that signing children seem to be more like English-speaking children than Italian-speaking children in terms of the timing of the acquisition of verb agreement. Even the youngest Italian-speaking children quoted above used the verb agreement morphology. Italian-speaking children do not produce verbs without agreement. They will occasionally use the wrong agreement, but they always use some agreement. The ASL-learning children, on the other hand, produce verbs with no agreement morphology. In ASL, null arguments must be "identified" by verbs that are marked for agreement. However, children are not marking any verbs for agreement, although they are using null arguments. That means that the children's utterances are not following the adult grammar.

Children who are around $2\frac{1}{2}$ to 3 years of age begin to use verb agreement morphology in ASL, especially when the person they are talking about is present with them. They also use null arguments with these "present referents," and when they use the agreement morphology, these null arguments are identified. However, at this age they do not yet use verb agreement with non-present referents.

At this point there is a change in children's use of arguments with non-present referents. From then until the time that they master verb agreement with non-present referents (around age 5), they do not use null arguments with non-present referents. If they did use them, they would not be identified. But from age 3 on, the deaf children only use null arguments when they are properly identified. By the age of 5, these children use both verb agreement and null arguments even with non-present referents, as illustrated in (7).

(7)   (Pam: 5;6)
      ₐPOUR_b SPILL-ON-HEAD; THEN _bPOUR_a SPILL-ON-HEAD.
      "(He-) poured on (-her) and spilled all over;
      then (she-) poured on (-him) and spilled all over."

We can summarize the data from children learning ASL in the following way:

(8)   **Null Argument and Verb Agreement Development**
      (1)   no verb agreement but null arguments are used
      (2)   verb agreement and null arguments used with present referents
      (3)   verb agreement and null arguments used with present and non-present referents

Null arguments are only allowed in ASL with agreement morphology. At the youngest stage, the children have not yet analyzed the agreement morphology – hence they do not have restrictions on the use of null arguments. But at the middle stage, they are using agreement morphology with present referents. Since they are not using it with non-present referents (for whatever reason), they cease using null arguments with non-present referents. However, they haven't changed their parameter, just their agreement morphology. We can tell that this is true because they use null arguments with present referents. Finally, at the last stage, they put it all together – correct agreement morphology and correct null arguments with non-present referents. This is illustrated in (9).

(9)   **Agreement**   **NAP**
      none   [+NA]
      present referents only   "
      present and non-present referents   "

    This analysis supports our hypothesis of Universal Grammar. According to this hypothesis, many things about language are innate. However, where languages differ, children must learn the particular facts about their language. When language differences can be captured by a parameter, then children only have to choose the correct setting on that parameter for their language. However, all languages differ with respect to the words and the agreement morphology, so these facts have to be learned by children individually. This learning might take time. Our hypothesis predicts that children will be very quick in their acquisition of the parts of language which are determined by Universal Grammar. However, they will be slow in those areas where languages differ the most, including the lexicon and morphology.

Conclusion

Universal Grammar provides children with innate knowledge of both universal principles and parameters which allow for limited cross-linguistic variation. One such parameter is the Null Argument Parameter, which determines whether or not a language allows subjects (and other arguments) to be covert. Italian allows null subjects, but English does not. ASL allows both subjects and objects to be null, but they must be identified by verb agreement morphology.

We saw that children acquiring ASL use null arguments from early on, as do children acquiring Italian. However, there is a difference: children learning Italian use verb agreement morphology from an early age, while children learning ASL take longer to fully use the agreement morphology. This affects their use of null arguments: if they were to use null arguments with verbs which are not marked for agreement, these arguments would not be identified. Children under 3 do use such unidentified null arguments; however, once children begin to acquire the verb agreement system they cease doing so. This study shows the intricate relationship between syntax and morphology, and the importance of considering children's morphological acquisition when studying related syntactic properties.

Note

1   Actually, there is another mechanism for identifying null arguments in ASL, so that sometimes the arguments of non-agreeing verbs can be null. However, we will only discuss the type of null argument that appears with agreeing verbs, to simplify the discussion.

Bibliographical Comments

The study by Hyams (1986) on English-speaking children's null subjects truly initiated the application of data from children's speech to the theory of parameter setting. Since then, many studies have looked at children's null subjects, with the goal of refining the details and applicability of this theory. One of several proposals that the correct account of children's use of null subjects is in processing limitations rather than a mis-set parameter was made by Boster (1997), whose account was detailed enough to include additional facts about subjectless sentences, as described in the text and beyond. The study summarized here of deaf children's determining the ASL setting on the NAP was by Lillo-Martin (1991).

31 Modularity and Modality

Introduction

In chapter 7 we introduced a theory of the mental architecture for language called the Modularity Hypothesis. This theory separates the processing of linguistic information from other kinds of cognitive functions. Since this theory was developed on the basis of data from spoken languages, it is open to question whether sign language is processed by the same linguistic module, or whether other processors are required. If there are significant effects of modality on language processing, this might undermine the Modularity Hypothesis as a hypothesis about the processing of language in general, restricting it to the processing of spoken languages. However, if sign languages are processed by the same module proposed for spoken languages, this would support the Modularity Hypothesis as a general theory about the mind. In this chapter, we will review the evidence regarding this issue. Although much more work needs to be done in this area, we will argue here that the evidence is consistent with a general modularity hypothesis.

In order to address this question, we will consider the properties of sign languages at each of the different levels of the grammar, as well as some data from psycholinguistics and neurolinguistics.

1 Modality and Grammar

According to the Modularity and Universal Grammar Hypotheses, a common set of linguistic principles applies across languages – and these principles are specific to language, rather than part of general cognitive processing. If sign languages adhere to these principles, then nothing special need be said about modality. Can the properties of sign languages be accounted for using general linguistic principles?

We argued in chapter 27 that American Sign Language (the most widely studied sign language) does adhere to the principles of UG. As far as is known, this is true. It is worthwhile, however, to point out those places where ASL has properties which might make it different from spoken languages – where the modality might have an influence on language structure. In the syntactic and morphological components of grammar, such potential differences arise in consideration of what some have called "spatial syntax."

In ASL, relations between different participants in a sentence are often portrayed using spatial locations. For example, the description of ASL verb agreement given in chapter 27 showed that referents in a sentence are associated with different locations in space. Then, a verb might move from the location of one of these referents, to identify the subject, to the location of another referent, to identify the object. Thus, it appears that space is being used to signify grammatical relations.

Although the form of agreement in ASL is thus spatial, is it necessary to refer to space when discussing the various aspects of the structure of the sentence? We argue that it is not – that it is sufficient to discuss the agreement facts outside of the form which this agreement takes, at least when discussing morphology and syntax. What is special about ASL is that the agreement forms, and the pronominal forms which also use these locations in space (e.g., the forms for "ME" and "YOU," discussed in chapter 27), often pick out a particular referent, rather than a class of referents based on features of person, number, or gender.

Compare this to the pronominal system of, say, English. In English, the pronouns pick out a class of referents – for example, "she" picks out third person singular female referents. In a particular discourse, there may be only one appropriate referent, but there may also be more than one, in which case the pronoun might be ambiguous. Take the following situation and sentence as an example.

(1)   Situation: Hillary, Tipper, Barbara, and Marilyn are having lunch together. George walks in and says: Isn't she smart!

Although you might think that George could only be talking about Barbara (for pragmatic reasons), of course the pronoun "she" could refer to any of the four women involved.

In contrast, in the same situation in an ASL discourse, the pronoun for SHE would point to the location of *one* of the women, unambiguously picking out the referent. Thus, in ASL, pronouns usually pick out particular referents, not classes of referents. This might well be a special property of sign languages.

Does this property require that ASL have a special notation or principles unique to it? No – the same notations and principles which are needed for spoken languages can be used here. Here is how.

When we discussed coreference between pronouns and other NPs in chapter 14, we needed a way to show which NPs were intended to be coreferential with which others. There we used the notation of italicizing coreferential NPs. This was sufficient for those purposes, since there was only one person the relevant NPs referred to. However, often more than one person is involved, and italicization would get confusing. Although italic is used, it is more common practice to use subscripts to identify referents. Consider the example in (2).

(2)   Ken accused Bill, and then he criticized him.

This example is quite ambiguous, since there are many options for the referents of "he" and "him." By adding subscripts, we can distinguish the various readings, some of which are given in (3).

(3)   a.   Ken$_i$ accused Bill$_j$, and then he$_i$ criticized him$_j$.
      b.   Ken$_i$ accused Bill$_j$, and then he$_j$ criticized him$_i$.
      c.   Ken$_i$ accused Bill$_j$, and then he$_i$ criticized him$_k$.

We interpret identical subscripts to indicate coreference, and non-identical subscripts to indicate disjoint reference. So, since "he" has the same subscript as "Ken" in (3a), they are intended to be coreferential; similarly "Bill" and "him" are coreferential in (3a). When a pronoun has a subscript which is not the same as another subscript in the sentence (as in (3c)), we assume it receives an extra-sentential reference; that is, it picks out someone in the discourse but not mentioned in the sentence. Of course, there is nothing special about using subscripts to convey this information. We could use the same type font, or color, or any other indication to show that coreference is intended. Subscripts are not theoretically relevant. The information they convey, however, is theoretically relevant. It is important for the theory that there is some way to mark NPs for their referents, and to have co-marked NPs be coreferential. These marks are called indices, and they are needed to account for reference facts and other facts about sentences in spoken language. It is assumed that every NP is marked with an index.

By marking NPs with indices, we can demonstrate the application of Principle C, among other things. Consider the examples in (4).

(4)   a.   George$_i$ thinks that he$_i$ is intelligent.
      b.   George$_i$ thinks that he$_j$ is intelligent.
      c.   *He$_i$ thinks that George$_i$ is intelligent.
      d.   He$_i$ thinks that George$_j$ is intelligent.

In (4a), the indices tell us that "George" and "he" are picking out the same person. This is a possible interpretation. (4b) shows that the same string of words can also be interpreted with "George" and "he" picking out different people, as indicated by the different indices. However, in (4c), "George" and "he" cannot refer to the same person, because this would violate Principle C. That is why the sentence is marked ungrammatical with the two NPs coindexed. In contrast, the same string of words, as in (4d), is grammatical, as long as "George" and "he" are understood to be different individuals. Thus, although we don't hear the different indices in English, the grammar needs to have some kind of mechanism to show what kinds of coreference are possible and impossible.

Now we can see what the special property of ASL is. In ASL, the indices are *overt*. We *can* see the indices – or at least, the pronouns are "pronounced" differently when the indices are different. A pronoun which corefers with Ken will be located in a different place from a pronoun which corefers with Bill. We will show this using subscripts on the sign glosses, as in example (5).

(5) a. $_a$KEN $_a$ACCUSE$_b$ $_b$BILL, $_a$PRONOUN $_a$CRITICIZE$_b$ $_b$PRONOUN.
         "Ken$_i$ accused Bill$_j$, and then he$_i$ criticized him$_j$."

     b. $_a$KEN $_a$ACCUSE$_b$ $_b$BILL, $_b$PRONOUN $_b$CRITICIZE$_a$ $_a$PRONOUN.
         "Ken$_i$ accused Bill$_j$, and then he$_j$ criticized him$_i$."

     c. $_a$KEN $_a$ACCUSE$_b$ $_b$BILL, $_a$PRONOUN $_a$CRITICIZE$_c$ $_c$PRONOUN.
         "Ken$_i$ accused Bill$_j$, and then he$_i$ criticized him$_k$."

In ASL, $_a$PRONOUN is pronounced differently from $_b$PRONOUN – they are directed at different locations in space. In English, of course, "he$_i$" is pronounced the same as "he$_j$." Although this special property will have to be stated for ASL, it is not a contradiction with UG. UG needs to have indices, for the reasons discussed above. The difference only comes out when the sentences are pronounced. In English, the pronouns with the different indices are pronounced the same; in ASL, pronouns with different indices are pronounced differently. Thus, this is only a lexical or phonological difference.

Let us now consider phonology in more detail. The phonology of a language describes its sound patterns. For sign languages, the equivalent of phonology describes how the pieces of signs are combined – the handshapes, the locations, and the movements of the signs. It might seem that the phonology of signed versus spoken languages would be quite different, since phonology refers to the output. But actually, the same principles that apply to spoken language phonology also apply to sign language phonology. Since we have not described these principles for spoken languages, we will not go into them here. However, a number of recent studies have found that the same kinds of notations and principles which are needed for spoken language phonology also apply to sign language phonology. The differences appear only at the most superficial levels – how the different patterns are pronounced. In spoken languages, the relevant

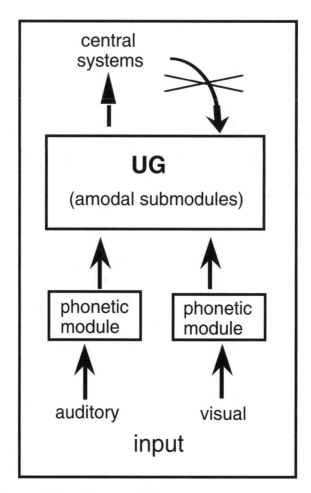

Figure 31.1   An amodal modularity model

features will discuss aspects of the tongue's position in the mouth, and the type of noise made with the voice box. In sign languages, the features concern the hands and movement. But the organizing principles around how these features are combined, and the rules which they are subject to, seem to be constant across signed and spoken languages.

The discussion up until now has thus claimed that the differences between signed and spoken languages are very superficial – only the actual pronunciation differs. We know that spoken languages will also differ along these lines. The words used will differ between languages, and the particular sounds that are used can vary widely. But, the fundamental claim of the Modularity and UG Hypotheses is that the principles and constraints governing how the sounds or words can combine will be universal. It seems that sign languages can also be included in the range of languages governed by UG, and processed by the language module – at least, according to what we can determine by examining their grammar. A model of the Modularity Hypothesis as applied to signed and spoken languages is offered in figure 31.1. The figure shows that the same principles of UG apply to both spoken and signed languages, even though the input comes from different sources (auditory and visual). For both modalities, the language module feeds the "central systems," or general cognitive processing, but cognition does not guide the workings of the language module. This is the essence of the Modularity Hypothesis as outlined in chapter 7.

We have argued from areas of the grammar that the facts about signed languages are completely consistent with the Modularity Hypothesis. As we saw in chapter 7, psycholinguistic evidence can also be brought to bear on this hypothesis. Is there any psycholinguistic evidence from signed languages for this hypothesis?

2 Modality and Psychological Reality

There are two types of evidence which will be summarized here. The first concerns how deaf signers process the pieces of their language. We will show that they do process it specially, just as speech is processed specially by hearing people. The second piece of evidence comes from language breakdown under brain damage.

In studies with hearing people, it has frequently been found that the sounds of language are processed differently from other sounds. Furthermore, adults who speak one language will not process in this special way the sounds of a language which they do not know (although young infants will, regardless of the language environment in which they find themselves). This result has been attributed to the language module. In particular, the phonetic processor – the first processor, which decodes the incoming sounds – will distinguish between sounds which are meaningful linguistically to the hearer and sounds which are not. This is evidence that the language module works separately from general cognitive processors.

Although not many studies in this area have been carried out, there is some evidence that the same is true for deaf signers. In particular, deaf signers process the movements used in signs quite differently than hearing non-signers do. When exactly the same physical stimulus is provided for deaf and hearing subjects, the hearing subjects do not treat the stimulus specially, but the deaf subjects do. This is arguably because for the hearing subjects, these movements are not meaningful, so they are processed by the general cognitive system. However, for the deaf subjects, these movements are pieces of signs – just as /ba/, /da/, and /ga/ are pieces of words for hearing subjects. Thus, for the deaf subjects, these movements are processed by the language module. This result is a strong first step towards establishing that sign languages are also processed by a special-purpose language module.

More evidence for this position comes from studies of patients who have brain damage, resulting in sign language aphasia. We reported in chapter 7 that damage to the left side of the brain often causes breakdown in language (aphasia) for hearing patients. Damage to the right side of the brain typically does not result in aphasia, but does result in spatial disabilities. Since the form of sign language is spatial, it is reasonable to wonder whether it would be processed more by the right hemisphere.

Several studies have found a striking difference between deaf patients with damage to the right versus left hemispheres. Like hearing patients, deaf signers who have left hemisphere brain damage have aphasia – in this case, sign aphasia. Some patients have very slow, awkward signing, like the speech of a Broca's aphasic. Others have more fluent signing which doesn't make sense, like another kind of aphasia called Wernicke's aphasia. However, these patients have generally intact spatial cognitive abilities.

In contrast, deaf signers who experience damage to the right hemisphere have severe spatial deficits. They don't seem to see things on the left side, a typical effect of right hemisphere lesions called left neglect. They may get lost in the hospital, and lose the ability to draw or show spatial relations, just like hearing patients with right hemisphere damage. However, the most important point is this: their signing is *not* impaired. They sign fluently and meaningfully, *even using the devices of "spatial" syntax*. This provides strong evidence that sign languages are processed in the left hemisphere, where language is processed, rather than in the right hemisphere. Thus, the type of processing which is required – linguistic versus non-linguistic – is more important for determining the location of the processing than the form of the input (auditory versus visual). This also supports the Modularity Hypothesis.

Conclusion

Although sign languages use a different modality from spoken languages, there are remarkable similarities in their properties and processing. These similarities support the Modularity and UG Hypotheses, by showing that even language in another modality adheres to the same principles which spoken languages display. The fact that deaf children acquire ASL in much the same fashion as hearing children acquire their native language (as long as there is sufficient input) also supports this view. It seems that humans are predisposed to learn language, by virtue of the Language Acquisition Device, containing Universal Grammar, which is a separate module of cognitive functioning. Whether the language is spoken or signed seems not to matter.

Bibliographical Comments

The Modularity Hypothesis for spoken languages was proposed by Fodor (1983). An extensive discussion of the hypothesis in its application to signed languages is provided in Lillo-Martin (1997). Sandler (1993) argues for the opposite conclusion – that the facts concerning the similarities and the differences between signed and spoken languages constitute evidence against Fodor's Modularity Hypothesis. Poizner (1983) and Poizner, Fok, and Bellugi (1989) present studies on the perception of signed linguistic information by signers and non-signers, showing that they process the information distinctly. Much of the work on aphasia in sign language users (and the lack of aphasia after right hemisphere damage) is presented in Poizner, Klima, and Bellugi (1987).

Part V Semantics and Philosophy of Language

Introduction

The goal of semantic theory is to provide a systematic account of a native speaker's semantic competence. As part of one's semantic competence, people are able to interpret words, phrases, and sentences. It seems obvious that the interpretation of phrases hinges on the meanings of the words that are contained in them, and that the interpretation of sentences depends on the phrases that they contain. This can be stated as a general principle: the meanings of words combine to yield the meanings of phrases, and the meanings of phrases combine to form the meanings of sentences. This general principle is called **compositionality**. There is one more condition under which lower-level meanings combine to form the meanings of higher-level expressions. The rules of semantic combinatorics respect the rules of syntax. That is, the ways in which word meanings and phrasal meanings are formed depend on the way words and phrases form constituents according to the rules of syntax. The majority of the chapters on semantics will be concerned with the principle of compositionality, and its role in child language development.

In our deliberations on compositionality, we will entertain the idea that the meaning of a sentence is a truth-value, either true or false. It is often valuable to know whether or not a sentence is true. For example, in reaching a conclusion on the basis of certain premises, it is crucial to know whether or not the premises are true. Obviously, whether a sentence is true or not depends on the semantic values of the words and phrases that it contains. That is not all there is to it, however. Whether a sentence is true or not also depends on the syntactic structure that is assigned to it. To see this, we simply need to point to two sentences with different truth-values, but which contain the same words. An example is: "Bill Clinton likes women" and "Women like Bill Clinton." Both sentences contain the same words, but one of these sentences may be true even if the other is false. This makes it clear that there are two parts to the process of semantic interpretation: (a) the meanings of the words, and (b) their mode of combination.

The idea that semantics mirrors syntactic structure was implicit in earlier chapters, for example when we discussed constituent structure and Phrase Structure rules. Recall that we motivated the introduction of PS rules by pointing out that the interpretation of phrases and sentences often hinged on the structure that was assigned to them. Let us illustrate the line of reasoning again, using the noun phrases that are italicized in the following examples.

(1) a. Cowboys are fond of *old corrals and sagebrush.*
         Paraphrase: Cowboys are fond of sagebrush and old corrals.
         Not: Cowboys are fond of old corrals and old sagebrush.

     b. Several *trial lawyers and accountants* were called in.
         Paraphrase: Several accountants and trial lawyers were called in.
         Not: Several trial lawyers and trial accountants were called in.

(2) Attach to wall using $\frac{3}{4}$-*inch nails or screws.*
     Paraphrase: Attach to wall using $\frac{3}{4}$-inch nails or $\frac{3}{4}$-inch screws.
     Not: Attach to wall using screws (of any size) or $\frac{3}{4}$-inch nails.

After reading the examples, you probably reached the interpretations of the italicized noun phrases as indicated in the paraphrases beneath the examples. The paraphrases suggest that the adjectives in (1) are interpreted as modifying the nouns that immediately follow them; the interpretation of the adjectives does not extend to the other noun within the NP. That is, "old" modifies "corrals" but not "sagebrush" in (1a), and "trial" modifies "lawyers" but not "accountants" in (1b). By contrast, the adjective "$\frac{3}{4}$-inch" modifies both of the Ns, "nails" and "screws," in (2). Observations like these were used in the chapters on Phrase Structure to motivate certain PS rules. The point was that different interpretation of linguistic expressions could be explained on the supposition that there were different structures for the different interpretations. Returning to the present examples, it seems reasonable to suppose that the italicized NPs in (1) are assigned one constituent structure, along the lines of (1'), whereas the italicized NP in (2) is assigned a different constituent structure, along the lines of (2').

(1') a. [old corrals] and sagebrush
      b. [trial lawyers] and accountants

(2') $\frac{3}{4}$-inch [nails and screws]

The preferences for assigning these particular constituent structures in (1) and (2) largely depends on general facts about the world, so-called **real world knowledge**. In the present examples, the relevant facts are that the expressions "old sagebrush" and "trial accountants" do not refer to sensible entities in the real world; although there are trial lawyers and other kinds of lawyers, the same distinction does not hold of accountants. On the other hand, both nails and screws are distinguished by length, so "$\frac{3}{4}$-inch" does make sense for both.

Having made the observation that two different structural analyses can be given to the same sequence of syntactic categories (i.e., Adj N Conj N), it follows that certain linguistic expressions are open to interpretation; that is, they are ambiguous. For these expressions, such as (3), our general knowledge of the world does not eliminate either of the possible interpretations. The reference set under discussion in (3) could be single men and single women, or it could be single men and all women, regardless of marital status. This ambiguity in interpretation can be accounted for on the hypothesis that the NP in (3) can have both the underlying structure of (1) and that of (2), as shown in (3').

(3)   *Single men and women* need not apply.

(3')   a.   [single men] and women
        b.   single [men and women]

These examples illustrate the relation between form and meaning that is stated in the Principle of Compositionality, due originally to the German logician Gottlob Frege:

The Principle of Compositionality
The meaning of a larger expression is a function of the meanings of its parts, and the syntactic rules that are used to combine them.

Although the inner workings of a compositional semantic system are complex, we will keep the machinery we introduce to the minimum, without avoiding the fundamental ideas and issues in semantics. We will be making several simplifying assumptions which we would like to acknowledge from the outset. One is the assumption that semantic representations are built step-by-step, tracing the structures that are built by PS rules. It is clear that, for certain constructions, the relationship between syntax and semantics is more complex than this. We have chosen not to focus on these constructions, however. In addition, we have chosen to avoid entirely any consideration of sentences which require syntactic transformations. Sentences of this kind are a central concern of current semantic theory, but there are two reasons for not including them in our deliberations. First, the technical machinery that is needed to understand these cases is exceedingly complex. The second reason for avoiding discussion of sentences which involve transformations is that relatively little is known at present about children's acquisition of sentences of this kind. Such sentences are the focus of current research in language acquisition, however, so we expect this state of affairs to change in the near future.

This last comment presupposes that we will be focusing on the acquisition of semantic knowledge, as a way of illustrating the key points about semantic theory, just as we focused on the acquisition of syntactic knowledge to illustrate the key issues in syntactic theory. This is correct. In the chapters that follow, we will examine certain research findings in the acquisition of semantics. Moreover, just as we concentrated on syntactic universals and their acquisition in the first parts of the book, this part explores a putatively universal semantic property, compositionality.

Before we introduce the mechanisms underlying compositionality, however, we wish to chart the waters of semantics on a larger scale, by focusing on a set of issues in the philosophy of language. This is the purpose of chapter 32, which introduces certain fundamental theories of the relationship between the meanings of linguistic expressions and the real world. This chapter on the philosophy of language focuses on several theories of meaning by looking at just one kind of linguistic expression, NPs. The focus will be on two kinds of NP, one called a **definite description**. Definite descriptions are NPs with the definite determiner, such as "the Theory of Relativity." The other kind of NP is a **name**, such as "Albert Einstein." Several proposals about the meaning of definite descriptions and names have been advanced in the literature on the philosophy of language. The first proposal we consider in this chapter is that the meaning of either kind of NP is simply its **reference**; that is, whatever it refers to in the world being talked about by the participants of some discourse. This proposal is called the **Referential Theory of Meaning**. We will call the individuals and the relations among individuals surrounding the participants of a given discourse the **domain of discourse**. According to the Referential Theory of Meaning, then, the meaning of a linguistic expression is whatever it refers to in the domain of discourse.

There are difficulties in maintaining the Referential Theory of Meaning. This was first observed by the German logician Frege, who posed interesting problems for the Referential Theory of Meaning. One problem was that of assigning a meaning to definite descriptions such as "the President of the United States," since this definite description refers to different individuals at different times. This suggests that the Referential Theory of Meaning is forced to maintain that a description's meaning changes from one time to another, a conclusion that is counter-intuitive at best.

As we will see, Frege developed an alternative to the Referential Theory of Meaning. He drew a distinction between the reference of a linguistic expression and its **sense**. According to Frege, the meaning of a linguistic expression was its sense, rather than its reference. We will explore Frege's approach further, in order to explain how the notion of the sense of a linguistic expression can be used to solve some of the problems that plague the Referential Theory of Meaning. Frege is also important because, as noted previously, he introduced the Principle of Compositionality. This principle will remain the primary focus of all of the chapters of this part.

32 Theories of Meaning

Introduction

One of the goals of semantics is to explain the "aboutness" relation that holds between linguistic expressions and the objects that they refer to in the world. So, let us start there. The first theory we consider is called the Referential Theory of Meaning. This theory is quite simple, so it is important to see why it fails before moving on to more complex theories.

1 The Referential Theory

The Referential Theory of Meaning proposes that the "meaning" of a linguistic expression is its reference. We will consider several subsequent accounts of proper names and definite descriptions that admit of both "meaning" and reference, but to avoid taking sides (right away), we will adopt the neutral phrase "semantic value," rather than "meaning," in order to describe the relation between words and their referents.

According to the Referential Theory of Meaning, then, the semantic value of a linguistic expression is its reference. We will coin other terms for reference, including **extension** and **denotation**. These terms are used almost interchangeably in describing the semantic relation that obtains between NPs and the entities these expressions pick out in the world. We will say that linguistic expressions denote (or refer to) objects. Putting it the other way around, we say that linguistic expressions have these entities as their extension (reference, denotation). For the present, it is important to note there are just two components to semantics, linguistic expressions and their reference. This is all there is to it, on the Referential Theory of Meaning.

If we look at proper names, such as "Albert Einstein," the Referential Theory of Meaning seems eminently reasonable. The reference of a name is a prime candidate for its semantic value. But under the theory, this idea is extended to all linguistic expressions. So, for instance, the semantic value of "cat" is the set of cats in the world, and the semantic value of the definite description "the cat" is a unique or most salient cat in the domain of discourse.

To evaluate the Referential Theory of Meaning, we shall introduce a linguistic principle, called the Law of Identity. The Law of Identity says that any two expressions with the same semantic value can be substituted freely in a sentence, without causing any change in the semantic value of the sentence that results from the substitution. Here is a simple example of how we might use the Law of Identity in a simple syllogism.

(1) Water is wet.
     H_2O is water.
     _____

     H_2O is wet.

This example conforms to the Law of Identity, because two expressions with the same semantic value (*water* and *H_2O*) are interchangeable without altering the truth of the sentence.

Let us provide another example in which the Referential Theory of Meaning gives the right result. We know that Bill Clinton is the President of the United States.[1] So, the semantic value of "Bill Clinton" is the same as the semantic value of the definite description "the President of the United States." Since both expressions have the same semantic value, they should mean the same thing, assuming that the Referential Theory of Meaning is correct. This means that, by the Law of Identity, we should be able to interchange the name "Bill Clinton" and the phrase "the President of the United States" in sentences without altering their truth-value. In some cases we can. Consider the following syllogisms.

(2) a.   Bill Clinton is on vacation in Hope.
     b.   Bill Clinton is the President of the United States.
          _____

     c.   The President of the United States is on vacation in Hope.

(3) a.   One person with laryngitis is Bill Clinton.
     b.   Bill Clinton is the President of the United States.
          _____

     c.   One person with laryngitis is the President of the United States.

According to the Referential Theory, the truth-value of the (a) and (c) versions of (2) and (3) should be the same. And, they are.

2 Problems with the Referential Theory

Two problems with the Referential Theory were first pointed out by Frege, the famous German logician. His arguments take the form of apparent counter-examples to the Law of Identity. Here is the form of the first argument he gave, as he originally set it out in the famous paper, "On sense and reference."

Suppose "a" and "b" are signs that refer to the same thing. If the Referential Theory of Meaning is correct, in this case, "a = a" must have the same semantic value as "a = b," since the semantic value of "a" is whatever "a" refers to, the semantic value of "b" is whatever "b" refers to, and "a" refers to the same thing as "b." But, "a = a" is true *a priori*. That is, we know the truth of "a = a" independent of any experience. (Sometimes it is said that "a = a" is an analytic or necessary truth.) By contrast, "a = b" is contingent – its truth must be established by experience. (This is sometimes called a synthetic statement.) Therefore "a = a" does not have the same semantic value as "a = b." According to the Referential Theory of Meaning, however, these two expressions should have the same semantic value. Since they do not, the theory is disconfirmed, and must be rejected.

To make Frege's argument concrete, we will consider several examples using English sentences. Most of our examples are adapted from ones given by Frege. In the first example, the linguistic expressions are both definite descriptions: *the morning star* and *the evening star*. As a matter of fact, these expressions refer to the same thing, the planet Venus. This is illustrated below.

(4)   The morning star is the evening star.

Still, "the morning star is the evening star" expresses something that someone might not already know.

By contrast, consider sentence (5).

(5)   The morning star is the morning star.

This sentence is altogether uninformative. Every English speaker knows this sentence to be true, regardless of what she might think that the definite description *the morning star* refers to, or even if she has no idea about what it refers to.

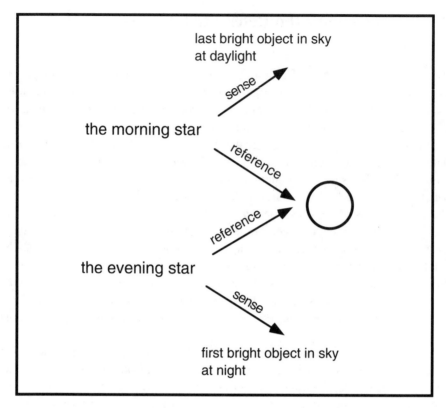

Figure 32.1   Reference versus sense

According to the Referential Theory of Meaning, however, the only difference between examples (4) and (5) is the substitution of *the morning star* for an NP with the same reference, *the evening star*. But, the substitution of NPs with the same semantic value (= reference) in a sentence should not affect its truth-value, if the Law of Identity is correct. The example shows, however, that the substitution of expressions with the same reference does affect the truth-value of certain sentences. As a matter of record, for many years people were unaware of the fact that the evening star, which was what they called the first bright object they saw in the sky at dusk, was actually the same thing as the morning star, which was what they called the last bright object in the sky at daybreak. It was discovered by astronomers that both objects are in fact the planet Venus. For all people knew before this discovery, however, the sentence *The morning star is the evening star* was false. But, no-one at the time would have doubted the truth of the sentence *The morning star is the morning star*. An illustration of this example is given in figure 32.1.

Frege's apparent counterexamples to the Referential Theory of Meaning lead to the same conclusion: either the Law of Identity is wrong, or the reference of a linguistic expression should not be taken to be its (only) semantic value. Frege argued for the latter view. He went on to propose an alternative theory, which is able to circumvent the counterexamples he raised to the Referential Theory.

Before we present his theory, let us consider another of Frege's arguments against the Referential Theory of Meaning. These arguments also appeal to the Law of Identity, but they hinge on other interesting linguistic constructions. One construction includes sentences with subordinate clauses that are connected to the main clause by a special class of verbs, *think, assert, believe, wonder*, etc. These are called "verbs of propositional attitude." In using such verbs, it is said that the (referent of the) subject NP bears some kind of attitude (of wondering, thinking, believing, and so on) towards a proposition (that something is the case).

Frege used sentences with verbs of propositional attitude as a second argument against the Referential Theory of Meaning. He observed that in sentences of the form "X believes that a = a" we may not always substitute an expression "b" that is equivalent in reference to "a" in the clause that follows a verb of propositional attitude. Substitutions of this kind can alter the truth-value of the sentence. Here's an example (taken from Bertrand Russell). Consider the following sentence:

(6)   King George III wondered if Scott was the author of *Waverley*.

As a matter of fact, Scott did write *Waverley*, so *Scott is the author of Waverley* is true. Even so, if we substitute the name *Scott* for the definite description *the author of Waverley* in sentence (6), the result is the (presumably) false sentence, *King George III wondered if Scott was Scott*.

Another example is (7).

(7)   a.   Dan Quayle believes Al Gore will be Al Gore in 2001.
      b.   Al Gore will be the President in 2001.
      _____
      c.   Dan Quayle believes Al Gore will be the President in 2001.

Let us assume for the sake of argument that the second premise (7b) is true. Whatever the status of this assumption, it is likely that the first premise (7a) is true. Even if the conclusion (7c) is true, as a matter of fact, the truth of the first premise and the conclusion depend on Dan Quayle's belief system in different ways. If Dan Quayle were to deny (7a), he would surely not be running for office in the next elections, whatever his degree of conviction about the conclusion (7c). However, the difference in truth-value between these statements results from the substitution of one linguistic expression for another one with the same reference, on the assumption that premise (7b) is true. According to the Referential

Theory of Meaning, then, assuming that (7b) is true would lead us to conclude that the premise (7a) and the conclusion (7c) should both receive the same truth-value. Clearly, there are circumstances in which Dan Quayle could deny (7c), though it is hard to imagine him denying the premise (7a).

3   Frege's Theory: Sense and Reference

In Frege's theory, words with the same reference may nevertheless have different semantic values. In addition to reference, Frege proposed that there is another component to linguistic representations, which he called a **sense**. According to Frege, the sense, not the reference, is the semantic value (or meaning) of a linguistic expression. A sense is what people grasp when they are said to know the meaning of a word. Frege considered the sense of a linguistic expression, not its reference, as its semantic value. Therefore, substitutions of expressions with different senses are prohibited by the Law of Identity, regardless of the reference of the expressions.

Frege suggested that, in addition to knowing the sense of a word, people also have **ideas** about words. Ideas were viewed as idiosyncratic/subjective/internal representations of a word. It is important not to confuse the notion of an idea and a sense. Ideas were assumed by Frege to be psychological properties of individuals such that different individuals could have different ideas about a word. By contrast, the sense of a word was taken to be a property that was shared by everyone who spoke the language.

Frege's solution to the apparent violations of the Law of Identity takes advantage of the tripartite distinction among: (i) a linguistic expression, (ii) its reference, and (iii) its sense. As noted, linguistic expressions may differ in sense, even if they have the same reference. The Law of Identity pertains to the senses of expressions, in Frege's view, rather than to their reference. By equating sense with meaning, Frege is able to explain why NPs with the same reference, but with different semantic values (= different senses), result in different truth-values. Therefore, Frege was able to salvage the Law of Identity, but only by abandoning the basic tenet of the Referential Theory of Meaning.

   (8)   Frege's solution

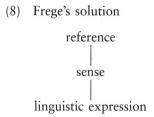

Let's return to the problematic cases for the Referential Theory of Meaning. One example concerned the substitutivity of definite descriptions with the same reference, as in examples (4) and (5).

(4)   The morning star is the evening star.

(5)   The morning star is the morning star.

In these examples, the definite descriptions *the morning star* and *the evening star* canNOT be interchanged without a shift in semantic interpretation (example (4) is contingent, whereas (5) is analytic). This posed a problem for the Referential Theory of Meaning because the semantic values of the definite descriptions were associated with their reference, and the definite descriptions in the two sentences have the same reference. This left their interpretive differences unexplained. According to Frege, however, although these expressions refer to the same thing, they differ in semantic value (that is, sense). That is why they cannot be substituted in the critical examples. By adding the layer of sense mediating a linguistic expression and its reference, Frege was able to maintain the Law of Identity while, at the same time, explaining the difference in interpretation between analytic and contingent sentences (figure 32.1).

A similar solution can be given to counterexamples involving verbs of propositional attitude, such as (9). Notice that the first premise could well be true, even if the conclusion is not, although these statements differ only by the substitution of expressions which refer to the same thing, as stated in the second premise.

(9)   King George III wondered if Scott was the author of *Waverley*.
      Scott was the author of *Waverley*.

      ――――――――――――――――――――――――――――――――――――

      King George III wondered if Scott was Scott.

The solution again appeals to the difference in sense between proper names and definite descriptions in the complement clauses of verbs of propositional attitude. In this linguistic construction, substitutions of expressions that differ in sense may result in changes in truth-value. It is said that the complement clauses of verbs of propositional attitude are **opaque**.

This ends our discussion of Frege. There are many other distinctions and interesting ideas in his writings. One idea that merits further attention is his argument that sentences have a reference, as well as a meaning. According to Frege, the reference of a sentence is its truth-value, true or false. There are interesting consequences of this hypothesis which we return to later. In our view, there is much to be gained from specifying the conditions under which sentences are true and false. In keeping with this, the general approach to semantic theory that began with Frege is called **truth-conditional semantics**.

4   Russell's Theory of Definite Descriptions

Frege handled the problematic cases for the Referential Theory of Meaning by adding a level of representation that mediates between a linguistic expression and its reference. He called this mediating representation a **sense**. The introduction of senses enabled Frege to circumvent the counterexamples he raised. The problems were avoided because, whatever the reference of two linguistic expressions, they might well differ in sense. It might be helpful to think of the sense of a linguistic expression as the means by which the reference of the linguistic expression is known. For example, we are all able to identify cats when they cross our paths. The sense of "cat," then, is whatever enables us to perform that feat of cat-identification.

By identifying sense with the semantic value of linguistic expressions, expressions with the same reference could not be expected to be exchanged without altering the semantic value (the truth-value) of the sentences involved. In this way, Frege maintained the Law of Identity, which holds that expressions with the same semantic value should be interchangeable in sentences, without influencing their truth.

Bertrand Russell proposed a different solution to the puzzles raised by Frege. Russell attempted to salvage the Referential Theory of Meaning without letting go of the Law of Identity. The purpose of this section is to introduce Russell's counterproposal.

Names and definite descriptions

Russell proposed a different way of handling the problematic cases. Instead of adding a mediating level of representation, according to which linguistic expressions could differ, he added to the repertoire of semantic values, such that different linguistic expressions receive different values. At the heart of Russell's proposal is the semantic value he gave to definite descriptions. According to Russell, the meaning of a name is its reference, just as the Referential Theory of Meaning would have it. However, Russell maintained that a definite description such as *the President of the United States* does not refer. Rather, a definite description was seen to be shorthand for a set of conditions which an individual may or may not satisfy. According to Russell, sentences of the form *The F is y* must satisfy the following three **conditions of attribution**:

(10) a. There exists something with attribute F.
     b. At most one thing has attribute F.
     c. That thing has attribute y.

Here is an example:

(11) The present king of France is bald.

Sentence (11) would be true on Russell's account if the following conditions were met:

(12) a. There exists someone who is presently king of France.
     b. At most one person is presently king of France.
     c. That person is bald.

Given this account of definite descriptions, Russell could handily respond to the puzzles that Frege had raised for the Referential Theory of Meaning. Recall that one of the problematic cases concerned the substitutivity of definite descriptions with the same reference, as in examples (13) and (14).

(13) The morning star is the evening star.

(14) The morning star is the morning star.

In these examples, the definite descriptions *the morning star* and *the evening star* cannot be interchanged without a shift in semantic interpretation; example (13) is contingent, whereas (14) is analytic. According to Russell, however, these expressions have different semantic values. It is one thing to say, as does (13), that something (and at most one thing) is a morning star and an evening star. Presumably, people called the last bright object they saw in the sky just before dawn, *the morning star*; and they called the first bright object they saw in the sky at dusk, *the evening star*. Different definite descriptions were used because of these different attributes. It was, therefore, an important empirical discovery that one object (the planet Venus) had both attributes. It is not a matter of empirical discovery at all, however, to find out that a bright object with the attribute of appearing in the sky before dawn also has the attribute of appearing in the sky before dawn, as stated in (14). Because the definite descriptions *the morning star* and *the evening star* have different semantic values, we should not expect them to be interchangeable in sentences without affecting their truth. Russell, like Frege, was therefore able to maintain the Law of Identity while, at the same time, explaining the difference in interpretation between analytic and contingent truths.

A similar solution could be given to counterexamples involving verbs of propositional attitude, such as (15), in which the first premise could be true even if the conclusion is not.

(15)   King George III wondered if Scott was the author of *Waverley*.
       Scott was the author of *Waverley*.

       _____

       King George III wondered if Scott was Scott.

Russell's account provides a simple solution to this puzzle: since proper names and definite descriptions have different semantic values, we should not expect them to be interchangeable in sentences without corresponding changes in truth-value.

Notice that Russell's solution does not require the postulation of another level of representation, such as Frege's level of senses. Although definite descriptions don't refer to specific individuals, as proper names do, they postulate the existence of some individual(s) or other that bears some attribute(s). In ontological terms, where the concern is with the existence and attributes of the entities in the real world, Russell's theory is consistent with the Referential Theory of Meaning.

5   Strawson's Objections

The British philosopher, Peter Strawson, added another wrinkle to the topic of definite descriptions. Strawson claimed that Russell's theory of definite descriptions produced the wrong results for sentences like the following:

(16)   The king of France is bald.

On Russell's account, this sentence is true if there is a king of France and he is bald, but it is false in any one of three circumstances: (i) there is a king of France, but he is not bald; (ii) there is no king of France; or (iii) there is more than one king of France. Strawson questioned whether the sentence in (16) was false in the latter two circumstances. Strawson argued that, according to our intuitions about what it means to say that a sentence is true or false, it seems odd to say that (16) is false if there is no king of France or if there was more than one. Rather, we would say that the speaker had failed to make a statement that could be judged to be either true or false.

A related point is that Russell's analysis has the counter-intuitive consequence of predicting that (17) should have three different interpretations.

(17) The king of France is not bald.

On Russell's account, this sentence means: (i) there is a king of France, but he is not bald; (ii) there is no king of France; or (iii) there is more than one king of France. In fact, the sentence has only the first of these interpretations; it does not appear to be three-ways ambiguous, according to our linguistic intuitions.

Based on these observations, Strawson concluded that a speaker who uses a definite description implies the existence of the individual denoted by it. If the definite description does not refer to an appropriate individual, then the sentence does not make either a true statement or a false statement – it is void of truth-value.

Strawson's own proposal was that two conditions must be satisfied to use a definite description successfully, that is, to make a true or false statement. First, the definite description must actually refer to someone. Let us call this the Condition of Reference. The second condition is that the individual referred to by the definite description must have the properties being attributed to him. Let us call this the Condition of Attribution. The difference between Strawson's account and Russell's account, then, boils down to this: for Russell, a definite description only needs to satisfy the Condition of Attribution in order to make a true or false assertion. As with names, the Condition of Reference must also be satisfied by definite descriptions, according to Strawson.

6 Donnellan's Viewpoint

The American philosopher, Keith Donnellan, challenged the view that definite descriptions are semantically distinct from names. On some occasions of use, they function just like names, in Donnellan's view. Donnellan also argues that, on other occasions, the same definite description may serve a different function, much like that conceived by Russell. We will explore Donnellan's proposals in this section.

Conditions of attribution and of reference

Donnellan distinguishes between two uses of definite descriptions. In some contexts a definite description has what he calls an attributive use; in other contexts, the same definite description is used referentially. It is essential to Donnellan's argument that the same definite description can be used either attributively or referentially in the same sentence, albeit on different occasions. It is also essential to his account that when a definite description is used attributively, it is not being used referentially, and when it is used referentially, it is not being used attributively. This entails that definite descriptions do not have an inherent semantic value. What decides how a definite description is interpreted is the **context** in which it is used. Finally, it is crucial to the account that sentences receive a truth-value on both of their uses.

The attributive use of definite descriptions

Here is one of Donnellan's main examples of a sentence that can be used either attributively or referentially.

(18)   Smith's murderer is insane.

We first consider how the definite description in this sentence (= *Smith's murderer*) might be used **attributively**. This requires a context in which *Smith's murderer* does not refer to anyone known to the speaker, yet it should be a context in which we might still say that the sentence is true or false. The context Donnellan offers is one in which Smith's body is discovered lying in a bloody heap on the floor, with many deep stab wounds. Upon discovering the body in this condition, the police inspector utters the sentence: *Smith's murderer is insane*. On this scenario, we may suppose further that there is no-one for the definite description "Smith's murderer" to refer to, since there is no-one else at the scene of the crime or in custody for the crime. Nevertheless, we would say, Donnellan suggests, that the sentence is true, as long as someone did indeed murder Smith in such a gruesome manner. Roughly, the interpretation that is given to the inspector's utterance is that whoever murdered Smith is insane.

It is important to note that, on this use of the definite description, it does not refer to anyone in particular. Yet, we would still maintain that the investigator said something that is true or false. On the other hand, if no-one murdered Smith, or if Smith did the damage to himself (somehow), then the sentence would be neither true nor false. The point is that the inspector doesn't have to use the definite description referentially for the sentence to be true. As long as someone murdered Smith, the sentence could be true. That person, whoever it is, can be said to be insane.

It is worth noting that the attributive use corresponds in many ways to the account of the semantics of definite descriptions advanced by Russell. Recall that, for Russell, there is no requirement that a definite description refers to someone – that is one of the criticisms of Russell's account levied by Strawson. There is a strong resemblance, then, between the attributive use of definite descriptions, according to Donnellan, and the conditions of attribution stated in

Russell's theory, where a definite description is shorthand for a list of attributes that some entity must satisfy for the sentences containing it to be true.

The referential use of definite descriptions

Sticking with the same sentence, *Smith's murderer is insane*, let us consider a context in which it is used **referentially**, but not attributively. In such a context there need be no-one who fits the description *Smith's murderer*. Nevertheless, the definite description could still be used to refer to a particular person, and we would be permitted to say that the sentence is true or false.

In this scenario, there is a man in custody, say Jones. It turns out (later) that Jones did not murder Smith. At the moment, however, the inspector thinks that Jones is guilty, and is questioning him about Smith's murder. Jones doesn't seem to understand anything. He doesn't know where he is or even who he is. He just babbles incoherently, rolls his eyes, and speaks to people who aren't in the room. When the inspector leaves the room, he says to a colleague: *Smith's murderer is insane*.

In this case, since Jones didn't murder Smith, there is no-one who fits the description "Smith's murderer." Still, what the inspector said is true, since Jones is indeed insane. The definite description *Smith's murderer* nevertheless succeeds in referring to Jones and, again, we would say that the inspector has uttered a sentence that is true.

Donnellan's proposals can be summarized as follows. Consider a sentence of the form: *The F is y*. On the attributive use of the definite description, if nothing is F, then nothing is y. A failure of the presupposition that something is F results in a sentence without a truth-value. However, the definite description can successfully be used attributively to pick out whoever has the characteristic F, even if this person is unknown. This use of definite descriptions is inconsistent with Strawson's theory, because Strawson required a definite description to refer to someone in order for the sentence containing it to receive a truth-value. Donnellan makes it clear that sentences with definite descriptions may be true or false, even if the definite description is not used attributively.

Next, consider the same sentence, but on a referential use. On the referential use of a definite description, the sentence can be judged for its truth-value based on whoever the definite description picks out. This use of definite descriptions is inconsistent with Russell's account. On the referential use, definite descriptions function just like names, and it does not matter to their truth or falsity whether the object being referred to has the attribute(s) mentioned in the description. This case argues against Russell's distinction between names and definite descriptions.

Donnellan's main point is that semantic values are not assigned to linguistic expressions once and for all; the semantic value depends on the context of its utterance. In order to understand the meaning of a linguistic expression, we need a description of the context in which it was used. According to Donnellan, it isn't appropriate to talk about the meaning of a sentence or a phrase but, rather, we must make clear the contexts in which sentences or phrases are used by speakers.

Here is a brief summary of concepts introduced in this chapter:

1 Referential Theory of Meaning

2 Frege's counterexamples
   - The Law of Identity
   - Analytic versus contingent truths
   - Verbs of propositional attitude

3 Frege's Theory
   - Linguistic Expression – Sense – Reference
   - Abandon the Referential Theory
   - Keep Law of Identity

4 Russell's Theory
   - Maintain the Referential Theory
   - Keep the Law of Identity
   - Conditions of Attribution: "the F is y"
     1 There exists something that is F
     2 At most one thing is F
     3 That thing is y

5 Strawson
   - Objections to Russell (e.g., negation)
   - Condition of Reference

6 Donnellan
   - Different contexts: Condition of Attribution, Condition of Reference

Note

1 This statement was accurate at the time the text was written. As we will see in chapter 36, when we consider the time at which an utterance is made the denotation of some NPs may change.

Bibliographical Comments

Frege's paper "On Sense and Reference" was originally published (in German) in 1892. Russell's response was presented in Russell (1905). The more recent philosophers' works referred to in this chapter are Strawson (1950) and Donnellan (1966). Most introductory texts begin with the observation that the domain of semantics includes the relation between linguistic expressions and "external reality" (recent examples include Chierchia and McConnell-Ginet, 1990, and Larson and Segal, 1995). We have called this view-point, which we attribute to Russell, the Referential Theory of Meaning. Both Frege and Russell use the law of identity in arguing for and against (respectively) the claim that linguistic expressions express a "sense," in addition to having reference.

33 Truth-Conditional Semantics

Introduction

The main goal of semantic theory is to provide a systematic account of the principles by which the meanings of linguistic expressions are determined. Semantics is concerned with meaning relationships among words, phrases, and sentences. We will limit our attention to declarative sentences, because these sentences have an important property – they are either true or false. In one tradition in semantic theory, a fundamental goal is to provide a system of rules which determine, for any given sentence, the conditions under which it is true. These conditions are called "truth conditions," so this branch of semantic theory is referred to as **truth-conditional semantics**.

Because there is an unlimited number of declarative sentences in any language, semantic theories must generate truth conditions by rule, rather than simply by listing them. This is a familiar argument. It was used earlier to motivate the need for recursive Phrase Structure (PS) rules, which combine syntactic constituents, Det, N, V, NP, VP, IP, and so on, to form the syntactic representations of an unlimited number of sentences. PS rules state certain relationships that hold among these constituents, namely relationships of dominance (mother/daughter) and precedence (left-to-right order). For example, a Det and an N combine, in that order, to form an NP; a (transitive) V and an NP combine, in that order, to form a VP. Proceeding upwards in the phrase marker, the NP and VP that were formed from "lower-level" constituents (Det, N, V, NP) are subsequently combined, to form an IP.

The addition of recursive rules to the syntactic component of the grammar enabled us to generate an unlimited number of sentences. Since we can also interpret an unlimited number of sentences, there is a similar need for recursive rules within the semantic component. The rules of semantic interpretation perform a similar function to that of PS rules; they combine lower-level constituents to form constituents at higher levels. The difference is in the nature of the constituents that are combined. The objects that are manipulated by semantic rules are not N, V, NP, VP, and IP. Rather, these rules combine the meaning counterparts to syntactic constituents. We will call these constituents of semantic representations, **semantic values**. Semantic rules combine semantic values just as PS rules combine syntactic constituents. So, for example, the semantic value of a Det combines with the semantic value of an N in order to produce the semantic value of an NP; the semantic value of a (transitive) V combines with the semantic value of an NP in order to produce the semantic value of a VP. In this way, the semantic values of higher-level constituents (e.g., NP, VP, IP) are formed on the basis of the semantic values of their parts, and the process of semantic composition proceeds in parallel to the rules of syntax. A system of semantic interpretation with these properties is said to be a "compositional semantics," because it conforms to the following Principle of Compositionality:

The Principle of Compositionality
The meaning of a linguistic expression is a function of the meanings of its parts, and the manner in which they are combined.

1   A Simplifying Assumption

This chapter makes the simplifying assumption that the Referential Theory of Meaning is correct: the semantic value of a linguistic expression is its reference (not its sense). Putting it differently, we will be working within an **extensional** system. In some logical systems, expressions with the same reference (or extension) can be substituted for each other. These are called extensional systems. We have offered reasons for thinking that equating meaning with reference is incorrect in certain cases (recall Frege's argument about the sentence "The morning star is the evening star"). For the moment, though, it is safe to ignore the problematic cases and proceed with this assumption in our demonstration of the inner workings of compositionality. Chapter 36 illustrates how certain modifications to the system enable us to handle the problematic cases. Since meaning is equated with reference in this chapter, the meaning of a sentence will be its truth-value (true or false). One goal of a compositional semantics, then, is to show how the meanings of words and phrases combine to derive a truth-value for the sentences that contain them.

2   Semantic Values within the Sentence

A compositional semantics begins with the assignment of semantic values to the most basic linguistic expressions, the Ns and Vs and so on. Then, these semantic values are combined in forming the values of higher-level expressions, the phrasal categories NP and VP and so on. Finally, the semantic values of phrase-level categories are combined to form the semantic value of the highest-level category, IP. The essential feature of a compositional system of semantic rules is that higher-level categories make use of the semantic values from which they are formed. In some systems, this is achieved by having the semantic rules for combining meanings correspond closely to the syntactic rules. In fact, in all of the cases we consider the semantic rules **mirror** syntactic PS rules. The semantic values of lower-level constituents are combined in precisely the same fashion as the syntactic categories themselves are combined. Some linguists have maintained that syntactic and semantic rules are in one-to-one correspondence – one semantic rule for each syntactic rule. Others deny that such a close correspondence can be achieved in all cases. One reason to favor such a correspondence, however, is that it guarantees that semantic values can be assigned to an unlimited number of linguistic expressions, including ones never encountered before. Recall that the PS rules are **recursive**. Because the syntax is recursive, the language is **productive**. If the semantic rules are based on the PS rules, then, the system will also have a semantics that is productive. This will ensure that speakers can understand novel sentences, for example. The principles of semantics must have this property since, as a matter of fact, any language user can readily understand linguistic expressions that they have not encountered before.

The extensions of certain NPs, proper names, are the individuals who bear the names. For example, the proper name *Sly Stallone* refers to the actor, Sylvester Stallone. The reference (or extension) of a common noun, such as *actor*, is a set of individuals; in this case, the set of actors. What is the semantic value of a VP? For present purposes, we will assume that the extension of a VP, such as *won an Oscar*, is also a set of individuals; in the present case, the set contains those individuals who have won Oscars. Sly Stallone will not be in that set, but Dustin Hoffman will be, along with Daniel Day-Lewis, John Wayne, and George C. Scott. This makes the sentence *Sly Stallone won an Oscar* false, whereas the sentence *Dustin Hoffman won an Oscar* is true.

It may appear circular to say that a noun or a verb phrase picks out a certain set of individuals, namely those individuals that are denoted by the noun or verb. To dispel the appearance of circularity, consider how we can tell whether or not someone knows the meaning of a linguistic expression. Take the noun *actor*. To know the meaning of *actor*, a speaker must know how to apply it correctly. That is, a speaker must know that it refers to actors. No doubt, there is more to knowing the meaning of a word than this, but at least part of knowing what a word means is to have the capacity to identify those entities that it refers to. For now, we will proceed as if this is all there is to the matter. In the next chapter we will confront this issue head-on.

Another feature of the system we are developing may seem odd. This is the fact that common nouns and VPs have the same kind of extension; both refer to sets of individuals. Adopting this view, however, has desirable consequences. For one, this makes it easy to state the semantic rules for determining the truth-values of sentences. Consider, for example, the sentence: *Good actors win Oscars*. This sentence will be true if the set of good actors **intersects** with the set of Oscar winners. A different semantic rule is required to derive the meaning of a sentence with a proper name, such as *Sly Stallone wins Oscars*. Such a sentence requires a rule that yields the truth-value "true" if and only if the individual, Sly Stallone, is **contained in** the set of Oscar winners. Since Sly Stallone has not yet won an Oscar, the sentence is false.[1]

The examples we have discussed in this chapter show that the simple notions of set intersection and set membership can be used to explain how meanings combine to yield truth-values in simple sentences. However, we overlooked certain details. One of the details that was not addressed was how the verb phrase "won an Oscar" was formed out of its constituent parts, "won" and "an" and "Oscar." The next two chapters establish general principles of composition, which apply to such cases. In other words, the chapters that follow are concerned with the inner workings of compositionality.

Note

1   This paragraph raises a problem for the view that there is a one-to-one correspondence between syntactic rules and semantic principles. Notice that the same syntactic rules are used in deriving sentences with proper names and ones with general terms. This paragraph suggests, however, that different semantic principles are required to interpret sentences with proper names versus ones with general terms.

Bibliographical Comments

As noted by Heim and Kratzer (1998), both symbolic logic and the formal semantics of natural language began with the work of Frege. As with Aristotle before him, Frege's concern was the semantic composition of sentences. Frege conjectured that statements could in general be partitioned into "unsaturated" parts (i.e., "functions") that become saturated when filled in by an appropriate constituent (i.e., "arguments"). The Fregian program was worked out in detail more recently by philosophers including David Lewis (1972) and Richard Montague (1974). Tarski (1944) and Davidson (1967) developed the idea that the meaning of sentences could be reduced to (recursive) statements about the conditions under which they are true.

34 Compositionality I

We now begin to state some of the principles for combining the semantic values of basic linguistic expressions to form the semantic values of higher-level expressions. The meanings of individual words are given by a **model**. The model determines the **domain of discourse**, that is, the individuals and the sets of individuals that are under discussion. To keep things simple, let us begin with a domain of discourse that contains just three people, a cat, and several things to eat. The names of the people are *Chelsea*, *Batman*, and *Lyle*. The cat is named *Cat 22*, because it has two extra claws. Figure 34.1 gives the extensions of these names.

Sometimes we will be forced to use written expressions to refer to semantic values of use. When this is done, we will represent the extension of a linguistic expression by capitalizing its first letter, and adding a prime (= ') to it. So, the individuals in the domain of discourse are: Chelsea', Cat 22', Batman' and Lyle'. It should be understood that these two ways of indicating the extension of a name are equivalent, with the alternatives illustrated in figure 34.2.

Also in the model are three Ns referring to food: *ice cream*, *grapes*, and *broccoli*. The semantic values of these Ns are given in figure 34.3, or by the following written expressions: Ice Cream', Grapes', and Broccoli'.

Besides individuals and food, our simple fragment of English contains two intransitive verbs, *sleeps* and *eats*.[1] As we discussed above, a straightforward way to represent the semantic value of an intransitive verb is as a set of individuals; the intransitive verb *sleeps* would refer to those individuals who sleep. Adopting this approach, the verb *sleeps* might pick out Chelsea and Cat 22. (Batman is a crime-fighter so he never sleeps, and Lyle sings and plays all night, every night, so he never sleeps.) Thus, the meaning of *sleeps* is as indicated in figure 34.4.

There is another way to represent the semantic value of an intransitive verb such as *sleeps*. This is to treat it as a special kind of function; one that assigns a truth-value to every individual in the model. Taking each individual in turn, this function indicates whether it is true or false that the individual sleeps. This kind of representation is called a **characteristic function**. The characteristic function associated with Sleeps', for example, associates "true" with all the individuals in the domain of discourse that sleep; otherwise, it assigns them the truth-value

Figure 34.1   Chelsea, Cat 22, Batman, and Lyle

Chelsea′ =

Figure 34.2   The extension of the name "Chelsea"

Figure 34.3   Ice Cream′, Grapes′, and Broccoli′

Figure 34.4   Sleeps′: the set

"false." Chelsea and Cat 22 are the only individuals who sleep; figure 34.5 thus represents the semantic value of the intransitive verb, *sleeps*.

As the figure shows, the semantic value of an intransitive verb is a function from individuals to truth-values. All individuals in the model (or domain of discourse) appear in the characteristic function.

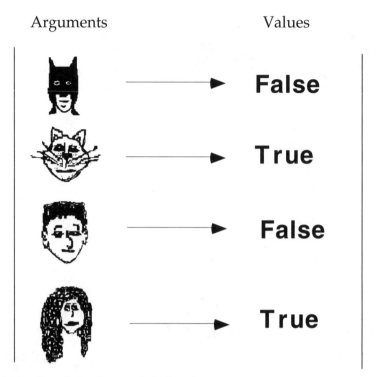

Figure 34.5   Sleeps': the characteristic function

It is important to appreciate that these alternative ways of representing the semantic value of an intransitive verb are logically equivalent. The representations contain exactly the same information. This should not be surprising, because specifying the individuals who sleep amounts to the same thing as deciding for each individual whether it is true or false that he or she sleeps.

Why go to the trouble of representing the semantic value of an intransitive verb as the characteristic function, rather than simply as the set itself? The answer is that representing semantic value in this way enables us to compose the semantic values of NPs and VPs in a straightforward way so as to yield truth-values.

Consider the sentence *Chelsea sleeps*. The semantic value of the intransitive verb, *sleeps*, is its characteristic function. The semantic value of the subject NP of the sentence, *Chelsea*, is an appropriate argument for this function. The value of the function applied to this argument appears on the right-hand side of the arrow. In this case, the value is true, so the sentence *Chelsea sleeps* is true (figure 34.6).

This is the first example of compositionality at work. Our goal was to derive the semantic value of a sentence (a truth-value) on the basis of the semantic

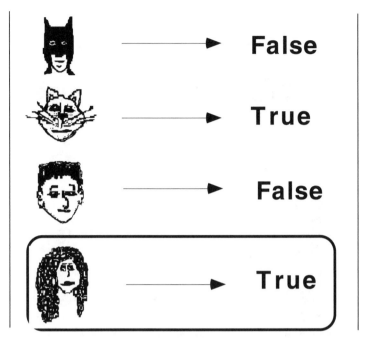

Figure 34.6 "Chelsea sleeps" is true

values of its parts. We chose a sentence that consists of just an intransitive verb and one kind of NP, a proper name. The semantic value of an intransitive verb was represented as a characteristic function from individuals (the argument of the function) to truth-values (the value of the function). The semantic value of a proper name is an individual. Intransitive VPs take the semantic value of NPs as arguments, and return the semantic value of a sentence, a truth-value.

The next example involves negation. The truth-value of a negative sentence is determined on the basis of the truth-value of the sentence without negation. Compare the following examples:

Chelsea sleeps.
Chelsea does not sleep.
Lyle sleeps.
Lyle does not sleep.

We saw that *Chelsea sleeps* is true. What about *Chelsea does not sleep*? Clearly, this must be false. We know this without even looking back at the semantic value of the intransitive verb *sleep*. Similarly, we determined that *Lyle sleeps* is false. From this it follows that *Lyle does not sleep* is true. These examples show us that the semantic value of a sentence with negation can be determined simply

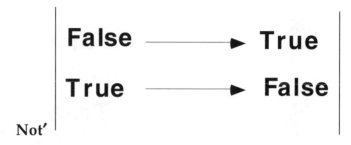

Not'

Figure 34.7   The semantic value of negation

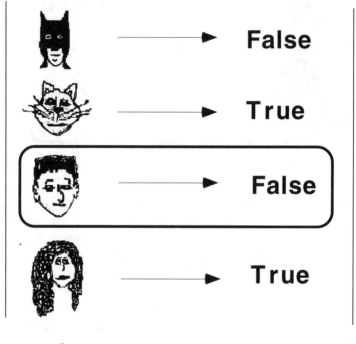

Sleeps'

Figure 34.8   "Lyle sleeps" is false

by considering the semantic value of the corresponding sentence without negation. The two sentences have opposite truth-values: if the first is true, then the second is false; if the first is false, then the second is true.

With these observations in mind, figure 34.7 shows how we will represent the semantic contribution of the negative word, *not*. Not' is a function from truth-values to truth-values. That is, the semantic value of the negative word, *not*, is a function from the semantic value of a sentence to the semantic value of a sentence. The truth-values, true and false, are its arguments, and they are its value.

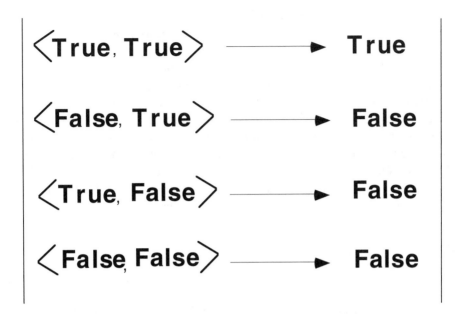

And′

Figure 34.9 The semantic value of "and"

We consider next how the process of compositionality can derive the semantic value of a sentence that is itself made up of sentences joined by conjunction. Such sentences are generated in the syntax by the following PS rule. In the rule, there are three occurrences of the syntactic constituent IP, and one occurrence of Conj.

IP → IP Conj IP

We know the semantic value of an IP: namely, a truth-value. It remains, then, to determine the semantic value of Conj. To this end, we will work through an example with the co-ordinating conjunction, *and*. The example is: *Chelsea sleeps and Lyle sleeps*.

The two sentences *Chelsea sleeps* and *Lyle sleeps* are conjoined clauses (joined by *and* in the example). We saw above that the first conjunct, *Chelsea sleeps*, is true. What about the second conjunct, *Lyle sleeps*? A cursory examination of the semantic value of the intransitive verb *sleeps* makes it clear that this sentence is false (figure 34.8).

So, *Chelsea sleeps* and *Lyle sleeps* are true and false respectively. What about the entire sentence, *Chelsea sleeps and Lyle sleeps*? Intuitively, this is false. That is, for the result of two sentences joined by *and* to be true, both sentences must be true. If either of them is false, or if both are, then the entire sentence is false. Therefore, the present example is false because one of its constituents is, namely *Lyle sleeps*.

These are the truth conditions associated with the conjunction *and*. In order to yield the truth-value "true," the sentences that are joined by *and* must both be true; otherwise, the result is the truth-value "false." This means that the semantic value of *and* can be given as a function with the pair of arguments, corresponding to the semantic values of the two sentences it joins. Based on these semantic values, it returns a truth-value, according to the schema in figure 34.9. This is the semantic value of one of the syntactic constituents that fall in the category Conj. In short, the semantic values of members of this category are functions from pairs of truth-values to a truth-value.

Note

1   We are discussing the meaning of *eats* that corresponds to *dines* and not the transitive verb *eats* that appears in sentences like *Bugs Bunny eats carrots*.

Bibliographical Comments

Characteristic functions of sets are depicted with arrows to graphically illustrate the relations between ordered pairs of entities, including both individuals and truth-values. The semantic structures presented in this chapter and also in chapter 35 are explained in greater detail in several introductory texts, including Cann (1995) and Chierchia and McConnell-Ginet (1990).

35 Compositionality II

The same kinds of mechanisms we described in the last chapter can be extended straightforwardly to provide a compositional treatment of more complex sentences, ones with transitive verbs, such as *likes*. The one difficulty is to come up with the semantic value of a transitive verb.

We proceed just as we did with intransitive verbs. First, the semantic value of a transitive verb is represented as a set, then this set is turned into a characteristic function. In terms of sets, the verb phrase meaning associated with *likes*, i.e., Likes', is not an unstructured set of individuals. Because Likes' is a transitive verb, it is associated with a set of **ordered pairs** of individuals. The individuals are ordered in pairs so we can tell who is doing the liking from who or what is being liked. Order is clearly needed, because person A could like person B, without B liking A. We will avoid even this level of complexity by simplifying the model such that it can only discuss who likes what food. Figure 35.1 graphically depicts the semantic value of Likes' in the domain of discourse under consideration. The set of ordered pairs indicates that Cat 22' and Batman' like Ice Cream', but not Grapes' or Broccoli', Lyle' likes Ice Cream' and Grapes', and Chelsea' only likes health food, namely Grapes' and Broccoli'.

It is logically equivalent to conceive of the semantic value of a transitive verb such as *likes* as a characteristic function. Using this perspective, figure 35.2 gives a graphic depiction of the semantic value of Likes'. It is useful to represent the semantic value of a transitive verb as a characteristic function in order to see more clearly how compositionality is achieved.

Step by step, here is how compositionality works for sentences with transitive verbs. First, the semantic value of the transitive verb combines with that of the direct object NP. The direct object NP represents the things that are liked: Ice Cream', Grapes', and Broccoli'. The semantic value of the direct object NP appears on the right-hand side of the graphic; this is the argument for the semantic value of the transitive verb, which is a characteristic function. Once the function corresponding to the transitive verb applies to this argument (the semantic value of the direct object NP) the result is another characteristic function. This second function should be familiar. It is of the same type as the characteristic function associated with an intransitive verb; it takes the subject

Figure 35.1 Likes': a set of ordered pairs

NP as its argument, and returns a truth-value. The next step, then, is to apply this characteristic function to an appropriate argument, the semantic value of a subject NP. The result of this functional application is a truth-value; just what we wanted.

Figure 35.3 illustrates how the semantic values of lower-level constituents combine according to their position in the phrase marker.

Let us turn next to a real sentence: *Lyle likes broccoli*. Our goal is to derive a truth-value for this sentence, based on the semantic values associated with its constituent parts. The only real trick in this case is to use the complex semantic value of the transitive verb *likes* to derive the truth-value of the sentence. The first step is to combine the semantic value of the transitive verb *likes* with the semantic value of the direct object NP, *broccoli* (figure 35.4).

Once the function corresponding to the transitive verb applies to this argument (the semantic value of the direct object NP), the result is another characteristic function (figure 35.5).

At this stage in the derivation of the sentence *Lyle likes broccoli*, we have obtained the semantic representation corresponding to the VP, *likes broccoli*. Notice that this characteristic function takes the same form as the semantic value corresponding to an intransitive verb, such as *sleep*. This is a nice result. It means that all VPs receive the same kind of semantic value, regardless of their internal contents (i.e., whether they contain a transitive or an intransitive verb).

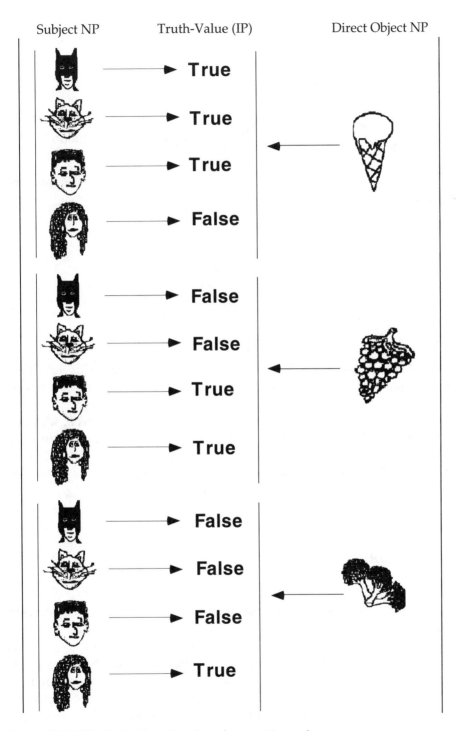

Figure 35.2 Likes': the semantic value of a transitive verb

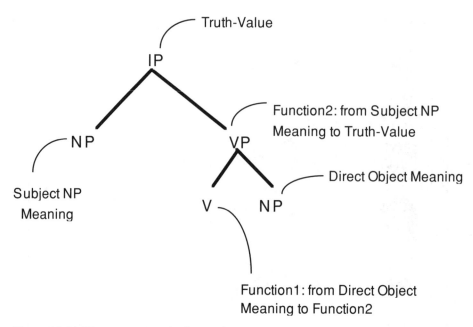

Figure 35.3 How semantics climbs up the syntactic tree

Let us take stock. Figure 35.6 shows where we are in the syntactic derivation, with the portion of the compositional process that has been completed shaded in.

It remains to combine the semantic value of the VP, *likes broccoli*, with that of the subject NP, *Lyle*. The semantic value of the VP is a characteristic function from individuals to truth-values; the semantic value of a subject NP, *Lyle*, is an individual. The result of applying the function to its argument is the truth-value "false." This is the result we were looking for.

Conclusion

This ends our demonstration of the inner workings of compositionality. To achieve compositionality, we focused on a semantic procedure called **functional application**. Some word or phrase semantic values were functions, while others were the arguments for these functions. For sentences with simple NP VP structure, the semantic value of the verb phrase was taken to be the function, and the semantic value of the noun phrase was its argument. The result of applying a function to an argument is called its value. The value obtained by applying a function associated with an intransitive verb to an NP argument is a truth-value,

Figure 35.4   Likes broccoli': the semantic values

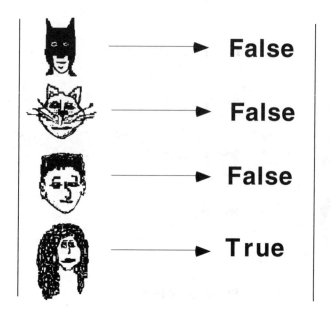

Likes Broccoli′

Figure 35.5   Likes broccoli′: the characteristic function

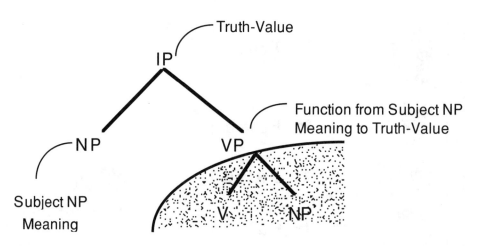

Figure 35.6   Semantics ends its climb up the syntactic tree

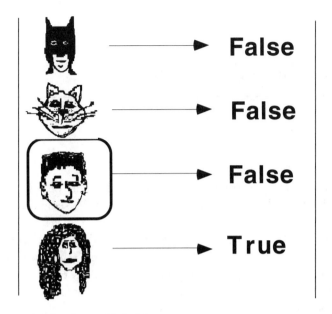

Figure 35.7 "Lyle likes broccoli" is false

that is, the semantic value of a sentence. In the case of transitive verbs, the value of the function after it applied to its initial argument was another function. This means that the procedure of functional application was undergone twice. After its second application, however, the same end-point was reached. The procedure led to the desired result, a truth-value for the sentence under consideration.

36　Intensional Semantics

The last two chapters illustrated how the semantic value of a sentence (which we took to be its truth-value) could be derived from the semantic values of the words and phrases it contained. This was to satisfy the Principle of Compositionality, a principle that lies at the heart of many theories of semantics. Even for a tiny fragment of English, providing a compositional semantic theory requires a lot of technical machinery. To keep things as simple as possible, we identified the semantic value of a linguistic expression with its reference (or extension). For many constructions little is lost by equating meaning with reference. Some linguistic expressions, however, cannot be handled within a system that identifies meaning with reference. In this chapter we will look at certain of the problematic linguistic expressions, and we will describe what is needed to provide them with a reasonable interpretation. Certain additions to the semantic theory are introduced, including **times** and **possible worlds**. Relativizing linguistic expressions to times and possible worlds makes the semantic theory **intensional**, a term that corresponds to what Frege called a **sense** (what is now commonly called an **intension**). The goal of this chapter is to show how intensional semantics works, and how it can be used to provide an account of the meanings of many different types of linguistic expressions. The chapter ends, however, by raising a problem that plagues even a system of intensional semantics.

1　The Problem: Sameness of Reference

The basic insight into the problem with extensional semantics was made by Frege. Recall that Frege argued against equating meaning and reference. If these are equated, he observed, then any two linguistic expressions with the same reference will have the same meaning. Frege advanced several counterexamples to this generalization. The counterexamples were linguistic constructions in which two expressions have the same reference, but not the same meaning.

One counterexample involved the sentences "The morning star is the evening star" and "The morning star is the morning star." Since the NP *the morning star* does in fact refer to the same entity as the NP *the evening star*, then substituting one of these expressions for the other should not alter the truth-value of sentences which contain them. However, this predicts (wrongly) that the sentence "The morning star is the evening star" means the same thing as "The morning star is the morning star." To see the difference in meaning, it should be noted that "The morning star is the morning star" is a **necessary truth** (i.e., it could never be false), but "The morning star is the evening star" is **contingent** (i.e., it happens to be true, but it is not a logical, or necessary, truth).

A similar argument will be used to unveil a weakness in the system of semantic representation that we presented in the last two chapters. There we took the meaning of a verb to be a **characteristic function**. For an intransitive verb (e.g., *sleep*), this was a function from a set of individuals (those picked out by the subject NP) to a truth-value, true or false. The meaning of a transitive verb was even more complex. It was represented as a function from individuals (the extension of the object NP) to a function from individuals (the extension of the subject NP) to truth-values. Even keeping things as simple as we could, we ended up with functions from individuals to functions from individuals to truth-values.

To see one source of potential problems with the identification of meaning with reference, we will begin by considering the semantic representation for two linguistic expressions, *walks on two legs*, and *talks*. The model under discussion contains all the characters from the previous chapter, and three new ones: Julia' (Roberts), Ronnie' (Reagan), and Tricky Dick' (Nixon). Now, suppose that every human in the model walks on two legs, but of course Cat 22' does not walk on two legs. Given this state of affairs, the semantic value of the VP *walks on two legs* can be given as the characteristic function in figure 36.1, which maps every human individual onto the truth-value "true," but which maps Cat 22' onto the truth-value "false."

Let us suppose, further, that every human in the model talks and that, not being human, Cat 22' does not talk. Therefore, the characteristic function associated with the VP *talks* will be the same as that associated with the VP *walks on two legs* (figure 36.2) even though the expressions mean different things.

It seems pretty clear that something has gone wrong, but what? The problem arises because the same individuals in the domain of discourse just happen to walk on two legs and talk. But even if this were true in larger domains, with many more individuals, we would not want to be forced to conclude on this basis that saying that someone walks on two legs is tantamount to saying that s/he talks. But this is just what is entailed by the assumption that sameness of reference entails sameness of meaning.

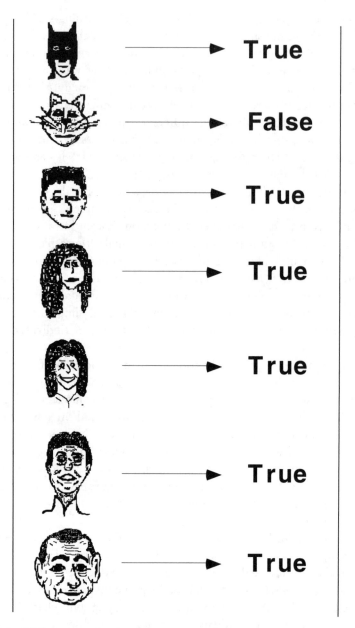

Figure 36.1   Walks on two legs'

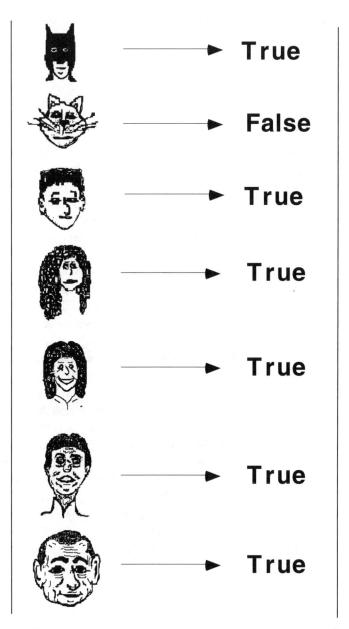

Figure 36.2 Talks'

There are further problems with analyzing meaning as extension, to which we now turn.

2   Times

There are certain critical features that are lacking in the system we have developed so far. One is the notion of time. This notion is needed even to assign the appropriate reference to certain definite descriptions, namely ones whose extension differs from time to time. Examples are *Miss America* and *the President of the United States*. No individual can be President of the United States for more than eight years. Therefore, the extension of the definite description *the President of the United States* changes at least every eight years, sometimes even more often. This makes it impossible to establish once and for all whether sentences like "Jimmy Carter is the President of the United States" are true or false. Rather, this sentence was true at some period of time, but it is false now. In order to evaluate linguistic expressions like this, therefore, we must **relativize** these expressions to particular times.

There is another type of linguistic expression that currently escapes us, but that can be handled once times are incorporated into the system. This is the class of adjectives that includes *former* and *future*, as in "former Celtic" or "future king." Consider, for example, the definite description *former player for the Boston Celtics*. Clearly, someone who is a former player for the Boston Celtics is not one who is within the extension of the NP *player for the Boston Celtics*. The meaning of *former* requires us to examine sets of individuals who do **not** currently fall within the extension of the noun. To evaluate the sentence "Larry Bird is a former player for the Boston Celtics," however, it does not suffice to know that Larry Bird is not a member of the Celtics now. What is needed is some way of referring to members of the team at earlier times, as well as at the present time. Examples like this point out the need to elaborate our semantics to include **times**.

3   Possible Worlds

Another feature is critical to an adequate semantic system. This involves the notion of a possible state of affairs (or possible world). To provide an adequate semantic theory, certain meanings of linguistic expressions must be relativized to possible states of affairs. For example, earlier in the chapter we mentioned

Frege's famous sentence "The morning star is the evening star," noting that it is a **contingent** truth. The point is that the reference of the NP *the morning star* turned out to be the same as the reference of *the evening star*, but this was a matter of fact, not a matter of logic. Things could have been otherwise, which is why the two names exist. People used two names because they thought, wrongly as it turned out, that they were describing two distinct heavenly objects. The point is that there was a possible state of affairs in which the two expressions had different referents, but this did not turn out to be the actual state of affairs. The notion **possible state of affairs**, or **possible world**, is central to many current semantic theories.

To avoid confusion, we advise you to think of a possible world as a possible state of affairs in *this* world. The term **possible world** suggests that a world other than our own is under consideration, for example, another planet that we can only see by telescope, or one in another galaxy that we can only visit by spacecraft. However, all of the examples we will discuss will involve possible states of the world we live in, that is, the real (or actual) world.

Many linguistic constructions illustrate the need for the semantic concept of a possible state of affairs. One case in point concerns sentences such as "If Kennedy had not been assassinated, the war in Viet Nam would have ended sooner," or "If I had studied harder, I could have gotten an 'A' in physics." Sentences like this are called **counterfactuals**. These sentences ask us to consider how the course of events in the actual world would have been altered, if certain events had been different. These sentences illustrate what we mean by a possible world, namely, a possible but not actual state of the real world. The point is that some such notion is needed in assigning the appropriate semantic values to certain linguistic expressions, such as counterfactual sentences.

4 Intensions

In the light of the inadequacies of an analysis of meaning in extensional terms, we will now formulate an **intensional semantics**. Within a system of intensional semantics, the meaning of a word is called an **intension**. It is important to note, though, that there is an intimate relationship between the intension of a linguistic expression and its **extension**. The key idea of intensional semantics is this: the meaning (sense or intension) of a linguistic expression is not its extension. Rather, the meaning of a linguistic expression is a *function from possible worlds and times to its extension*.

As always, examples will help to make the point clear. We saw earlier that some definite descriptions do not always pick out the same individuals at all times. An example is *the President of the United States*. This NP has different

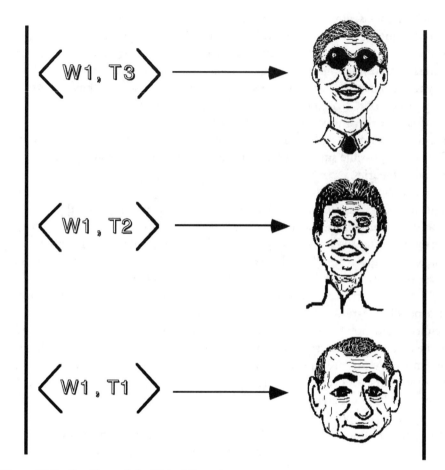

Figure 36.3   President of the United States'

individuals as its extension at different times in the actual world. Let us call the actual world, **W1**. Other possible worlds (other states of the actual world) will be given other numbers. Then, given that Richard Nixon was president before Ronald Reagan, and Reagan was president before Bill Clinton, we can provide an analysis of the meaning of the NP *the President of the United States* as in figure 36.3. The times **T1, T2,** and **T3** are in chronological order.

As we said above, we refer to the actual world as **W1**; other possible worlds will be given other numbers. These other possible worlds were needed, as we saw, to interpret counterfactual sentences. Consider the following sentence: *We wouldn't be in this mess if there had been a woman President the last eight years, instead of Clinton.* Whatever the truth of the sentence, it contains a clause that can be interpreted only if another possible world besides the actual world is considered. This is illustrated in figure 36.4.

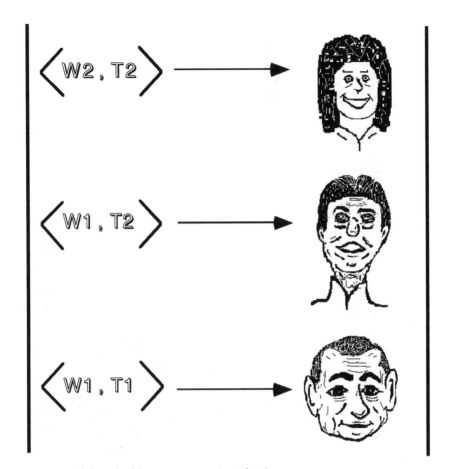

Figure 36.4 If there had been a woman President′

So far, we have seen how the use of possible worlds and times can help us avoid certain of the problems that arose with identifying meaning with reference. One problem with this view was that it led to the conclusion that certain definite descriptions must change in meaning at different times. To avoid this problem, we will assume that the meaning of such expressions are constant; they are functions from worlds and times to individuals. On the other hand, the reference of such definite descriptions do change from time to time.

There is another kind of NP with both a constant meaning and a constant reference. This is a proper name. The extension of a proper name is an individual. So, for example, the name *Ross Perot* refers to the individual Ross Perot (figure 36.5).

Most names pick out the same individual at all the times of their lives. Moreover, it would seem safe to say that even in different possible worlds, the same individual is being talked about. When we say things like "I wonder what

Figure 36.5   Ross Perot': extension

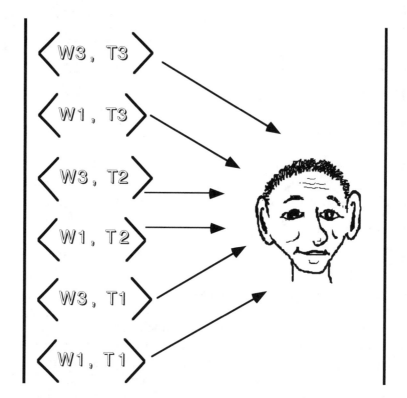

Figure 36.6   Ross Perot': intension

Ross Perot would be like with a mustache," we are talking about the same individual, but a different state of affairs than exists in the actual world.

Because names pick out the same individuals at different times, and across different possible worlds, they have been given a special status in the theory of semantics. They are called **rigid designators**. The main point to remember is the relation between the extension of a name and its intension. The intension of a name is a function from possible worlds and times to its extension, the person who bears the name. Figure 36.6 is a simple illustration of the rigid designator, Ross Perot'.

5 Solving Frege's Puzzles

Possible world semantics can cope with the difficulties that threaten semantic theories that equate meaning with reference. Suppose right now, in the actual world, everybody who eats hamburgers also eats pizza. Then, the meaning of "eats hamburgers" and "eats pizza" would be the same if meaning and reference were equated: a counter-intuitive result. However, if we add the level of intensionality, with its times and possible worlds, the problem vanishes.

To see this, it should suffice to notice that at least at some time, or in some possible world, the individuals who eat pizza and those who eat hamburgers will not be the same. In fact, we can easily imagine a state of affairs in which no-one eats hamburgers, because everyone is afraid of getting food poisoning. But in this state of affairs, we would not expect people to stop eating pizza. In another possible world everybody eats hamburgers, but no-one eats pizza, and so on. Because the extensions of these expressions differ in these different possible worlds, their intensions will be different.

We can now see how an intensional semantic system is able to handle some of the problematic cases for the Referential Theory of Meaning raised by Frege. Consider an example like one that Frege offered:

a. The morning star is the morning star.
b. The morning star is the evening star.

The (a) sentence is a logical truth, whereas the (b) sentence is contingent. This difference in meaning can be explained quite simply: the two NPs *the morning star* and *the evening star* do not refer to the same entity in all possible worlds; so, their meanings are not the same. On the other hand, (a) is true in every possible world; that is what makes it a logical truth.

Another puzzle raised by Frege concerned sentences with verbs of propositional attitude, such as *believe* and *wonder*. Earlier we gave the following example:

a. King George III wondered if Scott was the author of *Waverley*.
b. King George III wondered if Scott was Scott.

Since Scott is not the author of *Waverley* in some possible world, the first sentence could be true, so it made sense for King George to wonder who the author

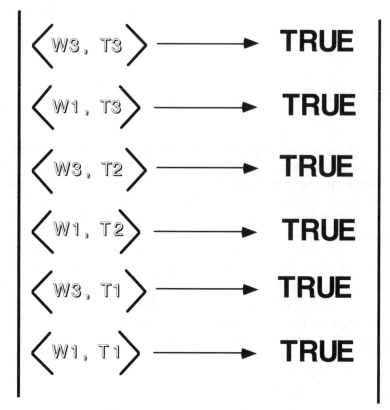

Figure 36.7   If John is 6′ tall then at least one person is 6′ tall

of *Waverley* was. It wouldn't make much sense for him to wonder whether Scott was Scott, since this statement (Scott is Scott) is a logical truth. Even if the extensions of "Scott" and "the author of *Waverley*" are the same, these expressions cannot be substituted one for the other, because this would stand in violation of the Law of Identity. The reason is simple. The two expressions don't mean the same thing, at least according to an intensional account of meaning.

6   A Problem Remains: Meaning and Truth

A meaning (or intension) is a function from possible worlds and times to the extension of a linguistic expression. It therefore follows that the meaning of a sentence is a function from possible worlds and times to truth-values. The notion of logical truth, or truth in all possible worlds, gives rise to a problem for intensional semantics, as we will now discuss.

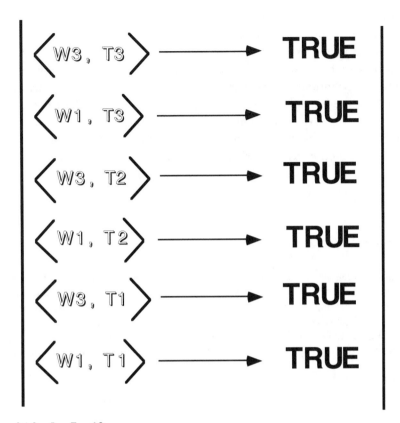

Figure 36.8 5 + 7 = 12

The problem for intensional semantics arises from the basic assumption that the meaning of a sentence is a function from possible worlds to truth-values. There is a simple proof that the meaning of a sentence cannot simply be such a function. The proof is this. Consider the following two sentences:

a. If John is 6′ tall then at least one person is 6′ tall.
b. 5 + 7 = 12

Both of these sentences are true. More than this, these sentences are **logically true**; they are true in all possible worlds. But if the meaning of sentences is a function from possible worlds to truth-values, then both of these sentences will have exactly the same meaning. This consequence follows from the fact that the value of the function from possible worlds and times is always the same, "true." Being logical truths, both sentences are true in every possible world, as represented in figures 36.7 and 36.8.

Clearly, the two sentences under consideration do not really mean the same thing. One is about numbers and one is about people's height. The problem is that, by associating the meaning of a sentence with functions, as we have, we lose the information that tells us what the sentences were about. One way out of this dilemma is to modify what we count as the meaning of a sentence. One approach is to have the meaning of a sentence include a description of the semantic contributions of the various parts of a sentence to its truth-value. Although we are interested in saying things that are true, much of the real work of semantic theory is in the steps that are performed along the way towards assigning a truth-value to a sentence. So the meaning of the sentence would not simply be a function from worlds and times to its truth-value; it would also include a record of the contributions of its component parts to its truth-value.

Bibliographical Comments

According to Frege, a linguistic expression has a sense, in addition to a reference. Frege described the sense of a linguistic expression as "the mode of presentation" of its reference. A way of interpreting what Frege meant by "mode of presentation" was proposed by Carnap (1947), who coined the term "intension" for this purpose. According to Carnap (also see Lewis, 1972), the intension of a linguistic expression is a function that yields an appropriate extension depending on various factors (sometimes called "possible worlds").

37 Learnability of Syntax and Semantics

The past few chapters have introduced the core linguistic notions of semantics along with some mechanisms that may be used to derive sentence meanings from the meanings of their constituent parts. All of these mechanisms fall within the semantic component of the language apparatus. We are ready now to begin discussion of the acquisition of semantic knowledge, especially the Principle of Compositionality. This chapter provides a backdrop against which we will discuss the so-called "logical problem of language acquisition." Essentially the "problem" is how children come to know so much given their limited experience. This issue was raised earlier in the context of syntactic principles. Clearly, the logical problem of language acquisition extends to semantic principles as well as to syntactic principles. In particular, the Principle of Compositionality itself places heavy constraints on the kinds of interpretations that can be assigned to sentences – the only interpretations that are possible are ones that are consistent with the syntactic structure that is attributed to the linguistic expressions.

In the three chapters that follow this one, we will examine children's understanding of three different linguistic constructions. Our goal is to demonstrate the interface conditions that hold between syntactic and semantic representations. One interface condition is the Principle of Compositionality; so, one goal is to see if young children adhere to this principle. The three constructions to be discussed are (a) noun phrases (with modifying phrases), (b) relative clauses, and (c) sentences with the determiner *every*, which is also known as a **universal quantifier**. As we will see, the literature on language development suggests that children interpret all three constructions differently from adults. What researchers make of the differences is not uniform, however. In the first two instances, researchers interpreted children's non-adult behavior as evidence that children and adults assign different syntactic structures to the constructions under investigation, that is, noun phrases with modifiers, and sentences with relative clauses. In other words, the claim for these two constructions is not that children lack compositionality; rather, the claim is that children use the same semantic mechanisms as adults do, but apply these mechanisms to different syntactic structures, resulting in different interpretations. Children's non-adult responses to the third construction (sentences with the universal quantifier, *every*) were construed differently, as evidence that children do indeed fail to adhere to the Principle of Compositionality.

The present chapter demonstrates that *any* differences between children and adults must be scrutinized with care, in light of the learnability problems that could arise. As we show, the road to the Final State of the language acquisition process, an adult grammar, is fraught with potential pitfalls if children make even the smallest of wrong turns.

1   Explanatory Adequacy

The theory of grammar in the generative framework attempts to achieve what Chomsky calls **explanatory adequacy**. Here is how Chomsky introduces the term:

> To the extent that a linguistic theory succeeds in selecting a descriptively adequate grammar on the basis of primary linguistic data, we can say that it meets the condition of *explanatory adequacy*.

As noted many times before, children can, in principle, learn any natural language on the basis of the primary linguistic data. This makes explanatory adequacy difficulty for a theory to achieve. A theory that explains how children in England become competent speakers of English could nevertheless fail to explain how children in the Netherlands become competent speakers of Dutch. Such a theory would fail to meet the condition of explanatory adequacy, however much insight might be gained from the theory about the linguistic competence of speakers of English.

In addition to setting the standards high, so as to explain learnability from a cross-linguistic perspective, explanatory adequacy is difficult for a linguistic theory to achieve even in the acquisition of a single language. The difficulty surfaces with the observation that the primary linguistic data are impoverished in certain respects (see chapters 2 and 4). In addition, there is considerable variation in individuals' linguistic experiences, even ones that are reared in the same linguistic community. Despite these features of the primary linguistic data, all children in the same linguistic community converge on an equivalent grammar, permitting mutual communication. Moreover, this occurs ubiquitously, regardless of the linguistic community. Finally, children accrue language competence remarkably fast (as compared to other cognitive skills), and make few wrong turns along the way (considering the possible wrong turns that could be taken). This chapter explores certain of the relevant features of the primary linguistic data and their potential impact on the course of language development.

2 Two Proposals about Phrase Structure

We will limit our discussion to the acquisition of noun phrases. More specifically, we focus on noun phrases in which the noun is modified by certain classes of modifiers. One class of modifiers under discussion includes **ordinals**, such as *first, second, third,* and so on. The other class contains adjectives such as *green, striped, furry, leather*. These are called "absolute" or "intersective" adjectives. Absolute adjectives can be contrasted with "relative" adjectives such as "big" or "expensive." The basic idea is that relative adjectives adapt their interpretation to the noun that they modify. A big ant is not big absolutely, but relative to the set of ants. By contrast, a red ant is not red *for an* ant; it is an ant and it is red.

Now we will look at how adjectives are introduced into noun phrases, in the syntax. It will be useful to consider two ways of introducing adjectives. The differences can be rendered using two different sets of PS rules, as indicated in (1a) and (1b). The rules in (1a) will be designated the **hierarchical analysis**, and those in (1b) will be designated the **flat-structure analysis**.

(1)   a.   i.   NP $\rightarrow$ Spec N'   Hierarchical analysis

           ii.   N' $\rightarrow$ AP $\left\{ \begin{matrix} N' \\ N \end{matrix} \right\}$

         iii.   N' $\rightarrow \left\{ \begin{matrix} N' \\ N \end{matrix} \right\}$ PP

         iv.   N' $\rightarrow$ N

     b.   i.   NP $\rightarrow$ Spec (AP) N   Flat-structure analysis

           ii.   NP $\rightarrow$ Spec N (PP)

The PS rules in (1a) should be familiar to you. The brackets in rules (ii) and (iii) mean that either choice is possible: an AP may be followed by an N' or by an N; a PP may follow either an N' or an N. In the previous chapters, we almost always used these rules with N on the right side of the arrow. However, in chapter 12 we noted that N' can be used in order to achieve recursion, that is, multiple adjectives preceding (or prepositional phrases following) a noun. In this set of rules, recursion is introduced in virtue of the intermediate category, N'.

The PS rules in (1b) lack the category N'. Instead, any number of adjectives may be introduced before a noun with no intermediate category. Similarly, any number of prepositional phrases may be introduced after a noun. These rules create "flat" structures in which multiple elements are dominated by the node NP.

The differences between these alternative sets of PS rules are not trivial. Linguists Norbert Hornstein and David Lightfoot showed the consequences of these alternative proposals and the learnability problems that would result if children made the incorrect choice. Let use see how these different sets of rules fare with respect to the process of one-substitution, which we discussed previously in chapter 11. The sentence in (2b) gives an example of one-substitution, in which *one* stands for *student*.

(2) a. The student with long hair is smarter than the student with short hair.
     b. The student with long hair is smarter than the one with short hair.

First we consider where the proform *one* is inserted into NP structures, according to the different rule systems. The structures in (3) show how the rules in (1a) derive the relevant phrases using the hierarchical analysis.

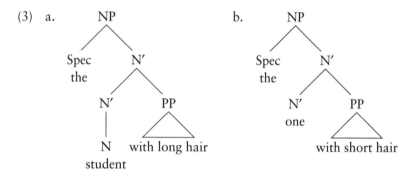

As we saw in chapter 11, the PS rules in (1a) are consistent with a principle that substitutes the proform *one* under identity with N′.

In constrast, the structures in (4) show how the rules in (1b), using the flat-structure analysis, must work to derive these phrases.

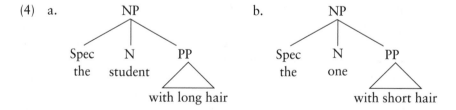

The important observation to make is that the PS rules in (1b) are consistent only with a linguistic principle according to which the proform *one* is substituted for a preceding N, since no intermediate category N′ is present in the structures they generate.

From the example given so far, either analysis seems to work. However, we will quickly observe that the flat-structure analysis is inadequate to account for further data. To see this, notice the difference in grammaticality between the following two sentences.

(5) The student with long hair is smarter than the one with short hair.

(6) *The student of philosophy is smarter than the one of linguistics.

Obviously the difference in grammaticality between examples (5) and (6) has to do with the PPs these sentences contain. Apparently the nominal constituent *student* cannot be replaced by the proform *one* when it is modified by one kind of PP, such as *of philosophy*, even though *one* can substitute for *student* when it is modified by other kinds of PPs, such as *with long hair*. Here is the intuition. The phrase *student with long hair* describes an individual with two properties: (a) that of being a student, and (b) that of having long hair. By contrast, the phrase *student of philosophy* describes individuals with a single property, that of being a student of philosophy; it makes little sense to say that someone is both a student and of philosophy.

Hence, we can see that the interpretation of proforms like *one* is restricted: the restriction is that *one* can only replace expressions whose semantic value is a **property**. In (5), the proform *one* can replace the nominal expression *student* because this expression within the NP denotes a property. In (6), on the other hand, there is only one expression that denotes a property, the entire phrase *student of philosophy*. This observation allows us to tighten the limits on the application of one-substitution so as to exclude (6), but permit (5).

This restriction does not mean that one-substitution will never apply when noun phrases contain expressions like *of philosophy*. Consider example (7).

(7) George is a student of philosophy and Michael is one too.

Notice that (7) is unambiguous. It states that Michael is a student of philosophy, not just a student. In this example, *one* substitutes for the N' *student of philosophy* (a property-denoting expression). It may help to appreciate the point by contrasting (7) with another example of one-substitution, that in (8).

(8) George is a student with long hair and Michael is one too.

Example (8) should be ambiguous, on the present account, since the proform *one* could be interpreted in two ways, either as replacing *student* or as replacing *student with long hair*. The reason that *one* can replace the larger phrase *student with long hair* in (8) is that a complex property can be derived by intersecting the two simple properties, (a) that of being a student, and (b) that of having long hair. (You will notice that this is by far the preferred interpretation of (8).)

The PS rules in (1a) enable us to render these semantic distinctions in the syntax. To see how, we propose that the following structures are associated with the different NPs, *the student with long hair*, and *the student of philosophy*.

(9) a.   b.

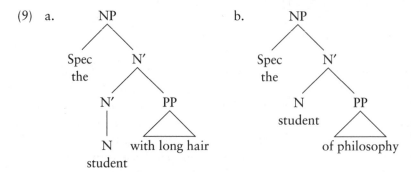

The structure in (9a) is identical to that given earlier in (3a). The structure in (9b) differs from that in (9a) by the omission of the node N′ immediately dominating *student* and nothing else. With these structures in hand, we can form a generalization that yields the facts that we want to explain, the acceptability of (5) but not (6), and the fact that (8) is ambiguous, but (7) is not. Not surprisingly, the generalization turns on the intermediate category N′. Notice that both *student* and *student with long hair* are immediately dominated by N′s in (9a), but only the phrase *student of philosophy* is in (9b). Now we can state the generalization: the proform *one* can substitute for N′ but not for N.

Given the PS rules in (1a), and the generalization that the proform *one* cannot substitute for N, it follows that *one* can replace *student* in (9a), but not in (9b). Either N′ in (9a) can be replaced by *one*, yielding the ambiguity in (8). In (9b), the proform *one* must substitute for *student of philosophy* because only this sequence of words is dominated by N′. Since there is only a single occurrence of N′ in (9b), there should be no ambiguity regarding the interpretation of *one* in examples like (7). In short, (1a) accounts for all the facts.

Consider next the flat-structure PS rules in (1b). The flat-structure analysis (FSA) falsely predicts that both (5) and (6) are grammatical. This is because the PS rules in (1b) are forced to assign the same structure to the NPs in (5) and (6). Given these PS rules, there is only one structural option for both of these NPs, as illustrated in (10). This means that the semantic difference in the nature of the PPs that modify *student* cannot be reflected in the syntax.

(10) a.   b.

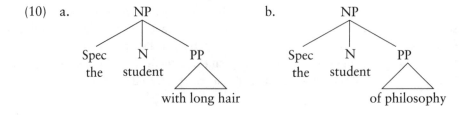

So far, we have offered an argument for the PS rules in (1a), and against the ones in (1b). Now let us ask what the impact of this proposal would be for the course of language development. Let us suppose, for the sake of discussion, that a child adopted the PS rules in (1b). Clearly, such a child would **overgenerate**. That is, the child would produce ungrammatical sentences like (6), in addition to grammatical ones like (5). This difference between children and adults is depicted in (11).

(11) *Child*

OK: The student with long hair is smarter than the one with short hair.

OK: The student of philosophy is smarter than the one of linguistics.

Adult

OK: The student with long hair is smarter than the one with short hair.

But Not: The student of philosophy is smarter than the one of linguistics.

When children produce extra sentences like the one in (11), which are not produced by adults, this is called **structural** (or **string**) **overgeneration**.

In addition to structural overgeneration, the child who adopted the PS rules in (1b) would lack an interpretive option that is available for adults, namely, the ability to interpret (8) to mean that Michael is a student with long hair, not just a student. This is called **semantic undergeneration**. This difference between children and adults is depicted in (12).

(12) *Child*

George is a student with long hair and Michael is one too.

= . . . and Michael is a student too.

≠ . . . and Michael is a student with long hair too.

Adult

George is a student with long hair and Michael is one too.

= . . . and Michael is a student too.

= . . . and Michael is a student with long hair too.

To summarize, the PS rules in (1a) characterize the adult grammar, and those in (1b) do not. So the question arises: if a child initially adopted the PS rules in (1b), would there be evidence from the available linguistic experience that would enable her to make the transition to the adult PS rules in (1a)? The next section sketches an argument that yields a negative conclusion, that is, an argument that children's experience could not lead them to overcome errors of either structural over- or semantic undergeneration. In other words, the argument is that children's primary linguistic evidence does not contain information that would compel children to abandon PS rules like those in (1b) in favor of ones like those in (1a).

3   The Problem of Structural Overgeneration

In the case of the structure of NPs, if children adopted non-adult PS rules like those in (1b), then there would not be readily available evidence from the linguistic environment to purge their grammars of the incorrect analysis. The data that would justify the abandonment of the illicit analysis could, in principle, be supplied by so-called negative evidence. Negative evidence is information about which sentences are deviant, from a grammatical point of view. For example, children could learn that the PS rules in (1b) are incorrect if they were confronted with the fact that (13) is ungrammatical (although it is unclear what they would make of that fact).

(13)   * The student of philosophy is smarter than the one of linguistics.

However, it is unlikely that negative evidence like this is available to children, at least not in sufficient abundance to account for the fact that every child converges on the adult grammar. Steven Pinker, a psycholinguist at MIT, summarizes the findings from studies of parental speech to children as follows:

> When parents are sensitive to the grammaticality of children's speech at all, the contingencies between their behavior and that of their children are noisy, indiscriminate, and inconsistent from child to child and age to age.

To conclude: since all children do, as a matter of fact, converge on the target grammar (presumably without negative evidence), it follows that children do not hypothesize the rules in (1b) in the first place; rather, they proceed with PS rules, with intermediate constituents like N', from the initial stages of language development. This ends our discussion of the problem of recovering from errors of structural overgeneration.

4   The Semantic Subset Problem

Next, we consider how children could recover from errors of semantic undergeneration. The source of the problem is the relationship between the meaning assigned by adults, and that which would be assigned by children using the flat-structure analysis (FSA). In sentences where the FSA and the adult analysis can be compared directly, it turns out that the set of circumstances that make a sentence true on the adult interpretation constitutes a **subset** of the circumstances that make the same sentence true on the child interpretation, that is, the interpretation generated by the FSA. Cases like this present special problems for language learnability, called **subset problems**.

To illustrate the predicament children would find themselves in, consider sentence (14). This sentence is ambiguous, as indicated by the paraphrases in (14a) and (14b). There is a strong preference to interpret (14) as (14a). That is, adults exhibit a preference for interpreting (14) to mean that Jeff is pulling a *heavy* box, not just that he is pulling a box. Nevertheless, the proform *one* is able to substitute over a smaller domain, as example (15) indicates.

(14)   Brian is pulling a heavy box and Jeff is pulling *one*, too.
    a. Brian is pulling a heavy box and Jeff is pulling a heavy box, too.
    b. Brian is pulling a heavy box and Jeff is pulling a box, too.

(15) Brian is pulling a heavy box, and Jeff is pulling a light one (*one* = box).

Children who adopt the flat-structure analysis of the phrase *a heavy box* should substitute *one* for *box*, not for *heavy box*. The reason is that the adjective *heavy* and the noun *box* do not form a constituent, according to the FSA. Children who adopt the FSA, then, would interpret sentence (14) to mean that Jeff is pulling a box, not that he is pulling a heavy box. The difference between children and adults would be readily apparent because, as we saw, the interpretation that is preferred by adults is for *one* to substitute for *heavy box*. But this interpretation would not be available to children.

Notice that the alternative interpretations under consideration are in a subset/superset relation. That is, the circumstances that make the preferred adult interpretation true (where *one* refers to *heavy box*) constitute a subset of those that make the child's interpretation true according to the FSA (where *one* refers to *box*). The reason is simple: someone who is pulling a heavy box is pulling a box. The reverse does not hold, however: someone who is pulling a box is not necessarily pulling a heavy box. That is, a subset problem arises because the extension of heavy-box′ is a subset of the extension of box′:

heavy-box′ $\subseteq$ box′

More generally, the extension (reference) of an expression corresponding to an N′ is a subset of the extension of the N below it in the phrase structure tree:

the extension of N′ $\subseteq$ the extension of N

Figure 37.1   "Brian is pulling a heavy box . . ."

The present example illustrates the point quite clearly. On the scenario under consideration, where adults assign a hierarchical analysis and children assign a flat-structure analysis, adults will allow *one* to refer to the set of *heavy boxes* in (14), whereas children can use *one* only to refer to *boxes*.

To appreciate the problem that this would pose for learnability, consider what the input to children will be, and what they will make of it. Continuing with the present example, adults would prefer to use (16) in situations where both Brian and Jeff are pulling heavy boxes, as in figure 37.1:

(16)   Brian is pulling a heavy box and Jeff is pulling one, too.

Adults are able to assign this interpretation because the combination of the Adj, *heavy*, and the N, *box*, forms a constituent, N'. For children with the FSA, however, the proform *one* can only substitute for N, because there is no N' on the FSA. As a consequence, the meaning that children assign to the same sentence makes it true in any circumstance in which Jeff is pulling a box, not just in circumstances in which he is pulling a heavy box. These children would consider the sentence true, for example, if Jeff is pulling a light box (figure 37.2). Note that the sentence would be judged by adults to be **false**, on the interpretation where *one* corefers with *heavy box*.

The problem for learnability is that children cannot **notice** that adults permit a reading that is not permitted in their grammars, namely the reading according to which both Brian and Jeff are pulling *heavy boxes*, not just *boxes*. This

Figure 37.2 "... and Jeff is pulling one too"

reading, although not available to children who adopt the FSA, is nevertheless consistent with these children's grammar, where *one* substitutes for N. Again, this follows from the observation that anyone who is pulling a heavy box is pulling a box.

Let us next ask why children would find it difficult to advance to the adult grammar. The reason for this can be seen by considering what the input to children would be like, on the assumption that adults have the hierarchical analysis. First, it should be clear that adults would not use the proform *one* in sentences like (17), which is repeated from the discussion above (= 6).

(17) *The student of philosophy is smarter than the one of linguistics.

Nor is it plausible to assume that parents (or other caretakers) inform children that sentences like (17) are ungrammatical. That is, it is unlikely that **negative evidence** is available to children on this matter. Other sources of information are also unlikely. For example, adults would avoid producing sentences like (16), where *one* substitutes for the N' *box* in contexts like the one in figure 37.2, where Jeff is pulling a light box (assuming that parents do not generally produce sentences that are false).

So far, we have made observations which indicate that children would lack certain evidence that could inform them that they have formed the incorrect generalization about one-substitution. There are, however, "exotic" contexts that point out the reading on which *one* and *heavy box* corefer. For example, the following sentence would provide this information in the context of the picture above:

(18) Brian is pulling a heavy box, but Jeff isn't pulling one.

It is clear that Jeff is pulling a box, so the child's FSA would lead them to judge (18) to be false in the context, whereas adults would judge it to be true.

We consider it to be highly unlikely that sentences like (18), produced in the right contexts, occur frequently in the experience of every child. If this is so, however, then at least some children whose grammars contained the rules in (1b) would not encounter the relevant sentence/meaning pairs. All of the data they would encounter would therefore confirm their hypothesis, and there would not be any reason to change it. These children would not converge on the adult grammar. But this leads to a contradiction, since all children do in fact become adult language users. To avoid the contradiction, we must jettison one of the assumptions that led to the learnability problem. The most reasonable assumption to abandon is that children adopt PS rules like (1b). To avoid the problem of learnability, as well as to provide adequate empirical coverage, we assume that, as an innate principle of Universal Grammar, children initially hypothesize rules like (1a) that establish intermediate-level syntactic constituents like N'.

The arguments presented in this chapter invite us to suppose that children make few errors of interpretation for NPs with modifiers. Logic dictates this, in light of the unsolvable problems that would arise if children made errors. But logic and real life do not always agree, which makes real life more interesting. This is the topic of the next three chapters.

Bibliographical Comments

The quote from Chomsky on explanatory adequacy is from his 1965 book, p. 25. The quote from Pinker is from Pinker (1990), p. 217. Other references concerning the lack of negative evidence were given in the Bibliographical Comments for chapter 1. The argument we give regarding the hierarchical structure of NPs and one-substitution is essentially that of Hornstein and Lightfoot (1981b) (cf. Baker, 1978, 1979).

38 Acquisition of NPs with Modifiers

This chapter is concerned with the relation between the semantic structure and the syntactic structure of noun phrases such as "the second striped ball." The relationship will be discussed in the context of non-adult responses children have been found to give to such NPs. A proposal that we consider is that the non-adult responses by children are the consequence of a different syntactic structure from that which adults assign to NPs. It will become clear, however, that this inference is based on several assumptions about the architecture of the language apparatus, including the assumption that children's (and adults') syntactic representations mirror their semantic representations, as dictated by the Principle of Compositionality. In the present example, researchers have interpreted children's non-adult behavior as evidence that children and adults assign different syntactic structures to noun phrases. This claim about syntax rests on the presumption that both children and adults adhere to the Principle of Compositionality. It is argued, therefore, that if children and adults interpret sentences differently, it must be because they assign different structural representations to the same strings of words.

This is one reason for discussing the phenomenon. Another reason is to illustrate other aspects of the language understanding system. In the final analysis we are led to conclude that the different interpretations of NPs by children and adults are not caused by differences in their syntactic representations. The differences are seen to reside outside the domain of the language apparatus entirely. This exonerates both syntax and semantics, leaving open the possibility that the real culprit could be a component of cognition that children can master on the basis of their experience.

1 Acquisition in the Real World

The proposal under discussion is that children go through stages of language development at which they lack intermediate-level constituents such as N'. Because these constituents introduce the hierarchical structure, it would follow that

Point to the second striped ball.

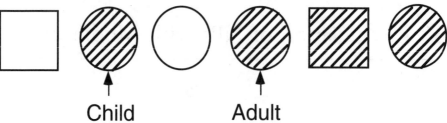

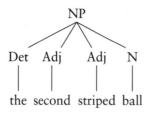

Figure 38.1 "Point to the second striped ball"

children lack the hierarchical structure that is characteristic of the adult NP; instead, children are hypothesized to initially assign a "flat" structure.

The relevant empirical observations were made by Edward Matthei and Thomas Roeper who discovered that 4- to 6-year-olds had difficulty in interpreting phrases such as "the second striped ball." What these researchers found was that children who were confronted with arrays like that in figure 38.1 often selected the ball which is second in the array and is also striped, rather than the second of the striped balls (counting from the left).

The empirical finding, then, is that children assign an interpretation that is not the one an adult would assign to expressions of this kind. This difference is attributed by Matthei to children's failure to adopt the same kind of hierarchical phrase structure for noun phrases that characterizes the adult grammar. Instead, he argues, they adopt a "flat-structure analysis" (FSA) for phrases like *second striped ball*. The claim is that children assign structural representations like that in (1), where adults would assign a hierarchical representation, as in (2).

(1) **Child analysis**　　　　(2) **Adult analysis**

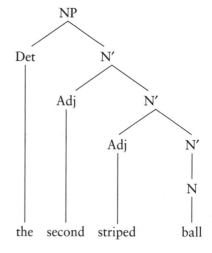

This conclusion is based on the assumption that children's erroneous responses are based on a non-adult semantic representation, and that children's (and adults') semantic representations directly inform us about the syntactic structures they assign. In other words, semantics mirrors syntax, as dictated by the Principle of Compositionality.

(3)   Input: "Point to the second striped ball"
Adults: Point to the second of the striped balls.
Children: Point to the object that is second in the array, and striped, and a ball.

Let us consider adults first. In pointing to the second of the striped balls, adults would appear to be applying the following procedure. First, they combine the meanings of *striped* and *ball*, to derive a semantic constituent *striped ball*, whose extension is the set of striped balls in the domain of discourse. The meaning of the ordinal *second* can be viewed as an instruction to search through that (presumably ordered) set, to identify the second member of the set.

The child's procedure would appear to lack the first step in the adult procedure, the formation of a set of striped balls. Instead, it appears that children view *second* as an instruction to find the second of the (presumably ordered) objects in the domain of discourse, and to see if it is both striped and a ball. In short, the meaning of the phrase *second striped ball* for the child seems to simply consist of the intersection of the meanings of its parts, *second*, *striped*, and *ball*.

(4)   Semantic analyses:

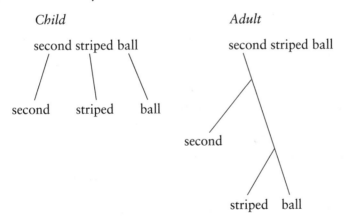

Assuming a compositional semantics, where the meanings of phrases are read off the syntax, it should now be clear why it made sense for Matthei to propose that children initially lack the intermediate category N'. The meanings of *striped*

and *ball* do not appear to be combined semantically, so it makes sense to infer that they do not combine syntactically.

Although this is a reasonable story, it leads headlong into the learnability problem we described in the previous chapter. Fortunately, it is not the only possible story. To see this, we need only note that children's responses may not be directly linked to their semantic/syntactic analysis of the input. There may be other factors intervening, as depicted in the following graphic.

Response ← ???? ← Semantic Analysis ← Phrase Structure ← Input

2   An Alternative Account

A paper by Henry Hamburger and Stephen Crain advances the idea that an alternative component of the language processor could be responsible for children's errors in responding to commands like "Point to the second striped ball." They observe that the logical structure of the necessary plan (non-linguistic, cognitive algorithm) for finding the "second striped ball" in an array is quite complex. This raises the possibility that plan complexity, not syntactic complexity, is the source of children's errors. An explanation of children's errors in terms of plan complexity has received empirical support. Differences in task demands associated with planning sometimes spell the difference between success and failure in comprehension, an observation that led Hamburger and Crain to study the complexity of the plans associated with phrases such as "the second striped ball" in detail.

Based on their proposal about the nature of the planning component underlying these linguistic expressions, Hamburger and Crain designed experiments designed to reduce the demands of the planning component while, at the same time, holding syntactic structure constant. A dramatic improvement in children's responses to phrases like "second striped ball" resulted from two changes in method, implemented in successive experiments. One change was the inclusion of a pretask session in which the children handled and counted homogeneous subsets of the items which were subsequently used in the test arrays. This experience is assumed to prime some of the planning required in the main experimental task. In addition, a dramatic improvement in performance on phrases like "second striped ball" resulted from first asking children to identify the "first striped ball," thus forcing them to plan and execute part of the plan used in interpreting the target phrase. Facilitating the planning aspects of the task by these simplifying maneuvers thus made it possible for children to reveal mastery of the syntax and semantics of such expressions.

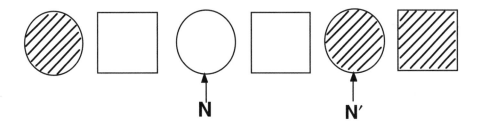

Point to the first striped ball; Point to the second one.

Figure 38.2 "Point to the first striped ball; point to the second one"

A positive result from the standpoint of learnability theory was also obtained in the Hamburger and Crain study. On the Hornstein and Lightfoot account, the proform "one" can substitute for an intermediate-level constituent like N' but, crucially, it cannot substitute for a lexical-level constituent like N. Based on this analysis, it is expected that as soon as children understood the meaning of ordinals they would permit "one" to corefer with "striped ball" in response to arrays like the one in figure 38.2. That is, they should sometimes point to the fifth ball in the array (again, counting from the left).

This is precisely what was found. In fact, children consistently used the proform *one* to corefer with expressions like "striped ball." Notice that using *one* in this way is incompatible with the flat-structure account, given the assumption that proforms corefer with a syntactic constituent. Since "striped ball" does not form a constituent on this account, children should only have been able to interpret "the second one" to mean the second ball, not the second "striped ball." The findings of the Hamburger and Crain experiment suggest that children, like adults, use proforms to corefer with intermediate-level syntactic constituents, as Hornstein and Lightfoot predict.

Based on these findings, we can draw the inference that children's responses do not represent the semantic (hence, syntactic) representations they assign to NPs; rather, the responses children gave reflect the response plan they generated in the test situation. Both semantics and syntax are exonerated.

This discussion leads us to draw the following moral. From the standpoint of language acquisition, any proposals about a divergence between children's and adults' grammars should be examined with care, to see whether or not they raise problems in language learnability. As we saw in the previous chapter, learnability problems arise because the input children receive from their linguistic environment doesn't generally contain the kind of data that would be useful in correcting erroneous hypotheses that children might make. Before children are attributed a non-adult grammatical representation, it is important to consider how children could possibly abandon their erroneous hypotheses in order to converge on the adult grammar.

Bibliographical Comments

The early tests examining children's understanding of NPs like "second striped ball" were conducted by Roeper (1972) and Matthei (1982). Hamburger and Crain (1984) made an extensive critique of these works and an alternative proposal. The work by Hornstein and Lightfoot referred to in this chapter (as in the previous one) was published in (1981b).

39 Relative Clauses

This chapter is about the acquisition of sentences that contain a restrictive relative clause. It is claimed in the literature that children interpret such sentences in a non-adult manner. The purported difference in interpretation between children and adults illustrates several important points about the nature of meaning representations and their relation to syntactic representations. Most importantly, the sentences under consideration, and the responses to them by children and adults, present a clear example of how semantic interpretation is seen to "piggyback" on syntactic structure, as dictated by the Principle of Compositionality. The explanations that have been offered to account for the observed differences in interpretation between children and adults all implicitly assume that the semantics component of UG adheres to compositionality.

Ultimately, we raise a problem with prior accounts of the differences in the way children and adults interpret sentences with relative clauses. The problem is one of learnability. On the accounts that have been proposed it is unclear how children could reach the Final State of language development, the adult grammatical system. This leads us to consider alternative explanations of children's non-adult responses. Discussion of the alternative account, and empirical evidence for it, are the concerns of the final section of the chapter.

1 The Flat Structure Hypothesis

The previous chapter was concerned with a flat-structure analysis of NPs. According to this hypothesis, children are seen to lack the hierarchical structure that is characteristic of adult syntactic representations. Instead, it is proposed that children assign "flat" phrasal structure. The present chapter centers on another construction, relative clauses. It has been claimed in the literature that children initially assign flat phrase structure to sentences with relative clauses. We offer both theoretical and empirical arguments against the flat-structure analysis of such sentences.

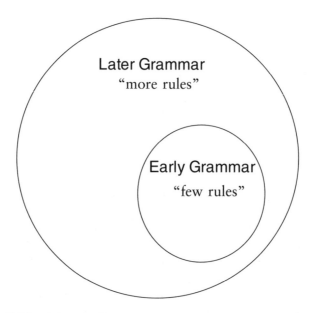

Figure 39.1 Children's intermediate grammars

At the core of any variant of the flat-structure analysis is the view that children advance in a *stepwise* fashion in making the transition to the adult system – small steps for small feet. At the time these flat-structure analyses of children's grammars were being formulated, phrase markers were viewed as the product of Phrase Structure rules alone, without the generalization achieved by X′-theory. On this account, therefore, it is reasonable to suppose that children's intermediate grammars, as well as their early grammars, comprise a *subset* of the rules and principles that characterize later stages, as depicted in figure 39.1.

From the perspective of language development, it may seem that the gradual accrual of structures in the target language would be advantageous. By generating only a subset of the structures that characterize the adult grammar, children would appear to be safeguarded against overgeneration, that is, producing sentences that are not in the target grammar. The flat-structure analysis introduces a different kind of learnability problem: namely, **semantic overgeneration**. As we will see, semantic overgeneration can be just as difficult for learners to overcome as **structural (string) overgeneration** or **semantic undergeneration**.

In the final analysis, the Flat Structure Hypothesis must therefore be wrong, because learners always succeed in acquiring the correct, adult analyses of every construction in their linguistic community. Both in the acquisition of NPs and in the acquisition of relative clauses, the Flat Structure Hypothesis is, indeed, wrong. It turns out that even the youngest children who have been tested in recent studies hypothesize the correct, adult linguistic analyses. The evidence for this is reported in the final two sections of the chapter.

2 Children's Understanding of Relative Clauses

The early literature on the acquisition of relative clauses made two claims. First, it was claimed that children and adults assign different syntactic representations to relative clauses. The second claim concerned the nature of this difference: children's misanalyses were claimed to be the result of the absence of certain rules from their grammars. The absence of these rules was supposed to cause children to use a flat, rather than hierarchical, structure for sentences with relative clauses. This proposal stems from experimental evidence seemingly demonstrating children's consistent misunderstanding of a certain relative clause construction.

The construction that was particularly problematic for children contained so-called OS relatives. Take a look at the example given in (1).

(1)   The dog pushed <u>the sheep</u> that ＿＿ jumped over the fence.
                       O   S

In (1), the relative clause "that jumped over the fence" modifies the noun in object position of the main clause (that is, *the sheep*). The "O" in the term "OS relatives" refers to this fact. The relative clause itself contains a superficially empty subject (that is, the subject of *jumped*). The "S" stands for this.

In the literature, the application of the Flat Structure Hypothesis to relative clauses is often called the **conjoined-clause analysis** of relative clauses. The idea behind the conjoined-clause analysis is that children go through a stage of development at which they have mastered "flat" conjoined clauses, but not the kind of recursive rules that are needed to generate hierarchical structures such as relative clauses. The assumption is that conjoined clauses are mastered earlier because they have "flatter" phrase structure than relative clauses.

As suggested by the Flat Structure Hypothesis, it is supposed that children have only a (proper) subset of the rules of the target grammar at this stage of development. It is supposed, further, that they incorrectly apply their existing rules (for interpreting conjoined clauses) to sentences that their grammar does not yet properly generate (namely, relative clauses). The result is a non-adult interpretation of sentences containing relative clauses (in the adult grammar).

Let us use sentence (1) to illustrate. In the adult grammar, this sentence contains the noun phrase, *the sheep*, and the relative clause, *that jumped over the fence*, within the same constituent. Assuming a compositional semantics, this explains why, for adults, the sheep is the agent of the jumping event.

However, according to the Flat Structure Hypothesis, children do not have access to the (recursive) rules needed to produce the appropriate hierarchical structure for a relative clause. Specifically, proponents of this hypothesis claimed that children do not have recursion within the NP; that is, they are unable to generate one NP inside another NP. According to the conjoined-clause analysis, the lack of the capacity to form recursive NP structures forces children to produce non-hierarchical, "flat" structures in interpreting sentences like (1). For children, then, the structures underlying sentences with relative clauses instead consist of conjoined clauses. Examples (2)–(3) illustrate the two possible ways to interpret the sentence. In (3a), the correct, relative clause interpretation is given. In (3b), the proposed "conjoined clause" interpretation is given.

(2)   The dog pushed the sheep that jumped over the fence.

(3)   a.   The dog pushed [the sheep that jumped over the fence]
      b.   [The dog pushed the sheep] [. . . jumped over the fence]

According to the conjoined-clause analysis, sentences like (2) would be assigned a structural analysis like (3b), which is appropriate for conjoined clauses.[1] Notice that in (3b) the NP *the sheep* is not part of the constituent containing the VP *jumped over the fence*, as it is in (3a), which is the structure underlying the sentence for adults. As a result of children's misanalysis of Phrase Structure, on this account, the sentence will be assigned the meaning in which the dog jumps over the fence.

In a series of experiments done with children, it was claimed that their responses indicated that indeed they followed the Flat Structure analysis of relative clauses like that in (1). The experiments that evoked non-adult responses from children typically used the research methodology of figure manipulation, or what is known as the act-out task. In these studies, the experimenter presents a sentence to children, and instructs them to act out the sentence (e.g., "do what I say") using toys and props that are present in the experimental workplace.

Using this technique for investigating the meanings children assign to sentences, several studies revealed that children consistently acted out OS sentences like (1) in a non-adult fashion. Many children who were asked to act out the meaning of (1) had the dog push the sheep, and then had *the dog* jump over the fence. Of course, for adults, (1) asserts that the sheep, not the dog, jumped over the fence. The Flat Structure Hypothesis was proposed to account for this non-adult behavior of children (see chapter 37).

The next section raises two theoretical problems for the conjoined-clause analysis of children's non-adult behavior. One concerns changes in linguistic theory. The second problem is learnability, that is, how children's grammars or language processing systems change, to become equivalent to those of adults.

3 Problems with the Conjoined-Clause Analysis

The conjoined-clause analysis proposes that children lack recursion in the NP. This may have made intuitive sense when it was initially formulated, within a linguistic theory that viewed grammars as sets of Phrase Structure rules. However, the proposal that children lack recursion in the NP makes less sense within current incarnations of linguistic theory. As discussed in chapter 9, it has been proposed that a general schema within Universal Grammar, called X′-theory, generates the phrasal structure assigned to sentences. The claim that children lack recursion in the NP therefore amounts to the claim that children have incomplete mastery of X′-theory. This is clearly inconsistent with the spirit of Universal Grammar; children's analyses of sentences with a relative clause would be aberrant, according to X′-theory.

There is another problem with the conjoined-clause analysis. Despite widespread acceptance of the account, it faces a learnability problem, to explain how children could recover from their mistake in hypothesizing the conjoined-clause analysis. This problem of "unlearning" must be confronted by any proposal that would have children assign incorrect analyses to sentences.

Is there evidence in the primary linguistic data to inform children that an error has been made? As noted earlier, learners must identify their errors solely on the basis of positive evidence, in the form of <sentence, meaning> pairs. Information about which sentences are *not* grammatical has been shown to be lacking in the input. In the present example, evidence about the well-formedness of sentences would not suffice to inform them of their error. Note, first, that children use the same sentences as adults, but assign them different interpretations. This can be represented as in (4).

(4)

Child	**Adult**
<sentence^{12}, meaning^{37}>	<sentence^{12}, meaning^{12}>

The conjoined-clause analysis of relative clauses constitutes a mistaken mapping between sentences and meanings. The incorrect meanings must somehow be purged from children's grammars. What is needed to jettison the conjoined-clause analysis is evidence that the meaning assigned to conjoined sentences can*not* also be assigned to sentences like (2), repeated here as (5). Therefore, children whose grammars imposed a conjoined-clause analysis of sentences with relative clauses (in the adult grammar) would require access to special linguistic input to inform them of their error.

(5) The dog pushed the sheep that jumped over the fence.

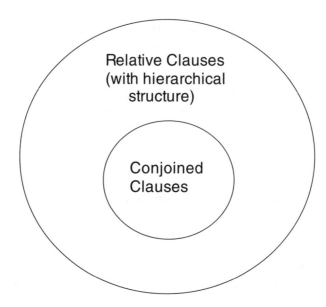

Figure 39.2   Development of clausal interpretation

At some point, of course, children will hear adults use sentences like (5) in a way that is not consistent with the conjoined-clause hypothesis. That is, children will hear (5) used to describe a context in which a sheep, not a dog, jumped over the fence. Will this suffice to cause them to abandon the conjoined-clause hypothesis? One argument against such a conclusion stems from the fact that many, perhaps most, sentences have more than one meaning. That is, the grammar that is internalized makes more than one meaning available for sentences. Therefore, learners who inferred that a sentence does not have some particular meaning simply because they do not hear it used with that meaning would be forced to throw out many legitimate sentence meanings.

Another possibility is that the input to children contains information about what sentences cannot mean. Even if this were true, which we doubt, it would be important to ascertain if this kind of evidence is available with sufficient regularity to ensure that every child receives it, at least by the time that she begins to correctly produce and comprehend sentences with relative clauses. As it turns out, children use such sentences correctly at quite an early age, as we will now show. Figure 39.2 depicts the situation. Children first assign conjoined-clause interpretations to sentences (even ones with a different meaning for adults). Later, children add to their linguistic repertoire, somehow learning to assign correct structures and their associated meaning to sentences with relative clauses.

The problem for children would be to find evidence from the environment that will compel them to abandon the conjoined-clause analysis. Adopting this analysis results in different meanings for sentences like (1) for children and adults. At first glance, it may seem that this poses no problem. Perhaps children simply abandon the meaning that they assign to such sentences when they encounter situations that make it clear that adults assign a different meaning. This won't work in general, however. As we said above, because many, perhaps most, sentences have more than one meaning, it follows that learners who adopted this strategy would be forced to discard many legitimate sentence meanings. It is more likely that children would add the new interpretation and keep the old one, leaving children with two meanings for a sentence that has only one meaning for adults. That is, children would find sentences like (1) ambiguous, whereas adults would find them unambiguous. As the graphic in (6) makes clear, the problem is "unlearning" the offending sentence meaning in the absence of negative evidence in the primary linguistic data. The problem is one of **semantic overgeneration**.

(6)

Child	Adult
$\langle \text{sentence}^{12}, \text{meaning}^{37} \rangle$	$\langle \text{sentence}^{12}, \text{meaning}^{12} \rangle$
$\langle \text{sentence}^{12}, \text{meaning}^{12} \rangle$	

These deliberations lead us to ask whether an alternative explanation of children's errors can be found. If so, then the problems of learnability can be circumvented.

4   Comprehension of Relative Clauses

In response to the problems with the conjoined-clause hypothesis, a number of experimental studies were undertaken to assess children's knowledge of relative clauses. These experiments used techniques other than the one which uncovered comprehension errors: the figure manipulation task. The findings from these new studies indicate that the source of children's errors in the earlier work is not a lack of syntactic knowledge. In experimental investigations using new methodological procedures, it has been amply demonstrated that children have mastery of relative clauses before their third birthday.

The new procedures were motivated by the observation that sentences with relative clauses often bear presuppositions that were not met in earlier studies. There are two presuppositions in (7).

(7)   The dog pushed the sheep that jumped over the fence.

First, (7) presupposes that at least two sheep are present in the context. If there is only a single sheep, there is no need to use the relative clause at all; one could just as well say "The dog pushed the sheep." The other presupposition is that one (but only one) of the sheep jumped over a fence prior to the utterance. It seems likely that previous studies failed to demonstrate early knowledge of relative clause constructions because they did not pay attention to these pragmatic presuppositions. For example, subjects were required to act out the meaning of a sentence such as (7) in contexts in which only one sheep was present. The typically poor performance by young children in these experiments was attributed to their ignorance of the linguistic properties of relative clause constructions. But suppose a child did know the linguistic properties but was also aware of the associated presuppositions. Such children might be unable to relate their correct understanding of the sentence structures to the inappropriate circumstances provided by the experiment. In other words, children were put in a position that required them to ignore either their knowledge of the syntax of relative clause structure or their knowledge of its pragmatics. Adult subjects may be able to "see through" the unnaturalness of an experimental task to the intentions of the experimenter, but it seems unrealistic to expect this of young children.

Following this line of reasoning, Hamburger and Crain made the apparently minor change of adding more sheep to the acting out situation for sentence (7). This simple change resulted in a much higher percentage of correct responses by children even younger than the ones tested in earlier research. The most frequent remaining "error" was made by the oldest children, who failed to act out the event described by the relative clause. This response by the older children was called the **Assertion Only** response by Hamburger and Crain, because these children acted out only the assertion made by sentence (8) – that the dog pushed the sheep – and not its presupposition – that there is one sheep that is distinguished from the others by the fact that it alone jumped over the fence.

(8) *The dog pushed the sheep* that jumped over the fence.

Hamburger and Crain argued, however, that the Assertion Only response is not really an error, but is precisely the kind of response that is compatible with perfect comprehension of the test sentences. They reasoned that it is appropriate to use (8) when the event described in a relative clause has **already** occurred. Responses of this type did not appear in previous studies, presumably because these studies failed to meet the presuppositions of the restrictive relative clause.

5   Elicitation of Relative Clauses

The most compelling evidence that young children do not lack the structural knowledge underlying relative clause formation comes from a second experiment in the Hamburger and Crain study. Using an elicited production task, pragmatic contexts were constructed in which the presuppositions of restrictive relative clauses were satisfied. We saw that contexts that are uniquely felicitous for a relative clause are ones in which there is a set of objects to restrict from; hence the term **restrictive** relative clause. Children were asked, therefore, to identify one from a set of identical toys. They were asked to describe the toy to a blindfolded observer. This prevented them from identifying the toy to the observer merely by pointing to it and saying "Point to this one." The property that differentiated the toy was not one that could be encoded merely with a noun (e.g., "the guard") or a prenominal adjective (e.g., "the big guard") or a prepositional phrase ("the guard with the gun"). Rather, it involved an action (e.g., "the guard that is shooting Darth Vader"). Young children reliably produce meaningful utterances with relative clauses when these conditions are met:

(9)   Jabba, please come over to point to the one that's asleep.   (3;5)
      Point to the one that's standing up.   (3;9)
      Point to the guy who's going to get killed.   (3;9)
      Point to the kangaroo that's eating the strawberry ice cream.   (3;11)

It should be mentioned that the possibility of imitation is excluded by the experimenter's care not to use any relative clause constructions in the elicitation situation. Also worth mentioning is the fact that the elicitation technique has been extended to younger children (as young as 2;8) and to the elicitation of a wider array of relative clause constructions, including relatives with object gaps (e.g., "the guard that Princess Leia is standing on"). Finally, comparable findings with 2- and 3-year-old children have also been obtained in Italian, in a study by Crain, McKee, and Emiliani.

Conclusion

The discovery that children understand, and even produce, sentences with relative clauses in appropriate circumstances supports the conclusion that children's performance failures in certain tasks should not be taken as evidence that this structure is missing from their grammars. Several other unaccommodating findings have been reinterpreted as reflecting the influence of task factors, and not as an indication of lack of structural competence. When questions about syntactic knowledge are asked in a different way, by adopting tasks that control as far as possible for the pragmatic demands of comprehension, children were found to succeed. We conclude that the failure in previous research to control for non-syntactic factors led to underestimates of children's grammatical capabilities in some cases. As a consequence of the new findings, the timetable for the acquisition of syntax has been brought more in line with the expectations of the theory of Universal Grammar which, as we saw, anticipates rapid acquisition of full knowledge without stages of successive approximation.

Note

1 The conjoined-clause analysis does *not* maintain that (1) is actually analyzed by children as (3b). If so, this would mean that they misinterpreted the word *that* as if it was the word *and*. Rather, the claim is that children misanalyze the **structure** of (1) as if it had the structure underlying (3b). We contend that children know both the structure and the pragmatic properties of sentences like (1).

Bibliographical Comments

Researchers who have claimed to find that children misunderstand relative clauses include deVilliers, Tager-Flusberg, Hakuta, and Cohen (1979), Goodluck and Tavakolian (1982), Sheldon (1974), and Tavakolian (1981), whose conjoined-clause analysis was extensively discussed in this chapter. The alternative proposal was presented by Hamburger and Crain (1982). The study of the acquisition of relative clauses in Italian mentioned in the chapter was reported in Crain, McKee, and Emiliani (1990).

40 Universal Quantification

In the adult grammar of English, the universal quantifier, *every*, is a determiner. It has the syntactic distribution and the semantic properties of determiners. We begin this chapter by looking at the semantics of *every*. Then we turn to the laboratory once again, to see when children master the semantics of universal quantification, and if the path of development is fraught with peril, as some researchers have proposed. As in the past two chapters, we will show that the perils are more imagined than real. New experimental findings are described, having emerged from methodological designs that are arguably superior to those used in previous research. These findings appear to support a strong UG picture of children's semantic competence.

Consider the question in (1), which asks about the content of figure 40.1.

(1) Is every farmer feeding a donkey?

For adults, the answer to the question in (1) is "yes." There are three farmers in the picture and each of them is feeding a donkey. The fact that there is a fourth donkey, which is not being fed by a farmer, is irrelevant in answering the question, as is the fact that there is a fox in the picture.

As this example illustrates, ordinarily the scope of the quantifier *every* is restricted in the adult grammar. It does not include every *object* in the domain of the discourse, nor does it include every *object mentioned* in the sentence. Rather, the scope of *every* is limited to those objects denoted by the noun within the NP that contains it.[1]

The semantic restriction on the interpretation of *every* conforms to the Principle of Compositionality. To see this, note first that the determiner, *every*, and the noun, *farmer*, form a constituent in the syntax; these constituents combine to make an NP. The Principle of Compositionality requires the semantic combinations of word meanings to mirror their syntactic combinations. It follows that the meaning of the determiner *every*, i.e., Every', and the meaning of the noun *farmer*, i.e., Farmer', combine to derive the meaning of the NP *every farmer*. We illustrate how meanings combine for the sentences in (2) and (3), where meanings that have been combined are joined by a plus, "+".

Figure 40.1   Every farmer is feeding a donkey: extra object condition

(2)   Every farmer is feeding a donkey.

(3)   every' + farmer' + is' + feeding' + a' + donkey'
      every' + farmer'   is' + feeding' + a' + donkey'
      every'   farmer'   is' + feeding'   a' + donkey'
                              is'   feeding'   a'   donkey'

Procedurally, the truth or falsity of the sentence *Every farmer is feeding a donkey* can be decided by examining every farmer in the conversational context, to verify that each one is feeding a donkey. Depending on the situation, the sentence can be verified without necessarily checking every donkey in the context. Once the relevant property of each of the farmers has been checked, the business of the compositional semantics has been completed, at least for adults.

1 Children's Understanding of Universal Quantification

Children are a different matter, however. The famous French psychologists Bärbel Inhelder and Jean Piaget observed that children do not consistently interpret questions like (1) or sentences like (2) in the same way as adults do. If shown a picture like that in figure 40.1 many 3- to 5-year-old children who are asked the question *Is every farmer feeding a donkey?* sometimes respond by saying "no." When asked to explain this answer (*Why not?*), children who have replied negatively usually point to the unfed donkey as the reason. On other occasions, the same children respond with the adult answer, "yes," to questions with the same form.

There is a similar finding for questions of a different form, with the universal quantifier *every* in a different position in the sentence:

(4) Is a farmer feeding every donkey?

For example, when asked the question in (4), if there are farmers that are not feeding donkeys in the context (even if a farmer is feeding every donkey), the same children sometimes offer the non-adult response, "no." When asked to justify this answer, these children point to the "extra" farmers. On other occasions, these children give the correct affirmative response to the same questions.

What is the source of the non-adult response? Children seem to be interpreting questions like (1) and (4) in the same way, as asking about the **symmetry** between farmers and donkeys, as if both questions can be answered affirmatively only if every farmer is feeding a donkey *and* every donkey is being fed by a farmer.

(1) Is every farmer feeding a donkey?
(4) Is a farmer feeding every donkey?

The negative responses by children have therefore been called the "symmetrical response." Children appear to demand symmetry between donkeys and farmers – the mapping must be one-to-one – in order for them to say "yes." Let us call any child that provides the symmetrical response, as well as the adult response, a symmetry child.

Returning to the source of the symmetrical response, the fact that both (1) and (4) contain only a single occurrence of the determiner *every* makes it appear that the universal quantifier *every* combines in meaning with both Ns, *farmer* and *donkey*, in questions like these. That is, it seems as if the symmetry child ignores the semantic restriction on the scope of determiners that is imposed by the Principle of Compositionality. Instead children seem to be permitting the scope of the universal quantifier to extend to both Ns, as if there were two occurrences of the quantifier, as illustrated in (5).

> (5) *Every* farmer is feeding a donkey,
>   and *every* donkey is being fed by a farmer.

Inhelder and Piaget attempted to explain children's symmetrical interpretation of questions like (1) and (4) in non-linguistic terms, as the result of their inability to distinguish part–whole relationships among sets. More recently, a linguistic account of children's comprehension failures, called the **symmetrical account**, has been advanced in the literature on language acquisition within the generative framework, by linguist William Philip. On the symmetrical account, children ignore the surface position of the universal quantifier in sentences like (1) and (4), permitting it to extend its interpretive range beyond the NP in which it is contained in the syntax. In other words, the symmetrical account maintains that children assign a non-compositional semantics to sentences with *every*.

2   Learnability Problems for the Symmetrical Account

Unfortunately, from the standpoint of learnability, the symmetry children are caught between the proverbial rock and hard place. Apparently, they sometimes access the adult interpretation and say "yes," but sometimes they access the symmetrical interpretation and say "no." Therefore, if the symmetry child supposes that adults have an equivalent grammar, then adults would also be expected to respond both "Yes" and "No" to questions like (1) and (4). Therein lies the problem. The symmetry child cannot learn anything she does not already know, because she knows the adult interpretation of sentences with the universal quantifier. The problem is the symmetry child knows too much; she can assign a non-adult interpretation as well as the adult interpretation. Therefore, the problem for the symmetry child is to expunge the symmetrical interpretation, and retain only the adult interpretation. In short, the problem is that sentences with universal quantification are *ambiguous* for the symmetry child.

As this discussion makes clear, the problem is one of **semantic overgeneration**. For illustrative purposes, let us pursue a few acquisition scenarios according to which children "unlearn" the symmetrical interpretation. One possible scenario is that children keep a mental record of the absence of certain responses by adults in certain situations. That is, if children could notice that adults never answer "no" to questions like *Is every farmer feeding a donkey?* in contexts like figure 40.1, then they could infer that adults do not assign the symmetrical interpretation to such questions. But, of course, learners cannot be expected to notice that certain events fail to occur. One notices only events that do occur.

Another possible source of "unlearning" is negative evidence. Adults could provide negative evidence in the form of corrective feedback when children *produce* sentences like *Every farmer is feeding a donkey*. Clearly, this won't work, for the following reason. When children access the symmetrical interpretation they will only produce sentences with a universal quantifier in contexts in which there is a one-to-one pairing of farmers and donkeys. But, notice that such contexts are entirely consistent with the adult interpretation; it is just that adults can produce the same sentences in other contexts as well, where the mapping is one-to-many.

From a learnability perspective, the symmetry child is in a precarious position. As we saw in the previous chapter, in the absence of abundant negative semantic evidence informing learners that certain meanings are not produced by the target grammar, any child grammar that spawns semantic overgeneration will fail to converge on the target grammar. Convergence fails because learners continually encounter evidence that is consistent with one of their interpretive options. In the present case, the available evidence is consistent with one of the interpretations assigned by the symmetry child, namely, the adult interpretation. Therefore, such a child will be unable to "unlearn" the symmetrical interpretation and, hence, will fail to converge on the adult grammar. The problem of "unlearning" arises because the symmetrical interpretation makes a sentence true in a subset of the circumstances corresponding to the adult interpretation – the symmetrical interpretation adds a further qualification to the truth conditions of sentences, beyond those imposed by the adult interpretation. On those occasions when children access the symmetrical interpretation, their interpretation will make a sentence true in a narrower range of circumstances than adults' responses require; but these situations also make the same sentences true on the adult interpretation.

If the results of the studies by Inhelder and Piaget are taken at face value, then it looks as though children don't adhere to compositionality early in the course of language development. Since this result doesn't comport either with the theory of Universal Grammar or with considerations of language learnability, we should look elsewhere for an explanation of the findings.

3   An Alternative Account

Based on the observations from the previous section, we are invited to ask if there was something in previous tasks, other than lack of knowledge of compositionality, that might explain children's non-adult responses. This section examines one possibility, namely that children's symmetrical responses are an artifact of the experimental design used to probe their linguistic knowledge of universal quantification.

As we have seen many times before, it is crucial in the investigation of children's linguistic competence to ensure that test sentences are presented in felicitous contexts. In the contexts provided for yes/no questions such as *Is every farmer feeding a donkey?*, felicitous usage dictates that both a "yes" answer and a "no" answer should be under consideration, at the point at which the question is asked. In tests of the symmetrical account, however, the target questions were not felicitous; this was because there was nothing in the pictures, such as figure 40.1, that corresponded to the negative answer to the question. Finding no point to the actual question being asked, children were prompted to sometimes infer that some other question was intended, namely a question about the symmetry between farmers and donkeys: i.e., "Is there a one-to-one mapping between farmers and donkeys?" The answer to this question is "no." On some trials, children were able to overlook the infelicity of asking a question whose answer is obvious. On these occasions, children produced the correct answer, "yes." In short, the symmetry child is one who tries to make sense of the questions posed to her.

We will illustrate the point by designing a better mousetrap. The same felicity conditions that pertain to yes/no questions also pertain to requests to indicate whether or not what someone said is true or false. For purposes of exposition, our hypothetical experiment uses the Truth-Value Judgment task, rather than a yes/no question task. Once we have described the workings of our hypothetical study, we can compare the design features of our study with the methodology used in previous studies which often evoked non-adult responses from children. Recall that in the TVJT, a story is acted out in front of children using toy props and characters. After the story is completed, a puppet, Kermit the Frog, presents the test sentence, as an assertion about what took place in the story. The child's task is to indicate if the test sentence accurately describes what happened in the story. Let us assume that children have the adult interpretation available to them, but not the symmetrical interpretation. We will design our study to reveal which interpretation they have.

As we discussed in chapter 15, it is useful to partition the story into four components, the **background**, the **assertion**, the **actual outcome**, and a **possible outcome**. As the story unfolds, there are three farmers, each holding a container of some food. In addition, let us suppose there are four donkeys and two dinosaurs waiting to be fed. This part of the story supplies the background. The background makes it clear that the farmers intend to feed something with the food, either the donkeys or the dinosaurs. In the present experiment, the actual outcome and the assertion are the same, *every farmer fed a donkey*. In order to distinguish the adult and the symmetrical interpretation, there should be an "extra" donkey at the conclusion of the story. That is, the farmers each feed one of the donkeys, but there are four donkeys, and one does not end up getting fed. If so, then the assertion will be true on the adult interpretation but not on the symmetrical interpretation. However, there is a possible outcome, according to which the assertion is false. The possible outcome is presented as the story unfolds. Each of the farmers considers feeding a dinosaur but, for one reason or another, they each end up feeding a donkey. The last event would mention the unfed donkey, to highlight the symmetrical interpretation, if it is available to children. At the conclusion of the story, Kermit the Frog produces the target sentence, (6), for evaluation by children.

(6)   Every farmer fed a donkey.
    (a) Background: Every farmer fed *so-and-so*.
    (b) Assertion: Every farmer fed *a donkey*.
    (c) Actual outcome: Every farmer fed a donkey.
    (d) Possible outcome: Some farmer(s) fed a dinosaur.

When the puppet's statement is made, there can be no doubt in the child's mind that every farmer fed a donkey, but also that there is one donkey that was not fed by a farmer. Therefore, children who access the symmetrical interpretation on any trial in the present study should answer "no," and when they are asked to explain why they gave this answer ("Why not?"), these children should point to the "extra" donkey, as in prior research. The main difference between the present study and prior research is the possible outcome, namely the option of feeding a dinosaur rather than a donkey. It should be clear to children that if the story had taken a different turn, the possible outcome could have been actualized, with at least one farmer feeding a dinosaur. The availability of the possible outcome satisfies the felicity condition for asking children to judge the truth or falsity of the target sentences. Without the possible outcome, children might be confused as to why they are asked to make a judgment about a sentence that is clearly true. The possible outcome tells them why: the sentence could have been false if things had turned out differently, as well they could have. It should be clear that this is related to the felicity condition described in chapter 15, called the condition of plausible dissent. The difference is that the present experiment induces "yes" responses for children who access the adult interpretation, rather than "no" responses. Therefore, this is simply the flip-side to the condition of plausible dissent; it could be called the condition of plausible assent.

   The experimental set-up employed in the studies reported by Philip did not satisfy the condition of plausible assent, because no alternative to the actual outcome was ever under consideration. We contend that this was the source of many children's non-adult responses in previous research. On this scenario, children made non-adult responses because the circumstances were inappropriate for a yes/no question (or a true/false judgment) on the adult interpretation of the question. Placed in this predicament, children were led to suppose that another question was intended, a question about the numerical correspondence between agents and objects. A child who inferred that the "extra" donkey was relevant to their interpretation would conclude that the correct answer is "no." It would also be clear to such a child that the correct answer would be "yes" if the extra donkey was not present. In short, the test questions were felicitous on the symmetrical interpretation but not on the adult interpretation.

Conclusion

This chapter presented empirical support for the view that the experimenters' failure to satisfy felicity conditions, and not the absence of compositionality in children's grammars, was responsible for children's non-adult judgments of sentences with the determiner *every* in earlier research. With our students and colleagues, we have conducted a series of studies which met the felicity conditions that we have just identified. The findings of these studies reveal a level of performance by children that is comparable to that of adults. Moreover, other studies of ours demonstrate that children, like adults, produce sentences with the universal quantifier, in appropriate contexts. We conclude, on the basis of the findings from seven studies of 4- to 6-year-olds, that young children do not lack grammatical competence with any aspect of universal quantification. This opens the door for further explorations of children's knowledge of semantics, and invites the conclusion that children adhere to the Principle of Compositionality from the earliest stages of language development.

Note

1   To see that the restriction on the scope of the universal quantifier, and all determiners, is not trivial, notice that this same restriction does not extend to adverbs, such as *only*. To see this, consider how to verify the truth or falsity of the sentence *Only farmers are feeding donkeys*. The procedure for verification of such a sentence would involve checking the domain of discourse to see that no individuals, other than farmers, are feeding donkeys. This includes checking entities not mentioned in the sentence.

Bibliographical Comments

Children's incorrect responses to questions with the universal quantifier were reported by Inhelder and Piaget (1964). Philip (1995) attempted to explain these observations by proposing that children and adults use different structures for such sentences (cf. also Roeper and deVilliers, 1991). A critique of this proposal and the alternative discussed here was presented by Crain, Thornton, Boster, Conway, Lillo-Martin, and Woodams (1996).

References

Akmajian, A., Demers, R. A., Farmer, A. K., and Harnish, R. M. (1995). *Linguistics: An Introduction to Language and Communication*. Cambridge, MA: MIT Press.

Akmajian, A., and Heny, F. W. (1975). *An Introduction to the Principles of Transformational Syntax*. Cambridge, MA: MIT Press.

Aksu-Koç, A. A., and Slobin, D. I. (1985). The Acquisition of Turkish. In D. I. Slobin (ed.), *The Crosslinguistic Study of Language Acquisition* (vol. 1, pp. 839–78). Hillsdale, NJ: Lawrence Erlbaum Associates.

Allen, R. (1984). *The Dialogues of Plato*. New Haven, CT: Yale University Press.

Aoun, J., Hornstein, N., and Sportiche, D. (1980). Some Aspects of Wide Scope Quantification. *Journal of Linguistic Research, 1*, 69–95.

Bach, E. (1971). Questions. *Linguistic Inquiry, 2*, 153–66.

Baker, C. L. (1970). Notes on the Description of English Questions: The Role of an Abstract Question Morpheme. *Foundations of Language, 6*, 197–219.

Baker, C. L. (1978). *Introduction to Generative Transformational Syntax*. Englewood Cliffs, NJ: Prentice-Hall.

Baker, C. L. (1979). Syntactic Theory and the Projection Problem. *Linguistic Inquiry, 10*, 533–81.

Baker, C. L., and McCarthy, J. J. (1981). *The Logical Problem of Language Acquisition*. Cambridge, MA: MIT Press.

Bellugi, U. (1965). The Development of Interrogative Structures in Children's Speech. In K. Reigel (ed.), *The Development of Language Functions* (pp. 103–37). Ann Arbor: Michigan Language Development Program.

Bellugi, U., Bihrle, A., Neville, H., Doherty, S., and Jernigan, T. (1992). Language, Cognition, and Brain Organization in a Neurodevelopmental Disorder. In M. Gunnar and C. Nelson (eds), *Developmental Behavioral Neuroscience: The Minnesota Symposia on Child Psychology*. Hillsdale, NJ: Lawrence Erlbaum Associates.

Berko, J. (1958). The Child's Learning of English Morphology. *Word, 14*, 150–7.

Berwick, R. (1985). *The Acquisition of Syntactic Knowledge*. Cambridge, MA: MIT Press.

Bloom, L. (1970). *Language Development: Form and Function in Emerging Grammars*. Cambridge, MA: MIT Press.

Bloom, P. (1993). *Language Acquisition: Core Readings*. Cambridge, MA: MIT Press.

Bloomfield, L. (1933). *Language*. New York: Holt.

Boster, C. T. (1997). Processing and Parameter Setting in Language Acquisition. Unpublished Ph.D., University of Connecticut, Storrs.

Bowerman, M. F. (1973). Structural Relationships in Children's Utterances: Syntactic or Semantic? In T. E. Moore (ed.), *Cognitive Development and the Acquisition of Language*. New York: Academic Press.

Broca, P. (1861). Perte de la parole. Romollissement chronique et destruction partielle du lobe anterieur gauche du cerveau. *Bulletin de la Société d'Anthropologie, 2*, 235.

Brown, R. (1973). *A First Language: The Early Stages*. Cambridge, MA: Harvard University Press.

Brown, R., Cazden, C., and Bellugi, U. (1969). The Child's Grammar from I to III. In J. P. Hill (ed.), *Minnesota Symposium on Child Psychology, Volume 2*. Minneapolis: University of Minnesota Press.

Brown, R., and Hanlon, C. (1970). Derivational Complexity and Order of Acquisition of Syntax. In J. Hayes (ed.), *Cognition and the Development of Language*. New York: Wiley.

Cann, R. (1995). *Formal Semantics: An Introduction*. Cambridge: Cambridge University Press.

Carnap, R. (1947, 1956). *Meaning and Necessity: A Study in Semantics and Modal Logic*. Chicago: University of Chicago Press.

Chen, D. (1998). Investigation of Word Order Acquisition in Early ASL. MS, University of Connecticut.

Chierchia, G., and McConnell-Ginet, S. (1990). *Meaning and Grammar: An Introduction to Semantics*. Cambridge, MA: MIT Press.

Chomsky, N. (1957). *Syntactic Structures*. The Hague: Mouton.

Chomsky, N. (1959). A Review of B. F. Skinner's *Verbal Behavior. Language, 35*, 26–58.

Chomsky, N. (1965). *Aspects of the Theory of Syntax*. Cambridge, MA: MIT Press.

Chomsky, N. (1970). Remarks on Nominalization. In R. Jacobs and P. Rosenbaum (eds), *Readings in English Transformational Grammar* (pp. 184–221). Waltham, MA: Ginn.

Chomsky, N. (1973). Conditions on Transformations. In S. R. Anderson and P. Kiparsky (eds), *A Festschrift for Morris Halle*. New York: Holt, Rinehart and Winston.

Chomsky, N. (1975). *The Logical Structure of Linguistic Theory*. New York: Plenum.

Chomsky, N. (1976). Conditions on Rules of Grammar. *Linguistic Analysis, 2*, 303–51.

Chomsky, N. (1977). On Wh-Movement. In P. Culicover, T. Wasow, and A. Akmajian (eds), *Formal Syntax*. New York: Academic Press.

Chomsky, N. (1981). *Lectures on Government and Binding*. Dordrecht: Foris.

Chomsky, N. (1986). *Barriers*. Cambridge, MA: MIT Press.

Chomsky, N., and Lasnik, H. (1977). Filters and Control. *Linguistic Inquiry, 8*, 425–504.

Clancy, P. M. (1985). The Acquisition of Japanese. In D. I. Slobin (ed.), *The Crosslinguistic Study of Language Acquisition* (vol. 1, pp. 373–524). Hillsdale, NJ: Lawrence Erlbaum Associates.

Cook, V. J., and Newson, M. (1996). *Chomsky's Universal Grammar: An Introduction (Second Edition)*. Oxford: Blackwell.

Crain, S. (1991). Language Acquisition in the Absence of Experience. *Behavioral and Brain Sciences, 14*, 597–650.

Crain, S., and McKee, C. (1986). Acquisition of Structural Restrictions on Anaphora. In S. Berman, J-W. Choe, and J. McDonough (eds), *Proceedings of the North Eastern Linguistic Society, 16*, 94–110. Amherst, MA: GLSA.

Crain, S., McKee, C., and Emiliani, M. (1990). Visiting Relatives in Italy. In J. deVilliers and L. Frazier (eds), *Language Processing and Language Acquisition* (pp. 335–56). Dordrecht: Reidel.

Crain, S., and Nakayama, M. (1987). Structure Dependence in Grammar Formation. *Language, 63*(3), 522–43.

Crain, S., Shankweiler, D., Macaruso, P., and Bar-Shalom, E. (1990). Working Memory and Comprehension of Spoken Sentences: Investigations of Children with Reading

Disorder. In G. Vallar and T. Shallice (eds), *Neuropsychological Disorders of Short-Term Memory* (pp. 477–508). Cambridge: Cambridge University Press.

Crain, S., and Thornton, R. (1991). Recharting the Course of Language Acquisition: Studies in Elicited Production. In N. A. Krasnegor, D. M. Rumbaugh, R. L. Schiefelbusch, and M. Studdert-Kennedy (eds), *Biobehavioral Foundations of Language Development* (pp. 321–37). Hillsdale, NJ: Lawrence Erlbaum Associates.

Crain, S., and Thornton, R. (1998). *Investigations in Universal Grammar: A Guide to Experiments on the Acquisition of Syntax and Semantics*. Cambridge, MA: MIT Press.

Crain, S., Thornton, R., Boster, C. T., Conway, L., Lillo-Martin, D., and Woodams, E. (1996). Quantification Without Qualification. *Language Acquisition, 5*, 83–153.

Cromer, R. (1991). *Language and Thought in Normal and Handicapped Children*. Oxford: Blackwell.

Davidson, D. (1967). Truth and Meaning. *Synthese, 17*, 304–23. Reprinted in A. P. Martinich (ed.), *The Philosophy of Language*. Oxford: Oxford University Press, 1985.

Dell, F. (1981). On the Learnability of Optional Phonological Rules. *Linguistic Inquiry, 12*, 31–7.

deVilliers, J., and deVilliers, P. (1985). The Acquisition of English. In D. I. Slobin (ed.), *The Crosslinguistic Study of Language Acquisition* (vol. 1, pp. 27–139). Hillsdale, NJ: Lawrence Erlbaum Associates.

deVilliers, J., Roeper, T., and Vainikka, A. (1990). The Acquisition of Long-Distance Rules. In L. Frazier and J. deVilliers (eds), *Language Processing and Language Acquisition* (pp. 257–97). Dordrecht: Kluwer Academic Publishers.

deVilliers, J., Tager-Flusberg, H., Hakuta, K., and Cohen, M. (1979). Children's Comprehension of Relative Clauses. *Journal of Psycholinguistic Research, 8*, 499–518.

Donnellan, K. (1966). Reference and Definite Descriptions. *Philosophical Review, 75*, 281–304.

Eimas, P. D. (1985). The Perception of Speech in Early Infancy. *Scientific American, 252*, 46–52.

Emonds, J. (1976). *A Transformational Approach to English Syntax: Root, Structure Preserving, and Local Transformations*. New York: Academic Press.

Erbaugh, M. (1992). The Acquisition of Mandarin. In D. I. Slobin (ed.), *The Crosslinguistic Study of Language Acquisition* (vol. 3, pp. 373–455). Hillsdale, NJ: Lawrence Erlbaum Associates.

Fiengo, R. (1977). On Trace Theory. *Linguistic Inquiry, 8*, 35–62.

Fodor, J. A. (1983). *The Modularity of Mind*. Cambridge, MA: MIT Press.

Fodor, J. A. (1985). Précis of *The Modularity of Mind*. *Behavioral and Brain Sciences, 8*, 1–42.

Forster, K. (1979). Levels of Processing and the Structure of the Language Processor. In W. E. Cooper and E. Walker (eds), *Sentence Processing: Psycholinguistic Studies Presented to Merrill Garrett* (pp. 27–85). Hillsdale, NJ: Lawrence Erlbaum Associates.

Frege, G. (1892). On Sense and Reference. In P. T. Geach and M. Black (eds), *Translations from the Philosophical Writings of Gottlob Frege (1952)* (pp. 56–78). Oxford: Basil Blackwell.

Garfield, J. L. (1989). *Modularity in Knowledge Representation and Natural-Language Understanding*. Cambridge, MA: MIT Press.

Gleason, H. A. (1961). *An Introduction to Descriptive Linguistics*. New York: Holt, Rinehart and Winston.

Gleitman, L. R., and Wanner, E. (1982). Language Acquisition: The State of the State of the Art. In E. Wanner and L. Gleitman (eds), *Language Acquisition: The State of the Art*. Cambridge: Cambridge University Press.

Goldin-Meadow, S., and Mylander, C. (1990). Beyond the Input Given: The Child's Role in the Acquisition of Language. *Language, 66*(2), 323–55.

Goodglass, H. (1993). *Understanding Aphasia*. San Diego: Academic Press.

Goodluck, H. (1991). *Language Acquisition: A Linguistic Introduction*. Oxford: Blackwell.

Goodluck, H., and Tavakolian, S. (1982). Competence and Processing in Children's Grammar of Relative Clauses. *Cognition*, 11, 1–27.

Guttman, N., and Kalish, H. I. (1956). Discriminability and Stimulus Generalization. *Journal of Experimental Psychology, 51*, 79–88.

Hamburger, H., and Crain, S. (1982). Relative Acquisition. In S. Kuczaj (ed.), *Language Development: Syntax and Semantics* (pp. 245–74). Hillsdale, NJ: Lawrence Erlbaum Associates.

Hamburger, H., and Crain, S. (1984). Acquisition of Cognitive Compiling. *Cognition*, 17, 85–136.

Harris, Z. S. (1951). *Methods in Structural Linguistics*. Chicago: University of Chicago Press.

Heim, I., and Kratzer, A. (1998). *Semantics in Generative Grammar*. Malden, MA: Blackwell Publishers.

Hockett, C. F. (1958). *A Course in Modern Linguistics*. New York: Macmillan.

Hollander, B. (1920). *In Search of the Soul*. New York: E. P. Dutton.

Hornstein, N. (1995). *Logical Form: From GB to Minimalism*. Oxford: Blackwell.

Hornstein, N., and Lightfoot, D. (eds) (1981a). *Explanations in Linguistics: The Logical Problem of Language Acquisition*. London: Longman.

Hornstein, N., and Lightfoot, D. (1981b). Introduction. In N. Hornstein and D. Lightfoot (eds), *Explanations in Linguistics: The Logical Problem of Language Acquisition* (pp. 9–31). London: Longman.

Huang, J. C.-T. (1982). Logical Relations in Chinese and the Theory of Grammar. Unpublished Ph.D. Dissertation, MIT.

Hyams, N. (1986). *Language Acquisition and the Theory of Parameters*. Dordrecht: Reidel.

Inhelder, B., and Piaget, J. (1964). *The Early Growth of Logic in the Child*. London: Routledge & Kegan Paul.

Jackendoff, R. (1977). *X′ Syntax: A Study of Phrase Structure*. Cambridge, MA: MIT Press.

Jaeggli, O. (1980). Remarks on *to* Contraction. *Linguistic Inquiry, 11*, 239–46.

Klima, E. S. (1964). Negation in English. In J. A. Fodor and J. J. Katz (eds), *The Structure of Language: Readings in the Philosophy of Language*. Englewood Cliffs, NJ: Prentice-Hall.

Klima, E. S., and Bellugi, U. (1979). *The Signs of Language*. Cambridge, MA: Harvard University Press.

Lakoff, G. (1970). Global Rules. *Language, 46*, 627–39.

Larson, R., and Segal, G. (1995). *Knowledge of Meaning: An Introduction to Semantic Theory*. Cambridge, MA: MIT Press.

Lasnik, H. (1976). Remarks on Coreference. *Linguistic Analysis, 2*, 1–22.

Lasnik, H. (1990). Syntax. In D. N. Osherson and H. Lasnik (eds), *An Invitation to Cognitive Science, Vol. 1: Language* (pp. 5–21). Cambridge, MA: MIT Press.

Lasnik, H., and Crain, S. (1985). On the Acquisition of Pronominal Reference. *Lingua, 65*, 135–54.

Lasnik, H., and Kupin, J. (1977). A Restrictive Theory of Transformational Grammar. *Theoretical Linguistics, 4*, 173–96.

Lasnik, H., and Saito, M. (1984). On the Nature of Proper Government. *Linguistic Inquiry, 15*, 235–89.

Lasnik, H., and Saito, M. (1992). *Move α*. Cambridge, MA: MIT Press.

Lasnik, H., and Uriagereka, J. (1988). *A Course in GB Syntax*. Cambridge, MA: MIT Press.

Lewis, D. (1972). General Semantics. In D. Davidson and G. Harman (eds), *Semantics for Natural Language*. Dordrecht: Reidel.

Lightfoot, D. (1982). *The Language Lottery*. Cambridge, MA: MIT Press.

Lillo-Martin, D. (1991). *Universal Grammar and American Sign Language: Setting the Null Argument Parameters*. Dordrecht: Kluwer Academic Publishers.

Lillo-Martin, D. (1992). Sentences as Islands: On the Boundedness of A'-Movement in American Sign Language. In H. Goodluck and M. Rochemont (eds), *Island Constraints* (pp. 259–74). Dordrecht: Kluwer Academic Publishers.

Lillo-Martin, D. (1997). The Modular Effects of Sign Language Acquisition. In M. Marschark, P. Siple, D. Lillo-Martin, R. Campbell, and V. Everhart (eds), *Relations of Language and Thought: The View from Sign Language and Deaf Children* (pp. 62–109). New York: Oxford University Press.

Lillo-Martin, D. (in press). Modality Effects and Modularity in Language Acquisition: The Acquisition of American Sign Language. In T. K. Bhatia and W. C. Ritchie (eds), *Handbook of Language Acquisition*. San Diego, CA: Academic Press.

Lillo-Martin, D., Boster, C. T., Matsuoka, K., and Nohara, M. (1996). Early and Late in Language Acquisition. In K. Matsuoka and A. Halbert (eds), *University of Connecticut Working Papers in Linguistics* (vol. 6, pp. 13–24). Cambridge, MA: MITWPL.

Matthei, E. (1982). The Acquisition of Prenominal Modifier Sequences. *Cognition, 11*, 301–32.

Matthews, R. J., and Demopoulos, W. (1989). *Learnability and Linguistic Theory*. Dordrecht: Kluwer Academic Publishers.

Mattingly, I. G., and Studdert-Kennedy, M. (eds) (1991). *Modularity and the Motor Theory of Speech Perception*. Hillsdale, NJ: Lawrence Erlbaum Associates.

May, R. (1977). The Grammar of Quantification. Unpublished Ph.D. Dissertation, MIT.

May, R. (1985). *Logical Form: Its Structure and Derivation*. Cambridge, MA: MIT Press.

McDaniel, D., Chiu, B., and Maxfield, T. (1995). Parameters for Wh-Movement Types: Evidence from Child Language. *Natural Language and Linguistic Theory, 13*, 709–53.

McDaniel, D., and McKee, C. (1992). Which Children did They Show Obey Strong Crossover? In H. Goodluck and M. Rochemont (eds), *Island Constraints: Theory, Acquisition and Processing* (pp. 275–94). Dordrecht: Kluwer Academic Publishers.

McNeil, D. (1970). *The Acquisition of Language: The Study of Developmental Psycholinguistics*. New York: Harper and Row.

Meier, R. P. (1982). Icons, Analogues, and Morphemes: The Acquisition of Verb Agreement in ASL. Unpublished Ph.D. Dissertation, University of California, San Diego.

Meier, R. P., and Newport, E. L. (1990). Out of the Hands of Babes: On a Possible Sign Advantage in Language Acquisition. *Language, 66*, 1–23.

Montague, R. (1974). *Formal Philosophy: Selected Papers of Richard Montague*, ed. R. H. Thomason. New Haven: Yale University Press.

Morgan, J. L., and Travis, L. L. (1989). Limits on Negative Information in Language Input. *Journal of Child Language, 16*, 531–52.

Nakayama, M. (1987). Performance Factors in Subject–Aux Inversion by Children. *Journal of Child Language, 14*, 113–25.

Neidle, C., Kegl, J., Bahan, B., Aarons, D., and MacLaughlin, D. (1997). Rightward WH-Movement in American Sign Language. In D. Beerman, D. LeBlanc, and H. van Riemsdijk (eds), *Rightward Movement* (pp. 247–78). Amsterdam: John Benjamins.

Newport, E., and Meier, R. (1985). The Acquisition of American Sign Language. In D. I. Slobin (ed.), *The Crosslinguistic Study of Language Acquisition* (vol. 1, pp. 881–938). Hillsdale, NJ: Lawrence Erlbaum Associates.

Newport, E. L., Gleitman, H., and Gleitman, L. R. (1977). Mother, I'd Rather do it Myself: Some Effects and Non-Effects of Maternal Speech Style. In C. Snow and C. Ferguson (eds), *Talking to Children: Language Input and Acquisition*. Cambridge: Cambridge University Press.

Park, T.-Z. (1970). Language Acquisition in a Korean Child. MS, Psychological Institute, University of Bern, Switzerland.

Pavlov, I. (1927). *Conditioned Reflexes*. Oxford: Oxford University Press.

Pesetsky, D. (1982). Complementizer-trace Phenomena and the Nominative Island Constraint. *The Linguistic Review, 1*, 297–343.

Petitto, L. A. (1983). From Gesture to Symbol: The Relationship Between Form and Meaning in the Acquisition of Personal Pronouns in American Sign Language. Unpublished Ph.D. Dissertation, Harvard University.

Petitto, L. A., and Marentette, P. F. (1991). Babbling in the Manual Mode: Evidence for the Ontogeny of Language. *Science, 251*, 1493–6.

Petronio, K., and Lillo-Martin, D. (1997). Wh-Movement and the Position of Spec CP: Evidence from American Sign Language. *Language, 73*, 18–57.

Philip, W. (1995). Event Quantification in the Acquisition of Universal Quantification. Unpublished Ph.D. Dissertation, University of Massachusetts, Amherst.

Pinker, S., (1990). Language Acquisition. In D. N. Osherson and H. Lasnik (eds), *An Invitation to Cognitive Science, Vol. 1: Language* (pp. 199–241). Cambridge, MA: MIT Press.

Pinker, S. (1995). Why the Child Holded the Baby Rabbits: A Case Study in Language Acquisition. In L. R. Gleitman and M. Liberman (eds), *An Invitation to Cognitive Science, Second Edition, Volume 1, Language* (pp. 107–33). Cambridge, MA: MIT Press.

Poizner, H. (1983). Perception of Movement in American Sign Language: Effects of Linguistic Structure and Linguistic Experience. *Perception and Psychophysics, 33*, 215–31.

Poizner, H., Fok, A., and Bellugi, U. (1989). The Interplay Between Perception of Language and Perception of Motion. *Language Sciences, 11*, 267–87.

Poizner, H., Klima, E. S., and Bellugi, U. (1987). *What the Hands Reveal about the Brain*. Cambridge, MA: MIT Press.

Postal, P. (1966). On So-Called "Pronouns" in English. In F. Dineen (ed.), *19th Monograph on Language and Linguistics*. Washington, DC: Georgetown University Press.

Postal, P. M. (1971). *Cross-over Phenomena*. New York: Holt, Rinehart and Winston.

Postal, P. M., and Pullum, G. K. (1982). The Contraction Debate. *Linguistic Inquiry, 13*, 122–38.

Radford, A. (1981). *Transformational Syntax: A Student's Guide to Chomsky's Extended Standard Theory*. Cambridge: Cambridge University Press.

Reilly, J. S., and McIntire, M. L. (1991). WHERE SHOE: The Acquisition of Wh-Questions in American Sign Language. *Papers and Reports in Child Language Development, 30*, 104–11.

Reinhart, T. (1976). The Syntactic Domain of Anaphora. Unpublished Doctoral Dissertation, MIT.

Riemsdijk, H. van, and Williams, E. (1986). *Introduction to the Theory of Grammar*. Cambridge, MA: MIT Press.

Rizzi, L. (1990). *Relativized Minimality*. Cambridge, MA: MIT Press.

Roeper, T. (1972). Approaches to a Theory of Language Acquisition with Examples from German Children. Unpublished Ph.D. Dissertation, Harvard University.

Roeper, T., and deVilliers, J. (1991). The Emergence of Bound Variable Structures. In T. Maxfield and B. Plunkett (eds), *University of Massachusetts Occasional Papers: Papers in the Acquisition of WH* (pp. 267–82). Amherst, MA: GLSA.

Roeper, T., Rooth, M., Mallish, L., and Akiyama, A. (1984). The Problem of Empty Categories and Bound Variables in Language Acquisition. MS, University of Massachusetts, Amherst.

Roeper, T., and Williams, E. (eds) (1987). *Parameter Setting*. Dordrecht: Reidel.

Ross, J. R. (1967). Constraints on Variables in Syntax. Unpublished Ph.D. Dissertation, MIT.

Rudin, C. (1988). On Multiple Questions and Multiple WH Fronting. *Natural Language and Linguistic Theory, 6*(4), 445–501.

Russell, B. (1905). On Denoting. *Mind, 14*, 479–93.

Sandler, W. (1993). Sign Language and Modularity. *Lingua, 89*, 315–51.

Sandler, W., and Lillo-Martin, D. (in preparation). *True Language Universals*. Cambridge: Cambridge University Press.

Selkirk, E. (1972). The Phrase Phonology of English and French. Unpublished Ph.D. Dissertation, MIT.

Sheldon, A. (1974). The Role of Parallel Function in the Acquisition of Relative Clauses in English. *Journal of Verbal Learning and Verbal Behavior, 13*, 272–81.

Skinner, B. F. (1938). *The Behavior of Organisms*. New York: Appleton-Century-Crofts.

Skinner, B. F. (1957). *Verbal Behavior*. New York: Appleton-Century-Crofts.

Slobin, D. I. (1966). The Acquisition of Russian as a Native Language. In F. Smith and G. A. Miller (eds), *The Genesis of Language: A Psycholinguistic Approach* (pp. 129–48). Cambridge, MA: MIT Press.

Slobin, D. I. (ed.) (1985). *The Crosslinguistic Study of Language Acquisition*. Hillsdale, NJ: Lawrence Erlbaum Associates.

Snow, C., and Ferguson, C. (1977). *Talking to Children: Language Input and Acquisition*. Cambridge: Cambridge University Press.

Solan, L. (1983). *Pronominal Reference: Child Language and the Theory of Grammar*. Dordrecht: Reidel.

Stemmer, N. (1981). A Note on Empiricism and Structure-Dependence. *Journal of Child Language, 8*, 649–63.

Stokoe, W. C., Casterline, D., and Croneberg, C. (1965). *Dictionary of American Sign Language*. Washington, DC: Gallaudet College Press.

Stowell, T. (1981). Origins of Phrase Structure. Unpublished Ph.D. Dissertation, MIT.

Strawson, P. (1950). On Referring. *Mind, 59*, 320–44.

Stromswold, K. (1990). *Learnability and the Acquisition of Auxiliaries*. Unpublished Ph.D. Dissertation, MIT.

Tarski, A. (1944). The Semantic Conception of Truth. *Philosophy and Phenomenological Research, 4*, 341–75. Reprinted in A. P. Martinich (ed.), *The Philosophy of Language*. Oxford: Oxford University Press, 1985.

Tavakolian, S. (1978). Children's Comprehension of Pronominal Subjects and Missing Subjects in Complicated Sentences. In H. Goodluck and L. Solan (eds), *UMass Occasional Papers in Linguistics: Papers in the Structure and Development of Child Language* (pp. 145–52). Amherst, MA: GLSA.

Tavakolian, S. (1981). The Conjoined-Clause Analysis of Relative Clauses. In S. Tavakolian (ed.), *Language Acquisition and Linguistic Theory*. Cambridge, MA: MIT Press.

Thorndike, E. L. (1898). Animal Intelligence: An Experimental Study of the Associative Processes in Animals. *Psychological Monographs, 2.*

Thornton, R. (1990). Adventures in Long-Distance Moving: The Acquisition of Complex WH-Questions. Unpublished Ph.D. Dissertation, The University of Connecticut, Storrs.

Thornton, R. (1995). Referentiality and Wh-Movement in Child English: Juvenile D-Linkuency. *Language Acquisition, 4*(1–2), 139–75.

Thornton, R., and Crain, S. (1994). Successful Cyclic Movement. In T. Hoekstra and B. D. Schwartz (eds), *Language Acquisition Studies in Generative Grammar* (pp. 215–52). Amsterdam/Philadelphia: John Benjamins.

Valian, V. (1986). Syntactic Categories in the Speech of Young Children. *Developmental Psychology, 22,* 562–79.

Vihman, M. M., Macken, M. A., Miller, R., Simmons, H., and Miller, J. (1985). From Babbling to Speech: A Re-Assessment of the Continuity Issue. *Language, 61*(2), 397–445.

Wasow, T. (1972). Anaphoric Relations in English. Unpublished Ph.D. Dissertation, MIT.

Wexler, K., and Culicover, P. (1980). *Formal Principles of Language Acquisition.* Cambridge, MA: MIT Press.

Whitaker, H., and Whitaker, H. A. (1976). *Studies in Neurolinguistics: Vol. 2.* New York: Academic Press.

Wilbur, R. B. (1987). *American Sign Language: Linguistic and Applied Dimensions.* Boston, MA: College-Hill Press.

Wode, H. (1971). Some Stages in the Acquisition of Questions by Monolingual Children. *Word, 27,* 261–310.

Zurif, E. (1995). Brain Regions of Relevance to Syntactic Processing. In L. R. Gleitman and M. Liberman (eds), *An Invitation to Cognitive Science, Second Edition, Volume 1, Language* (pp. 381–97). Cambridge, MA: MIT Press.

Index

 Also from Blackwell Publishers...

ENGLISH GRAMMAR
A GENERATIVE PERSPECTIVE
Liliane Haegeman and Jacqueline Guéron
0-631-18839-8 paperback
0-631-18838-X hardcover

ESSENTIAL INTRODUCTORY LINGUISTICS
Grover Hudson
0-631-20304-4 paperback
0-631-20303-6 hardcover

THE DEVELOPMENT OF LANGUAGE
ACQUISITION, CHANGE, AND EVOLUTION
David Lightfoot
0-631-21060-1 paperback
0-631-21059-8 hardcover

MINIMALIST ANALYSIS
Howard Lasnik
0-631-21094-6 paperback
0-631-21093-8 hardcover

A COURSE IN PHONOLOGY
Iggy Roca and Wyn Johnson
0-631-21346-5 paperback
0-631-21345-7 hardcover

PROPER ENGLISH:
MYTHS AND MISUNDERSTANDINGS ABOUT LANGUAGE
Ronald Wardhaugh
0-631-21269-8 paperback
0-631-21268-X hardcover

A WORKBOOK IN THE STRUCTURE OF ENGLISH:
LINGUISTIC PRINCIPLES AND LANGUAGE ACQUISITION
William Rutherford
0-631-20479-2 paperback
0-631-20478-4 hardcover

LANGUAGE ACQUISITION:
A LINGUISTIC INTRODUCTION
Helen Goodluck
0-631-17386-2 paperback

HANDBOOK OF CHILD LANGUAGE, THE
Edited by Paul Fletcher and Brian MacWhinney
0-631-20312-5 paperback

TO ORDER CALL :
1-800-216-2522 (N. America orders only) or
24-hour freephone on 0500 008205
(UK orders only)

VISIT US ON THE WEB : http://www.blackwellpublishers.co.uk